HYSTERICAL
PERSONALITY

HYSTERICAL PERSONALITY

EDITED BY

MARDI J. HOROWITZ, M.D.

Professor of Psychiatry

University of California

San Francisco

JASON ARONSON, INC.
New York, N.Y.

Bibliography: pp. 24
Includes Index.

1. Hysteria.   I.   Horowitz, Mardi Jon, 1934-
[DNLM: 1. Hysterical personality. WM173 H9995]
RC532.H9   616.8'52   77-73100

ISBN: 0-87668-264-6

Library of Congress Catalog Number: 77-73100

Manufactured in the United States of America

The contributors dedicate this work to the
ideal of the University of California:
fiat lux.
This is not pure nostalgic love of institution:
the motto is central to the treatment of
hysterical personality disorders.

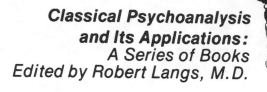

Classical Psychoanalysis
and Its Applications:
A Series of Books
Edited by Robert Langs, M.D.

Series Introduction

It is most gratifying to include in this series a second work by Mardi Horowitz. As editor of this volume on hysterical personality, Horowitz has shaped what is perhaps the definitive treatment of the subject. He is quite fortunate to have had available for this undertaking a group of erudite and sensitive analysts and social scientists who have studied and clarified virtually every important dimension of this personality constellation. The diverse approaches of his contributors afford the book an especially broad scope, while the clinical contributions provide an ultimate understanding of the psychopathology and treatment of patients suffering hysterical disorders. This volume, an exemplary interdisciplinary work, integrates classical psychoanalysis with other social sciences, demonstrating once again how each of these disciplines can enrich and extend the others.

Robert Langs, M.D.

Contributors

David W. Allen, M. D.

Clinical professor of psychiatry, Langley Porter Institute, University of California, San Francisco; faculty, San Francisco Psychoanalytic Institute

C. Clifford Attkisson, Ph. D.

Assistant professor of psychiatry in residence, Langley Porter Institute, University of California, San Francisco

Kay H. Blacker, M. D.

Clinical professor of psychiatry and associate dean for Hospital Educational Affairs, University of California School of Medicine, Davis; training analyst, San Francisco Psychoanalytic Institute

Mardi J. Horowitz, M. D.

Professor of psychiatry and director, Psychotherapy Evaluation and Study Center, Langley Porter Institute, University of California, San Francisco; faculty, San Franisco Psychoanalytic Institute

Aubrey Metcalf, M. D.

Associate clinical professor of psychiatry; supervising child psychiatrist, Children's Service, Langley Porter Institute, University of California, San Francisco

Lydia Temoshok, Ph. D.

Assistant professor, graduate faculty, New School for Social Research, New York

Joe P. Tupin, M. D.

Professor of psychiatry and vice-chairman, Department of Psychiatry, University of California School of Medicine, Davis

Ilza Veith, Ph. D.

Professor and vice-chairman, Department of History of Health Sciences, School of Medicine, University of California, San Francisco; professor of psychiatry, Langley Porter Institute, University of California, San Francisco

Preface

This is a book by friends. While the academic location of contributors may suggest that the pages herein represent the official position statement on hysterical personality of the northern components of the University of California system, this is hardly the case; the clustering is due only to the evolution of the work. A series of psychiatry grand rounds at Langley Porter Institute was arranged in sequence, and many of the present contributors spoke on hysterical personality. The result was a synergistic presentation of ideas, followed by many requests for a repetition of "hysteria month." This book is the answer to those requests.

Since we deal with a typology that goes to the roots of recorded history, the fine, scholarly view by Ilza Veith is an apt beginning. Only a brief Introduction defining the typology precedes it. Kay Blacker and Joe Tupin continue to trace the history into modern times and bring the typology up to date in chapter 2. The hysterical personality is shaped by social roles and other cultural factors in ways illustrated by an epidemiological review in the next chapter by Lydia Temoshok and Clifford Attkisson. A part of this chapter covers information presented in the preceding chapter. The two chapters, however, follow different lines of approach: the former the clinical approach, here the epidemiological approach. The result is a complementary understanding of psychological and social contributions to the formation and manifestation of hysterical personality. We consider hysterical personality to be not only a behavior pattern and set of core conflicts and interpersonal fantasies, but also a developmental defect. In chapter 4, Aubrey

Metcalf, a child psychiatrist, reconsiders developmental theories of how a hysterical personality may be formed and comments on the significance of the virtual absence of such diagnoses in child psychiatry clinics. In chapter 5 David Allen begins the discussion of treatment by covering the patterns of relationship and communication that occur in the psychotherapy or psychoanalysis of persons of this character type, with a special focus on the typical impediments to working through areas of conflict. My final chapter explores the structural basis for the manifestations of hysterical personality and describes how process and development in treatment lead to structural change.

As editor, I will take the perquisite of thanking Nancy Wilner for her extensive and invaluable help in putting this manuscript together in all its facets. Phyllis Cameron prepared many drafts of the text and Jordan Horowitz assembled the concluding bibliography.

MARDI J. HOROWITZ, M.D.

Contents

HYSTERICAL
PERSONALITY

Introduction:

The Core Characteristics of Hysterical Personality

MARDI J. HOROWITZ M. D.

Personality classification has been a human activity throughout history, and an important paradox has always haunted the effort: personality typology groups persons together by the very attributes that highlight their individual differences. One may generalize on the traits of a hysterical personality, but no particular person will ever precisely fit the description. The study of any individual must consider those traits that differ from type as well as those that conform to it.

Many kinds of personality classification exist. Those in psychiatry focus on disorders of interpersonal functions and are based on empirical observations of frequent signs. Of these psychiatric categories, hysterical personality is one of the most venerable, but as is characteristic of this typology, there is still dispute over inclusive traits and nomenclature: hysterical personality or histrionic personality disorder. The second edition of the *Diagnostic and Statistical Manual* of the American Psychiatric Association (*DSM II*) (1968) defines it this way: "Hysterical Personality (Histrionic Personality Disorder): These behavior patterns are characterized by excitability, emotional instability, overreactivity, and self-dramatization. This self-dramatization is always attention seeking and often seductive, whether or not the patient is aware of its purpose. These personalities are also immature, self-centered, often vain, and usually dependent on others" (p. 43).

Psychodynamic investigations amplify and correct these behavioral observations. The official description overemphasizes dramatic acts because it omits the disordered perceptual, cognitive, and verbal communication patterns that are also observed. These information-processing attributes may be decisive explanatory concepts, useful in the conceptualization of etiology and in the construction of rational approaches to treatment.

A landmark in the theory of personality disorders was the focus on the relationship between acts, thought, and the person's style of processing and organizing information (Shapiro 1965; Gardner and others 1959). Shapiro, for example, in his examination of hysterical personality gives the global perceptual manner, impressionistic groupings of constructs, and shallow repertoire of memories the central thematic importance they deserve. Such cognitive and experiential attributes are complementary to the defense mechanisms of denial and repression, previously and repeatedly observed by psychoanalysts working with hysterical personalities (Breuer and Freud 1893-1895). Earlier, such characteristics of *form* were taken for granted, and not described in detail, because attention was riveted to *contents*, to symbolic derivatives and the acting out of unconscious and unresolved oedipal fantasies. These observations of information-processing style must be added to the classical descriptors of behavior.

Observations are facilitated if one defines the kind of time intervals to be scanned in the search for recurrent patterns. One scans a life cycle of months and years for long-order patterns, relying on clinical histories for the relevant data. For hysterical personality, observations may include frequent relationships in which the person fulfills a childlike role in relation to a care-taker, a waiflike role in relation to either an abandoning or rescuing person, and a helpless or sexually exploited role in relation to an aggressor. These patterns of recurrent interpersonal behavior suggest an inner map or mental schemata that produces equivalent fantasies, role models, and self-images. To find medium-order patterns, one scans hours or days; interaction during the diagnostic interview may itself provide the raw data. Recognizable patterns include displays of variable emotions, attention-seeking behavior, behavioral provocativeness without self-recognition of intent, and suggestibility. One scans much smaller time intervals—minutes and seconds—to observe patterns of information processing. Unclear verbal statements, use of language for effect on others rather than for meaning, choice of

TABLE 1

Common Patterns in the Hysterical Personality

Long-Order Patterns: Interpersonal Relations
_____

Repetitive, impulsive, stereotyped interpersonal relationships often characterized by victim-aggressor, child-parent, and rescue or rape themes

"Cardboard" fantasies and caricaturelike roles for self and others to play

Drifting but possibly dramatic lives with an existential sense that reality is not really real, frequent experience of self as not in control and not responsible

Medium-Order Patterns: Traits
_____

Attention-seeking behaviors, possibly including demands for attention and/or the use of charm, vivacity, displays of sex appeal, childlikeness, passivity, or infirmity

Fluid change in mood and emotion, excitable, episodically flooded with feeling

Inconsistency of attitudes, suggestibility

Short-Order Patterns: Information Processing Style
_____

Global deployment of attention

Unclear, inhibited, or incomplete statements of ideas and feelings, possibly with lack of details or clear labels in communication, nonverbal communications not translated into words or conscious meanings

Only partial or unidirectional associational lines

Short circuit to apparent completion of problematic thoughts global rather than specific labels for experience, and shallowness (in the sense of a failure to understand ideational implications) are typical short-order patterns. Common traits, organized by these time intervals, are summarized in table 1. Taken altogether, this cluster of characteristics is the operational definition of hysterical personality used by the authors of this book.

Historically, patterns of thought, feeling, and action were matters for spiritual rather than medical observation. But activities and failures of the body are in the domain of healing arts and sciences. Hysterical personalities tend to speak the language of the body, and through this communicative media they enter the portals of medical psychology. First, isolated hysterical symptoms were observed and conceptualized. Only after centuries of empirical observation were complex hysterical neuroses (conversion and dissociation reactions) clearly described. Not until recent decades were these neurotic symptoms clearly distinguished from the disordered interpersonal styles of the prototypic hysterical personality. The next two chapters retrace that historical course.

REFERENCES

American Psychiatric Association (1968). *Diagnostic and Statistical Manual of Mental Disorders (DSM II)*. Washington, D.C.

Breuer, S., and Freud, S. (1893-1895). Studies on hysteria. *Standard Edition* 2.

Gardner, R., Holzman, P. S., Klein, G. S., Linton, H., and Spence, D. P. (1959).Cognitive controls: a study of individual consistencies in cognitive behavior. *Psychological Issues* 1: 1-186

Shapiro, D. (1965). *Neurotic Styles*. New York: Basic Books.

CHAPTER 1

Four Thousand Years of Hysteria

ILZA VEITH, Ph. D.

The mention of the history of hysteria generally evokes the mental image of Freud in Vienna, of Bernheim and Liébault in Nancy, of Charcot and the Salpêtrière in Paris. Few appreciate how much further back it goes, and how long, how diffuse, and how complex it is. Having pursued this long and unbroken history of hysteria, I became so vitally interested in the subject that I spent more than four years on its investigation in order to write a book about it (Veith 1965). It is for this reason that I will share with you some of my observations on "four thousand years of hysteria."

Four thousand years seems a magic number in the study of the history of medicine, for the few diseases that we can trace back to the beginnings of human documentation can be followed back that far, that is, into the history of Egyptian antiquity. The earliest diseases that are that old are an interesting and quite disparate mixture. Their physical evidence speaks of tooth decay and arthritis; both can be diagnosed in many of the ancient mummies that have been preserved. Examples of poliomyelitis and Paget's disease are pictured in stone relief and sculptures that have been excavated by Egyptologists. Melancholia, or rather depression, diabetes, and hysteria are described in the earliest medical papyri which date back to the nineteenth century B.C.

But before embarking upon my history of hysteria, I must stress that during the long span of the disease, the concept of hysteria has undergone many changes in its etiology and treatment and even in its manifestations, and that much of what used to be denoted as hysteria would now no longer be so designated. Also, many symptoms and signs now recognized as part of the complex syndrome of hysteria and hysterial personality were formerly not recognized as belonging within this complex.

There is ample evidence that the awareness of hysteria goes back to ancient Egypt; and for this reason I wish to introduce you to the Daily Life Room of the Ancient Egyptians at the Metropolitan Museum of Art in New York City. There we find an irregular piece of limestone, only six by seven centimeters in size, which presumably contains the oldest existing medical prescription in the history of medicine. According to the Egyptologist von Ofele, such limestone tablets, known as *ostracon,* were used as cheap substitutes for papyrus; and the one here discussed is estimated to date from approximately 1500 B.C.

The ingredients of such prescriptions mainly consisted of precious and semiprecious stones, among which lapis lazuli predominated, as it was treasured for its blue color, which seemed especially pertinent to the treatment of mood disorders. These stones were ground up and used for fumigation to be applied to the patient whenever "the ball in the throat," now known as *globus hystericus,* was a prominent symptom. This ball in the throat was believed to be caused by a dislocation of the uterus upwards.

This earliest belief in the migrating uterus influenced most subsequent etiological speculations. It is responsible for the name *hysteria,* as well as for the belief that it was an affliction of women only. The association of hysteria with the female generative system was in essence an expression of awareness of the malign effect of disordered sexual activity on emotional stability. But these concepts go back to man's earliest speculations about health and disease, long before the term *hysteria* had been coined, and they indicate the prominent role that sexual life played in general well-being, even in remote antiquity. They are documented in the first recorded medical literature of ancient Egypt, two thousand years before Christ. And, as will become evident, they persisted with minor modifications in all Western cultures and throughout all periods well into the nineteenth century.

HYSTERIA IN ANCIENT EGYPT

The earliest sources of recorded medicine emanated from the two great centers of culture—the Egyptian and the Mesopotamian. Of these, the Egyptian records play the important part in the story of the evolution of the concepts of hysteria. Knowledge of Egyptian medicine is derived chiefly from a small number of surviving papyri. The oldest of these, in fact, deals specifically with the subject of hysteria. This document is known as the *Kahun Papyrus,* after the ancient Egyptian city in whose ruins the papyrus was found, and dates from about 1900 B.C. It is incomplete; only fragments have survived (Griffith 1897). These were evidently part of a small treatise describing a series of morbid states, all attributed to displacement of the uterus. Each brief enumeration of symptoms is followed by the physician's pronouncement on the nature of the case and his recommendations for appropriate treatment.

Of the diseases mentioned in this document, most of those that are defined clearly enough to be recognizable would be classed today as hysterical disorders. Significantly, even the ancient Egyptian physicians suspected the "hysterical" basis for the complaints. This is not specifically stated in the text but is implied by the fact that the complaints are listed under the heading of "Disorders of the Uterus" and, further, by the fact that the treatment recommended was directed toward that organ. For at that early time, it was taken for granted that certain behavioral disorders were associated with the generative organs and with aberrations in the position of the womb. This was so firmly established that no other explanation for the symptoms was even so much as suggested. A few illustrative cases are cited: "a woman who loves bed; she does not rise and does not shake it," another woman "who is ill in seeing" and who has a pain in her neck, a third "woman pained in her teeth and jaws; she knows not how to open her mouth," and, finally, "woman aching in all her limbs with pain to the sockets of her eyes." These and similar disturbances were believed to be caused by "starvation" of the uterus or by its upward dislocation with a consequent crowding of the other organs.[1] The physician's efforts were therefore quite logically directed toward nourishing the hungry organ or returning it to the place from which it had strayed.

Observations of patients with prolapse may have lent credibility to the uterine-displacement theory in hysteria, although it is noteworthy that this easily recognized anomaly was never associated with the bizarre phenomena then believed to be characteristic of hysteria. In the absence of any systematic knowledge of anatomy in general, and of the female generative organs in particular, the notion of a mobile and migratory uterus would not be as abusrd as it might sound. Yet, despite the unshakable belief in the role of the wandering uterus, there is no mention in the *Kahun Papyrus* of direct manipulation to restore it to its normal position. Instead, attempts were made to lure or drive the organ back, as if it were a living, independent organism. The parts were fumigated with precious and sweet-smelling substances to attract the womb; or evil-tasting and foul-smelling substances were ingested or inhaled to repel the organ and drive it away from the upper part of the body where it was thought to have wandered. So deeply ingrained did these methods become that they were carried over into recent times, long after their original rationale had been forgotten. Thus, strong-smelling herbs such as valerian and asafetida in the form of aromatics, sedatives, and antispasmodics were still recommended as specific antihystericals in medical and pharmacological textbooks as late as the early twentieth century (Strümpel 1911, Sollman 1918).

The preoccupation with hysterical manifestations in the *Kahun Papyrus* was not an isolated phenomenon in the medical literature of ancient Egypt. This is suggested by the fact that at least one other and even more important specimen along the small number of known medical papyri deals extensively with this subject. Named after the German Egyptologist George Ebers, who first published its facsimile, the *Papyrus Ebers* (Ebbell 1947) dates back to the sixteenth century B.C. It has been called the greatest Egyptian medical document, and it is most certainly the largest of the antique Egyptian medical texts to have been discovered; moreover, it is complete and well preserved.[2]

The chapter entitled "Diseases of Women," dealing largely with hysteria, goes far beyond the therapeutic suggestions in the *Kahun Papyrus*. Among the elaborations is the detailed prescription "to cause a woman's womb to go to its place." The remedies and their modes of application show the highly imaginative approaches by which control of hysterical symptoms was attempted. One prescription, a potion composed of tar from the wood of a ship and the dregs of beer, was, by its evil taste, supposed to induce the descent of the uterus. Other recipes list ointments, compounded from a variety of unpleasant ingredients, that were used to rub the affected parts of the body in order to drive down the uterus. One such ointment was composed of dry excrement moistened with beer: "The fingers of the woman are rubbed with it; thou shalt apply it to all her limbs and to her diseased place" (pp. 108-109).

The *Papyrus Ebers*, in agreement with the methods of the earlier *Kahun Papyrus*, also recommends applying a variety of fragrant and aromatic substances to attract the uterus from below. Further modes of treatment are described wherein fumigation by means of fragrant and powerful substances is used, similar to the ground lapis lazuli in the ostracon prescription mentioned earlier. Also among these: "dry excrement of men is placed on frankincense, and the woman is fumigated therewith; let the fumes thereof enter into her vulva." Although the medicinal use of highly unappetizing substances was far from uncommon in ancient Egypt, this particular prescription suggests a deliberate choice. The implication of gratifying the uterus with discharges from the opposite sex cannot be disregarded. As a final measure "to cause the womb to go back to its place: an ibis of wax is placed on charcoal and let the fumes thereof enter into her vulva" (pp. 108-109).

This last merits special comment, since it alone of the remedies mentioned in the papyri introduces a magico-religious element to the otherwise entirely rational basis of treatment. For, bizarre as these therapeutic measures may seem to us, they are entirely reasonable within the framework of the then existing concepts of the pathogenesis of hysterical disorders. Fumigation with pleasing scents could, with reason, be expected to entice a wandering uterus back to its normal seat deep in the pelvis. But to incorporate the aromatic agents into a waxen bird appears to go beyond reason: it becomes comprehensible only on realizing that the ibis was the symbol of the god Thoth. This male deity ranked among the most powerful in the Egyptian pantheon. He personified the moon and was related to the sun; as the inventor of the art of writing he became the scribe of all the other gods and partook of their work; and since he was also believed to be the owner of secret books, he was considered the god of wisdom (Frankfort 1948). He was revered as an author of books on medicine and functioned as physician to the gods and the protector of all who were ill (Roeder 1916). In the favoring of the patient's pudenda with the fumes of the waxen image of Thoth, we see a combination of rational medical treatment with symbolism in its appeal to the powers of the god. This specific instance of the ibis used for vulvar insufflation inevitably gives rise to further speculations that bear on modern psychological theories. The employment of the image of a powerful male deity to lure back a wandering female organ is highly suggestive of the nature of the underlying ideas concerning hysteria, even if they are nowhere spelled out in detail.

HIPPOCRATES: THE RATIONAL
GREEK VIEW OF HYSTERIA

It was apparently inevitable that some traces of older, and even foreign, medical theories would find their way into Greek medicine, and it was probably by this route that Egyptian notions about the nature of the uterus and its migratory propensities were perpetuated in the *Corpus Hippocraticum*.

In the Egyptian papyri the disturbances resulting from the movement of the womb were described, but they had not yet been given a specific appellation. This step was taken in the Hippocratic writings where the connection of the uterus *(hystera)* with the disease resulting from its disturbances is first expressed by the term *hysteria*. It appears in the thirty-fifth Hippocratic aphorism, which reads: "When a woman suffers from hysteria or difficult labor an attack of sneezing is beneficial." In light of the Egyptian prescriptions this might mean that the spasm of sneezing would push the uterus back in place.

In Greek literature the term "hysteria" is more frequently used in its adjectival form ("hysterical") and is applied to such conditions as certain forms of respiratory difficulty in which the choking sensation was believed to be due to the pressure of the displaced uterus. Similarly, the *globus hystericus* could be explained on the basis of such organic malposition. This phenomenon was thought to occur primarily in mature women who were deprived of sexual relations; prolonged continence was believed to result in demonstrable organic changes in the womb. The thinking ran that in such situations the uterus dries up and loses weight and, in its search for moisture, rises toward the hypochondrium, thus impeding the flow of breath which was supposed normally to descend into the abdominal cavity. If the organ comes to rest in this position it causes convulsions similar to those of epilepsy. If it mounts higher and attaches itself to the heart the patient feels anxiety and oppression and begins to vomit. When it fastens itself to the liver the patient loses her voice and grits her teeth, and her complexion turns ashen. If the uterus lodges in the loins, the woman feels a hard ball, or lump, in her side. But when it mounts as high as the head, it causes pain around the eyes and nose, the head feels heavy, and drowsiness and lethargy set in. Beyond these specific symptoms, the movement of the womb generally produces palpitations and excessive perspiration and convulsions similar to those observed in epilepsy (Hippocrates 1851). The anatomical difficulties in the way of such free and extensive migrations were apparently of no concern to these writers. This may in part be due to an overwhelming igorance of bodily structure and particularly that of the female generative system.

Perhaps our best inferences about the intuition of ancient clinicians can be drawn from analysis of the treatments frequently proposed for persons with hysteria. Attention, strong stimuli and genital insertions are prominent. For example, the physician was to undertake a manual examination to search for the dislodged uterus, taking special care to avoid touching the liver; also a bandage was to be applied below the hypochondria to prevent further ascension of the womb. Into the forcibly opened mouth of the patient the physician was to pour strongly perfumed wine. Fetid fumigations for the nose and aromatic ones for the uterus were to help return the organ to its normal abode.

Although all symptoms were thought to appear in both widows and spinsters, the after-treatment of both types of patients were different. Immediately following the attack, all patients were to be given a strong purgative and subsequently a draught of ass's milk. To the widow one then applies aromatic fumigations to the uterus: a pessary with buprested,[3] and in the morning one with bitter almonds. After a two-day interval an aromatic injection is given into the uterus, and the following morning one applies a pessary soaked in mint. After a one-day interval there will again be aromatic fumigations. While this is what one should do for the widow, it is best that she remarry and become pregnant. So far as the spinster is concerned, the physician advises her to take a husband; he applies nothing to the uterus nor does he administer any purgatives; instead he gives fleabane[4] and castor oil to drink in wine on an empty stomach. The woman is not to inhale or anoint her head with perfumes.

The treatments of hysterical disorders in the Hippocratic texts are similar to those in Egyptian papyri and were directed toward achieving the same purpose. In disturbances that were diagnosed as "suffocation of the womb" two types of fumigation were used to induce the uterus to move downward: those with malodorous substances which were to be inhaled or sweet-scented aromas which were applied below. Elderly virgins as well as widows, including those who had had children, were thought to be particularly vulnerable to hysterical afflictions caused by irregular menses; marriage was recommended to them as the speediest way of achieving a cure (Hippocrates 1851). It is this recommendation that translates the sexual element, implied initially in the earliest concepts of hysteria, into tangible terms. As will be seen in subsequent pages, it continued to be among the standard therapies for more than two thousand years.

HYSTERIA AND THE DREAM CULT
OF AESCULAPIUS

Contemporary with Hippocrates and his scientific school of medicine, there existed in Greece a healing cult dedicated to Aesculapius, the Greek god of medicine. The temples of Aesculapius were generally situated in localities of natural beauty, which provided a pleasing environment to the patient. After an initial period of sacrifices, ablutions, and fasting, the patient was placed on a couch in one of many small rooms that surrounded the main temple and was told to rest; cure was to be wrought by the god Aesculapius, who would appear in a dream. A number of votive tablets found at the temple sites tell of the dreams and the visions the patients experienced during their temple sleep. In most cases, it seems Aesculapius appeared to them and brought about their recovery by words alone or by manipulation at the site of the malady. The god carried a staff and was often accompanied by one or more of the large snakes which abounded in the temples. Sometimes the patients felt that they were touched or licked by these snakes. According to the tablets, cure was the almost invariable result of these dreams. It was a distinctly psychotherapeutic atmosphere in which these cures were undertaken, with rudiments of many of the procedures that were to endure through the millennia to the present day. Even the couch, of a fame then scarcely foreseeable, was in evidence.

The following cases taken from inscriptions that were excavated at the site of the great Aesculapian temple in Epidaurus (Edelstein and Edelstein 1945) are example that would seem to confirm this impression:

Inscription 3. A man, whose fingers with the exception of one were paralyzed, came as a suppliant to the god. While looking at the tablets in the temple, he expressed incredulity regarding the cure and scoffed at the inscriptions. But in his sleep he saw a vision. It seemed to him that he was playing at dice below the Temple, and was about to cast the dice [when] the god appeared, sprang upon his hand, and stretched out his [the patient's] fingers. When the god had stepped aside it seemed to the patient that he could bend his hand and [he] stretched out all his fingers one by one. When he had straightened them all the god asked him if he would still be incredulous of the inscriptions on the tablets in the Temple. He answered that he would not, [and the god said to him:] "Since, then, formerly you did not believe in the cures, though they were not incredible, for the future your name shall be 'Incredulous.'" When day dawned, he walked out sound.

Inscription 4. Ambrosia of Athens, blind of one eye. She came as a suppliant to the god. As she walked about in the Temple, she laughed at some of the cures as incredible and impossible that the lame and the blind should be healed by merely seeing a dream. In her sleep she had a vision. It seemed to her that the god stood by her, and said that he would cure her, but that in payment he would ask her to dedicate to the Temple a silver pig, as a memorial of her ignorance. After saying this, he cut the diseased eyeball, and poured in some drug.

Inscription 5. A voiceless boy. He came as suppliant to the Temple for his voice. When he had performed the preliminary sacrifices, and fulfilled the usual rites, the temple servant, who brings in the fire for the god, looking at the boy's father, demanded he should promise to bring within a year the thank-offering for the cure if he obtained that for which he had come. The boy suddenly said, "I promise." His father was startled at this, and asked him to repeat it. The boy repeated the words and after that became well. [pp. 230-235]

The subject of fees is frequently mentioned in these inscriptions, and it appears that thank-offerings of sacrificial animals, objects of art, votive tablets, or precious metals were usually expected. That they were essential in the healing ritual is confirmed by the inscriptions recording the histories of two blind men whose sight was restored but who lost it again after refusing to make the prearranged donation to the temple. The size of the fees varied according to the patients' means, and from the poor even the smallest and most insignificant offerings were graciously accepted. Large fees, however, were expected from wealthy patients, and some were encouraged to donate buildings, baths, or add other structures to the temples. (Among the largest recorded gifts was that of Phalysios of Naupaktos, who donated two thousand gold pieces in return for the recovery of his vision.)

Apparently, many patients suffering from transitory blindness, probably of hysterical origin, sought help at the temples. The following inscription deals with another case of this nature:

Inscription 18. Alketas of Haleis. This blind man had a dream. It seemed to him that the god came up to him and opened his eyes with his fingers. And that he first saw the trees of the Temple. At daybreak, he walked out restored to health. [Edelstein and Edelstein, p. 233]

Evidently the Aesculapian priest-healers did not recognize the hysterical substrate of these temple patients, but treated them for the symptomatic complaints which had brought them to the sanctuaries. The priests, who had no medical training, were not baffled by the absence of structural lesions which might account for the symptoms; nor were they astonished at the complacency of the patients in the face of gross objective disability. *La belle indifference* was an aspect of the illness that was not to be described until two millennia later, and in a totally different cultural setting.

GRAECO-ROMAN RATIONALITY

Conventional symptoms were not associated with hysteria by ancient Greek healers, be they priests or hippocratic physicians. The latter recognized hysteria only in paroxismal outbreaks of behavior disorders, which came to be described as attacks or fits, and also caused the frequent confusion of hysteria with epilepsy. It was in the effort to forestall such confusion of the two diseases that several Graeco-Roman authors called attention to the need of differential diagnosis of hysteria and epilepsy.

For the purposes of a differential diagnosis, the theory of the migrating uterus was used to confirm the essential differences between hysteria and epilepsy, and even apoplexy. Although all Graeco-Roman authors were concerned with such differential diagnosis, the one most active in this specific field was Caelius Aurelianus whose important volume *On Acute Diseases and On Chronic Diseases* contains the most important notations on that subject. So far as the acute form of the disease is concerned we should quote the following description.

An hysterical suffocation may be distinguished from catalepsy chiefly by the drawing up of the womb so that it appears to bulge out above the navel or abdomen, and also by the presence of pain in these parts before the time of the attack. And sometimes the patients are found to have been accustomed to attacks over a long period of time.

Their pulse is small, rapid, and weak; the neck is distended, eyelids meet and there is a chill numbness of the body. [pp. 173-174]

Apoplexy may also be distinguished from epilepsy, for epileptics are shaken by convulsions of the whole body and foam at the mouth, whereas this is never true of apoplectics. Furthermore, epileptics usually can stand up after an attack without having suffered any impairment in their general condition, whereas apoplectics suffer a paralysis of parts of the body. Again, apoplexy is always considered an acute and swift disease, while epilepsy is generally found to be chronic as well. [p. 333]

Under the category of chronic diseases the following passages are most revealing:

Epilepsy attacks bodies at all seasons and especially in the spring. Hysterical suffocation in women is often found to resemble epilepsy, for in either case the patient is bereft of her senses. But the diseases may be distinguished, for toward the end of an attack of epilepsy there is foaming at the mouth and nostrils. This completes our account of the special signs indicative of epilepsy. [p. 485]

Now many of the symptoms here found are similar to those found in other diseases. Thus loss of reason also occurs in mania and phrenitis, loss of voice in lethargy and suffocation, apoplexy, epilepsy, and catalepsy. But those who suffer from worms never foam at the mouth. On the other hand, hysterical suffocation always involves an ascent of the uterus and usually occurs in adult life after an affection of the uterus. [p. 887]

ST. AUGUSTINE:
MEDIEVAL ASPECTS OF HYSTERIA

This somatic, or rather uterine, concept of hysteria which had originated in ancient Egypt remained in force well into the Middle Ages and even beyond; it was somewhat eclipsed in the medieval times as a result of St. Augustine's dictum: "There are no diseases that do not arise from witchery and hence from the mind." This statement was considered particularly applicable to the recognition and treatment of hysteria and hence led to a curious dichotomy of attitudes in regard to the etiology and treatment of that disease. When hysteria was considered in terms of its traditional uterine causation it was treated medically, that is, by fumigation and sweet-smelling substances. But when the Augustinian concept of witchery prevailed, treatment was taken over by the clergy and consisted of exorcism and torture. As being a victim of supernatural disease denoted the heretic, the patients so diagnosed came into the hands of the law, namely, the Inquisition, in which case the patients were questioned under torture for having exposed themselves to the allure of the devil or witchcraft and were punished for it—often by death. Once the aberration of a belief in witches and its dire consequences had come into being, numberless deluded inquisitors obtained confessions of devilish intercourse with even greater numbers of equally deluded witches who confessed to an unending variety of supernatural crimes; most of these in earlier periods, would simply have been grouped under the category of hysteria. But the treatment of a disease that was characterized by odd behavior fell under the authority of the priest. Of course, a great many of the medieval monks were trained in the practice of medicine, and they could give medical as well as spiritual care. But it was predominantly the pure cleric, not the medically trained monk, who gave medieval medicine its superhuman stamp.

Perhaps the best example for this removal of all physical considerations from the realm of medicine can be found in a work that was actually composed during the Renaissance, but which is unsurpassed as a prototype of medieval reasoning. This work, the *Malleus Maleficarum* (the "Witches' Hammer") stemmed from the pen of two Dominican monks, Johann Sprenger and Heinrich Kraemer, who had been appointed Inquisitors of Northern Germany by Pope Innocent VIII. Fortified by a Papal Bull of 1481, these two men composed a work that relegated any mental and physical aberration from the norm as deviltry, witchery, and evil. The volume became the guidebook for the Inquisition and went through nearly twenty editions within two centuries. The 1928 edition rendered it in English.

In the course of the Middle Ages the differentiation between the mentally sick, the witch, and the heretic had become less and less sharply defined, and in the thirteenth century, they were considered synonymous by most persons. Eventually, however, all diseases came into the realm of witchery. This can be illustrated by the following statement emanating from the pen of the two Inquisitors.

> There is no part in our body that they [the witches] would not injure. Most of the time they make the human being possessed and thus they are left to the devils to be tortured with unheard of pains. They even get into carnal relations with them. . . . Unfortunately, the number of such witches is very great in every province; more than that, there is no locality too small for a witch to find. Yet Inquisitors and Judges who could avenge these open offenses against God and Nature are so few and far between. Men and beast die as a result of the evil of these women and no one thinks of the fact that these things are perpetrated by witches. Many suffer constantly of severest diseases and are not even aware that they are bewitched.

It is interesting that most of the victims of witchery were men and that there are vastly more witches than wizards in the mental world of the two Inquisitors. While almost any known disease was described and ascribed to witchery, the disturbances encountered most frequently relate to the reproductive organs. Sexual disorders, impotence, perversion, and delusions of the loss of sexual organs occur with remarkable frequency.

In view of the fact that the two authors of *Malleus Maleficarum* were monks and subordinates to the laws of celibacy, their preoccupation with these subjects is quite remarkable. Even more so, perhaps, is their attitude toward women, who, they felt, by their very nature, were prone to enter into a compact with the devil. It almost appears as if they considered the state of femaleness a disease itself, when they exclaimed: "What else is woman but a foe to friendship, an unescapable punishment, a necessary evil, a natural temptation, a desirable calamity, a domestic danger, a delectable detriment, an evil of nature, painted with fair colours! Therefore if it be a sin to divorce her when she ought to be kept, it is indeed a necessary torture; for either we commit adultery by divorcing her, or we must endure daily strife." Thus women, inferior by nature, lying, vicious, and hopelessly impure, are naturally the most serviceable and most willing tools of the devil.

Woman is also proven to be constitutionally inferior because "it should be noted that there was a defect in the formation of the first woman, since she was formed from a bent rib, that is, a rib of the breast, which is bent as it were in a contrary direction to a man. And since through this defect she is an imperfect animal, she always deceives."

EXIT THE CLERGY AND
ENTER THE RENAISSANCE

The end of medieval thought was clearly expressed in the writings of Paracelsus of Hohenheim (1493-1540) who insisted on the clear and distinct division between the religious and medical aspects of mental disease. This declaration of independence of clerical interference in the treatment of mental patients is most clearly expressed in the following statement by Paracelsus:

In nature there are not only diseases which afflict our body and our health, but many others which deprive us of sound reason and these are the most serious. While speaking about the natural diseases, and observing to what extent and how seriously they afflict various parts of our body, we must not forget to explain the origin of the diseases which deprive man of reason, as we know from experience that they develop out of man's disposition. The present-day clergy of Europe attribute such diseases to ghostly beings and threefold spirits; we are not inclined to believe them. For nature proves that such statements by earthly gods are quite incorrect and that nature is the sole origin of diseases. [Sigerist 1941, p. 142]

In spite of this rational approach, however, that excluded the supernatural from any consideration of disease, Paracelsus returned to the most ancient and confused uterine etiology of hysteria. Once again we read in his pages the idea of the mitigating uterus, although he went even further by denoting his belief in the sexual causation of hysteria by calling it *hysteria lasciva*.

THE GREAT ENGLISH CLINICIANS

A century and a half later we cannot discern any fundamental change in the hysteria concept, even in the writings of as sophisticated a physician as Richard Mead (1673-1754), who was the most successful physician of his time in England. His enormous success was expressed not only by the vast numbers of patients who flocked to his consulting rooms, but also by the great wealth he had accumulated and invested in important collections of art and antiques.

So far as Richard Mead's views on hysteria are concerned, we find that they belie his otherwise advanced medical attitude. One should have assumed that his large medical practice might have informed him that hysteria was not restricted to women, but, evidently, custom had blinded Mead to such an observation, for he says in his essay "The Hysterical Disease":

> There is no disease so vexatious to women as that called hysterical. It is common to maids, wives, and widows; and although it may not be attended with great danger, yet it is frequently very terrifying; and moreover, it sometimes deprives them of their senses as effectually as if they had been seized with an epileptick fit.

> When a woman has fallen into a hysterical fit, blood-letting will be of use, if she has strength to bear it; if not, cupping-glasses are to be applied to her groins and hips. But if she continues long in it, it will be proper to put the snuff of a candle, or some other thing of a foetid smell to her nostrils, in order to rouse her. In the meantime, her thighs and legs ought to be rubbed.

> When she is recovered from the fit, proper means must be used to prevent a relapse. If she be liable to obstructions [amenorrhea], and not regular, the menstrual discharges are to be promoted. The strong-smelling gums and steel medicines are very serviceable; and it is beneficial to use exercise. But the disturbances of the mind generally require proper remedies. [Mead 1792, p. 565]

Finally, recalls Mead,

> Hippocrates after prescribing castor and many other medicines wisely says, that a woman's best remedy is to marry, and bear children. [p. 565]

So far, we see that most physicians considered hysteria a purely somatic affliction without the remotest suspicion that the extreme behavioral changes might be caused by anything but physical alterations of the body. The first emphatic doubts of this assumption were voiced by two seventeenth-century physicians, Charles Le Pois, better known as Carolus Piso, and, more important, Thomas Sydenham, the most distinguished English physician of his century. Piso simply dissociated hysteria from the uterus, while Sydenham, associating hysteria with such psychological disturbances as "antecedent sorrows," saw it as a clearly psychiatric affliction.

Although Sydenham deeply influenced contemporary medicine with his writings on gout, chorea, and epidemic diseases, his important essay on hysteria was evidently ignored; it was too abrupt a contradiction to the traditional theories on that disease, in as much as he not only excluded the uterus from the etiology, but also included the "male subjects" among its victims (see Veith 1965). The following passage from the essential part of Sydenham's (1848) study of hysteria:

> Of all chronic diseases hysteria—unless I err—is the commonest; since just as fevers—taken with their accompaniments—equal two-thirds of the number of all chronic diseases taken together, so do hysterical complaints (or complaints so called) make one half of the remaining third. As to females, if we except those who lead a hard and hardy life, there is rarely one who is wholly free from them—and females, be it remembered, form one half of the adults of the world. Then, again, such male subjects as lead a sedentary or studious life, and grow pale over their books and papers, are similarly affected; since, however much, antiquity may have laid the blame of hysteria upon the uterus, hypochondriasis (which we impute to some obstruction of the spleen or viscera) is as like it, as one egg is to another. True, indeed, it is that women are more subject than males. [p. 85]

First recognition of conversion hysteria. Proceeding from this introduction, Sydenham first of all warned:

> The frequency of hysteria is no less remarkable than the multiformity of the shapes which it puts on. Few of the maladies of miserable

mortality are not imitated by it. Whatever part of the body it attacks, it will create the proper symptom of that part. Hence, without skill and sagacity the physician will be deceived; so as to refer the symptoms to some essential disease of the part in question, and not to the effects of hysteria. [p. 85]

He then described the various manifestations which he recognized to be of hysterical origin, listing among them recurring violent headaches, occasionally following by vomiting, violent coughing, and spasms of the colon. Sydenham cautioned that differential diagnosis of pains of apparently visceral origin may be difficult: "It may be hysteria or it may be a calculus; and unless there have been some antecedent mental emotion . . . the former may be mistaken for the latter."[5] He found it even more difficult to diagnose cases where pain in the bladder and retention of urine occurred. In connection with "hysteria on the stomach," Sydenham observed continuous vomiting and diarrhea.

He turned from hysterical afflictions of the internal organs to those of the external parts, "the muscular flesh of the jaws, shoulders, hands, legs and ankles, sometimes causing pain and sometimes swelling." Even some forms of toothache were not exempted from his list of hysterical complaints, and "of all pains . . . the most certain [to be of hysterical nature] is the pain in the back." Polyuria he considered an almost unfailing symptom of hysteria in females, and of hypochondriasis in males.

Syndenham's recognition of the emotional concomitants of these physical disturbances was equally perspicacious. He wrote of the incurable despair of patients, their belief that they must suffer all the evil that befalls mankind, their presentiment of further unhappiness. He described their propensity to anger, jealousy, and suspicion and pointed to their very occasional intervals of joy, hope, and cheerfulness; their daytime moods, mirrored by their dreams, were haunted by sad forebodings. "All is caprice," he said; "they love without measure those whom they will soon hate without reason."

With deep compassion for these patients, Sydenham compared their physical and mental sufferings to life in a purgatory wherein they expiate crimes committed in a previous state. Yet he emphasized that these men and women were not insane. He even went so far as to say that "those who thus suffer are persons of prudent judgment, persons who in their profundity of meditation and the wisdom of their speech far surpass those whose minds have never been exerted by such stimuli." Despite Sydenham's insistence on the sanity of the hysterical patient, he nevertheless recognized the manifestations to be of mental origin. Jorden had believed them to have their origin in the head, and Willis, in the brain; and both the authors were aware of the frequent association of emotional disturbances with hysterical phenomena (Veith 1965). Yet the definite inclusion of hysteria itself among afflictions of the mind was the contribution of Thomas Sydenham.

Among the mental symptoms described by Sydenham is depression. Some of the patients showing evidence of this today would be diagnosed as suffering from the cyclic form of this emotional imbalance. It is, of course, not to be expected that a physician of Sydenham's day could differentiate between hysteria and manic-depressive illness in view of the dearth of information on mental disease in the seventeenth century.

Sydenham's explanation of the pathogenesis of hysterical disorders included remote or external as well as proximate and direct causes. He explained the former as follows:

> The remote or external causes of hysteria are over-ordinate actions of the body; and still oftener over-ordinate commotions of the mind, arising from sudden bursts of anger, pain, fear or other similar emotions. Hence, as often as females consult me concerning such, or such bodily ailments as are difficult to be determined by the usual rules for diagnosis, I never fail to carefully inquire whether they are not worse sufferers when trouble, low-spirits, or any mental perturbation takes hold of them. If so, I put down the symptoms for hysterical; a diagnosis which becomes all the more certain whenever a large quantity of limpid crystalline urine has been voided. To such, and such like mental emotions bodily derangements may be added, e.g., long fasting and over-free evacuations (whether from bleeding, purging, or emetics) which have been too much for the system to bear up against. [p. 85]

Sydenham's choice of hypochondriasis as a corresponding male form of hysteria was deliberate. Since the time of antiquity, the hypochondrium, that is, the region beneath the ribs, had been accorded a similar role in the emotional and behavioral distress of the male to that the uterus played in similar distress in the female. Just as "uterine suffocation" was held to give rise to mental and physical disorders in women, "hypochondriacal suffocation" was held to cause numerous derangements in the abdominal viscera of men, specifically the spleen. In fact, the involvement of the spleen was considered synonymous with melancholy, and was the cause of that form of melancholy concerned with physical complaints.

In Sydenham's day, the word *hypochondriasis* simply meant male hysteria; it did not have the connotation of a morbid preoccupation with impaired physical health. This extended meaning was added by later writers, particularly Jean Pierre Falret in the nineteenth century, who described false beliefs concerning an impaired state of health as the major characteristic of hypochondriasis.

What sort of person was the hysteric, male and female, of Sydenham's day and of the many previous centuries? The patient was a composite of one whom we would now describe as manic depressive, or simply as a depressive person, perhaps even at times a schizophrenic, and, most frequently, a patient who was given to fits and seizures from a variety of diseases. In fact, we will never know how real were these fits and seizures and how much they arose from the cultural expectations of contemporary society. One always seems to discover the sense of someone presenting a performance behind each patient whose hysterical fit is being described. As we shall see in the subsequent pages, this "acting out" of the hysterical personality continued to be described by physicians until well into the twentieth century.

But, to return to Sydenham, that clinician's mode of treatment of the hysteric was entirely reasonable within the framework of contemporary etiological concepts. Since the hysterical fits or paroxysms were both strenuous and tiring to the patient, Sydenham generally prescribed anodyne medicine to soothe the patient and to alleviate the coexistent pain. He did mention the common practice of bloodletting but was careful to point out that venesection had to be performed with great caution in hysteria as the patient—already weakened—might not be able to tolerate further depletion of life-

giving energy. Another substance, however, prescribed by Sydenham, was extremely farsighted in view of the general degree of
seventeenth century understanding of body chemistry: it was his
prescription of iron filings to "strengthen his patients' blood."

This prescription requires a further explanation. It was intended
to counteract the pallor of chlorosis, the so-called green sickness of
which so many of the young ladies of society suffered and
languished, and which caused weakness and lassitude in addition to
the desirable and presumably aristocratic pallor. Furthermore, as
hysteria was often seen as an accompaniment of menstrual
disorders, either of an excessive menstrual discharge or amenorrhea,
it was believed by Sydenham that the iron filings prescribed by him
would either help supplement the excessive loss of blood or
stimulate the flow of blood if it had ceased owing to the hysterical
diathesis. In male patients the iron filings were thought to fulfill their
purpose in relation to bleeding hemorrhoids or, conversely, in
relation to hemorrhoids that failed to bleed. Even if Sydenham had
overcome the belief in the uterine causation of hysteria, he was still
enough a child of his time to believe in the need of increased
evacuation of body waste and body humors as vehicles toward
ridding the patient of the besetting illness; hence menstrual or
hemorrhoidal blood served well to carry out the excessive fullness
that had caused hysteria.

Even though the languid behavior and unnatural pallor of his
hysterical patients were hallowed in the respective social circles,
these symptoms were not immune to Sydenham's therapeutic zeal,
and to counteract them, he prescribed physical exercise, specifically
horseback riding, to his patients. Oddly enough, in doing so he
seemed to follow the traditional approach to hysteria, for those
physicians who continued to see hysteria as a result of the migrating
uterus necessarily interpreted horseback riding, and approved of it,
as a means of physically agitating the patient and thus giving the
uterus a chance to return to its natural abode in the pelvis.

HYSTERIA IN THE AMERICAN COLONIES

As Sydenham did not have a university affiliation, his followers
and disciples were essentially composed from among his readers,
and none was as zealous a reader and follower as was the Puritan

minister-physician Cotton Mather of the American Colony in Massachusetts.

Although he is, perhaps, best known for his involvement with the Salem witchcraft trials, it is his authorship of the first colonial medical book, *The Angel of Bethesda,* rather than the Salem trials, that involves him in our study of the history of hysteria.

It is amusing to read Cotton Mather's chapters on hysteria and hypochondriasis because of their great similarity—if not identity—with the writings of Sydenham, who admittedly was Cotton Mather's model and medical inspiration. Furthermore, Cotton Mather's medical writings reveal his theological background, as he combined the theological with the scientific approach to diagnosis, therapy, and prognosis (Beall and Shryock 1954). This may be exemplified with the following passage from *The Angel of Bethesda:*

> By practising, the Art of Curing by Consolation, you may carry on the Experiment. I propound then: Lett the Physician with all possible Ingenuity of Conversation, find out, what Matter of Anxiety there may have been upon the Mind of the Patient; what there is that has made his Life uneasy to him. Having discovered the Burden, lett him use all the Ways he can devise, to take it off. Offer him such thoughts as may be the best Anodynes for his distressed Mind; especially the right Thoughts of the Righteous, and the Ways to a Composure upon religious Principles. Give him a Prospect, if you can, of sound Deliverance from his Distresses, or some Abatement of them. Raise in him as bright Thoughts as may be; and scatter the Clouds, remove the Loads, by which his Mind is perplexed withal; especially, by representing and magnifying the Mercy of God in Christ unto him. [Beall and Shyrock, pp. 145-146]

(Note, incidentally, that in Mather's book only the masculine pronoun is used when referring to hysterical patients.)

In the pattern laid out by Sydenham, Cotton Mather recommends strenuous exercise, particularly horseback riding for his hysterical patients, perhaps without being aware that this remedy was a carry-over from the ancient rationale of returning the uterus to its proper abode by shaking the patient upon a galloping horse.

The rationale of this treatment is reemphasized once again by the brilliant English physician Bernard de Mandeville (1670-1733), who wrote a very imaginative treatise on hysteria and hypochondriasis (1711). The entire book consists of a dialogue between a hypothetical patient, named Mismomedon, and an equally hypothetical physician whom he called Philopirio. Mismomedon consults the physician concerning his wife who was suffering from melancholia and his daughter who was suffering from hysteria. In response Philopirio prescribed a vigorous regimen of horseback riding, passive exercise, and massage for the hysterical daughter which required at least three hours both in the morning and in the afternoon. The father, taken aback by the severity of that regimen, respectfully inquired whether this therapy, which seemed rather innovative to him, could not be replaced by the older, time-honored remedy; namely whether marriage might not be as effective as all these exercises. The doctor's reply was decidedly negative for a variety of reasons which he detailed with great clarity:

I never prescribe an uncertain Remedy, that may prove worse than the Disease; for not to speak of the many inconveniences, the advising it often puts People to. In the first place it may fail, and then there are two People made unhappy instead of one; Secondly, it may but half Cure the Woman, who lingering under the remainder of her Disease, may have a dozen Children, that shall all inherit it. A physician has a publick Trust reposed in him: His Prescriptions by assisting some ought never to prejudice other; besides that a Young Lady has no reason with the same Fortune to expect such an agreeable Match, whilst she labours under so deplorable an Infirmity, as if she was in perfect Health; therefore let her either be first Cured, and then Marry without being injurious to her self, her Husband, or her Posterity; or else remain single, with this Comfort at least in her Affliction that she is not liable of entailing it upon others. [Mandeville 1711]

This brief answer is replete with new thought. Countless physicians had recommended such marriages, but none before had expressed an interest in the results of a marriage of a hysterical patient or in the fate of her spouse and children. The fact that marriage might fail to bring a cure, that the children might be

affected, and that unhappiness might be multiplied had never
before been the concern of physicians. Needless to say, de
Mandeville's exceptional therapy in no way weakened the tendency
of later physicians to advise marriage.

The foregoing discussion makes it evident that with the exception
of Carolus Piso, Thomas Sydenham, and Cotton Mather, the
concept of hysteria as a physical disease had barely changed in two
thousand years.

ENTER NEUROSIS

It is interesting that even the man who introduced the word
neurosis still clung to the somatic etiology of hysteria. He was
William Cullen (1717-1790), an outstanding Scottish physician and
the leader of the English clinical teachers of the eighteenth century,
who was also instrumental in the founding of the medical school of
Glasgow. Like most previous students of hysteria, Cullen also was
far from being a psychiatrist, a medical specialty which had not yet
come into existence. The existence of a psychiatric patient was a
misfortune that concerned the entire family, all of whom therefore
consulted the physician about the treatment. Hence Cullen, who
introduced the word "neuorsis" did so not from a psychiatric point
of view, but in an effort to account for disease in a systematic
fashion. This naturally required an enormous simplification of all
physiological phenomena. In spite of—or perhaps because of—its
simplicity, Cullen's *First Lines of the Practice of Physic* (1796) was
for fifty years the authoritative medical text in Europe as well as in
this country.

Although Cullen is identified with the term *neurology,* there is a
great disparity between his and the modern scientific interpretation
of this word; his conception of the nervous system bore little relation
to the modern definition. In short, he saw all of life as a function of
nervous energy, and disease as a nervous disorder. What these
terms actually signified was never made clear. As did other
physicians of his time, he attempted to establish a classification of
diseases. By his definition all diseases had to be related to disorders
of the nervous system, and since only two deviations from this

system could be envisaged—namely, excessive or diminished tonus—the limits for nosological arrangement of all the ailments of body and mind were extremely narrow. Within this tight complex he recognized only four principal categories of disease: fevers, cachexias, local disorders, and "neuroses," which also comprised hysteria. Despite his belief that all disease was manifested by deviations in tone, which represented malfunction of the nervous system, somehow a category of disorders characterized by spasm or atony was segregated from the rest and included under the term "neurosis." It was for this reason, and not because of its psychic concomitants, that hysteria, obviously a spastic or convulsive disorder, fell under the heading of "neurosis."

Cullen's neurological and neuropathological contributions stopped with his nosological arrangement, at least so far as hysteria was concerned. Indeed, this man, who thought himself to be a ruthless innovator and whom the world regarded as the creator of a totally new system of medicine, contributed not a single new idea to the etiology and therapy of hysterical disorders. Yet, out of a welter of earlier and rarely acknowledged sources, he created the impression of an entirely new concept, convincing enough to gain important adherents all over Europe and even in America.

Like most authors on the subject, Cullen introduced his discussion of hysteria with a description of the general character of the illness. He drew the traditional picture of a paroxysmal attack preceded by the voiding of large quantities of limpid urine and accompanied by a globus, loss of consciousness, general muscular contraction, including the anal sphincter, and subsequent retention of urine. These paroxysms alternated with bouts of laughter and crying, "false imagination," and some degree of delirium. Ostensibly from his own observations, he found the disease to be more frequent in women than in men, especially from the age of puberty to thirty-five years. He saw it related to the menstrual period, to young widowhood, and to passions of the sensitive mind. "It occurs especially in those females who are liable to the Nymphomania; and the Nosologists have properly enough marked one of the varieties of the disease by the title of *Hysteria Libidinosa*" (Cullen, p. 104). Clearly, this refers to Sauvages, whose *Nosologie* furnished the word and the concept for hysteria libidinosa. It is probably also from this source that Cullen found support for his notion that hysteria and hypochondria were totally different diseases. It is important to reiterate that the meaning of Cullen's term "neurosis" bore little relation to its modern connotation (Riese 1958). Indeed, it is difficult to follow Cullen's thought about a definition of neurosis.

As to the pathogenesis of hysteria, Cullen was lost in a maze of confusion. For instance, as to the etiology, he thought it would "be obvious that its paroxysm began in the alimentary canal, which is afterwards communicated to the brain, and to a great part of the nervous system," and then he went on to correlate it with menstrual difficulties "and with the diseases that depend on the state of the genitals." He concluded by agreeing with the time-worn deduction "that the physicians have at all times judged rightly in considering this disease as an affection of the uterus and other parts of the genital system." The only innovation is that for the first time the ovaries were included in the picture of hysteria and were mentioned as being particularly affected in this disease. Cullen made no pretense of explaining by what means genital disturbances affected the brain and caused the hysterical convulsions. His study of epilepsy had convinced him that this disease was caused by a dilation of the blood vessels in the brain. This led him to suggest that hysteria might result from a turgescence of blood in the genital system. Having established this arbitrary analogy, he concluded that the indications of treatment were the same in both diseases.

Among Cullen's most important pupils was the great American Benjamin Rush (1745-1813), the youngest of the three physicians who signed the Declaration of Independence. Rush also was a great admirer of Thomas Syndenham, whose writings he edited and annotated. While Rush (1809) in general took over Cullen's etiological concepts, he was also an astute observer and, without stating it explicitly, made it evident that he had come to realize that "nervous disorders" such as hysteria could not simply be explained in terms of somatic disease but were due in large part to altered circumstances of life. Furthermore, it was Benjamin Rush's belief that rising standards of living, which increase the pace of civilizations, also led to an increase of disease in general and hysteria in particular.

In comparing England to ancient Rome, Rush said: "It was only in the decline of the [Roman] empire that physicians vied with the emperors of Rome in magnificence and splendor." And deploring the effect of the English pattern and influence upon the colonies, Rush stated: "the same effects of a civil war upon the hysteria, were observed by Doctor Cullen in Scotland, in the years 1745 and 1746." Hysteria, or the "nervous fever," unlike other illnesses, seem to have enjoyed a distinct social prestige which was violated by American democracy (Rush 1812): "The *hysteric* and *hypochondriac disorders*, once peculiar to the chambers of the great are now to be found in our kitchens and workshops. All these diseases have been produced by our having deserted the simple diet, and manners, of our ancestors" (p. 157).

But, then, it was not purely the external influence and the power of imitation that increased the number of patients in the Philadelphia hospitals; it was also the political events that engaged the emotions to such an extent that illness resulted. Rush (1809) described this phenomenon as follows: "It may perhaps help to extend our ideas of the influence of the [political] passions upon diseases, to add, that when either love, jealousy, grief, or even devotion, wholly engross the female mind, they seldom fail, in like manner, to cure or to suspend hysterical complaints" (p. 238).

These excerpts from Rush's writings clearly imply that hysteria was considered a disease of the better classes and that it conveyed its own social distinction. This was clear also in Sydenham's writings, although neither Sydenham nor Rush wished to engage in a sociological stratification of the respective values of various diseases. The implication of hysteria as a disease of the wealthy and prominent reflects in particular on the general medical practice of the sixteenth to the eighteenth century, which was engaged in taking care of the upper classes. Evidently the hysterics among the lower classes either went unnoticed or were sent to the poorhouses.

FRENCH VIEWS ON HYSTERIA

In contrast to the English and American medical milieu, it is interesting to note that in France, which subsequently became the *fons et origo* (well and origin) of all further hysteria study and research, social distinctions did not arise. The patients were seen not within the framework of private practice but within the framework of such famous public institutions as the Bicêtre and the Sâlpêtrière, two public French insane asylums, the first, from its inception, for men patients and the second for women. Le Bicêtre has achieved its everlasting fame because it was here that Philipe Pinel literally struck the chains off the insane patients, freeing the inmates from their fetters. Beyond that heroic measure—which well fitted into the spirit of the French Revolution inasmuch as it gave egalite to all including the mentally deranged—Pinel also devised a very logical nosological system which he used in order to segregate patients according to the nature of their afflictions. Like most classificatory efforts subsequent to Cullen, Pinel's nosology also included a class of diseases called the "Neuroses." In Pinel's use, the term *neuroses* came close to the present understanding of psychoneuroses as it included hysteria. This affliction was described under the section "Genital Disorders of Women." By placing hysteria into this section, Pinel indicated that he recognized hysterical conditions in women only, but like other physicians before him, Pinel described similar afflictions in men under different nosological designations. Thus, sterility and frigidity, as well as nymphomania, were part of the *furor uterinus,* which was "for the woman what satyriasis is for the man."

Nymphomania, which Pinel considered as part of the totality of hysteria, he believed to be caused by a combination of lascivious reading, severe domestic discipline, and a secluded homelife. Naturally, masturbation was believed to be an aggravating factor in the development of hysteria. According to Pinel (1813), the disease evolves as follows:

> In the beginning the imagination is constantly obsessed by lascivious or obscure matters. The patient is in a state of sadness and restlessness; she becomes taciturn, seeks solitude, loses sleep and appetite, conducts a private battle between sentiments of modesty and the impulse towards frantic desires. In the second phase she abandons herself to her voluptuous leanings, she stops fighting them, she forgets all rules of modesty and propriety; her looks and actions are provocative, her gestures indecent; she begins to solicit at the moment

of the approach of the first man, she makes efforts to throw herself in his arms. She threatens and flares up if the man tries to resist her. In the third phase her mental alienation is complete, her obscenity disgusting, her fury blind with the only desire to wound and to revile. She is on fire though without fever, and finally, she manifests all the different symptoms of a violently maniacal condition. [p. 287]

Pinel's subsequent case histories intimately relate "violent hysterical reactions" to specific forms of sexual deprivation, such as that caused by marriage to an impotent husband, or the separation from a socially undesirable lover. The symptoms of the hysterical fits or the so-called violent reactions were frequent tears without apparent cause, somber and taciturn behavior, inability to speak, discoloration of the face caused by a periodic tightening of the throat, and feelings and fears of strangulation. The patient furthermore suffered from congestion of her salivary gland followed by abundant salivation similar to that following mercury treatment. Because of a sudden muscular rigidity, the patient was unable to open her mouth and developed an opisthotonoslike contortion with a barely perceptible pulse, slow but regular respiration. The bowels became constipated and her urine copious and limpid.

Though perhaps somewhat more detailed than that of his predecessors and successors, Pinel's listing of symptoms demonstrates that "hysterical fits" had remained the same throughout the millennia and were to remain the same even when Sigmund Freud came to treat hysteria. Pinel brought an end to the "fits" by bringing about the *evacuation sexuelle;* that is, as soon as menstruation was restored, he found that all physical symptoms of hysteria were terminated, with apathy, depression, and anorexia as the only remaining signs of the essential disturbance. When the patient was sent to the country for fresh air and physical exercise, her menstruation became regular and she was cured of her hysteria. In the case of male hysteria similar beneficial effects were obtained by inducing bleeding of the hemorrhoids which, as could be assumed, were ubiquitous and dormant in the entire male population. In the case of women hysterics, Pinel insisted that in order to prevent a relapse, marriage should be consummated before the beginnings of winter.

Pinel's extensive preoccupation with hysteria shows a different concept from that of his predecessors. He was aware of the somatic manifestations and their physical concomitants, but they in no way minimized his belief in the "moral," or rather psychogenic, origin of the disease. Involved here was a predisposition to emotional instability to which there was added prurient stimulation by voluptuous conversation and reading of pornographic literature, abuse of sexual pleasure, including masturbation, or, more seriously, deprivation of sexual enjoyment after long periods of great indulgence.

Pinel's most important contribution to the understanding of hysteria was his deviation from the purely mechanical uterine etiology and from the increasingly sterile and repetitive neurological basis that had emanated from Great Britain for close to two hundred years. To be sure, the early efforts of British physicians to supplant the belief in witchcraft by one in the affliction of the brain and the nervous system were important and forward-looking steps. Equally significant were the findings of Willis (1664) and Whytt (1767) which demonstrated at postmortem examinations that there were no pathological changes in the uteri of hysterical patients and that, for this reason, the cause of the disease must be found elsewhere.

Because of his specialized interest and major hospital appointments, Pinel had vastly greater experience with mentally disturbed patients than had any of his predecessors. He was able to establish clinical pictures of the various mental diseases. His concept of behavioral disorders without demonstrable organic changes in the nervous system was also confirmed by postmortem examinations. Pinel thus freed the brain, as Willis and Whytt had freed the uterus, from any organic etiological connection with hysteria. In a similar fashion, his identification of amenorrhea, nymphomania, and sexual abstinence as hysterical manifestations was not a simple restatement of an older view but the direct outcome of his own observations. This reintroduction of sexual factors as a major component in hysteria pointed the way to later developments that culminated with the work of Freud.

HYSTERIA COMES TO VIENNA

In spite of its long history, hysteria attained its major fame and importance with the arrival of Sigmund Freud, whose theories and practices of psychoanalysis initially were based entirely on his work with hysterical patients. The bridge between Pinel and Freud spanned several streams of thought, however, and involved so many personalities that only a few of them can be discussed here. Outstanding among these is Baron Ernst von Feuchtérsleben (1806-1849) in whose book *The Principles of Medical Psychology* (1845) the terms *psychosis* and *psychiatric* were introduced in their modern sense and psychosis was differentiated from neurosis.[7] His emphasis upon the psychic elements grew out of his admiration and emulation of "the philanthropic Pinel," whom he credited with "being the first who positively recommended the psychical method of cure" (p. 65). The term *psychiatry* in the form of *Psychiaterie* is, of course, derived from the Greek *psyche* meaning "mind," and *iatros*, meaning "physician," and made its earliest appearance in 1808 in the writings of Johann Christian Reil.[8]

Feuchtérsleben, a Viennese, was the first of a long series of prominent authorities on mental diseases to emanate from the German-speaking school. The initial Italian leadership in both general medicine and in psychiatry had been assumed successively by France and Britain. Austria and Germany lagged behind until the nineteenth century, when they rapidly gained world dominance in all the medical sciences.

At this juncture, Feuchtérsleben concurred with a new and rather surprising trend that became manifest in the thinking regarding mental disease. As in the evolution of medical thought, which some two millennia earlier moved from religious and magical concepts toward philosophical ones, psychiatry in the eighteenth century emerged from the realm of mysticism and turned to philosophy. The dominant figure was Immanuel Kant (1724-1804), who claimed the traditional hegemony of the philosopher over matters dealing with the soul and all other factors relating to mind and emotions. On the basis of his own studies on perception and the nature of the human senses and their aberrations, Kant (1929) adjudged himself an authority on mental disturbances superior to physicians, even to those who were psychiatrically oriented.[9]

Kant's immersion in psychiatry was so deep that he proposed his own classification of mental diseases as his contemporaries in other countries were doing. He postulated that the various aberrations could be equated with stages of the civilization of man. Thus, primitive man was free from the dangers of mental disease, whereas the growing complexities of civilization posed increasing threats to man's personal freedom and hence his psychological balance. Doubtless, the intellectual climate that fostered Rousseau's belief in the "noble savage" and in the superior virtues of a return to nature contributed to these views.

Feuchtérsleben's (1845) praise of Kant was extravagant. He described him as "the man who in profundity and acuteness, far exceeded all of us, who have mounted upon his shoulder" (p. 17). Despite this admiration, Feuchtérsleben resented Kant's excluding the physician from the study of psychology and the practice of psychiatry. He vigorously held that both these fields were distinctly the medical man's business: "The question in dispute is, properly speaking, not whether the mind can become diseased, but whether the task of treating independent states of the mind by education, instruction, etc., is to be considered as belonging to the province of the physician or not. The present state of the world seems to reply in the negative, because since these moral influences are confided to the parents, teachers, the clergy, etc., and by diseases, in a nonfigurative sense, only the somatic are understood, the physician has to do with them alone" (p. 72). In keeping with his convictions about the unity of body and mind, he believed that only the physician was competent to comprehend and treat disturbances of the mind.

Although Feuchtérsleben discussed hysteria in a specific chapter, his previously mentioned views were obviously related to his ideas on hysteria, and much additional information is to be found scattered throughout his entire volume. He termed hysteria a "sister condition" to hypochondriasis, as did his predecessors—the former occurring primarily in the female and the latter in the male. The two were distinguished from one another by "the psychoorganic difference between the two sexes."

Hypochondriasis by that time had come closer to its present meaning and represented primarily an exaggerated fear of physical disease. This apprehension was augmented by the ever present threat of syphilis or of mercury poisoning following a course of its treatment. So prevalent was this form of hypochondriasis that it was noted as a "species" by some nosologists and termed *syphilis imaginaria.* Hypochondriacs were believed to be relatively immune to epidemics and contagious diseases because "of the concentration of their attention on themselves, and their consequently diminished receptivity for the external world" (Feuchtérsleben, p. 226). This withdrawal explains the early nineteenth-century synonyms for hypochondriasis, namely, "melancholy" and "spleen," as it was called in England.[10] It was a form of depression which "if it did attack women, which sometimes happens, they are generally masculine Amazonian women" (p. 225). By the same token it was Feuchtérsleben's belief that "when men were attacked by genuine hysterical fits (globus hystericus, etc.) which certainly does occur, they are for the most part effeminate men." Because of the greater delicacy of their nervous systems, women manifested hysteria more by abnormal peripheral motor and sensory phenomena than by the changes in mood so often displayed by men. This nervous sensitivity was supposed to result in a hyperirritability of the spinal cord which became known as *neuralgia spinalis.* The consequent exaggeration of reflex actions which were initiated by sexual factors resulted in the hyperkinetic responses of hysterical convulsions.

Other symptoms analyzed by Feuchtérsleben were localized pains in various parts of the body and "hyperaphia," a condition of such extreme and general sensitivity that even the slightest touch was intolerable. He also listed the *globus hystericus,* and further the *clavus hystericus,* the feeling as if a nail were being driven into a certain spot on the head. He spoke of transient swellings, "anathymiasis," which appear in various regions; and of tonic and clonic convulsions which terminate in sudden and unrestrained laughter.

The psychogenic predispositions to both hysteria and hypochondriasis were selfishness, overprivilege with satiety and boredom, excessive scholarliness, as well as the misfortunes of life. In women he blamed particularly "the female education," which he called the bane of our times because it combined everything that could heighten sensibility, weaken spontaneity, give emphasis to the sexual sphere, and sanction the feelings and impulse that relate to it. This artificially heightened persistence of sexual tension unfortunately was not relieved because of a rapid succession of pregnancies or impotence of husbands. Women in the middle of their childbearing period were found by Feuchtérsleben to be particularly disposed toward hysteria, although he also encountered it during puberty and the climacterium. But most frequently he saw it in those who remained unmarried "and in whom both the want of exercise in those sexual functions intended by nature for use and disappointed desire or hope, or at least the feeling of having failed in their earthly destination, are to be taken into account" (p. 228). Freud's colleagues would have been considerably less shocked by Freud's emphasis on sex had they been more conversant with the older literature on the subject of hysteria.

Although Feuchtérsleben spoke of hysteria and hypochondriasis, he did not consider them to be distinct entities. Rather, he believed that they symptomatically represented the effect of a multitude of noxious circumstances upon a sensitive organism. As such, they were a stage in the life history of the susceptible individual and their outcome varied. They might yield to treatment and subside entirely.

Guided by these principles, Feuchtérsleben geared his therapy to three aspects of the disease: its causes, its manifestations, and the prevention of recurrences. In the Hippocratic tradition, he asserted that the prime art of the psychiatrist is to know when to do nothing. Such therapeutic restraint applied particularly to administration of narcotics, which were so prevalent in Feuchtérsleben's day. He considered them contraindicated because their blunting of the sensorium impaired the efficacy of psychotherapy. He also cautioned against their injurious side effects, notably a progressive mental deterioration. It is strange that with his wide experience and perspicacity he failed, as did his predecessors, to recognize, or at least to mention, the hazards of narcotic addiction. In quite a modern-sounding manner he advised the physician to establish rapport with the patient without, however, permitting too great a familiarity, which would interfere with the doctor's influence. Insofar as possible, the patient should be treated as if he were sound of mind, and he must be permitted "himself to continue to spin the thread which has been held out to him" (p. 357).

As a further adjunct to treatment, Feuchtérsleben felt there should be continuous and intensified investigation of the patient's dreams, "not because it is to be considered a spiritual divination, but because as the *unconscious language* [of the mind], it often very clearly shows, to those who can comprehend its meaning, the state of the patient though he himself is not aware of this (pp. 197-198). He urged that "the interpretation of dreams deserves the attention and study of the physician." Half a century later Freud answered this call.

Kant had suggested that "perhaps without the wearying but salutary pain of dreams, sleep would be death." Feuchtérsleben fully agreed, believing, as do many modern investigators, that one never sleeps without dreaming. He was certain that dreams were frequently psychologically significant because they shed light on powerful but obscured ideas. "Dreams may give a man historical information respecting himself, . . . and the forgotten images of bygone days rise up and show the mind its former shape" (p. 166). Feuchtérsleben believed that in pathological states of the mind "the old Adam appears, and is in every sense interesting to the psychological physician (p. 166). He considered such glimpses into the patient's emotional past especially revealing in the transitory states of hysteria and hypochondriasis.

Feuchtérsleben was strikingly in advance of his day. Most of his contemporaries still thought of dreams in terms of fortune-telling and superstition.[11] Where he praised the art of doing nothing, his colleagues drugged and purged. Above all, he had the courage to speak of hysteria, and indeed of all mental aberrations, as transitory stages between health and disease, while the others of his period established rigid classifications that allowed little leeway for recovery or change. Gentle and humorous though he was, he could not help criticizing his predecessors and colleagues for having made "excursions for pleasure, rather than voyages of discovery in the domain of medical psychology."

Feuchtérsleben's most famous German colleague was Wilhelm Griesinger (1817-1868), whose book entitled *Mental Pathology and Therapeutics* was also published in 1845.[12] The two men shared the same interests, but their beliefs were worlds apart—the worlds of Berlin and Vienna. Although both were exposed to similar intellectual influences, Griesinger severed his ties with philosophy, and Kant played no part in his evolving ideas of psychic disorders. To students of psychiatry, Griesinger represented science, Feuchtérsleben literature. The former was diligently read; the latter was scanned for enjoyment and perhaps was not taken quite seriously. Griesinger was the embodiment of the new German science which was to blossom so luxuriantly. The nineteenth century is recognized as the period of the most rapid development in the history of the medical sciences, and the unprecedented acceleration of progress in our time is but a continuation of the powerful thrusts that began over one hundred fifty years ago.

Two other famous German professors, both dedicated to the emerging belief in the scientific basis of medicine, shaped Griesinger's orientation. Johann Lukas Schönlein (1793-1864) was among the first to turn from romantic natural philosophy to the scientific school of natural history. As professor of medicine at the University of Berlin, he introduced clinical teaching into Germany and with it the use of the vernacular in 1840. Carl R. A. Wunderlich (1815-1877), under whom Griesinger worked as an assistant, displayed his scientific bent by introducing clinical thermometry (1868) as an integral part of medicine.[13] Griesinger extended this approach to psychiatry when he succeeded to the professorship of clinical medicine and of mental science at the University of Berlin.

Griesinger's magnum opus on the pathology and therapy of mental illness (1845) bears witness to his scientific convictions. Even hysteria, the most unclassifiable and multiform of all afflictions, found a neat place in his scheme as one form and cause of insanity. Although this arrangement reveals some of his bias—he thought of hysteria largely in somatic terms—his assumption was not entirely rigid, nor did he believe that hysteria must necessarily lead to insanity. At any rate, he discussed all aspects of the disease in one chapter, compactly and precisely, without wandering into the realm of hypothesis or philosophy.

In spite of its conciseness and positive wording, Griesinger's work lacks the clarity and the modern pertinence of Feuchtérsleben's writings. He saw hysteria as a nonspecific affliction of the nervous system with variable manifestations arising in different parts of the "nervous apparatus" and almost always accompanied by psychological disturbances. He attributed these disturbances to a conglomeration of causes, including the ancient implication of the uterus, some superficially understood neurological and psychological concepts, and congenital emotional predisposition.

Griesinger maintained that in the majority of the ordinary mild cases, hysteria could not *as yet* be considered a mental disease. He did, however, conceptualize personality aspects of hysterical character. He listed traits which he had come to consider characteristic of hysteria and which were generally exhibited in these light forms and sometimes accompanied by sensory-motor anomalies: "immoderate sensitiveness, especially to the slightest reproach [in which there is a] tendency to refer everything to themselves, great irritability, great change of disposition on the least, or even from no, external motive" (p. 179). Other marks of these patients were volatile humor and many apparently senseless caprices. He stated that hysterical women often exhibit unusually active intelligence and "tender sympathy" for other females.

He suggested that hysteria also carried with it a great many negative traits, such as inclination toward deception and prevarication, jealousy, malice, and other sorts of misbehavior. Sydenham's compassion and Feuchtersleben's empathy are completely lacking in Griesinger's writings; his patients were censurable for these unattractive traits. Soon many other voices were heard charging that the behavioral aberrations of hysteria were willful misdemeanors. The more serious cases took the form of episodes of maniacal behavior, sometimes observed in very young girls, which "manifest themselves by vociferation, singing, cursing, aimless wandering; occasionally by more formal delirium, attempts at suicide, nymphomaniacal excitement; occasionally by delirium of a religious or demoniacal character; or there are attacks of all kinds of noisy and perverse, but still coherent, actions. In either case they retain but slight remembrance of what took place during the disorder" (p. 180).

Griesinger identified a further variation of the disease as a chronic form of hysterical insanity. This variation begins with a gradual increase in the severity of the habitual manifestations. The symptoms become more persistent and more intense and the patient becomes progressively less able to exert self-control. Although Griesinger did not offer a reason for this aggravation, he noted that it often followed violent emotional disturbances, weakness from a variety of acute diseases, or menstrual irregularities.

The diagnosis, according to Griesinger, was based on three factors: a hereditary disposition; the patient's earlier history of globus hystericus, convulsive attacks, local anesthesias and hyperesthesias, or paralyses; and the presence of local diseases of the genital organs, which were "of the greatest importance in regard to prognosis and treatment" (p. 181). Griesinger insisted that all local diseases of the uterus, ovaries, and vagina were likely to be followed by hysteria, which then may gradually progress into insanity (p. 201). Obviously, therefore, the possibility of such local disease should be uppermost in mind when hysterical patients were studied.

Griesinger's reversion to a somatic explanation for hysterical disturbances by implicating the sexual organs almost to the exclusion of everything else must be looked upon as a regression from the enlightened psychiatric concepts of Pinel and Feuchtérsleben. His writings reveal a gross lack of logic and an obtuseness which probably represented an inability to see and comprehend whatever was not consonant with his preconceived ideas. This is evident also in the nature of the arguments he used to deny the hysterogenic role of ungratified sexual desires and needs: "Some cases may doubtless be attributable to nonsatisfaction of the sexual appetite; but this is, as a rule, much overrated, as the existence of hysteria in girls who have not reached the age of puberty, its great frequency amongst married women—the frequent injurious influence of marriage, pregnancy, and childbirth, and the frequency of the affection amongst prostitutes, show" (p. 181).

Paradoxical, too, in light of Griesinger's uncritical acceptance of female pelvic disease as the almost exclusive cause of hysteria, was his recognition of its occasional occurrence in young men. He reported having seen many such cases and having "recently observed one with distinct globus and convulsions in a young married, very anemic man whose wife was pregnant" (p. 181). Regrettably he did not elaborate on this brief history, which suggests a wealth of interpretations. Nor did he offer any etiological explanations for hysteria in men. His discussion of male hysteria was very brief. Nevertheless, its existence being recognized by this most important and widely read German psychiatrist evoked no hostility, whereas less than thirty years later a comparable statement subjected Freud to a torrent of ridicule and abuse.

There have always been factions in the direction of medical investigation; and if today the favorite subject of medical scientists is organ-transplant surgery and the study of immunity and the factors that bring it about, the nineteenth century concentrated on hysteria and exhaustive descriptions of the hysterical personality, which came to be a logical outgrowth of the emotional climate of the Victorian era. Of the men engaged in hysteria research some have remained entirely unknown to posterity and have blossomed but once in their writings on hysteria. Others have gained undying fame from their treatment of the same subject. Among the former is the British physician Robert Brudenell Carter, who has entered the annals of history almost exclusively as an ophthalmological surgeon.

Oddly enough it was Carter (1853), who wrote explicitly and informatively on repression, particularly of "sexual passion," and its detrimental effect on both men and women. In fact it was perhaps Carter's very explicitness on the subject of sexual or erotic passion in both sexes which made his writings unacceptable to his contemporaries, although most of them shared his strong aversion to the hysterical personality as it was generally exhibited by the patients who were so afflicted. Thus another contemporary, the French physician Jules Falret, characterizes the hysteric as follows in his essay on "folie raisonnante on folie morale" (1890), originally presented before the Société Médico-Psychologique in 1866.

These patients are veritable actresses; they do not know of a greater pleasure than to deceive . . . all those with whom they come in touch. The hysterics who exaggerate their convulsive movement . . . make an equal travesty and exaggeration of the movements of their soul, their ideas, and their acts. . . . In one word, the life of the hysteric is nothing but one perpetual falsehood; they affect the airs of piety and devotion and let themselves be taken for saints while at the same time secretly abandoning themselves to the most shameful actions; and at home, before their husbands and children, making the most violent scenes in which they employ the coarsest and often most obscene language and given themselves up to the most disorderly actions. [p. 502]

It is only necessary, Falret repeats, to have received the pitiable confidences of the husbands of hysterical women in order to gain an idea of what life is with these patients. All their passions, including the sexual, are exaggerated, he warns. Some are so dominated by erotic impulses that unable to find satisfaction with their husbands, they turn to all kinds of immoral conduct. Others, carried away by senseless jealousy, ruin their domestic life; and yet another group derive distorted pleasure from tyrannizing over their husbands in public. Physicians, unfamiliar with these emotional debauches, might mistake them for simple viciousness. The very immensity of treachery and perversity is in itself diagnostic and indicates beyond question that such hysterical women are truly deranged, despite the appearance of reason they maintain before society.

One country of this abnormally oriented world failed to share the otherwise prevalent antipathetic reaction to hysteria in the latter part of the nineteenth century. During the decades in which the rapidly changing views on hysteria were being recorded more or less simultaneously throughout the Old World, a new voice was beginning to make itself heard. The American Colonies had given way to the Republic and the frontier was rapidly being pushed westward.

Evidently the young country still remembered the days so vividly when women were scarce and when those men who wished to found a family had to beg for their wives to be sent from England. Indeed so precious was the bridal cargo that for a considerable period they could be obtained only in return for an equal weight of tobacco which was the most sought-after colonial product. It was this historical memory that must have accounted for the uncommon appreciative regard and unfailing attentive respect shown by American men to their wives and to women in general.

The physicians of the American Colonies were generally busy with the treatment of accidents, heat prostration, and frostbites, and above all with the various epidemics of smallpox, cholera, and yellow fever that ravaged the sparse population and against which their meager medical talents were powerless. So that there was little time left to delve into the mystery of neurological and psychiatric disturbances. The Civil War, however, triggered renewed interest in this field, as the large number of casualties imposed upon physicians the challenge of differentiating between actual nerve injury, shell shock, hysteria, and malingering. The doctors had the particularly difficult task of exposing the willful misrepresentations for what they were. All other categories of neuropsychiatric casualties had to be treated.

Outstanding among those who accepted this double challenge and met it with comprehension and success was Silas Weir Mitchell (1829-1914), who was Queen Victoria's junior by ten years and a contemporary of Robert B. Carter. Mitchell has been hailed as one of the founders of American neurology and neurophysiology, and his merits in the field of psychiatry were as widely acclaimed as was his fame as a physician and popular author of novels and poems.

Silas Mitchell's interest in clinical neurology, aroused by the large number of Civil War casualties, so occupied his energies that his researches, perforce, had to be put aside. Assigned to the army hospitals that had been established in and about Philadelphia with facilities to take care of as many as twenty-six thousand sick and wounded soldiers, Mitchell found vast numbers suffering with nerve injuries and their sequelae. Because of his earlier concern with neurology, he eagerly assumed responsibility for the care of those patients whom his colleagues were glad to relinquish in light of the prevailing ignorance about such problems. Mitchell's competence so pleased the surgeon-general William A. Hammond that finally a hospital for neural disorders was created at Turner's Lane, near Philadelphia, in Auguest 1862, and pavillons were built for four hundred men. It became the model for the concentration of certain types of injuries in specific centers, a model which was very effectively used by both Great Britain and the United States in World War II. The selected patients assigned to Mitchell and his colleagues included cases of tremendous variety and interest. At one time, he reported, there were eighty epileptic patients, every kind of nerve wound, palsies, singular choreas, and stump disorders.

The neurological work of Mitchell is given such prominence in this account because of the close relationship between organic nerve injuries, hysteria, and malingering. His paper "On Malingering, Especially in Regard to Simulation of Diseases of the Nervous System," written with Keen and Morehouse (1864), represents one of the significant studies on the tenuous distinction between assumed and genuine disability. Closely allied to malingering was "nostalgia," a frequently identified cause of disability among the soldiers, about which Mitchell wrote with interest and sympathy:

> Cases of nostalgia, homesickness, were serious additions to the perils of wounds and disease, and a disorder we rarely see nowadays. I regret that no careful study was made of what was in some instances an interesting psychic malady, making men hysteric and incurable except by discharge. Today, aided by German perplexities, we would ask the victim a hundred and twenty-one questions, consult their subconscious mind and their dreams, as to why they wanted to go home and do no better than let them go as hopeless.[14]

These reminiscences expressed in 1913 reflect Mitchell's excellent memory of the war, which had ended nearly half a century earlier, and they throw light on the preoccupation with psychiatry that filled a great part of his later life. Alert and active until his death in 1914 at the age of eight-five, he lived long enough to span the teachings of Benjamin Rush, whom he never ceased to admire, and those of Sigmund Freud, who was just then becoming known in the United States. Mitchell's ironical attitude toward the "German perplexities" of psychoanalysis is well portrayed in his words on "nostalgia."

The complete survival of Freud's ideas is in striking contrast to the almost total oblivion into which those of Mitchell have fallen, although Mitchell's work was immensely influential in its day. Also, in spite of Mitchell's negative attitude toward psychoanalysis, he helped in no small measure, though quite inadvertently, to pave the way for its ready acceptance in the United States by his initiation of noninstitutional treatment of neuroses.

Most of Mitchell's neurotic patients, like many of Freud's, were women suffering from hysteria. It was for their management that he wrote his first psychiatric treatise, *Fat and Blood* (1877). This strange title was an expression of the then not uncommon belief that "moral" or psychiatric treatment could be effective only in persons with good physical health. The cases he thus treated were "chiefly women of the clan well known to every physician—nervous women, who as a rule are thin, and lack blood." Most of them had previously "run the gauntlet of nerve-doctors, gynaecologists, plaster jackets, braces, water-treatment, and all the phantastic variety of other cures" (pp. 27, 28), and still remained invalids "unable to attend the duties of life and sources alike of discomfort to themselves and anxiety to others." He saw the general development of the disease as follows:

> The woman grows pale and thin, eats little, or if she eats does not profit by it. Everything wearies her—to sew, to write, to read, to walk—and by and by the sofa or the bed is her only comfort. Every effort is paid for dearly, and she describes herself as aching and sore, as sleeping ill, and as needing constant stimulus, and endless tonics. Then comes the mischievous role of bromides, opium, chloral, and brandy. If the case did not begin with uterine troubles they soon appear, and are usually treated in vain if the general means employed to build up the bodily health fail, as in many of these cases they do fail. The same remark applies to the dyspepsias and constipation which further annoy the patient and embarrass the treatment. If such a person is emotional she does not fail to become more so, and even the firmest women lose self-control at last under incessant feebleness. [pp. 27-28]

If these events were not interrupted, these women were destined to become permanently bedridden and to furnish the most lamentable examples of all the strange phenomena of hysteria. Mitchell saw "the self-sacrificing love and over-careful sympathy of a mother, a sister, or some other devoted relative" as a further aggravation of the burden that tended to destroy the patient. He applauded Oliver Wendell Holmes's incisive description of a hysterical girl as "a vampire who sucks the blood [of] the healthy people around her." For this reason Mitchell introduced his famous "rest cure,"which entailed a specified period of bedrest away from the influence of the oversolicitous families, believing, as did Carter, that "once [you] separate the patient from the moral and physical surroundings which have become part of her life of sickness, and you will have made a change which will be in itself beneficial, and will enormously aid in the treatment which is to follow" (p. 28).

Although Mitchell's book was entitled *Fat and Blood,* he was fully aware that fat itself was not synonymous with health and that obesity was frequently a symptom of a profound disturbance. But he reasoned that since great exertion, periods of prolonged emotional strain, and physical illness frequently resulted in rapid loss of weight, a slight surplus of fat should be possessed by every individual. Many of his patients suffered from "nervous exhaustion" or were emaciated and anemic from continuous dyspepsia and were therefore already depleted of fat resources. For these in particular he prescribed a rest cure—not the pleasurable escape that was often sought by neurotic patients. He said, "To lie abed half the day, and sew a little and read a little, and be interesting and excite sympathy, is all very well, but when they are bidden to stay in bed a month, and neither to read, write, nor sew, and to have one nurse—who is not a relative—then rest becomes for some women a rather bitter medicine, and they are glad enough to accept the order to rise and go about when the doctor issues a mandate which has become pleasantly welcome and eagerly looked for" (p. 41).

Although Mitchell realized that some patients might take to such treatment with "morbid delight," he felt that they could be handled by a discerning physician. To forestall the weakening of the body by enforced bedrest, he prescribed a great deal of passive exercise in the form of massage and electrical stimulation. He observed that this regimen accompanied by a light but nutritious diet generally evoked a sense of immediate relief and often an abrupt disappearance of all the earlier symptoms. However, rest, isolation from former harmful influences, diet, and passive exercise furnished only the frame for the actual treatment; the substance was supplied by the physician in the form of "moral medication," or psychotherapy. This consisted largely of long conversation with the patient, eliciting, often in writing, her life history and the circumstances preceding the onset of the hysterical state.

It is significant to see how much Mitchell and Freud, the contemporaries who never met each other, had in common when we read in Mitchell's later study (1881): "I make use of some of the curious self-analyses which patients who have recovered have placed at my disposal. Both for what they betray and what they conceal these histories are valuable, and especially so when they come from women of educated intelligence. The elements out of which these disorders arise are deeply human, and exist in all of us, in varying amount" (pp. 50-51). It is interesting that these statements preceded Freud's publications by several years.

Mitchell was extremely resourceful in his moral therapy. He "urged and scolded, and teased and bribed, and decoyed along the road to heatlh; but this is what it means to treat hysteria. There is no short cut; no royal road" (p. 51). He was an extraordinarily charming man, erudite and entertaining, and doubtless most attractive to his female patients. His resourcefulness in dealing with them was almost boundless. One of his most astounding approaches is related by his biographer A. B. Burr and concerns one of his patients who refused to obey Mitchell's order that she leave her bed. When all arguments and orders proved futile, he finally threatened: "If you are not out of bed in five minutes—I'll get into it with you!" Even this threat proved to be without effect and Mitchell began to undress; but when he was about to remove his trousers the patient left her bed in haste. While this story may be apocryphal, since Mitchell does not relate it himself, it was well known during his lifetime and apparently was never denied by him.

It is strange indeed that with all his intimate contacts and understanding of his female patients, he was, unlike so many other students of hysteria, so little impressed with the etiological role of sexual deprivation. Although he spoke of the "false relationships with husbands" that could cause neuroses, he nevertheless categorically rejected all sexual implications. He described Freud's writings as "filthy things" that should be consigned to the fire. On one occasion, however, speaking before the American Neurological Association in Philadelphia on May 21, 1908, in a somewhat mellower mood, he admitted an "intellectual welcome" and an open mind to "psychopathic analysis." And he went on to say: "I most gladly read the elaborate and novel studies in psychologic diagnosis, the laboratory aids, the association test, the mind-probing examinations. They are interesting and even fascinating, although at times men do seem to me to reach by wandering ways facts of individual history more simply to be discovered by less cumbersome methods."

Mitchell (1888) admitted that he had often been asked whether his constant contact "with the nervous weaknesses, the petty moral deformities" of his female patients had not lessened his esteem for women. He answered with an emphatic denial: "The largest knowledge finds the largest excuses"; and the physician aware of the many possible educational errors and the marital difficulties will not condemn the patient but understand and help her.

> The priest hears the crime or folly of the hour, but to the physician are oftener told the long, sad tales of the whole life, its far-away mistakes, its failures, and its faults. None may be quite foreign to his purpose or needs. The causes of breakdowns and nervous disaster, and consequent emotional disturbances and their bitter fruit, are often to be sought in the remote past. He may dislike the quest, but he cannot avoid it. If he be a student of character, it will have for him a personal interest as well as the relative value of its applicative side. The moral world of the sickbed explains in a measure some of the things that are strange in daily life, and the man who does not know sick women does not know women. [p. 10]

The women of Mitchell's day cherished this special concern and thrived under his benevolent protection. But Mitchell's day ended on the eve of World War I, and at its close women had renounced all the special frailties and privileges that Mitchell had found so endearing and that had provided the basis for his therapy. The last vestige of Victorian reticence had also disappeared, and the new climate of thought, thoroughly receptive to Freudian views, had little interest in Mitchell's tranquil methods or in his efforts to put "wholesome fat" on women who were rigorously dieting to achieve the figures of young boys.

Similarly forgiving and sympathetic toward his female hysterical patients was Sigmund Freud, whose method of psychoanalysis evolved from his treatment of hysterics. In order to follow that development we must rethink our way through various fads and psychic phenomena.

Franz Anton Mesmer's theory of "animal magnetism," the curative effect of which he displayed in the salons of Vienna and Paris, ran afoul of the contemporary scientific and medical profession of France and was condemned in 1784 as simple "imagination" by a royal commission that had been appointed by Louis XVI. Although Mesmer had withdrawn into obscurity after the verdict of the royal commission, animal magnetism continued to be practiced by other believers. In France it was the Marquis de Puységur, no physician but a country gentleman, who continued to magnetize persons who came to him for help. By inducing what he called "somnabulistic sleep," he brought about striking personality changes in some patients. The publicity attendant upon the Marquis' claims of cure led to the appointment of yet another investigative commission; again a verdict adverse to the movement was issued.

Because of the negative verdicts of the two investigative commissions, the evolution from animal magnetism to hypnosis could not take place in France but happened in England, where Mesmerism had been introduced upon its expulsion from France. James Braid, a Scotsman, was the first thoroughly serious physician to concern himself with the investigation of the phenomenon of mesmeric sleep. As a surgeon, he not only saw its potential for inducing unawareness of pain, but also employed it with success in his own practice. To divert animal magnetism from its earlier odious association with Mesmer, that is, from charlatanism, Braid renamed it neurypnology, neurohypnosis, or hypnosis. It is interesting that Braid of Great Britain discovered this method of surgical analgesia in 1845, exactly two years before the discovery of ether anesthesia in the United States.

Braid was a remarkable surgeon, inasmuch as he saw the value of hypnosis beyond its role as a pain-killer in surgical operations and discovered its value in the treatment and cure of functional disorders. He was among the first to emphasize the distinction between functional and organic diseases and to recognize the value of suggestion in the former. Mesmer's "animal magnetism" had been so successfully driven out of France that no one recognized it when it returned under the name of hypnosis, and when Jean-Martin Charcot, the greatest neurological scientist of his day, employed hypnotism in his study and treatment of hysteria

CHARCOT

It is so well known as to scarcely need restatement that it was at Charcot's clinic in France that Sigmund Freud watched the application of hypnosis to hysterical patients and found the patients absolutely responsive to hypnotic suggestion. But what is far less well known is that Charcot, who was so vitally important to the history of hysteria and psychiatry in general, was very much misled by his devoted assistants in his exaggerated confidence in certain aspects of hypnotism. The collapse of these hypotheses cost him much of the fame and respect which his earlier labors had brought him.

Jean-Martin Charcot was born in Paris in 1825, a contemporary of the German Wilhelm Griesinger, the British Robert Brudenell Carter, the Austrian Baron von Feuchtérsleben, and the American Silas Weir Mitchell. As Charcot passed through the various stages of a French academic career, he had shown signs of great promise, publishing widely on different medical subjects, but he evinced little interest in the pathology and clinical correlation of diseases of the nervous system. At the age of thirty-seven he was made physician to the Salpêtrière Hospital, which attained its first major publicity in connection with Pinel's work. It usually housed some five thousand neurotic indigents, epileptics, and insane paitents, many of whom were deemed incurable. With this extraordinary number and variety of patient material, Charcot's orientation changed. According to his biographer, Guillain (1955), "It was during a period of only eight years, between 1862 and 1870, that Charcot structured his magnificent masterpieces by his descriptions of multiple sclerosis, the tabetic arthropathies, amyotrophic lateral sclerosis, and the localization of lesions of the spinal cord. These studies established his fame as a scientist and provided a magnificent beginning for his additional contributions to neurology and neuropathology. He also proved to be a superb teacher and later attracted students from all parts of the world.

After ten years as chief of the medical services at the Salpêtrière, Charcot was nominated to the professorship of pathological anatomy at the University of Paris. He occupied this chair until 1882, when he was appointed to the newly established professorship in diseases of the nervous system at the same institution. Although he maintained an interest in organic neurologic disorders throughout his teaching career, in his later years he was chiefly concerned with investigation of the neuroses, hysteria, and hypnotism.

This interest logically grew out of his life at the Salpêtrière; but his shift from organic neurological and neuropathological studies to hysteria was the accidental result of an administrative arrangement at that hospital. As related by Pierre Marie, one of Charot's students, certain parts of the ancient buildings that composed the Salpêtrière had become so decrepit that they had to be abandoned. The inmates were transferred to other divisions, and the nonpsychotic epileptics and the hysterics were separated from the insane. Since the first two groups manifested episodic behavior, it was considered logical to house them together and to establish a special section, called the *quartier des épileptiques simples* or the "division of simple epileptics." This service was assigned to Charcot as the senior physician, who suddenly found himself surrounded by the problems of hysteria.

Pierre Marie explained the results of this anomalous condition. Whereas in this new situation the seizures of the epileptics remained unchanged in frequency and severity, the hysterics were greatly affected by their constant exposure to epileptic patients. Because of the tendency to mimic, especially in young hysterics, they began to imitate every phase of epileptic seizures; the tonic and the clonic convulsions, the subsequent hallucinations, and finally Charcot's "bizarre postures."

Unfortunately Charcot failed to recognize this imitation at first and believed that a new entity was manifest, which he termed "hystero-epilepsy." Only much later did he realize the absurdity of this designation, and he called attention to the great difference between the clinical form as well as the substratum of a true epileptic attack which had been classed under the name of epileptiform hysteria (Charcot 1877, p. 304).

In the meantime, having immersed himself specifically in the study of hysteria, he noted that the *grandes* paroxysms, which to him represented "hysteria major," always occurred in an identical manner in the same patient. As mentioned earlier, such convulsive attacks had become rare in his day, but, as mimicked epileptic fits, they appeared to occur frequently in the Salpêtrière, Charcot distinguished these seizures of "hystero-epilepsy" from the veiled manifestations that he called "hysteria minor." He noted narrowing of the field of vision as well as disturbances of skin sensitivity, which included hemianesthesia. When these two somatic manifestations occurred simultaneously, they were characterized as the physical stigmata of hysteria. Thus he defined hysteria as a specific neurosis that manifests itself by periodic attacks and permanent stigmata. In so doing he was in essence defining a disposition, a personality which tended to have episodic hysterical attacks.

Charcot was among those who knew that the same symptoms could be found in men as well as women. He wrote in one of his lectures: "Keep it well in mind and this should not require a great effort, that the word 'hysteria' means nothing, and little by little you will acquire the habit of speaking of hysteria in man without thinking in any way of the uterus" (1877, p. 37). Since, however, the Salpêtrière was a hospital for female patients, most of Charcot's patients were women, and among them he found symptoms that had not previously been recorded: spontaneous pains in the region of the ovaries and the mammary glands. This suggested to Charcot that these regions were "hysterogenic zones."

Contrary to all previous observers, Charcot described the attacks as being quite uniform in all his patients. The paroxysm itself, he said, consisted of the four stages that he had described in hystero-epilepsy, as will be detailed later in this chapter. With a similar attempt at systematization, he arranged the stigmata in three categories: (1) the sensory disturbances, which included the anesthesias and hyperesthesias, (2) the disturbances of the special senses, such as deafness and narrowing of the field of vision, and (3) the motor disturbances. He was aware, of course, that all these impairments were functional, but that they mimicked organic disease. Charcot never doubted that the paroxysm would invariably unfold into the major hysteric crisis with its four well-defined phases. It seems never to have occurred to him that the patients might be acting out what they knew was expected of them; or that the repetition of these dramatic crises at the precise time of lectures and demonstrations before an appreciative audience of physicians and medical students may have been engineered by his assistants as a misguided expression of helpfulness. The means by which it is believed this was achieved will be described later.

Charcot is popularly credited with recognizing the role of the emotions in the production of hysteria. Although it has been shown above that he was far from the first to do so, his pronouncements, coming as they did from the leading figure in neuropsychiatry, were not only more acceptable but also spread to a much wider medical public. Among his observations was the role of suggestion in creating certain symptoms, such as artificially induced paralysis, and he stated that "in the matter of suggestion, what is done can be undone." Charcot also knew of the narrow and often barely perceptible line that seems to divide hysteria from malingering, which often evaporated to amalgamate the two states. He expressed his admiration (Charcot 1889a) for "the ruse, the sagacity, and the unyielding tenacity that especially the women, who are under the influence of a severe neurosis, display in order to deceive . . . particularly when the victim of the deceit happens to be a physician" (p. 368).

Even more than his predecessors, Charcot attributed a major significance to psychic trauma in the production of hysterical attacks and for this reason urged the removal of patients from the psychopathogenic environment:

It would not be possible for me to insist too much on the capital importance which attaches to isolation in the treatment of hysteria. Without doubt, the psychic element plays a very important part in most of the cases of this malady, even when it is not the predominating feature. I have held firmly to this doctrine for nearly fifteen years, and all that I have seen during that time—everything that I have observed by day—tends only to confirm me in that opinion. Yes, it is necessary to separate both children and adults from their father and their mother, whose influence, as experience teaches, is particularly pernicious.

Experience shows repeatedly, though it is not always easy to understand the reason, that it is the mothers whose influence is so deleterious, who will hear no argument, and will only yield in general the last extremity. [1889a, p. 210]

The validity of the observations in terms of the position held today is obvious. Again, they were more acceptable coming from Charcot than from Carter, the relatively unknown practitioner in the English countryside, or from the Americans, Mitchell and Holmes, though all these men were prominent in their own countries. Similarly, the phenomenon of hysterical contagion, first noted by Baglivi (Veith 1965, p. 147) and afterwards observed by so many others, was described by Charcot as explaining some of the mass hysterias in the convents of the Middle Ages and the Renaissance.

Charcot's formula for treatment of hysteria was largely limited to symptomatic therapy. It consisted of two approaches. The first was psychological and was directed toward the neutralizing of the original psychic trauma and assuring patients that their afflictions were curable. He insisted on a change of their "moral environment," and he demanded submission to a certain amount of discipline. His second approach was the traditional effort directed toward the reinvigorating of organs and extremities and stimulating the muscles to alleviate concurrent symptomatic impairment.

On the whole, however, it appears that Charcot was far less intensely concerned with therapy than with scientific analysis of the disease. This has been elaborated by Thomas Szasz (1961), who suggested that Charcot's primary role as a professor of neurology was to increase knowledge of the diseases of the nervous system and to teach students and physicians. But more significant than this, perhaps, was his aloof personality, which could not identify itself with the miseries of his patients, particularly since the inmates of the Salpêtrière were the dregs of society. For these reasons, he more drastically differed in his physician-patient relationships than had Mitchell, whose nervous ladies were part of his own social milieu.

That Charcot, the most scientific and productive of all neurologists of his day, should ever be actively involved with hypnotism is astounding. It can only be explained as the result of his broad interest in all aspects of brain function, including the new field of psychology. Up to his time, the study of mental function had been almost exclusively in the hands of scholars and philosophers. Charcot felt that such knowledge could add a new dimension to understanding diseases of the nervous system, and he therefore invited several psychologists to join in his research, as part of his effort to combine all elements, including hypnotism, that had any bearing on mental processes. His interest awakened, he made a systematic study of the subject beginning with the writings of Braid, and then introduced hypnotism into his own program at the Salpêtrière in 1878. At the outset a prudent and conservative orientation was developed and applied to these investigations. But soon this caution gave way to uncritical and enthusiastic reports of spectacular findings that were totally unsupported by scientific proof. Thus, as intimated above, Charcot's concern with hypnotism led him into error that proved to have catastrophic repercussions. It would appear that Charcot first visualized hypnotism primarily as a diagnostic agent rather than an important therapeutic tool. In fact, in the beginning he became convinced that mere susceptibility to hypnotism indicated that the subject was potentially hysterical, and he never deviated from this view.

Significantly, Charcot never induced the trance state himself but relegated this duty to his assistants. It has been assumed that unbeknown to Charcot these men conditioned the patients to perform according to their chief's expectations. Thus the eminent neuroscientist was led into serious error by the well-meaning efforts of his faithful associates. The regular responses to implanted suggestion, of which he was unaware, gave him reason to believe that the hysterical patients' uniform reactions to hypnotism were characteristic of the disease; and on these convictions he staked his scientific reputation.

Charcot concluded from these studies that "major hypnotism" could only be induced in grave hysterics and that the manifestations of major hypnotism were always a reenactment of a typical grand paroxysm. In the paralyses that so often followed the attack, Charcot reported an exaggerated patella tendon reflex on the side that was paralyzed. He also claimed to be able to transfer analgesia or anesthesia from the affected side to the opposite side by means of magnets. To him, this constituted a diagnostic tool far more reliable than any previous one for recognizing the confusing malingering, which the disease so closely resembled. And this Charcot proclaimed with the full authority of his fame and official position.

Although the French Academy of Sciences had repeatedly condemned all work on magnetism, it could not ignore serious pronouncements by the world's leading neurologist. Despite the fact that its approval in 1882 was grudging and partial, it was nevertheless sufficient to lift the onus from hypnotism and make further research possible. Just two years later a group of investigators, who came to be known as the "Nancy School," took advantage of this new freedom. This school was to rival and challenge Charcot's work at the Salpêtrière until his death in 1892. The challengers were A. A. Liébault, a local medical practitioner, and Hyppolyte Bernheim, a professor at the University of Nancy. Their approach to hypnosis differed radically from Charcot's. They hypnotized patients themselves, were unconcerned with the reflexes and contractures brought about by hypnosis, and operated with words alone, without recourse to instruments and magnets. Moreover, they were decidedly interested in the therapeutic use of hypnotism, and Bernheim recorded a great number of speedy cures of hysterical disorders. Like Braid, they completely denied the existence of any fluid passing from hypnotizer to patient and strongly maintained that whatever influence was exerted was entirely psychological.

Bernheim insisted that the hypnotic state was nothing more than sleep brought about by suggestion and that it accentuated the effects of suggestion by removing intellectual control. Both Liébault and Berheim found that susceptibility to hypnosis was not restricted to neuropaths and that although impressionability varied from person to person, most persons were susceptible. Bernheim postulated that hysteria was not actually a disease at all and that everyone was potentially more or less hysterical.[15] According to his definition, hysteria consisted simply of attacks occurring in persons whose psychological reactions to emotional traumata were exaggerated or distorted. Bernheim coined the expression *hystérisables* for such persons, and a series of attacks he called "hysterical diathesis." This tendency toward hysteria could be corrected through emotional education or guidance, which was in reality a form of suggestion. Bernheim himself readily admitted that hysterics were especially suggestible, but he emphatically denied that suggestibility in itself was a pathological condition.

The question of augmented suggestibility in connection with hypnosis led to a reexamination of the problem of criminal suggestion, and contrary to Braid, Maudsley, and Charcot, the followers of the Nancy School agreed that hypnosis might constitute a definite danger. This was but one aspect of the differences between the Nancy School and Charcot; indeed the Nancy School considered the work of Charcot completely invalid as it related to hysteria.

Bernheim's initial pronouncements were restrained, but they became forceful after Charcot's pupils attacked his work as unscientific and published their own extraordinary claims, such as their ability to transfer diseases to hysterics by way of magnets. Bernheim, in turn, openly expressed his doubts about the soundness of Charcot's observations of exaggerated reflexes,[16] and finally suggested that the patients had been subjected to specialized training before being studied by Charcot, that they had not undergone natural hypnosis but were "suffering from a suggestive hysterical neurosis."

As the battle waxed, the confines of scholarly scientific publications were transcended, and a bitter public polemic ensued. Bernheim, presenting his case in 1891 in a leading newspaper, *Le Temps,* said that "the hypnotism of the Salpêtrière is an artificial product, the outcome of training." Babinski, one of a group of prominent neurologists who supported Charcot, replied in an article in the *Gazette Hebdomadaire* criticizing the vagueness of the psychological notions of the Nancy School and their overemphasis on suggestion without any attempt at its definition. But the Nancy School gradually gained adherents and Charcot's position became increasingly untenable. Eventually the few voices raised in his behalf also fell silent, and, at the time of his death in 1892, the Nancy School claimed full victory.

Without the stimulus of a running battle with their strong adversary, the Nancy School lost much of its momentum, and the medical world at large became indifferent to the subject of hypnotism. Publications on hypnotism, which had numbered in the thousands in the 1870s and 1880s dwindled to a small trickle at the turn of the century and soon ceased altogether. Contemplating this rapid decay, Pierre Janet (1901b) wrote: "No one repudiated hypnotism, no one denied the power of suggestion; people simply ceased to talk about [them]" (p. 200). Nevertheless, an indirect though important relationship has linked modern psychiatry, particularly psychoanalysis, to the work of the two rival schools, and hypnotism played a significant part in the early stages of Freud's work.

One of Charcot's greatest assets was, of course, his ability to attract extremely promising students and to give them superb training. From his school there came Pierre Marie (1853-1940), the most brilliant of his pupils in neurology, who described many hitherto unknown forms of nervous system disease. There was Charcot's Polish assistant, Joseph Babinski (1857-1932), who is known for the great-toe reflex that bears his name and for his contributions to the knowledge of cerebellar disorders. There was also the great psychologist Pierre Janet, and Sigmund Freud, who was but briefly under Charcot's tutelage, was decisively influenced by him. These are the leading and best-known from among dozens of distinguished neurologists who flocked to the lectures of Charcot from all over the world. He left an indelible mark upon his pupils, who were fiercely proud of their teacher, even if they could not always defend his mistakes. The extent of his influence is most evident when we realize that three of his most outstanding pupils, Janet, Babinski, and Freud, devoted years of their lives to the very subject that had occupied their teacher so intently during his last decade. Pierre Marie, the fourth of this distinguished quartet, who himself had never been involved in Charcot's studies on hysteria, gently spoke of the unfortunate experiments with hypnotism as his teacher's "slight failing" (Guillain 1955, p. 174).

There is evidence that shortly before his death, Charcot had begun to reconsider his theories on hysteria. The first sign of a different and fresh point of view can be detected in his article "La foi qui guerit" ("Faith Healing"), which was published simultaneously in London and Paris (1892). He was encouraged to write this article by the editors of the *New Review* who, after publishing the experiences of a famous explorer when visiting a religious sanctuary, consulted Charcot concerning his own views on miraculous healing. These he set forth in a most interesting manner, for the subject had long been of concern to him, as, he thought, it should be to every physician: "the goal of medicine being the cure of patients without distinction as to what curative process is used" (Guillain 1955, p. 177). For this reason the ability to heal by faith appeared to him a most valuable attainment because he felt it to be often effective when all other means failed.

Charcot further states: "The cure of a particular symptom directly produced by faith healing, which is commonly called a miracle cure, is as one can show in the majority of cases a natural phenomenon that has occurred in all ages, among the most varied civilizations and religions, and even a phenomenon that is actually observed in all geographic regions" (quoted in Guillain, p. 178). He then stressed that faith healing should be limited to diseases that do not require any other tangible intervention beyond the power of the mind over the body. He debated this subject with many of his colleagues with whose writings he was conversant. He quoted Hack Tuke's small treatise on the influence of the mind upon the body (1872), and he agreed with Russel Reynolds (1869), who spoke of "paralysis dependent upon an idea." Yet his article was far from a summary of the contemporary literature on the subject. The depth of his personal involvement with the topic is evident from his references to the pilgrimages to the Christian shrines, to the sanctuaries of Egypt, and to the temples of Aesculapius. In all of them he recognized three common elements: anticipation of the cure, autosuggestion, and the contagiousness of shared belief in recovery. But most significant, in view of his earlier opinions on hysteria, was his final paragraph (quoted in Guillain 1955):

In summary, I believe that for those who wish to practice it, faith healing requires a special patience and special kinds of disease which are susceptible to the influence that the mind possesses over the body. Hysteric patients possess an eminently favorable mental picture for the cultivation of faith healing, because they are in the first place suggestible, either through suggestions coming from without or more especially because they possess of themselves a very powerful element of autosuggestion. Among these individuals, both men and women, the influence of the mind over the body is sufficiently effective to precipitate a recovery from some diseases, which, because of our past ignorance, were considered incurable. Does this mean that from now on we know everything about faith healing and that every day we shall see its frontiers retract under the influence of scientific discoveries? Certainly not. We must always search into everything, we must know how to be patient. I am still among the first to admit: "There are more things in heaven and earth than are dreamed of in your philosophy." [p. 179]

This paragraph reveals that Charcot did not cling to preconceived notions of the nature of hysteria, and it disputes the frequently voiced criticism that Charcot's orientation was purely organic. That this is so is also borne out by the notes of George Guinon (1925), Charcot's last private secretary, who described some of the conversations he had had with the master shortly before the latter's death. These indicate that Charcot had planned to revise his entire work on the pathology of the nervous system because he had come to the conclusion "that his concept of hysteria had become decadent . . . [that he] had foreseen the need of dismembering his theory on hysteria and was preparing to dynamite the edifice to which he had personally contributed so much in building" (pp. 511-512). In offering this revelation, Guinon was conscious of the incongruity that he, a secretary, apparently alone knew of Charcot's contemplated changes and that only he was aware of the critical turn of mind that the master had directed against himself.

CHARCOT'S SUCCESSORS

Just when Charcot must have been contemplating these radical changes in his own thinking on hysteria, his pupil Pierre Janet, in 1893, completed a book entitled *The Mental State of Hystericals* (1901a). This work was based on Janet's dissertation for the Doctor of Medicine degree. The degree was awarded to him in 1893, when he was thiry-four years old and after he had made a name for himself as a philosopher and author of studies on Bacon and Malebranche. In his brief and somewhat contradictory preface to this publication, Charcot generously recommended it to the medical public. He emphasized not only that Janet had been his pupil but also that the studies upon which the text was based had been conducted during his service at the Salpêtrière and merely confirmed a thought often expressed in his own lectures "that hysteria is largely a *mental malady*" (p. v; emphasis mine) and that it could be understood and treated only if this feature was constantly borne in mind. Janet, in turn, frequently and gratefully referred to the inspiration he had derived from his "eminent master," but he made it clear that the book was the result of his own studies and researches, and that "the largest portion of these observations are new" (p. xv).

In the definition of hysteria, Janet agreed with Paul Briquet, the author of another monumental treatise on hysteria (1859), that hysteria is a general disease which modifies the whole organism and that for this reason the interrelations of the psychological and the physiological phenomena should be minutely investigated. "It is thus only," Janet stated, "that medicine will be able to acquire the knowledge of the whole man and understand the diseases that affect the whole organism."

His method of research was limited to close and careful observation, for he thoroughly distrusted psychological experimentation. The statement he made to this effect (1901a) is significant and has lost little of its validity in the intervening three quarters of a century.

We must distrust complicated experiments on the mind, which are not easy to make; they are often sufficient to upset the mental state we wish to study. Psychology is not yet advanced enough to admit of many precise measures. The general nature of the phenomena, their thousand variations, their changeable conditions, are not sufficiently known for us to boast of measuring any one isolated fact. It is useless and even dangerous to take a microscope and engage in rough anatomy; we expose ourselves thus in not knowing what we look at. We believe that we should, before all, know well our subject in his life, his education, his disposition, his ideas, and that we should be convinced that we can never know him enough. We must then place this person in simple and well-determined circumstances, and note exactly on the spur of the moment what he will do and say. To examine his acts and words is as yet the best means of knowing men, and we find it neither useless nor wearisome to write down the wandering speeches of a lunatic. [pp. xiv-xv]

He thus prepared the reader for the detailed case histories and the circumstantial descriptions of actions, words, and phases spoken or written by the patients. These he saw as "instructive documents" and the "graphics of pathological psychology," which naturally had to be interpreted but which must never be ignored.

The small group of patients presented in such detail were culled from the vast numbers he had treated. The sum of his observations led him to the conclusion that hysterical symptoms fall into two different forms: They are either essential and temporary, or they are permanent, that is, they persist until the last indications of the disease have disappeared. This difference, less clearly analyzed, had been characterized by earlier writers as "stigmata" and "accidents." Although Janet found this terminology not entirely satisfactory, he retained it and simply focused attention on the mental aspects of both. In so doing he introduced a new and extremely interesting insight into a disease whose apparently protean manifestations and infinite variety of symptoms had baffled untold generations of physicians. The analysis of the *mental* aspects of the disease completely altered the picture. What initially appeared to be varied and disconnected fell into a consistent and coherent pattern when subjected to the analysis of its psychological counterparts. In this way Janet differentiated hysteria from all other mental disturbances.

Janet recognized five groups of mental stigmata: anesthesia, amnesia, abulia,[17] motor disturbance, and modifications of the character. The last-mentioned was divided into two components, the intelligence and the emotions. In the former he generally noted a deterioration; in the latter, exaggerated reactions to a diminished number of emotions because of the fact that "these patients are in general very indifferent, at least to all that is not directly connected with a small number of fixed ideas" (Janet 1901a, p. xv).

The mental accidents he divided among suggestion and subconscious acts, fixed ideas, convulsive attacks, somnambulisms, and deliria. There is little doubt that among the patients who provided him with this detailed symptomatology there were—as there had been among Charcot's patients—many who suffered from severe psychoses and whose hysteria, if it existed at all, was superimposed upon an even more serious disease. But although he was unable, or unwilling, always to make a differential diagnosis, he nevertheless presented a novel and penetrating picture of the psychology of hysteria. Indeed the book is so rich and original that a summary of it can hardly be given; a discussion of a few of the highlights must suffice. Of special interest here is Janet's opinion concerning the behavioral peculiarities of the hysterical patients. Again, he quotes Briquet: "It is impossible to enter into this description, which would come nearer a romance of morals and manners than a medical clinique, but hystericals, having attracted attention these many years, have a reputation and a legend" (Janet 1901a, pp. 214-215).

Convention had come to attribute to hysterics a certain characteristic mode of conduct that Janet wished to analyze. He was interested primarily in their alleged sexual proclivities, for "after having accused hystericals of all crimes of witchcraft, and having reproached them with cohabiting every Saturday with the devil, disguised as a he-goat, people have long preserved a vague remembrance of these superstitions, and have maintained that these patients had an eminently erotic disposition (p. 215). Janet was so convinced of the absurdity of this notion, which he considered a relic of the uterine theory, that he ignored the possibility that that theory might have been formulated from the erotic disposition.

Dismissing the role of the uterus as absurd, Janet then claimed that the time had come to investigate the reputed hypereroticism of hysterical patients. From his study of hundreds of cases, he found that such erotic disposition does exist in hysteria but only to the same degree as do all other fixed ideas. In 120 patients so studied there were but four in which sexuality played an altogether prominent role. And even in this manifestation, he felt, there was nothing strange or pathological. Amorous passions and sexual desires simply were normal to the young inmates of the Salpêtrière, as they were among all groups of young women. Hysterical patients were as disposed to talk of love, to see its evidence, and to read descriptions of it as were all other elements in the population. "Why should their minds, so ready to receive impressions, so docile to all influences, resist this one?" In their hysterical delirium he had often heard patients speak of love, of husbands, of men, of rape, and of pregnancy. These, he believed, must be paramount in the patients' thoughts, for "you cannot put into your delirium what is not in your mind." The same is true also for the contents of dreams.

But Janet simply could not accept the traditional beliefs of exaggerated sexual preoccupation in hysteria and stated flatly that with a very few exceptions, "the hystericals are, in general, not any more erotic than normal persons." He maintained, to the contrary, that they are rather more frequently frigid than sensual and that they are more likely to forget their former attachments than to increase them. The reason for this, Janet believed, was simply due to the shrinking of their emotional radius, to their increasing egocentricity, their preoccupation with their own concerns, and their indifference to demands and expectations from others. Even the tendency toward simulation and mendacity he attributed simply to their forgetfulness or to lack of interest in their own earlier statements, promises, or facts of life, rather than to defects of conscience.

It is for this reason also, according to Janet, that hysteria, which was formerly considered a most variable and protean malady, was actually extraordinarily predictable and repetitious in each individual patient. He observed that early in the course of the disease patients organized their fixed ideas and their resulting manifestations; they tended to organize their emotional patterns, movements, and ideas—whether borrowed or their own—and weave them all together to "transform them more or less through a kind of subconscious meditation." But exacerbations in illnesses of longer standing were systematized and uniform and could not be altered. Thus, far from being too labile, the hysterical patient was not sufficiently so. Absorbed in their preoccupation with their fixed ideas, the patients retained a constant emotional climate that was unaffected by and unadaptable to all external influences.

The *idée fixe* that characterizes hysteria is developed "below consciousness" and remains "outside of normal consciousness. . . .

The subconscious character of the fixed ideas ... plays an important part in the therapeutics of these affections" (pp. 411-412). Referring to an earlier work, Janet stated: "We formerly showed that it was necessary to look up, so to say, these subconscious phenomena in order to attack them, and that one could not treat the hysterical accident before having reached those deep layers of thought within which the fixed idea was concealed" (p. 412).

This thought is undoubtedly what modern psychology has come to consider Freudian, and it is regrettable for historical reasons that Janet failed to cite the place where his earlier demonstrations were made and documented. He referred gently to the work of his Austrian colleagues but firmly claimed priority, viz: "We are happy to see today MM. Breuer and Freud express the same idea ...[when they say that] it is necessary to make the patient conscious of the provocative event, and to bring it into full light. As soon as the subject recognizes his fixed ideas, the [hysterical] accidents are bound to disappear [see Breuer and Freud 1893-1895, p. 6]." Despite his pleasure with Breuer and Freud's verification of his already "somewhat old" interpretations of subconsciously fixed ideas in hystericals, he scouted their claims of easy cure. In concluding these deliberations, he said, "in any case, it is certain that this discovery of the subconscious phenomena is an indispensable preliminary" (Janet 1901a, p. 290). Whether this statement of Janet's is intentionally enigmatic concerning the priority of the discovery of the subconscious phenomena in hysteria or whether Janet simply took it for granted that it was his will remain unresolved.

Freud (1925), too, seems to have been troubled by this question, for he stated somewhat curiously, "I always treated Janet with respect, since his discoveries coincided to a considerable extent with those of Breuer, which were made earlier but were published later than his" (p. 31). Later, this respect dwindled when Janet became less than enthusiastic about the importation of psychoanalytic ideas into France. On that occasion, Freud reports in his autobiography: "Janet behaved ill, showed ignorance of the facts, and used ugly arguments. And finally he revealed himself to my eyes and destroyed the value of his own work by declaring that when he had spoken of 'unconscious' mental acts he had meant nothing by the phrase—it had been no more than a façon de parler" (p. 31). This was but a part of Freud's polemic.

In Zilboorg's opinion (1941), Freud was somewhat unfair in accusing Janet of such total lack of comprehension. The latter's definition of "unconscious" also included the sense of "automatic" actions, and, indeed, he was the first to have brought out fully the significance of the automatic behavior of the hysterical patient. Nor was his use of the word "subconscious" actually entirely lacking in its present dynamic connotation, as the following brief excerpts quite clearly show: "The subconscious act may influence consciousness even before its execution; it may call forth vague impulses which the patient calls 'desires,' the origin of which he does not understand. . . . Let us take a step further; subconscious ideas, before any kind of manifestation, may through the association of images, create real hallucinations which will suddenly invade the consciousness" (p. 26). The real weaknesses in Janet's position were his etiological theories. He believed in "provocative agents" of hysterical accidents, but these were mostly of a physical nature and included hemorrhages, chronic diseases, localized infections, typhoid fever, autointoxication, organic diseases of the nervous system, and various alcoholic and other intoxications. He did admit a few psychological alternatives, such as "physical or moral shocks, overwork . . . painful emotions, and especially a succession of that sort of emotion the effects of which are cumulative" (1901a, p. 526). All these provocative agents appeared to Janet to have one feature in common: they weakened the organism and increased the depression of the nervous system. The vulnerability to their injurious effect was particularly great during the state of "moral" or emotional puberty that follows physical pubescence and occurs at different ages in various countries and climates. The many problems typical of this period of life can bring about a condition which Janet termed "psychological insufficiency." If this happens in minds already unstable because of hereditary influences, the resulting damage generally takes the form of hysteria.

Janet devoted little space to the treatment of hysteria. It is clear, however, that he utilized both suggestion and the manipulation of environment. In the former he thought himself in full agreement with Bernheim (1886) of the Nancy School, in the latter he followed the pattern of his teacher Charcot in separating his patients from their earlier influences and environments. In his apparent indifference to the therapy of hysteria, Janet also followed in Charcot's footsteps; that is, he concerned himself primarily with the control of manifestations of the disease and its predisposing factors. Bernheim, who was more clinically inclined, spoke logically of "desuggestion" as the true therapy of hysteria, a subtle difference not mentioned by Janet.

Hysteria was a dominant interest in Janet's professional life, and even toward the term "hysteria" he displayed a rather sentimental attachment: "The word 'hysteria' should be preserved, although its primitive meaning has much changed. It would be very difficult to modify it nowadays, and truly it has so great and beautiful a history that it would be painful to give it up" (Janet 1901a, p. 527). This attitude remained throughout the succeeding decades of his rising fame and mounting success, during which time he continued to lecture and write on the subject. In an impressive series of lectures delivered at Harvard University in 1906 on the occasion of the inauguration of the new medical school buildings, he devoted fifteen sessions to the subject of hysteria.

Janet's devotion to the word "hysteria," and his desire to preserve it, even though it had become etymologically meaningless, was not shared by all of Charcot's disciples. Babinski created a new term, *pithiatisme,* which to him expressed the disease's most important features, since it combined the Greek words, *peithō* ("I persuade") and *iatos* ("curable"), believing that amenability to cure by persuasion was not only the most important characteristic of hysteria but also that it was of diagnostic importance. Although the term still lingers in the current medical dictionaries, it failed to become part of the general medical vocabulary.

Babinski's great number of publications on hysteria beginning in the early 1890s had made him an authority on the subject. Soon after the outbreak of the First World War, concern with hysteria became of enormous practical importance, since this was one of the totally disabling diseases among the soldiers of all armies. Moreover, the problem of distinguishing the malingerer from the hysteric that had faced Mitchel and Keen in the Civil War had become even more pressing in this much larger international conflict. Actually, it is hard to see how Babinski's "pithiatismic" concept could have been very helpful in this dilemma, although his discussion of treatment is a very positive and optimistic one (Babinski and Froment 1918, p. 290-304).

From the preceding accounts, it can be seen that Charcot's influence extended to a group of brilliant pupils who inherited their master's interest in hysteria. Beyond this, however, Charcot's tremendous renown gave the subject of hysteria a dignity that resulted in the publication of voluminous treatises not only by Charcot's disciples but also by such famous authorities as Kraepelin, Moebius, and Kretschmer in Germany, and Daniel Hack Tuke in England. While their ideas quite naturally varied to a considerable degree, there is a consistent pattern recognizable, one that marks the further evolution of the theories of Charcot. This unifying belief lies in the acceptance of suggestion as the governing aspect of hysteria, both in its etiology and in its treatment.

FREUD

This, then, was the status of world thought on hysteria when Freud burst upon the awareness of his contemporaries. The revolution created by him in psychiatry in particular and in Western thought as a whole had been anticipated in part by many of his predecessors, some of whom have been quoted in this chapter (see Riese 1958). Nevertheless, his major role in establishing current concepts of mental function and its disturbances is beyond challenge. It was specifically his interest in and study of hysteria that formed the starting point of psychoanalysis and led to the formulation of those ideas on the illness which have not as yet been superseded. For this reason, a summary of Freud's concern with hysteria forms a fitting conclusion to this chapter.

In the preceding pages we have traced the introduction and development of neurosis, both the word and the concept from the initial somatic interpretation to a psychological one. Today the word *psychoneurosis* as applied to hysteria is self-descriptive and hardly requires any explanation. Although Freud's *Autobiographical Study*, his contributions *On the History of the Psycho-Analytic Movement*, and Ernest Jones's *Life of Freud* have made the beginnings of psychoanalysis a familiar story, a very brief reiteration of it is necessary here to bring out the supremely important role played by hysteria in its development.

It was hysteria that brought Freud in touch with Josef Breuer, one of the most distinguished Viennese internists, whose large and busy practice included patients suffering from that disease; among Breuer's patients was Miss Anna O., whose treatment lasted two years and whose case is one of the most famous in the annals of psychoanalysis. Breuer related to Freud the history of Miss Anna O. during the course of his therapy with her from 1880 to 1882. Freud's intense interest was aroused by the case, particularly since he greatly admired Breuer, who was his senior by fourteen years; he spoke of him as a man of superior intelligence to whom he was soon bound by ties of close friendship.

Breuer's approach to Miss Anna O.'s hysteria was a completely novel one and provided both physicians a much more profound insight into the causes and meaning of hysterical symptoms than had ever been gained before. Quite accidentally, Breuer had observed that the symptoms could be corrected if the patient could be induced while under hypnosis to put into words the fantasy from which she suffered at the moment. This one experience with a single patient suggested to Breuer his method of treatment, although the patient when awake was unable to trace any connection between her illness and any previous experience of her life. Through hypnosis Breuer was readily able to produce the missing links. From Breuer's notes of the case, Freud became convinced that this man was coming closer to an understanding of the nature of psychoneurosis than anyone had before.

Freud's involvement with hysteria and his friendship with Breuer occurred early in his medical career—even before he had decided to devote all his energies to psychiatry, although in his original decision to study medicine he had been motivated by a "curiosity which was . . . directed . . . towards human concerns." This led him first toward neurology. He became intensely involved in the field of neuroanatomy, and while still a junior resident he began to publish short papers on various neuroanatomical subjects. Indeed, he was so successful a diagnostician that the fame of his "diagnoses and their postmortem confirmation" brought him large audiences of admiring American physicians (Freud 1925, p. 11). Yet, in spite of his serious interest in neurology and neuroanatomy at the University of Vienna, he said that he felt himself drawn elsewhere and "in the distance shone the great name of Charcot" (p. 11). Freud received his appointment as lecturer in neuropathology in the spring of 1885, and shortly thereafter, with the help of his mentor Professor Brücke, he was awarded a very generous travel fellowship for his studies with Charcot at the Salpêtrière.

Initially, Charcot paid no personal attention to Freud, who was simply one of a large number of foreigners attending the famous clinical demonstrations. But when one day in Freud's hearing Charcot expressed his regret that his work had as yet not found a German translator, Freud offered to undertake this task. Charcot accepted gratefully and henceforth admitted Freud to the circle of his personal acquaintances and to all the work that was conducted at the Salpêtrière.

In contrast to many other more critical visitors, Freud was deeply impressed with Charcot's work on hysteria and said that "Charcot had proved, for instance, the genuineness of hysterical phenomena and their conformity to laws, . . . the frequent occurrence of hysteria in men"; and, furthermore, that artificially [that is, hypnotically] produced hysteria closely resembled the spontaneous attacks. In spite, however, of his hero worship of Charcot, Freud confessed that many of the demonstrations provoked in him and in other visitors a sense of astonishment and an inclination to skepticism (see also Munthe 1930, pp. 300-303, 320-321), and he therefore decided to tell Charcot of his impressions of Breuer's work. But Freud related that 'the master' "showed no interest in my first outline of the subject, so that I never returned to it and allowed it to pass from my mind" (Freud 1925, pp. 19-20).[18] Freud's receptivity to Charcot's method's can be explained by the fact that he was intellectually prepared to favor the therapeutic use of hypnotic suggestion. For, following Breuer's example, Freud himself had used hypnosis for the purpose of eliciting from patients their own stories about the origin of their symptoms, which, when awake, they would have been unable to recall or unwilling to divulge.

On his return to Vienna in 1886, Freud was even more convinced of the universal relevance of Breuer's theories. He said that "the state of things which he [Breuer] had discovered seemed to me to be of so fundamental a nature that I could not believe it could fail to be present in any case of hysteria if it had been proved to occur in a single one" (1925, p. 25). Yet only a great deal of experience could confirm this supposition. In order to test Breuer's theory and to prove his own belief in it, Freud began to repeat Breuer's methods on his own patients with the eventual exclusion of all other therapeutic approaches. He recorded his own observations and case histories minutely and then suggested to Breuer that they jointly publish their combined experiences with this new therapy of hysteria. Initially, Breuer objected strongly to the plan of a joint publication, but he consented after he had become aware that Pierre Janet's book had meanwhile anticipated some of his own important findings, among them the need to trace hysterical symptoms back to the causative events in the patient's life and the need to remove these symptoms by means of a recreation under hypnosis of the original situation.

The first joint publication of Breuer and Freud was brief; it was entitled "On the Psychical Mechanism of Hysterical Phenomena" (1893). In this preliminary article the authors submitted the opinion that in hysteria the patients reexperience the original psychic trauma. Their physical symptoms that heretofore had been regarded as spontaneous random manifestations were thus closely related to the original causal event. This publication was succeeded in 1895 by a larger volume entitled *Studies on Hysteria*. Although this now appears in the *Standard Edition* (Breuer and Freud 1893-1895), Freud emphasized that it was largely the product of Breuer's practical experience, while his contribution was the formulation of the theory. At any rate, the major object of this book was less the definition of the nature of hysteria than the elucidation of its symptoms. In the case of Anna O., the first patient with whom

Breuer used hypnotic suggestion to recall the precipitating event, it was revealed that her symptoms could be traced back to a severe illness of her father, whom she had been nursing with affectionate devotion. From these revelations Breuer interpreted the meaning of all her symptoms: They were converted reminiscences of those stressful situations she had then experienced. After complete recall of these situations under hypnosis and unreserved expression of those emotions she had originally suppressed, the symptoms gradually disappeared and their return was prevented.

For this therapeutic method Breuer had found the designation *catharsis,* the results of which were highly satisfactory. The theory of catharsis was in no way involved with the subject of sexuality as an etiological agent. This was to a much greater extent Freud's contribution, for the case histories that he contributed to their first volume were characterized by sexual factors, whereas Breuer wrote of Anna O. that her "sexual side was extraordinarily underdeveloped" (in Freud 1925, p. 22).

The subsequent stages of Freud's work were devoted to the gradual transition from catharsis to psychoanalysis. In the course of this evolution, Breuer withdrew from the collaboration and left Freud as "the sole administrator of his legacy (Freud 1925, p. 22). The reasons for Breuer's withdrawal were not to any large degree ideological; rather, his medical practice did not permit him the time for intensive involvement with psychiatric patients, whereas Freud, on his return from Paris, had devoted his professional life solely to the practice of psychiatry. His reasons for giving up neurology are revealed in the following:

This implied, of course, that I abandoned the treatment of organic nervous diseases; but that was of little importance. For on the one hand the prospects in the treatment of such disorders were in any case never promising, while on the other hand, in the private practice of a physician working in a large town, the quantity of such patients was nothing compared to the crowds of neurotics, whose number seemed further multiplied by the manner in which they hurried, with their troubles unsolved, from one physician to another. And apart from this, there was something positively seductive in working with hypnotism. For the first time there was a sense of having overcome one's helplessness, and it was highly flattering to enjoy the reputation of being a miracle-worker. [1925, p. 17]

Freud's favorable inclination toward the use of hypnotism evolved in a fashion similar to that of Braid; it originated while he was still a medical student. He had attended a public exhibition by a well-known "magnetist" and, on noticing that one of the subjects turned deathly pale under hypnosis, he became convinced of the genuineness of the phenomenon. Although a scientific explanation of this observation was soon forthcoming, the professor of psychiatry in Austria and Germany remained convinced that hypnosis was dangerous as well as fraudulent and that all those employing it in their practice should be treated with contempt.

During his stay with Charcot, Freud had seen Europe's most prominent and gifted neurologists make use of hypnotism at the Salpêtrière in the production of symptoms and in their removal. Soon after his return from Paris, he became aware of the use of suggestion by the school at Nancy, where Liébault and Bernheim made extensive and remarkably successful use of suggestion for therapeutic purposes, with or without hypnosis. Under these influences Freud employed hypnotic suggestion almost as the sole psychotherapeutic method in the first years of his activity in private practice. To his chagrin, however, he found himself unable to induce deep hypnosis in every patient—a disadvantage inherent in all hypnotic treatment. In order to perfect himself in his hypnotic technique, he decided in 1889 to go to Nancy to observe the work of the two physicians of that school. There he "received the profoundest impression of the possibility that there could be mental processes which nevertheless remained hidden from the consciousness of men" (1925, p. 17). It is interesting that at the time when Freud journeyed to Nancy, a stereotyped image of the hysteric must have been in existence so that beyond the designation of "hysteric" there was no need for any further description. This is evident in Freud's statement: "Thinking it would be instructive, I had persuaded one of my patients to follow me to Nancy. This patient was a very highly gifted hysteric, a woman of good birth, who had been handed over to me because no one knew what to do with her" (1925, pp. 17-18).

Freud felt obliged to show his appreciation for the travel grant from the university that had made his study trip possible by giving a report before the Viennese Medical Society on his impressions during his stay in Paris. His talk was badly received, and some of those present bluntly declared that much of it was incredible (Freud 1925, p. 15). This adverse reaction referred particularly to his reports on having seen hysteria in *men* at the Salpêtrière; and one of the physicians in his audience, "an old surgeon, actually broke out with the exclamation: 'But my dear Sir, how can you talk such nonsense? Hysteron . . . means the uterus, so how can a man be hysterical'" (1925, p. 15). Freud's Viennese colleagues also made it impossible for him to demonstrate his findings; they refused him permission to work with or observe their patients. Only once was he applauded— when outside the hospital he accidentally came upon a man suffering from an obvious hysterical hemianesthesia and succeeded in presenting him to the same medical society; but in spite of their approbation on this occasion, Freud failed to arouse his colleagues' interest in his work. Their persistent denial of his observations extended to include the production of hysterical paralyses by suggestion, at that a phenomenon accepted all over the world as one of the most frequent etiologic agencies.

The general, persistent, and unconcealed rejection of his ideas became increasingly irritating to Freud. For various reasons he withdrew completely from academic life and from participation in the work of the local medical society; in fact, he completely discontinued the treatment of organic nervous diseases and limited his practice to the treatment of psychoneurotic disorders. In an interesting observation of the reversal of current evaluations, Karl Menninger (1963) calls attention to the greater scientific potential of Freud's clinical practice in contrast to his research work: "It was with neurological studies of sensation that Freud began his scientific career and his research work led to the discovery of the local obliteration of sensation through injected chemicals (cocaine, etc.). When he then turned to clinical work, the phenomena of blocked sensation were of particular interest to him, as they appeared in 'hysterical' patients, and in experiments with hypnosis" (p. 109).

In reminiscing in his *Autobiographical Study* about the writing of the *Studies on Hysteria,* Freud wrote: "It would have been difficult to guess what an importance sexuality has in the aetiology of the neuroses." This importance he began to appreciate later in his own increasing practice, when he learned what had been suggested over and over again by other physicians for nearly two thousand years, "that it was not *any* kind of emotional excitation that was in action behind the phenomena of the neurosis, but habitually one of a sexual nature, whether it was a current sexual conflict or the effect of earlier sexual experiences." Only many years later did he realize that in associating hysteria with sexuality, he "was going back to the very beginnings of medicine and reviving a thought of Plato's" (1925, pp. 23-24).[19]

The discovery of the importance of sexual factors in the etiology of hysteria induced Freud to examine the sexual life of his many neurasthenic patients. "This experiment cost me, it is true, my popularity as a doctor, but it brought me convictions which today, almost thirty years later, have lost none of their force" (1925, p. 24). Eventually, Freud came to regard *all* neuroses as being the results of the disturbed sexual functions, that is, he thought of "actual" neuroses as the direct morbid expression of such disturbances and the psychoneuroses as their mental expression. The mechanism by which he visualized the physical act of intercourse to exert its influence is quite obscure and very difficult to comprehend in the light of the terms which he used. In the *Autobiographical Study* he states: "It [sexuality] had a somatic side as well, and it was possible to assign chemical processes to it and to attribute sexual excitement to the presence of some particular, though at present unknown, substances" (p. 25). In coming to these conclusions, Freud thought that he had proved sexuality to be a physical phenomenon and not something purely mental as had hitherto been believed. Freud held that its somatic side was responsible for the production of certain chemical processes producing specific substances. That these hypotheses are vaguely reminiscent of the theories underlying the "vapors," and those of Galen concerning the hysterogenic effect of retained sperm resulting from unaccustomed sexual continence (see

Veith 1965) is all the more striking because Freud appeared totally unaware of the historical background and earlier humoral theories. Indeed, far from believing he had proved the veracity of old historical beliefs, Freud was pleased to have found a way of relating psychiatry to modern science and the burgeoning field of chemistry, and hence he considered his own hypotheses of distinct scientific merit. His preoccupation with psychotherapy left him no time to pursue further the chemical alterations behind those neuroses which he termed "actual"; nor was anyone else sufficiently interested in taking up this aspect of Freud's work. Even thirty years later, when writing his *Autobiographical Study,* he proudly spoke of these "early findings," saying, "They strike me as being the first rough outlines of what is probably a far more complicated subject. But on the whole they seem to me still to hold good." A rather startling comment regarding the role of sexual disturbance reads: "All that I am asserting is that the symptoms of these patients are not mentally determined or removable by analysis, but that they must be regarded as direct toxic consequences of disturbed sexual chemical processes" (p. 26). Perhaps if the term *endocrinological* were substituted for *chemical,* his views might not strike us as quite so bizarre, even though the physico-chemical effects of sexual intercourse are not prominently encountered in modern writings on normal or morbid sexuality.

In spite of his earlier withdrawal from an academic career and from participation in the work of learned societies, Freud used the years that followed the publication of the *Studies on Hysteria* to read papers dealing with the role of sexuality in the production of neuroses before a number of medical societies outside Vienna, but his work was received only with disbelief and disapproval. For some time after the publication of their joint work, Breuer continued to express his support of Freud's theories but without materially improving the general medical reaction to them. Breuer's loyalty, however, stopped short of fully accepting Freud's concept of the sexual etiology of neuroses. The reason for Breuer's adverse reaction to these theories was, perhaps, his own experience with his first famous patient, Anna O., whose case history he had been reluctant to detail fully to Freud, later saying that her sexual feelings were remarkably underdeveloped. Long after the conclusion of Anna O.'s treatment, Freud was able to reconstruct the final events that accounted for Breuer's silence on the subject. Her reaction, according to Freud (1925, p. 26), appears to have been the first recorded "transference love," a phenomenon becoming manifest after catharsis has been accomplished. This is one of the earliest mentions of "transference," a factor, Freud stated, which is allowed to play the decisive part in determining the therapeutic results of analysis. In his transference the patient, initially quite unconsciously, acts out upon the analyst those emotional experiences that had their origin in his earliest attachments during the repressed period of his childhood (1925, p. 42). Miss Anna O.'s expression of her transference had been so embarrassing to Breuer and the memory of this event so painful to him that Freud's continued emphasis on sexual factors in hysteria served as a permanent uncomfortable reminder of his own awkwardness in the face of such manifestation. It seems to have been for this reason that Breuer disociated himself generally from Freud's etiological speculations (Breuer and Freud 1893). Nevertheless, he too appreciated the effect of the sexual drives on mental stability and said: "The sexual instinct is undoubtedly the most powerful source of persisting increases of excitation (and consequently of neuroses)" (1893, p. 200). And, later on: "I do not think I am exaggerating when I assert that *the great majority of severe neuroses in women have their origin in the marriage bed*" (p. 246). In view of the frequent assertion that the emphasis on sexuality was a preoccupation peculiar to Freud and that it was his special contribution to psychoanalysis, it may be of interest to present Breuer's footnote to the above-quoted italicized statement.

It is a most unfortunate thing that clinical medicine ignores one of the most important of all the pathogenic factors or at least only hints at it delicately. This is certainly a subject in which the acquired knowledge of experienced physicians should be communicated to their juniors, who as a rule blindly overlook sexuality—at all events so far as their patients are concerned. [1893, p. 246n]

In spite of this positive statement, there must have remained in Breuer's mind reservations and qualifications of his belief in the sexual etiology of neuroses. Breuer's doubts about the all-importance of sexuality became evident in a letter from Freud to his friend Fliess, written in 1893, the year of the publication of *Studies on Hysteria*. At that time in a formal address to the Physicians' Collegium, Breuer spontaneously declared his own belief in the sexual etiology of neuroses. However, when Freud later on approached him to thank him for this public testimony, Breuer strangely remarked, "All the same, I don't believe it." Breuer's lack of concurrence with all the theories of his coauthor was matched by Freud's gradual departure from the use of hypnosis and his development of the psychoanalytic method—his distinctive contribution to psychiatry. The reasons for this shift arose from Freud's growing belief in the possibility of exploring the patients' unconscious and repressed memories without altering his mental state by inducing hypnosis. This belief was superimposed upon his failure, mentioned above, to induce hypnosis in some of his patients. Instead, he attempted to put them in a state of deep "concentration," aided by a mild pressure of his hand and having the patient lie down and close his eyes. This method, which was described by him as "pressure technique," initiated Freud's use of the recumbent position during psychoanalysis, a position he maintained even after he had given up the method of concentration and laying-on of hands (1893-1895, p. 110).

So far as hysteria was concerned, it seemed surprising to both Breuer and Freud that events experienced so long ago continued to operate with such intensity that their recollection should not be subject to the process of wearing away to which most memories succumb. The state of intactness of the memory, they felt, depended on the extent of the reaction to the event that had originally produced the effect. The concept "reaction" included such reflexes as tears, rage, anger, and acts of revenge. Both Breuer and Freud suggested that a sufficiently strong reaction discharged the affect completely, that is, it lead to the abreaction of the effect of the event. Breuer and Freud retained the old distinction between chronic hysteria and (acute) hysterical attacks and called attention to Charcot's schematic description of the four phases that were believed to characterize all major hysterical attacks. Freud's local reference to Charcot's favorite theory was made in 1893, the year after Charcot's death and long after French medicine had discredited as fictitious his theories on the four phases of hysteria.

In enumerating Charcot's four phases of hysteria—the epileptoid phase, the phase of large movements, the hallucinatory phase *(attitudes passionelles)*, and the phase of terminal delirium—Freud, speaking of Charcot as though he were still alive, said that "Charcot derives all those forms of hysterical attack which are in practice met with more often than the complete *grande attaque*" (1893-1895, p. 13). Freud's and Breuer's own observations tended to confirm the existence of Charcot's third phase, that is, the *attitudes passionelles:* "Where this is present in a well-marked form, it exhibits the hallucinatory reproduction of a memory which was important in bringing about the onset of the hysteria—the memory either of a single major trauma or of a series of interconnected part-traumas (such as underlie common hysteria)" (1893, p. 14). Then they suggested that the symptom is always a symbol of a repressed traumatic memory. Similarly, they found that an attack could be provoked under hypnosis and that such artificially provoked seizures would then serve an ancient need, namely the establishment of a differential diagnosis of hysteria and epilepsy. And on this occasion they gave a description of the usual manifestations of hysteria which would also serve to explain the symptoms of Freud's patient who accompanied him to Nancy.

> The motor phenomena of hysterical attacks can be interpreted partly as universal forms of reaction appropriate to the affect accompanying the memory (such as kicking about and waving the arms and legs, which even young babies do), partly as a direct expression of these memories; but in part, like the hysterical stigmata found among the chronic symptoms, they cannot be explained in this way. [1893-1895, p. 15]

It is this description of the hysterical patient's extraordinary behavior that helps, in a way, to explain why hysteria has become an apparently infrequent illness. In this century behavior that includes "kicking about" and "waving the arms and legs" is met with distaste and lack of sympathy and is tolerated at best only among shrieking mobs of teenage girls in response to their current singing idols. Whether it is true or not, it has been suggested that, unlike the psychotic patient, the person suffering from hysteria retains a sense of reality in the course of the seizure and is thus able to control his manifestations and to keep them within the limits permissible in his contemporary setting. The fainting ladies of the Victorian period would be unacceptable today, partly because they would fail completely to evoke any sympathetic response in their social environment and partly because the skill of fainting gracefully has almost disappeared. With the increasing awareness of conversion reactions and the popularization of psychiatric literature, the "old fashioned" somatic expressions of hysteria have become suspect among the more sophisticated classes; hence most physicians observe that obvious conversion symptoms are now rarely encountered and, if at all, only among the uneducated of the lower social strata. Thus previous types of hysterical attacks have become subjectively unrewarding. The helpful concern that was shown for hysterical women throughout the ages until early in this century has given way to uncomprehending indifference.

From the above it can be seen that Freud's studies on hysteria, instead of endowing this illness with greater significance, actually divested it of much of the mystical importance it had held for more than two millennia. With much of the Freudian terminology having become part of sophisticated language, expressions such as "psychosomatic," "flight into illness," and "secondary gain" are understood by the potentially hysterical and by many others who are unwilling to make the hysteric a focus of attention. If, as has been stated, hysteria is primarily a means of achieving ego satisfaction, this lack of attention could easily account for the reduced incidence of classical forms of the illness. Thus, it may not be too paradoxical to state that it was the intensified understanding of the cause of hysteria by leading psychiatrists during this century that contributed to the near-disappearance of certain forms of this disease.

This apparent disappearance of classical hysteria, a long-cherished disease entity, was recently documented by the exclusion of hysteria from among the American Psychiatric Association classificatory system of mental diseases and by its replacement with the designations of conversion reaction, associative reaction, and hysterical personality. Nevertheless, the designation has by no means disappeared from the medical vocabulary. Regardless of time, reason, and efforts, the average physician, the neurologists, and many psychiatrists still associate with the designation of "hysteric" a hyperexcitable female patient and the prevarications usually associated with the Münchhausen syndrome which in the hysteric may either be a conversion symptom or pure fabrication. In spite of Charcot's efforts to explain the disease, there are several false concepts still related to hysteria—such as the disproportionate number of female patients versus the near-nonexistence of males so afflicted—that appear to be impossible to eradicate. Another such false concept is the disease description of hystero-epilepsy that had been mistakenly discovered and described by Charcot. It is true that few physicians, and even fewer psychiatrists, are burdened by this unwieldly designation, but oddly enough it persists in some popular medical dictionaries where it is described as if Charcot had never refuted his own theories concerning this disease complex. Thus it reads: "*Hysteroepilepsy:* A form of hysteria in which there are nervous explosions of a violent character. The attack begins usually with epileptoid convulsions. The next stage is one of emotional attitudes in which the patient gives dramatic expression to feelings of anger, disgust, surprise, joy, or other intense emotion; the final stage is one of delirium. The complete attack lasts from five or ten minutes to half an hour."

This atavistic documentation of an absurd, long-defunct, and never useful description is not the only one carefully preserved in *Stedman's Medical Dictionary,* but there are other embellishments of the basic word, such as "hysteroerotic," "hysterofrenatory," "hysterocatalepsy," and several others, which lead their forlorn and unsolicited existences in the pages of this and other medical dictionaries, and perhaps they are also preserved in the more obscure papers of medical literature at large.

NOTES

1. Although the nature of the uterine abnormality was sometimes interpreted as a starvation of the organ, a much more frequent explanation was that the uterus was displaced. Displacements in various directions produced their effects by pressing on contiguous structures.

2. The others are the *Edwin Smith Papyrus*, which deals with surgery and which was composed around 1600 B.C.; the *Hearst Papyrus*, which contains prescriptions similar to those in the *Papyrus Ebers;* the *Berlin Medical Papyrus*, which is assumed to have been written about 1250 B.C. and which also contains prescriptions in an unsystematic arrangement; and finally the *London Medical Papyrus*, which was probably written about 1350 B.C. and which, although containing a few prescriptions, consists chiefly of incantations against a variety of diseases.

3. Any of a large family of poisonous beetles (Buprestidae) with short notched antennae and long bodies tapering at the rear.

4. A member of the Aster family.

5. All subsequent quotations from Sydenham are taken from the "Epistolary Dissertation" (Sydenham 1848).

6. A copy of this manuscript was made available to me by the Massachusetts Historical Society.

7. The physicians practicing "psychiatrics" were referred to by Feuchtérsleben (1847) as "psychological physicians," "psychopathic physicians" and "psychiatric physicians."

8. Johann Christian Reil (1759-1813), whom Feuchtérsleben quotes frequently and with much respect, was an extraordinary personality. He was not only the founder and original editor of the first scientific periodical, the *Archiv für die Physiologie* which later became the epoch-making *Müller's Archiv,* but he was also a neurologist of considerable acumen and is known in this field for the "island of Reil" in the brain. Of particular importance to this study is the fact that he was the first to found a journal of psychiatry, the *Magazin für psychische Heilkunde* (1805-1806), which he subsequently change into his *Beytrage* (1808-1812). His pupil C. F. Nasse continued the journal under the title *Zeitschrift für psychische*

Ärzte (1818-1822). Reil shared Pinel's devotion to the humane treatment of the insane and published his *Rhapsodieen über die Anwendung der psychischen Kurmethode auf Geisteszerrüttungen* in 1803 to this effect. Strangely enough, however, his "psychological method of healing" included the stimulation of violent reactions. Reil believed in arousing anger, hostility, and guilt feelings, the latter by means of a theater in mental hospitals where employees would take roles of judges, prosecutors, avenging angels, and reviving corpses who would judge patients' behavior and possible transgressions or sins.

9. This authority was acknowledged even by a physician of the stature of C. W. Hufeland (1762-1836), who submitted one of his books to the criticism of Kant because it touched upon mental health. Kant, in turn, sent to Hufeland a very small book of his own, which carried the disproportionately lengthy title *Von der Macht des Gemüths durch den blossen Vorsatz Seiner krankhaften Gefühle Meister zu sein* ("On the Power of the Mind to master One's Pathological Feelings [Sensation] through Sheer Will Power").

10. Where there continued a belief in a national disposition.

11. C. G. Carus (1831), however, was on the verge of a deeper understanding.

12. This work was also published in English translation by the Sydenham Society after a more customary and conservative passage of time and period of appraisal in 1867, twenty-two years after its first appearance.

13. Wunderlich's famous work on the relationship of animal to disease (1868) formed the foundation of our present clinical thermometry.

14. From a lecture, "The Medical Department of the Civil War," delivered before the Physicians Club of Chicago in February 1913.

15. This view was independently voiced by Bernheim's younger German contemporary, the Leipzig neurologist Paul Julius Moebius (1853-1907).

16. Much earlier, while Charcot was at the very height of his fame, S. Weir Mitchell admitted his own frustration with the healing success of the

magnetic "metal cure" and said that he had "never once witnessed the phenomenon of transfer of the analgesia or anaesthesia to the opposite side—a phenomenon which seems to be undeniably frequent in the hands of as admirable an observer as Charcot," S. Weir Mitchell (1881, p. 24).

17. *Abulia:* loss or marked diminution of willpower.

18. The German edition uses the expression *der Meister*, translated as "the great man" in the English edition, pp. 33-34.

19. He refers to the statement from Plato's *Timaeus:* "The womb is an animal which longs to generate children. When it remains barren too long after puberty, it is distressed and sorely disturbed."

REFERENCES

Aurelianus, C. (1950). *On Acute Diseases and on Chronic Diseases*. Trans. I. E. Drablin. Chicago: University of Chicago Press.

Babinski, J., and Froment, J. (1918). *Hysteria or Pithiasm and Reflex Nervous Disorders in the Neurology of War*. London: University of London Press.

Beall, O., and Shryock, R. (1954). *Cotton Mather: First Significant Figures in American Medicine*. Baltimore: Johns Hopkins Press.

Bernheim, H. (1886). *Suggestive Therapeutics*. Trans. C. A. Hert. Westport, Conn.: Associated Booksellers, 1957.

Breuer, J., and Freud, S. (1893-1895). Studies in hysteria. *Standard Edition 2*.

Bríquet, P. (1859). *Traité Clinique et Thérapeutique de L'hystérie*. Paris: Baillière.

Carter, R. B. (1853). *On the Pathology and Treatment of Hysteria*. London: John Churchill.

Carus, C. G. (1831). *Vorlesungen über Psychologic*. Leipzig: Gerhard Fleischer.

Charcot, J. M. (1877). *Lectures on the Diseases of the Nervous System*. Trans. G. Sigerson. London: New Sydenham Society.

———(1889a). Isolation in the treatment of hysteria. In *Clinical Lectures on Diseases of the Nervous System*, vol. 3, trans. T. Savell. London: New Sydenham Society.

———(1889b). *Leçons du Mardi à la Salpêtrière, Policlinique du 19 Mars*. Paris: Felix Alcair.

———(1892). Faith healing. *New Review and Revue Hebdomadaire* December, pp. 112-132.

Cullen, W. (1796). *First Lines of the Practice of Physic*. With practical and expository notes by John Rotheram. Edinburgh, 1896.

Ebbell, B., trans. (1947) *The Papyrus Ebers, The Greatest Egyptian Medical Document*. Copenhagen: Leven and Mucksguard.

Edelstein, E., and Edelstein, L. (1945). *Asclepios: A Collection and Interpretation of the Testimonies*. Baltimore: Johns Hopkins Press.

Falret, J. (1866). *Études Cliniques Sur les Maladies Mentales et Nerveuses*. Paris: Baillière, 1890.

Feuchtérsleben, E. Von. (1845). *The Principles of Medical Psychology*. Ed. B. G. Babington. London: New Sydenham Society, 1847.

Frankfort, H. (1948). *Kingship and the Gods: A Study of Ancient Near Eastern Religion as the Integration of Society and Nature*. Chicago: University of Chicago Press.

Freud, S. (1914). On the history of the psycho-analytic movement. *Standard Edition* 14: 3-66.

———(1925). Autobiographical study. *Standard Edition* 20: 3-76.

Griesinger, W. (1845). *Mental Pathology and Therapeutics*. Trans. C. L. Roberson and J. Rutherford. London: New Sydenham Society, 1867.

Griffith, F. L., ed. (1897). *Papyri Petri, Hieratic Papyri from Kahun and Gurob; Principally of the Middle Kingdom. Vol. 1: Literary, Medical and Mathematical Papyri from Kahun*. London: Bernard Quaritch.

Guillain, G. (1955). *J. M. Charcot, 1825-1893: His Life—His Work*. Ed. and trans. P. Bailey. New York: Hoeber, 1959.

Guinon G. (1925). Charcot intime. In *Paris Medical* (May 1925) pp. 511-526

Hippocrates (1851). *Oeuvres Complète d'Hippocrate*. Fols. 1, 7, 8. Trans. E. Littre. Paris: Ballière, 1851.

Janet, P. (1901a). *The Mental State of Hystericals: A Study of Mental Stigmata and Mental Accidents*. Trans. C. R. Carson. New York: Putnam.

———(1901b). *Psychological Healing: A Historical and Clerical Study*. Trans. E. and C. Paul. New York: Macmillan, 1925.

Kant, E. (1929). *On the Power of the Mind to Master One's Pathological Feelings Through Sheer Will Power*. Leipzig: Philipp Reklam.

Keen, W. W., Mitchell, S. W., and Morehouse, G. R. (1864). On malingering, especially in regard to stimulation of diseases of the nervous system. *American Journal of the Medical Sciences* 47: 367-394.

Leigh, D. (1961). *The Historical Development of British Psychiatry*. New York: Pergamon.

Malleus Maleficarum (1951). Trans. M. Summers. London: Pushkin.

Mandeville, B. de (1711). *A Treatise of the Hypochondriak and Hysterick.* London: Deylen Leach.

Mead, R. (1762). *The Medical Works of Richard Mead.* Section 4. London.

Menninger, K. (1963). *The Vital Balance.* New York: Viking.

Mitchell, S. W. (1877). *Fat and Blood: and How to Make Them.* Philadelphia: Lippincott.

———(1881). *Lectures on Diseases of the Nervous System, Especially in Women.* Philadelphia: Henry C. Lias.

———(1888). *Doctor and Patient.* Philadelphia: Lippincott.

Murthe, A. (1930). *The Story of San Michele.* New York: Dutton.

Pinel, P. (1813). *Nosographie Philosophique ou la Méthode de l'Analyse Appliquée à la Médicine.* 5th ed. Paris: Brosson, 1813.

Reynolds, R. (1869). Remarks on paralysis and other disorders of motion and sensation. Department on idea. *British Medical Journal,* July.

Riese, W. (1958). The history of the term and conception of neurosis in pre-Freudian origins of psychoanalysis. In *Science and Psychoanalysis,* vol. 1, ed. J. Masserman. New York: Grune and Stratton.

Roeder, G. (1916). *Urkunden zur Religion des alten Agyptens.* Jena.

Rush, B. (1809). An account of the influence . . . of the American Revolution upon the human body. In *Medical Inquiries and Observations,* 3rd ed. Philadelphia: Hopkins and Earle.

——— (1812). *Medical Inquiries and Observations upon the Diseases of the Mind.* Philadelphia: Gregg.

Sigerist, H., ed. (1941). *Four Treatises by Paracelsus.* Baltimore: Johns Hopkins Press.

Sollman, T. (1918). *A Manual of Pharmacology.* Philadelphia.

Strümpel, A. (1911). *A Textbook of Medicine for Students and Practitioners.* New York.

Sydenham, T. (1848). *Works of Thomas Sydenham, M.D.* Trans. R. G. Latham. London.

Szasz, T. (1961). *The Myth of Mental Illness: Foundations of a Theory of Personal Conduct.* New York: Hoeber and Harper.

Tuke, D. H. (1872). *Illustrations of the Influence of the Mind upon the Body in Health and Disease, Designed to Elucidate the Action of the Imagination.* London.

Veith, I. (1965). *Hysteria: The History of a Disease.* Chicago: University of Chicago Press.

Whytt, R. (1767). *Observations on the Nature, Causes, and Cure of those Disorders which have been commonly called Nervous, Hypochondriac, or Hysteric: to which are prefixed some remarks on the Sympathy of the Nerves.* Edinburg: Balfour.

Willis, T. (1664). *Cereleri anatome, cui accessit nervorum descripto et usus.* London.

Wunderlick, C. (1868). *Das Verhalten der Eigenwarme in Krankheiten.* Leipzig.

Zilboorg, G. (1941). *A History of Medical Psychology.* New York: Norton.

CHAPTER 2

Hysteria and Hysterical Structures: Developmental and Social Theories

KAY H. BLACKER, M.D.
JOE P. TUPIN, M.D.

In the historical review of chapter one, both hysterical symptoms and efforts to describe a hysterical character structure were traced through two millennia. Continuing the narrative, we will trace the main concepts during the twentieth century. To begin this review of the modern era, we return to the point where Ilza Veith concluded; the origins of psychoanalysis.

PSYCHOANALYTIC THEORIES

The psychoanalytic understanding of hysterical behavior began with Breuer's observation of his patient, Anna O. Since hysterical behaviors cannot be understood outside of the context in which they occur, it is helpful to understand the physician who made the observations, as well as the young woman who produced the phenomena.

Joseph Breuer was a highly respected, forty-year-old physician at the time Anna's family contacted him to aid their daughter. He was a "doctor's doctor"; his diagnostic skills and medical acumen were so well recognized and acknowledged by his medical colleagues that he was a physician to many of them. His career had been distinguished. As a young man at twenty-six and again at thiry-two, he had made important scientific observations regarding human physiology that are acknowledged as basic contributions even today. He was described by colleagues and family as a gentle, sensitive man with an inquiring, scientific spirit.

Breuer's scientific training with his teacher, Brücke, gave him a thorough grounding in empirical observation. He was caught up in the philosophical zeitgeist of his time, that is, the attempt to explain all phenomena on physical grounds. His extensive and clear descriptions of Anna O. reflected his attempt to apply strict scientific principles to the bewildering phenomena—the complicated montage—of symptoms that unfolded before him.

In his famous study of respiratory physiology which he published at age twenty-six, Breuer "conceived the idea of self-regulatory process—a hypothesis of feedback control mechanisms which proved to have wide, general applicability. . . . [he] devised novel techniques which permitted observation of the natural excitatory processes occurring in pulmonary tissue during expansion and contraction of the lungs" (Schlessinger et al. 1967, p. 408).

Previous investigators had either stimulated or severed the vagus nerve, which had precluded observation of the normal physiological state and prevented the identification of a feedback control mechanism. Breuer's subsequent physiological investigation of the semicircular canals follows the same pattern. Again, meticulous dissection and a patient approach enabled him to make observations that were not possible when utilizing the blunt methods of his predecessors.

Breuer's work with Anna shows the same dedication and meticulous attention to detail he had utilized in making his earlier physiological discoveries. His approach enabled him to discover psychological processes that had not been observable utilizing the medical treatments of his day. He was with this young woman almost daily for two years, and his descriptions are a model of Germanic scientific exactitude. Paradoxically, while his intense, focused attention enabled him to make the crucial observations, his attention also unknowingly encouraged a proliferation of symptoms and intensification of the illness (see Gedo et al. 1964).

Anna was the second of four children of a wealthy, orthodox Jewish, mercantile family. Two younger sisters died in early childhood. She had a brother two years her senior. Although there is little mention of her mother in the famous case report, material from Anna's later life suggests they were close. Her difficulties began after her father developed symptoms of a pulmonary illness which continued in an unremitting fashion, resulting in his death nine months later (see Pollock 1968, 1973).

Breuer saw this young woman as bubbling over with intellectual vitality and smothered by the monotonous existence in her puritanically minded family. He felt she gained relief by "indulging in systematic daydreaming, which she described as her 'private theatre' . . . She pursued this activity almost continuously while engaged in her household duties, which she discharged unexceptionally" (Breuer and Freud 1893-1895, p. 22). Breuer felt that this habitual daydreaming played an important role in the development of her illness.

He described a variegated illness, one filled with symptoms of many types: disturbance of vision, paralysis to the point of contractures, paresthesias, and altered states of consciousness. The form of Anna's difficulties varied in relationship to the course of her father's terminal illness:

> . . . two entirely distinct stages of consciousness were present which alternated very frequently and without warning and which became more and more differentiated in the course of the illness. In one of these states she recognized her surroundings; she was melancholy and anxious but relatively normal. In the other state she hallucinated and was naughty—that is to say, she was abusive, used to throw cushions at people, so far as the contractures at various times allowed, tore buttons off her bed clothes and linen with those of her fingers which she could move, and so on. [Breuer and Freud 1893-1895, p. 24]

Gradually the doctor and the patient became aware of variations in her disorders and both began to sense some regularity in these variations:

> And now for the first time the psychical mechanism of the disorder became clear. As I knew, she had felt very much offended over something and had determined not to speak of it. When I guessed this and obliged her to talk about it, the inhibition, which had made any other kind of utterance impossible as well, disappeared. [Breuer and Freud 1893-1895, p. 25]

> She aptly described this procedure, speaking seriously, as a talking cure, while she referred to it jokingly as chimney-sweeping. [Breuer and Freud 1893-1895, p.30)

Breuer became increasingly attuned to this phenomena and observed:

> This was because every one of the spontaneous products of her imagination and every event which had been assimilated by the pathological part of her mind persisted as a psychical stimulus until it had been narrated in her hypnosis, after which it completely ceased to operate. [Breuer and Freud 1893-1895, p. 32]

These observations prompted Breuer and Freud to advance their now familiar formulation: "hysterics suffer mainly from reminiscences" (Breuer and Freud 1893-1895, p. 7).

In 1893, Breuer and Freud hypothesized that hysterical symptoms were caused by intense memories or ideas of events; these they termed *psychic traumas*. They postulated that the recollection of these traumas formed an irritant that resulted in psychical splitting, a process which accomplished the removal of the memory from consciousness and which formed the basis for hysteria. They suggested two reasons why they felt the traumas were not experienced in a normal fashion and why the memory of them failed to wear away or diminish: first, because "it was a question of things which the patient wished to forget, and therefore intentionally repressed from his conscious thought and inhibited and suppressed" (Breuer and Freud 1893-1895, p. 10). Simply stated, the trauma was viewed to be actively isolated by the patient's mind because its content and associated affects posed serious threat to the emotional well-being or self-concept of the patient. Second, because the memories "originated during the prevalence of severely paralyzing affects, such as fright, or during positively abnormal psychical states, such as the semihypnotic twilight state of daydreaming, autohypnosis, and so on" (Breuer and Freud 1893-1895, p. 11). Breuer named this state "hypnoid" and felt that the nature of the state made a normal reaction to an event impossible. This postulate is remarkably close to a modern theory developed out of neurophysiological laboratories which is termed "state dependent learning" (Weingartner and Faillace 1971).

Breuer did not continue with the cathartic method or even his investigation of hysterical symptoms after Anna O. He was frightened off by an outpouring of love for him by Anna. Freud, on the other hand, continued his own work and became increasingly impressed that the psychological factor was the cause of the psychic splitting and the formation of hysterical symptoms. In 1894 Freud stated, "I was repeatedly able to show that the splitting of the content of consciousness is a result of an *act of will* on the part of the patient; that is to say, *it is initiated by an effort of will whose motive can be specified* (italics mine). By this I do not, of course, mean that the patient intends to bring about a splitting of consciousness. His intention is a different one; but, instead of attaining its aim, he produces a splitting of consciousness" (Freud 1893-1899, p. 46). Freud specified that this splitting occurred when "an occurrence of incompatibility took place in their ideational life—that is to say, . . . the ego was faced with an experience, idea, or feeling which aroused such distressing affect that the subject decided to forget about it because he had no confidence in his power to resolve the contradiction between the incompatible idea and his ego by means of thought—activity" (1893-1899, p. 47). "In females," Freud further stated, "incompatible ideas of this sort arise chiefly on the soil of sexual experience and sensation" (1893-1899, p. 47). He proposed that the emotions which were pushed away or suppressed were expressed in another form: "But the sum of excitation which has been detached from [the idea] must be put to another use. . . . In hysteria, the incompatible idea is rendered innocuous by its sum of excitation being transformed to something somatic. For this I should like to propose the name of conversion" (1893-1899, p. 49).

Initially, Freud believed his female hysterical patients when they told him they had been sexually molested when children. Only with further clinical experience did he recognize that he was at that period "unable to distinguish with certainty between falsifications made by hysterics in their memories of childhood and traces of real events" (Freud 1901-1905, p. 274). With this added information he revised his theory in the following way: "They [hysterical symptoms] were now no longer to be regarded as direct derivatives of the repressed memories of childhood experiences; but between the symptoms and the childish impressions, there were inserted the patient's fantasies (or imaginary memories)" (Freud 1901-1905, p. 274). Such fantasies were usually unconsciously manufactured attempts to conceal a variety of infantile sexual wishes and activities. It was these wishes and activities which Freud now viewed as producing the splitting and conversion symptoms.

The richness of his new theory is readily observable in the famous Dora case (Freud 1901-1905). In this paper, Freud used the case material to illustrate his recent discoveries of childhood sexuality and his more sophisticated knowledge of mental functioning. The case is a complicated tale involving not only the difficulties of a bright and stubborn young woman, but also of a complex relationship between two families, and a series of falsifications on the part of the father. What is crucial to our modern understanding of hysteria, however, is Freud's discussion of the many hysterical symptoms. With Dora, Freud clearly recognized and detailed the multiple determination of a single symptom. Dora both loved and felt betrayed by her father; her father's friend, Herr K.; and the wife of her father's friend, Frau K. Her symptoms seemed to be expressions of both heterosexual and homosexual love, guilt, anger, and rage influenced by a severe repression of early childhood masturbatory activities—activities which Freud had been able to decipher from Dora's dream reports.

This strong-willed young woman broke off treatment after three months. After publishing this case report and a paper on the etiology of hysteria in 1906, Freud left the investigation of hysterical phenomena. He did not proceed further than the explanations he provided in the Dora case, in which he stressed the multidetermined nature of hysterical symptoms and the repression of infantile sexual wishes and activities.

Although Freud did not attempt to organize and integrate his theories, others did. There resulted from these efforts, and the addition of later psychoanalytic concepts, a symmetrical, generally agreed-upon formulation of hysterical symptoms. Freud's theories of libidinal development and of the Oedipus complex were amalgamated into a stereotype. According to this stereotype, hysterical symptoms arise from repressed sexual wishes. These strivings are unable to achieve expression or sublimation because of oedipal fears—that is, because of fear of punishment from the parent of the same sex. According to this formulation, this conflict induces a psychic regression and the production of symptoms. For example, the globus hystericus was felt to represent sexual excitement displaced upwards from the vagina to the throat. Vomiting was interpreted as concern about oral impregnation.

Fenichel (1945), in his encyclopedic summary of psychoanalytic phenomena and theories, felt secure enough to state: "Conversion hysteria is the classical subject matter of psychoanalysis. As a matter of fact, the psychoanalytic method was discovered, tested, and perfected through the study of hysterical patients; . . . the technique of psychoanalysis still remains most easily applicable to cases of hysteria, and it is the psychoanalytic treatment of hysteria that continued to yield the best therapeutic results" (p. 230). And he continues: "Freud's statement that the oedipal complex is the nuclear complex of the neuroses is particularly valid in hysteria, which remains on the level of the phallic phase of sexual development" (p. 231). Although early analysts were aware of preoedipal conflicts in hysterical patients, they considered these conflicts to represent regressions from oedipal struggles, not fixations at earlier developmental levels: "And between the original Oedipus fantasies and the latter daydreams there are inserted infantile masturbatory fantasy, whose Oedipus character is sometimes rather distorted. The conflicts which were originally connected with the Oedipus complex frequently are displaced onto the act of masturbation. That is why so frequently the struggle against masturbation is found as the unconscious content of hysterical symptoms" (Fenichel, p. 231).

This stereotyped formulation held sway for many years until clinical experience demonstrated its fallacies. Many analysts had begun to question the alleged ease with which hysterics were thought to be treated by psychoanalysis and psychotherapy, and in 1953 Marmor brought together much of the analytic experience that raised questions concerning the oedipal formulation of hysteria. Many analysts had found that although symptom relief might occur early and dramatically in the course of treatment, it was more often a form of transference compliance than of major and enduring personality change. Often this compliance and the associated wish to be loved and protected became the major source of resistance to further maturation. For example, Wittels (1930) as early as the 1920s had noted the difficulty that the hysterical character had in freeing himself from fixation at an infantile level. To Wittels, the hysteric remained as a child confusing fantasy and reality. Reich (1933) formulated his theoretical understanding in terms of conflict at the genital phase of development, but in his descriptions he stressed preoedipal developmental facts: "in as much as pregenital, oral, anal, and urethral strivings form a part of the hysterical character— as is always the case" (p. 206).

Marmor argued that the oral mechanisms and symptoms are always conspicuous in hysteria, for example, globus hystericus, vomiting, anorexia, bulemia, history of prolonged thumb sucking in childhood. He stated the preoedipal conflicts played a greater role in determining the dynamics of hysteria than had been generally assumed. To him, the incestuous dream of the hysteric concealed, behind the symbolic wish to cohabit with the mother (or father), a deeper wish to be loved and protected by her (or him) to the exclusion of the rest of the world. He held, for example, that the phallus in a dream represented, in the deepest sense, the breast. Marmor felt that much of the sexuality of the hysteric was a sham, primarily because it expressed a pregenital oral-receptive wish rather than a genital one.

The distress and surprise of the hysterical woman when her seductiveness leads her to being approached genitally is consequently understandable. She is being approached as a woman when what she really desires is to be taken as a child. Repeatedly, one hears the hysterical woman say, "If only a man would just kiss me and hold me in his arms instead of wanting sex!" This theme of the hysterical woman's wanting to be held—not seduced—was developed further by Hollender (1971).

Marmor maintained that oedipal conflicts played a prominent role in the hysteric's psychopathology. He felt, however, that early oral fixations gave the subsequent Oedipus complex of the hysteric a strong pregenital cast. He felt it was possible to note in the oedipal history of most hysterics either intense frustration of oral-receptive needs as a consequence of early rejection by parents or an excessive gratification of these needs. Either, Marmor postulated, resulted in preoedipal fixations. He also speculated that the greater frequency of hysteria in women as compared to men may be a cultural phenomenon. He felt that the oral receptivity, dependency, and passivity were perhaps more easily expressed by women in our society since they were acceptable feminine traits. We agree with Marmor's speculation and will have more to say about this later.

A recent article by Melitta Sperling (1973), describing many years of analytic work with hysterical patients, probably summarizes today's psychoanalytic conceptualization. Sperling described a woman much like Freud's Dora. The symptomatology was remarkably similar, consisting of "frequent attacks of severe difficulty in breathing, associated with rapid heart beat, dizziness, and fainting spells. She also had coughing spells which often lasted for a month, attacks of 'laryngitis' which resulted in her becoming aphonic for days at a time, and migraine headaches" (pp. 745-746). Sperling noted that in her patient, "the whole body and bodily functions were highly sexualized. Vagina and anus, the womb and the rectum, sexual functions and secretions, were mixed up with anal functions and excretions and then displaced from the genital and anal areas to the oral cavity and respiratory system, including the nose" (p. 752). The basic issue in the dynamics of this patient, and the many other hysterics Sperling had worked with during her thirty years of analytic experience, was the fear of attaching herself to the analyst and then being unable to bear losing the analyst. The patient had recurrent dreams in which the outstanding feeling was that of being alone in an empty street. She saw the analyst as a mother whom she feared would disappoint her and leave her.

Sperling stressed the primitive and destructive meanings of hysterical symptoms: "It [the quality of object relations in these patients] is a special form of symbiotic mother-child relationship in which the mother, because of her own pathological needs, does not permit overt expression of aggression, self-assertion, and rebellion against her, but puts a premium on submission and dependence and rewards the child by special care given to him when he is sick. The child early learns to repress aggressive and other impulses and affects objectionable to his mother" (pp. 763-764). According to Sperling's understanding of hysteria and conversion symptoms, "the concept of the preoedipal mother transference, its role in the production of negative therapeutic reactions, and the technique of recognizing and analyzing it are of utmost importance in the treatment of patients with conversion symptoms" (pp. 766-767). She felt that oedipal conflicts and adult sexual wishes and conflicts can serve as the trigger for the development of hysterical symptomatology. However, in her view the conversion symptoms per se are only understandable in terms of the early relationships between the mothering parent and the child: "It would seem that conversion is possible only in a state of regression to pregenital, symbiotic phases of development. All conversion is therefore pregenital by nature" (p. 769).

Freud's initial theories concerning hysterical symptoms focused on their sexual meaning and the sexual conflicts involved. These concepts in turn were reformulated by other analysts in terms of the Oedipus complex. Sperling's paper is the most recent in a long series of reports detailing the pregenital components of hysterical symptoms. These later papers have stressed the primitive type of object relationships in hysterical patients resulting from disturbances in early mothering and the importance of the aggressive impulses, as well as the sexual ones, in the formation of hysterical symptoms.

Some of the confusion within psychoanalytic theories was further clarified when, in 1959, Rangell pointed out the error of equating the symptom of conversion with the concept of hysteria: "There was lingered on the general automatic association of conversion with hysteria, so the two have been indissolubly linked. Tell an analyst conversion, and he adds hysteria. . . . This automatic associating has long since outlived its usefulness and even longer its accuracy" (p. 633).

Rangell amassed evidence that the conversion process itself "is employed to express forbidden wishes throughout the entire gamut of psychopathological symptomatology" (p. 636) and is not merely limited to the expression of adult genital sexual conflicts in hysterical patients. The conversion mechanism is seen to be a process which can be placed into operation at any or all phases of conflictual pressure. For example, "a stiff neck can, via its hypercathected voluntary musculature, symbolically represent a forbidden erection based upon incestuous wishes" (p. 639). It can also, as in catatonia, symbolically represent and archaic and primitive level of functioning, such as a restraining of an aggressive discharge toward the outer world.

Rangell suggested the term "conversion" be used in the following manner: "Conversion, as we would restrict it, is a sequel to conflicts, mild or severe. It is an act of ego process, in the direction of symptom formulation (p. 645). They (conversion symptoms) are all of the nature of pathological defensive formations in the service of maintaining homeostasis" (p. 646). Indeed, it is uncertain as to whether or not conversion symptoms are more frequently found in connection with other hysterical symptoms. Two investigators, Chodoff and Lyons (1958), state there is no association, while others (see Guze 1975) claim there is a common, although not an invariable, association with hysteria.

Thus the classical theory of genital libidinal fixation and incestuous yearnings has given way to a broader, richer, and more complex formulation emphasizing pregenital elements and ego functions. This new picture, developing from Marmor's amalgamation of classical libidinal theory with ego psychology, emphasizes oral fixations, the close relation to addiction, depression, and schizophrenia. It appears that within an individual patient there is a heterogenous mixture of fixations and conflicts. And when we begin to compare hysterical patients to one another, we find they differ greatly and can best be described as existing at points on a continuum of disorders marked by two polarities, the "good genital" and "bad oral hysteric" (Easser and Lesser 1965, Kernberg 1967, Zetzel 1968, Lazare 1970). This spectrum essentially reflects the degree of ego impairment and/or the level of ego development achieved in the course of maturation. The usefulness of the concept of a continuum of disorders relative to the structure of an individual's personality, which in turn is determined by the level of fixations and conflicts, will be further developed below.

AFFECTIVE THEORY: HYSTEROID DYSPHORIA

Kline and Davis (1969), in a brief passage in their book, describe a patient type which they call *hysteroid dysphoria*. They describe the behavior of these patients as characterized by emotionality, irresponsibility, shallowness, giddy affect, and shortsighted action. They are further characterized as seductive, manipulative, exploitive, exhibitionistic, egocentric, and narcissistic. Kline and Davis comment that the patients' thinking is determined by emotions and, as a consequence, is illogical. But, they point out, "although these patients refer to their dysphoric mood as 'depression' the essential characteristics of the pathologic depressive mood are not salient. They are prone to oversleep and overeat. Although they may express themselves disparagingly, they are activity oriented and successfully strive to engage in new, rewarding situations. . . . We view these character traits as secondary to the primary affective disturbance" (p. 185). Placing an affective disturbance at the base of hysteria is predicated on clinical observation and research reports suggesting that some of these patients improve on monoamine oxidase inhibitors. The authors imply that since this condition responds to a pharmacologic intervention, biologic factors play an important role in its genesis.

There seems to be little evidence that this formulation is true. More likely, as the hysteric is confronted with heightened intrapsychic or interpersonal conflict, depressive symptoms develop. This has been noted to accompany aging and the loss of youthful attractiveness.

NEUROBIOLOGICAL THEORY

Ludwig (1972) has postulated that the basic defect in hysteria is biologic, stemming from two distinctive patterns: (1) violent motor reactions and (2) a sham death reflex. Violent motor reaction is described as an "instinctive defense reaction against disturbing or external stimuli" (p. 772). Once a threatening situation is perceived, be it real or fantasy, a person responds with an "overproduction of aimless motions," (p. 773) and should this prove successful it is then reinforced. The sham death reflex has been noted in a number of animals and is characterized by "partial loss of reaction to other stimuli, and often a well-marked analgesia" (p. 773).

The symptoms arising from these two defects include such things as fugue states, convulsive paroxysms, dreamy states, various fits and spells, blindness, and deafness. Ludwig further suggests that when these are combined with operant conditioning and regressive activity the total picture of hysteria evolves. Unfortunately, he does not clearly differentiate between hysterical personality, conversion, and dissociative symptoms. He further elaborates a concept of "selective depression of awareness of a bodily function brought on by corticofugal inhibition of afferent stimulation at the level of the brain stem reticular formation" (p. 774). This, he concludes, is an attention dysfunction, leading to "a constant state of distraction manifest by dissociation between attention and certain sources of afferent stimulation with a simultaneous diversion of attention to nonsymptom-related areas" (p. 775). Defect in this area may relate to dysfunction of memory, attention, control and field articulation.

This theory is such a radical departure from traditional concepts that full evaluation must await further elaboration of detail and empirical validation or refutation. Although a biological factor is suggested by the work of Guze, and of Kline and Davis, there is no basis to assume that it fits the pattern suggested by Ludwig. Furthermore, the behavioral deficits described, generally familiar to clinicians and typical hysterics, are not a priori a function of a biologic substrate defect as is the apparent case in animals.

SOCIAL THEORIES

Halleck (1967) points out that the earliest dynamic descriptions of the hysterical personality emphasized unresolved oedipal conflicts as the primary determinant of the disorder and goes on to point out the importance of early nurturant problems. In addition to this core psychoanalytic formulation, Halleck adds a social-cultural dimension, a position echoed by other authors. He notes that in our society "a man who feels deprived can deny his needs for others and turn upon and attack those he perceives as having rejected him. Such behavior is usually characterized as a form of sociopathy" (p. 753). He goes on to say that "the American girl, however, is not expected to deny her dependency needs and has little opportunity to express aggression directly. The female child is more likely to adapt to deprivation by seeking to bind people through relationships in which she assumes a highly dependent role" (p. 753). Sociopathy roles, he points out, are rarely available to women in our society, although it is sometimes possible for lower class and adolescent women. Thus, he postulates that cultural determinants play an active role in personality formation. These roles, however, are perhaps changing as a result of the feminist movement. For example, the rates of crime, of violence, and of suicide are now increasing among women.

Hollender (1971) points out that a hysterical life style is fostered in a society in which female children are encouraged to be "childlike, relatively helpless and a man's plaything" (p. 21). He postulates that the ideal climate for the production of hysterical personalities existed in the "plantation society of the antebellum South" (p. 21). He summarizes by saying hysterical personality as a life style is fostered by social forces in little girls who are attractive in terms of appearance and personality. The individual psychodynamic pattern that "adds oil to the fire is maternal deprivation and turning to father for mothering" (p. 24). Hollender points out that "since many, perhaps most women, show some hysterical traits and no precise quantification is possible, it would be technically correct but cumbersome to say that a person is more or less a hysterical personality" (p. 17). "Furthermore," he states, "some women find it possible to be more flexible because they did not adopt the socially positive hysterical pattern to a marked degree or with deep intensity. In these instances an explanation may be found in the fact that the socially psychodynamic forces did not play into and amplify (or distort) the socially fostered lifestyle" (p. 23). Lastly, he asserts that "beneath the facade of grown women, they are little girls" (p. 26).

Lerner (1974) reviews much of the literature relevant to the question of social determinants as they relate to hysterical personality and subscribes to the point of view that there are many cultural expectations of women's behavior that are captured in the hysteric's personality style. Lastly, Chodoff and Lyons (1958) point out that nearly all of the papers about hysterical personality have been written by men. Luisada, Peele, and Pittard (1974) go a step further in speculating that the literature on hysterical personality written by women might have much more to say about male

hysterics, thus emphasizing the last link in the social determinant—
the eye of the beholder.

Halleck (1967) presents a convincing although largely antidotal
case for his formulations. His ideas are likely to be accepted with less
critical review than are Ludwig's or Kline and Davis's because of
their "fit" with current general assumptions about the importance of
childrearing practices and cultural patterns on psychopathology.
However, as with much of dynamic psychiatry, empirical validation
is lacking and unlikely to be immediately forthcoming.

FAMILIAL THEORY

Purtell, Robins, and Cohen (1951), Perley and Guze (1962), Guze
(1975), and several other psychiatrists at Washington University in
St. Louis describe a syndrome—Briquet's syndrome—which, they
assert, is hysteria. The syndrome is characterized by multiple,
varied somatic complaints, an early age of onset, disordered sexual
functioning, dysphoric mood, and multiple operations. A more
extensive description is given below (p. 116). Investigators
(Arkonac and Guze 1963) feel they have found evidence that this
syndrome is a familial condition. In addition, they have found an
increased incidence of sociopathic behavior in the first-degree male
relatives of females they have identified as hysteric (Woerner and
Guze 1968). They postulate a genetic transmission but do not
describe the genetic mechanism nor the biologic aberration which
results. The data are based on carefully done epidemiologic studies
of family groups. The two significant problems, however, are: first,
whether hysteria as they define it is the same as hysteria as usually
thought of by today's psychiatrists, and second, whether a positive
family tree invariably implies a genetic, biologic linkage for the
shared characteristic, or whether the characteristic is the consequence of a shared environment and learned behavior.

Guze's work is careful, statistically sound, and clearly epidemiological in nature. Such descriptive and correlational studies,
described in the next chapter, provide the basis for experimental
investigation but do not conducively establish a genetic origin over a
psychodynamic one. Studies of adopted children using large

populations, careful sampling, and rigorous diagnostic standards might clarify the nature-nurture point.

CULTURAL THEORIES

We know of no attempts that compare the manifestations of hysterical personality among varying cultures. However, individuals with hysterical symptoms are found in all cultures. Indeed the form that the hysterical symptom assumes seems to be culturally defined. This suggests that the forms are learned and have symbolic meanings. In some cultures periods of dissociation and symbolic and ritualized behaviors occur only in men, while in others they occur only in women. In addition, these hysterical symptoms and states occur within specific age groups and at predictable times. The variation from culture to culture is in marked contrast to the fixed stereotyped behavior of schizophrenic patients. Schizophrenic patients seem to manifest similar behaviors across cultures, and evidence suggests the severe schizophrenias can be diagnosed without reference to culture. In schizophrenia, of course, the content of delusions will be determined by the beliefs of a culture; but the form of the behavior, such as personal disorganization, withdrawal, and so on, is similar (Crocetti and Lemkau 1967).

Anthropologists have studied hysterical behaviors in many cultures. Langness (1967) found the concept of hysterical psychosis (developed by Hirsch and Hollander in 1964 and further elaborated in 1969) useful in organizing field observations. It is these more blatant and gross hysterical symptoms that have been most clearly described within the cultural studies. Langness's review and discussion may be the most complete. Foulks's work (1972) on Arctic hysteria is the most intensive investigation of a single syndrome. Hysterical behaviors vary from subculture to subculture within the United States. La Barre's 1956 description of the snake-handling cults of Appalachia is a classic (LaBarre 1969). Other authors have pointed out that minicultures, such as Army basic training camps, will increase the incidence and determine the form of hysterical behaviors (Rabkin 1964).

Perhaps a most convincing demonstration that severe dissociative and wildly destructive behavior can be learned and is highly symbolic is illustrated by the history of the "running amok" syndrome in Indonesia. Running amok occurred in males. At a time of stress a male entered a dissociated state and began killing in an indiscriminate fashion, until he was killed. The Dutch decreased the incidence by changing the rules of the game. The Dutch authorities insisted that when a man ran amok, he be captured, not killed. After capture he was sentenced to a lifetime of work on a road gang. Within a few years, the syndrome essentially disappeared.

Ralph Linton (1956) summarizes: "Hysterical phenomena are everywhere very decidedly culturally patterned. In fact, if one knows a culture, one can predict what form hysterias are going to take in that society—or pretty near so. This is the strongest possible argument in favor of the thesis that, whatever the etiology and dynamics of hysteria may be, its symptoms are extensively and intensively shaped by culture" (p. 132).

OBSERVATIONS OF CHILDREN

There are no studies of hysterical personalities in children (see chapter 3); however, hysterical symptoms including conversion reactions do occur in childhood. Their incidence and distribution according to age are unknown as is their natural history. Although Freud described Little Hans in 1904, reports on hysterical behavior in children in the psychiatric and pediatric literature have been infrequent. Proctor's paper (1958) summarized much of the relevant literature. His interest was stimulated by the high frequency of hysterical symptoms in a clinical population he worked with in North Carolina. Interestingly, 56 percent of his sample of patients were male. Proctor suggested an explanation for the disparity of the diagnosis of hysterical symptoms in male children as compared with adult males: "Within the framework of social acceptance and approval, hysterical mechanisms could be readily used by the male in childhood, but not in later life. Such traits are more socially and culturally acceptable for women than for men, and thus it would seem that hysteria would be more acceptable to women" (p. 439).

Although the exact incidence of hysterical symptoms in childhood remains unknown, the experience of Rock (1971) suggests that the symptoms are not uncommon. Rock, a child psychiatrist, working in conjunction with the Walter Reed General Hospital in Washington, D.C., and the Tripler General Hospital in Honolulu, diagnosed ten cases of conversion reactions in children in approximately two years. The children's ages ranged from three to thirteen. "In each instance, some threat to the dependence relationship between the parent-child had recently taken place; some minor trauma or illness had fixed the symptom; and the child's consequent inability to function at his appropriate age level appeared as a consequence of depressive feelings based on these areas of psychic trauma" (p. 91).

The highlighting of the dependency relationship between the parent and the child as the primarily dynamic issue involved in the symptom formation in these children is remarkably similar to the formulation derived by Sperling from her analytic studies of conversion symptoms in adults.

The reports by Proctor and Rock suggest that conversion reactions in children are more frequent than our past literature would indicate. Rock's report suggests that the incidence is directly proportional to the alertness and knowledge of the physician. He stresses that the diagnosis should be considered in every case of sensory, motor, or neuromuscular disorder in children, and not be made only by exclusion, for the sooner the diagnosis is made, the better the possibility for preventing permanent physical disabilities and more severe psychological disabilities.

BEHAVIORAL THEORY

Since hysteria is a traditional psychopathological term developed out of dynamic psychology, begavior therapists have written very little on the concept. Behavioral therapy, however, had been extensively applied to hysterical symptoms. Buss (1966) is a good introduction to the manner in which behaviorists think, while Yates surveys the many applications of behavior therapy to patients with hysterical symptoms. Brady's articles demonstrate interesting applications of behavioral techniques to the treatment of hysterical blindness (Brady and Lind 1961) and to a variety of female sexual problems (Brady 1967).

The approach of a behavioral therapist to a patient with hysterical symptoms, determined by a therapist's orientation, is probably changing with innovations in this field. A therapist trained by Wolpe (1969) would proceed with systematic desensitization, that is, the pairing of fearful images with relaxation; whereas one trained to use "implosive therapy" (Stampfl and Lewis 1967) would force a similar patient to confront his fears immediately and directly. On the other hand, a behaviorist influenced by Skinner (1953) would focus on the use of positive and negative reinforcements or rewards to encourage a phobic patient to approach and master a fearful situation.

At this point in the development of behavioral therapy, it appears that most therapists use a variety of behavioral techniques. In addition, as behaviorists have applied their theories to the complicated problems of people, as well as to the behaviors of laboratory animals, some have become impressed by factors described by dynamic psychotherapists, such as the power of the relationship or transference to alter behavior. Some behaviorists have incorporated these understandings into their treatment approaches.

ATTEMPT AT CLARIFICATION OF THEORIES OF HYSTERIA

There are, clearly, many theories of hysteria. At times, it may even seem there are as many theories as there are observations. Indeed, it seems physicians have been both attracted and repulsed by the phenomenon throughout the ages. For example, hysteria as an official diagnosis has disappeared and reappeared in the official psychiatric diagnostic nomenclature. Although hysteria was a common diagnosis in psychiatry, there was no diagnostic entity listed for hysteria in the first diagnostic manual of the American Psychiatic Association (*DSM I*), (1952); however, a diagnostic heading for hysteria appeared in *DSM II* (1968).

It is useful to review the descriptions of hysterical phenomena and to consider these descriptions in relation to the current usage of the term *hysteria*. Hysteria has been used to refer to a wide variety of symptoms. Prominent in the descriptions have been disturbances of the genito-urinary systems of the neurological and voluntary muscular systems, the appearance of altered states of consciousness including the presence of multiple personalities, extreme emotional instability including transient psychotic states, and a style of thinking and of experiencing the world characterized by a massive use of repression and denial. You will note that parts of these descriptions or attributes appear in most of the current conceptualizations of hysteria.

Currently the word "hysteria" is commonly used in the lay press to refer to extreme emotionality, as in "She (he) is acting hysterically." Hysteria often appears as a catchall term designating general emotional upheaval associated with the acute trauma of accidents, death, or other holocausts. The word also usually carries a strong negative connotation.

Hysteria appears as an official psychiatric diagnosis in the second *Diagnostic and Statistical Manual* of the American Psychiatric Association (*DSM II*, 1968), in the syndrome *hysterical neurosis.* According to the manual, hysterical neurosis is "characterized by an involuntary psychogenic loss or disorder of function." This diagnosis includes two subtypes: hysterical neurosis, conversion type and hysterical neurosis, dissociative type. In the conversion type, the special senses, are affected, causing such symptoms as blindness, deafness, anosmia, anesthesia, paresthesia, paralysis, ataxia, akinesia, and dyskinesia. "In the dissociative type," states the manual, "alternations may occur in the patient's state of consciousness or in his identity to produce such symptoms as amnesia, somnambulism, fugue, and multiple personality."

Hysteria also appears in the manual as *hysterical personality.* Hysterical personality, as described in *DSM II*, is a syndrome characterized by excitability, emotional instability, overreactivity, self-dramatization, attention seeking, immaturity, vanity, and unusual dependence (p. 43). This diagnosis is made from observations of manifest personality traits.

Yet another concept of hysteria can be found in the current psychiatric literature. This concept, referred to earlier, is described by a group of St. Louis investigators (Woodruff, Goodwin, and Guze 1974) as having at its base the descriptions of the nineteenth-century French physician, Paul Bríquet (1859). According to the St. Louis group, Briquet's syndrome has an early onset, usually before age twenty, almost invariably before thirty. It appears almost exclusively in females. It is characterized by multiple chronic physical complaints, many hospitalizations, multiple surgeries, and in addition, sexual symptoms, anxiety, and depression.

It should be stressed that "St. Louis" hysteria is a medical syndrome defined in the following manner: "for a diagnosis of hysteria, the patient must have twenty symptoms (medically unexplained) in at least nine of the ten symptom groups" (Cadoret and King 1974). The relationship of "St. Louis" hysteria, so narrowly defined in terms of conversion reactions and psychosomatic dysfunction, to the usual psychiatrists' ideas of hysteria, which include cognitive style, interpersonal patterns of relating, personality organization, and so on, is unknown. There is most probably some overlap, but the amount is uncertain. Research into this area is badly needed if we are to further clarify our thinking.

Hysteria is also found in the current psychiatric and anthropological literature as referring to a type of transient psychotic state called *hysterical psychosis* (Richman and White 1970). This syndrome has a documented existence and can be differentiated from other psychogenic psychoses. It is usually sudden in onset, short-lived, precipitated by actual object loss or other significant stress, and has no long-term sinister prognosis of psychotic deterioration. The psychodynamics of an episode are usually blatantly evident. Manifestations may include hallucinations, delusions, depersonalization, bizarre behavior, and labile affect. As noted earlier, variations of this disorder have been described in many cultures.

HYSTERICAL PERSONALITY

We believe there have been refinements in the recent clinical descriptions of patients that now make it possible to better conceptualize the phenomena of hysteria within the concept of hysterical personality. The crucial ideas for this advance arise from two broad streams. The first is the development of the psychoanalytic concept of character. The second is the development of subtypes of hysteria—the "good" and "bad hysterics"—which has arisen out of experience with a wide range of hysterical patients undergoing psychoanalytic treatment.

As you will recall, initial psychoanalytic research into psychopathology focused on the instinctual and symbolic content, on the impulses and fantasies. Later, there gradually developed an interest in the enduring characteristics or typologies of patients. Freud (1908), Abraham (1912), and others began to describe patient types. Their first descriptions were couched in terms of libidinal development and fixations; for example, Abraham's description of the anal character type and Freud's delineation of erotic, obsessional, and narcissistic types.

A further shift occurred when Reich (1933) focused on repetitive patterns of behavior which he felt were caused by a fixation of libidinal energy bound by psychological mechanisms and muscle tone. He called this combination of psychological and somatic factors "character armor." According to Reich, conflict between impulse and defense was fixed into enduring psychological somatic patterns, destined to be repeated over and over. Anna Freud's observations (1936), parallel in time, contributed further to understanding patterns of psychological defenses and the organization of personality.

Hartmann's contributions (1958) stressed the integrative and adaptive capacities of the ego. He postulated that there were enduring capacities within each individual's ego which arose independently of psychological conflict. He termed these independent capacities "autonomous ego functions." Hartmann felt these perceptive and cognitive functions were derived from innate biological givens or potentials. He assumed these functions could remain independent of psychological conflict or could become involved in and influenced by conflict. His suggestions added an important dimension to the psychoanalytic model of personality, for personality structure was now seen as resulting from interactions between conflict-free ego capacities and psychological conflict.

Erikson (1950) added to this personality model through his observations on the contributions of culture to personality. He pointed out how a culture may either reinforce or interfere with the development of a person's emergent use of particular types of psychological defenses. He described the process by which cultures shape the personalities of their members into adaptive personality types for given geographical and social environments.

Shapiro (1965) evolved the concept of neurotic style out of the broader psychoanalytic concept of character by focusing upon the question, How does the individual operate? This new concept highlighted the patterns of operation of ego functions, not the forces that motivate these functions. According to Shapiro, these styles were most apparent within controlled observational settings, such as psychoanalytic sessions or psychological test interviews. Shapiro illustrated his concept of neurotic style in the following way:

Suppose we observe an Indian, whose culture is unfamiliar, performing a strange dance with great intensity. As we watch, puzzled, we may notice there is a drought and that this is an agricultural community; we consider the possibility that this is a prayerful dance designed to bring rain and that possibility that it is an expression of apprehension as well. By careful observation, we may be able to decipher certain regular gestures that confirm our guess. There is no doubt that at this point we have achieved a significant measure of understanding. But the limitations of that understanding become apparent if we only consider that nearby, watching, is a non-Indian farmer who also suffers from the drought but who does not join in the dancing. It does not occur to him to perform these gestures; instead he goes home and worries. The Indian dances not only because there is a drought but also because he is an Indian. His dancing follows observed attitudes and ways of thinking—a frame of mind that is likely to be long standing and relatively stable. Knowledge of these stable forms adds another dimension of plausibility, of sense to his behavior. [p. 16]

The concept of neurotic style focuses on the transformations occurring between the push or drive and the particular constellation of defenses employed by an individual. In the sample above, the desire for rain resulted in differing behaviors: the rain dance by the Indian and the fretting by the non-Indian.

The hysterical neurotic style described by Shapiro is based upon a pervasive use of repression: "What we mean most often by repression is forgetting . . . the loss not of affect, but of ideational contents from consciousness" (p. 109). Shapiro thus utilized the observations and ideas that Freud postulated in 1896, when Freud suggested that in hysterics ideational content was split from consciousness. Shapiro amplifies Freud's concept as he relates this psychical maneuver not only to the conversion symptom, but to a characteristic ongoing process, an enduring part of an individual's personality. Shapiro supports his thesis by pointing out that when a clinician inquires for a specific description from a hysteric, he is likely to get "not facts but impressions. These impressions may be interesting and communicative, and they are often very vivid, but they remain impressions—not detailed, not quite sharply defined, and certainly not technical" (p. 111). Such responses from hysteric patients indicate that ideas, concepts, and facts are not easily available to them. Shapiro stresses as characteristic features of hysterical cognition: "the relative absence of active concentration, the susceptibility to transient, impressive influences, in a relatively nonfactual subjective world" (p. 116).

Shapiro's description of hysterical neurotic style also stresses the extreme emotionality found in this style. Emotionality, as well as repression, is distinctive of the style. To an observer a hysteric's emotions seem exaggerated and unconvincing. To others, hysterics do not seem to be sincere. Indeed, hysterics often seem surprised when others do take them seriously, when they find that a logical sequence of their own statements and actions has come to pass. "This attitude becomes apparent, sometimes, in the form of astonishment or incredulity on the part of hysterical people when a consequence of some action of their own or of circumstances of which they were aware comes to pass, a consequence that may have been completely predictable to everyone else" (Shapiro, p. 122). Their extreme variation in emotion also seems to defend against still other emotion. Their subjective world seems to lie at a great distance from an intellectual understanding of their own behavior.

Zetzel (1968) was perhaps the first to describe subtypes of hysterics. She observed wide variation in the character or personality structure among patients who sought psychoanalysis because of hysterical symptoms. She called the polar types in the patient mix she observed the "good hysteric" and the "bad hysteric." "Good" referred to patients who had predominantly genital or oedipal conflicts, relatively mature personality structures, and who did well in psychoanalytic treatment. "Bad" referred to patients who had predominantly preoedipal conflicts, defects in ego and personality structure, and who did poorly in psychoanalytic treatment.

Lazare (1971) further developed Zetzel's concept. He emphasized the developmental, characterological, and behavioral aspects of the hysterical spectrum. The "good hysterics" appear to come from intact families with adequate early mothering; while the "bad hysterics" seem to come from chaotic family backgrounds, with mothers who were often absent, seriously depressed, or who offered poor models for identification. The psychopathology is more pervasive throughout the personality of the "bad hysteric," the sexuality more perverse, the behavior more blatant. While in the "good hysteric" the symptoms are more isolated, ego alien, the sexual difficulties are at a genital level and secondary to inhibition, and the behaviors are more modulated. The "good hysteric" is usually the more successful in school, at work, socially, and in psychotherapy.

TOWARD A STRUCTURAL MODEL

The concept of neurotic style, coupled with the genetic, characterological, and behavioral features provided by the hysterical subtypes, now makes possible a new model. This model is based on an understanding of an individual's character and the contributions to this structure of the relative amounts of preoedipal and oedipal conflicts. The structure is assumed to be derived from the biological and experiential components of an individual's life history, that is, the relative admixtures of intactness of family, physical and emotional health of parents, richness and type of education and social milieus.

We view symptoms as existing within the matrix of a hysterical character structure. We place emphasis upon the matrix, the structure. We view the symptom as an epiphenomena. This conceptualization constitutes an almost total reversal of the early views in which hysteria was equated with hysterical symptoms.

This new model enables us to emphasize those enduring

personality traits that have been associated with the hysterical personality. Chodoff and Lyons (1958), for example, identified with the following: dependence, egocentricity, emotionality, exhibitionism, fear of sexuality, sexual provocativeness, and suggestibility. Lazare and others (1966, 1970), using factor analytic techniques, found: aggression, emotionality, oral aggression, obstinacy, exhibitionism, egocentricity, and sexual provocativeness. In contrast to Chodoff and Lyons, they did not find dependence, fear of sexuality, and suggestibility to be striking in their population. In Lazare's studies, however, there was an overlapping of oral, obsessive, and hysterical personality traits in some patients. These findings are in accord with our view that hysterical personality traits occur along a psychosexual continuum of psychosexual development.

Female hysterics have been described as "caricatures of femininity" (Chodoff and Lyons 1958). We have broadened this concept to a "caricature of sexual role." Caricature, of course, means a likeness or imitation that is so distorted or inferior as to seem ludicrous. The phrase "caricature of sexual role" is a convenient notation which allows us to stress two ideas which we see as central to the understanding of hysteria. The first is that a failure of a firm sexual identity is always part of hysterical structure, and the second is that such a failure is central to hysterical difficulties in men as well as women.

It is important to think in symmetrical terms. We believe the male counterpart of the overly feminine female hysteric is the hypermasculine, pseudosociopathic Don Juan male. (Don Juan is used here to refer to the seventeenth-century seducer of women, not to Carlos Castaneda's teacher.) We believe that the hypermasculine male hysteric is characterized by all of the essential features found in female hysterics, and thus should be thought of in the same diagnostic, descriptive, prognostic, etiologic, and therapeutic manner. Thus in both males and females, the behavioral manifestations are a "caricature of sex role."

Abse (1959) has written perceptively of males with hysterical symptoms who attempt to gain a strong male identification through hypermasculine activities, such as daredevil motorcycle riding. It seems to us and to several other authors—Kolb (1973), Malmquist (1971), Halleck (1967), and MacKinnon and Michels (1971)—that there must be two types of male hysterics: the passive, effeminate, often homosexual male; and the assertive, pseudohypermasculine, aggressive hypersexual (Don Juan) male.

Recently, Luisada, Peele, and Pittard (1974) studied twenty-seven men admitted for inpatient treatment who fit the DSM II criteria for hysterical personality. The majority had a history of suicidal gestures or threats. There was a frequent family history of mental illness, usually alcoholism. Fathers were described as being unassertive or as being absent during the patient's childhood. The subjects had poor educational and occupational success. Most were heterosexual, and half had been married. Few, however, had stable marriages. Many of those who were married had older wives, and "all had disturbed sexual relations ranging from fears of inadequacy to unhappy homosexual relationships" (p. 19). The majority abused alcohol or drugs and had criminal records of drunkenness or robbery. Striking effeminacy was noted in four patients and hypermasculinity in two. Antisocial behavior was typical of the group. Physical complaints were common in some patients, but there was no indication of overuse of surgery. Problems in sexual performance did not predominate; social problems were more common.

To restate our hypothesis, the common theme in male and female hysterics is a caricature of sex-role; thus, instead of only looking for effeminate characteristics in the male, one should also look for pseudomasculine or hypermasculine characteristics which stem from the same general genetic-dynamic base as the hyperfeminine characteristics in the female. Thus the conflict, defensive structure, cognition, perception, and interpersonal styles are the same in males and females; but the most common behavioral manifestations are mirror images, pseudofemininity in the female and pseudomasculinity in the male.

CHARACTEROLOGICAL PATTERNS

Previous authors have emphasized various attributes of the hysteric, and consequently we find a personality pattern description determined, at least in part, by the perspective of the author. We assert that the following descriptors constitute the core characteristics of a hysterical personality. Some of these behaviors occur more commonly than others and prominence varies among individuals; each behavior may have a range and variety of expression. These descriptors are a synthesis of the literature and our clinical experience.

The core descriptors are aggressive behavior, emotionality, sexual problems, obstinacy, exhibitionism, egocentricity, and sexual provocativeness and dependency. These behaviors express sexual confusion, pseudomasculine and pseudofeminine adaptation, and a false maturity. Unique perceptual, cognitive, and communicative styles complete the descriptive picture; these will be discussed in chapter 6.

Core determinants of the personality style are two: (1) early maternal deprivation and (2) distorted resolution of the oedipal situation and of the emergent sexual role identification. Psychosocial, psychosexual, and ego function perspectives will be related to this developmental model. Zetzel's good-bad (oral-genital) polarity is in actuality a continuum which reflects the two predominant developmental stages where significant conflicts begin. Not only is there a make-believe quality to the sexual identity of hysterics but there is also a similar "as if" quality in other aspects of their behavior. Thus, maturity is more apparent than real—a pseudoadult facade as is suggested by the term child-woman, which some authors have applied to the female hysteric. There is both a distortion of gender role and a false maturity. The "little girl" quality of some female hysterics is well recognized. A similar "little boy" quality in the male hysteric is frequently seen when illness or injury intervenes, and a break occurs in the shell of the counterphobic bravado.

Table 1 gives examples of the manifestations of the diagnostic descriptors for pseudofeminine and pseudomasculine adaptations. Looking down the list of descriptors, some are more culturally consistent with a pseudomasculine adaptation, while others are more consistent with direct expression by the pseudofeminine individual. For example, aggression is more commonly directly expressed by males, while emotionality and dependency are more culturally consistent with the feminine role. Obstinacy, exhibition-

TABLE 1

PSEUDOFEMININE EXPRESSION	DIAGNOSTIC DESCRIPTORS	PSEUDOMASCULINE EXPRESSION
subtle, indirect manipulation, competitive with males, dominant, easily angered, argues, sarcastic, pouts but controlled, provokes guilt in others	Aggression	direct, threatens others with verbal or physical fights, fights to prove self, bombastic, resists dependency
poor emotional control, sentimental, romantic, cries easily, behavioral and emotional overreaction, intense emotional response, calms quickly, diffuse, shallow, labile	Emotionality	impulsive, transient, superficial affect, may deny feelings or be sentimental
frigid, avoids sexual encounters, surprise at men's response to sexual provocativeness	Sexual Problems	sexual exploitation, Don Juanism, hypermasculine
stubborn, will not give in on "rights"—feminine prerogatives	Obstinacy	stubborn on masculine issues, for example, independence and nondominance by females
dress, cosmetics, posture and gait, or any attribute including defects or needs used to attract attention	Exhibitionism	show of strength, bravery or tolerance of pain, dress attracts attention, flashy cars or gadgets
own needs first, sensitive to critical remarks, vulnerable to slights	Egocentricity	self-interest first, body image very important, uses others, vulnerable to slights
flirtatious, cat-and-mouse games with men, romantic, coy, coquettish	Sexual Provocativeness	flirtatious, frequent affairs of fact or fantasy, conquest important
protests for independence but rarely acts, may abuse drugs or alcohol	Dependency	pseudo hypermasculinity, disabled with relatively minor illnesses and injuries

ism, egocentricity, and sexual provocativeness seem to be directly expressed by both males and females.

The better integrated (genital, or "good") hysteric may adapt reasonably well, particularly in aggressive or creative pursuits. Some males may act out aggressively and antisocially; they may be gang or group leaders and may develop strong, although somewhat superficial, relationships. There is some capacity for closeness in the family and outside, but he usually continues to be somewhat irresponsible and egocentric. Vanity and bravado characterize the pseudofeminine and the pseudomasculine individual. Turbulent interpersonal affairs, particularly those with sexual relationships, are common.

The more genitally fixated, less oral, less narcissistically vulnerable hysteric may be ambitious and successful with fairly good employment and educational records. However, under stress there may be a development of either depressive or psychosomatic complaints. This may come at the time of growing older with the loss of physical attractiveness and virility, or in association with rejection from a sexual partner. Repression is the central mechanism and is reflected in the cognitive and perceptual style of the hysteric.

The more pregenitally fixated or more narcissistically vulnerable hysteric is characterized by ego weakness with poor integration of personality elements and poor differentiation of internal and external reality. The diffuseness of cognition and affect is more pronounced and under stress quickly regresses to a passive, depressed, or psychotic role with a serious risk of suicide. They have few problem-solving techniques—acting out, regression, or sickness frequently being their only resource. Negative self-concepts and poor self-esteem are common. There is poor adaptation with an unstable, unpredictable, and lonely adjustment. Relationships may be intense but quite chaotic and unpredictable with primitive aggressive outbursts, intense jealousy, and possessiveness. There may be grandiose beliefs in self. A variety of sexual behaviors may be attempted with little investment or satisfaction. Often there is an abuse of drugs or alcohol. The caricature of femininity or masculinity is often more bizarre.

In the infantile hysteric with a pseudomasculine adjustment, aggressiveness and sexual exploitation may be common; whereas in the hysteric with pseudofeminine adjustment, promiscuous and jealous behavior, characterized by strong emotional outbursts, are common. There is a poor vocational and educational record, and often behavior, particularly in the pseudomasculine hysteric, leads to arrest. Sex partners are seen only as temporarily relieving sexual needs and providing marginal nurturance. While relationships may be confused and primitive, they are of vast importance as a buffer for poor self-esteem. Nurturance is eagerly sought, but it is also inevitably distrusted. This combination, of course, produces chaotic relationships with others. The person may be inconsistent, irresponsible, sadistic, or masochistic, rarely integrating into group or gang behavior. He is, at best, a follower on the periphery of a group. With distress, he may act with impulsive aggressive behavior. Depression or psychosis may be associated with violence or suicide attempts. Physical complaints are very common.

Both the biologic male and female have the potential for developing a pseudomasculine or pseudofeminine adjustment. The pseudomasculine adaptation in the male is the supermale, Don Juan, he-man. He may be attracted to physically active, risk-taking kinds of activities and jobs. He is frequently pushed to demonstrate his power and strength. This may be effected through a variety of extralegal maneuvers which may get him into recurrent trouble with legal authorities. This sociopathiclike behavior may be confused with the true sociopath; however, the hysteric will show splitting of his personality. The underlying dependency in many of his antisocial acts will seem exaggerated, often grotesque and bizarre, in contrast to the true sociopath, whose actions and personality are more integrated and, in one sense, more mature.

The pseudosociopathic Don Juan represents one end of a continuum. At the other end is peudofemininity in its most extreme form: the dependent, passive, coy, exhibitionistic, manipulative, Southern belle type. Between these polarities, both for males and females, lies a range of sexual and characterological adaptations which may have a mixture of both feminine and masculine elements all the while maintaining many of the core descriptors noted previously. Pseudofeminine adjustment in males has been recognized for some time and may be associated with homosexuality. In biologic females, pseudomasculine adjustment seems to be less well described and recognized, and most likely would represent the "butch" adaptation of the lesbian.

SUMMARY OF BEHAVIORAL DESCRIPTORS
BY AGE AND SEX

The protypical descriptions given below may aid in evaluating individuals for diagnostic and therapeutic purposes. We have chosen to describe three ages: teenage, adulthood, and middle age.

Men

Teenage. The more primitive, oral, pseudomasculine male hysteric may seek membership in gangs or small socially deviant groups. He will tend to remain distant and unintegrated and may drift away as he grows older. His behavior may be so bizarre and impulsive as to make him an outcast even within a subculture of social deviancy. Thus, he may become a loner with bouts of alcohol or drug abuse, and aggressive and other impulsive exhibitionistic acts. He may develop an intense, though very dependent-dominant relationship with a girl, a relationship that will be turbulent and unstable. He will achieve little in educational or vocational success; exhibitionism and egocentricity will be manifest through demanding, impulsive, risk-taking behavior with insistence upon loyalty from associates. He will use sexuality to satisfy dependency and nurturant needs.

The more integrated, oedipal male hysteric will have many of the same elements but with a higher probability of "success" and satisfying outcomes. Thus, friendships will be more stable and less exploitive. Gang membership may occur but central, even leadership roles may be achieved. Impulsivity and risk-taking will be less bizarre and self-destructive. Heterosexual relationships will develop but may be more stable with some give and take. Success may be achieved in athletic, selective academic, or vocational areas. Exhibitionistic, vain behavior will be reflected in clothes and manner. He may sustain and attract prolonged loyalties and will often be found to be likeable and attractive to others. Aggression and fighting will occur, but that, like sexuality, will be less compulsively and exploitively pursued.

Adult. At this stage, the oral, primitive, male hysteric will have developed a very lonely life style, often characterized by overt criminal behavior, alcohol or drug abuse. He may have experienced jail terms or other brushes with the law. Regular aggressive behavior may be centered around alcohol use or automobiles. Drug taking may have become a serious problem. Interpersonal relationships will have deteriorated and sexual behavior will be more clearly a compulsive act serving nurturant needs. Heterosexual relationships will be turbulent. There will be little academic or vocational success and the individual will drift from one impulsive, risk-taking, exhibitionistic act to the next. Emergent egodystonic feelings will be dealt with by drinking and compulsive sexuality.

The more successful, integrated hysteric may well achieve a reasonably satisfying and socially acceptable kind of behavior. He may be attracted to educational and vocational opportunities that reward egocentric and exhibitionistic needs. Long-range goals may be formulated and sought and occasionally achieved. Aggressive behavior may be channeled into leadership activities or into competitive behaviors necessary to success in certain kinds of business. Vanity is reflected in clothes, automobiles, and choice of sexual partners. Marriage may develop but will be unstable and unrewarding with frequent extramarital liaisons and alcohol abuse.

Middle age. The primitive male hysteric by this time will have had a heavy involvement in alcohol or socially deviant behavior. He may have experienced long periods of incarceration or serious physical damage from alcohol abuse. His risk-taking behavior may have led to accidents, causing serious injury or even death. Industrial accidents with chronic disability are common. A life style characterized by aimless drifting, transient interpersonal relationships, and marginal sexual adjustment is present. Exhibitionism and egocentricity are lessened by the development of depression, social isolation, and the appearance of chronic physical complaints. Overreaction to injury and illness and excessive complaints of pain or other physical problems will be visible. Exploitation of others through dependency will become prominent, overt aggression will take a more verbal form.

The better integrated, middle-aged male hysteric may persist much as he did through early adulthood, with some stability of vocational interest and even a large measure of financial success. Exhibitionism and egocentricity continue and may be manifest in interpersonal relationships, dress, excesses, and "flashy" use of money. Fighting is only manifest through verbal exchanges. Vanity and egocentricity may lead to poor business decisions. Communication may be poor with family and coworkers and increasing autocratic behaviors may develop.

Women
Teenage. The oral female hysteric will follow a pattern much like her male counterpart. After early attempts to integrate herself into a gang or some socially deviant or outcast subgroup of peers, she will gradually drift away, developing a lonely life style marked with a lack of success in academic, interpersonal, or vocational pursuits. Impulsivity is more likely to be reflected in sexual rather than in aggressive behavior. Exhibitionism will center around seductive behavior that will depend heavily on clothes and behavioral mannerisms. This exhibitionism may at times be perceived as bizarre. She will be seen as being "too available." Clinging dependence may alternate with aggressive, angry behavior toward others. Interpersonal relationships are chaotic and unstable, leaving those around her puzzled, angry, and hurt. Sex serves to achieve her nurturant and dependent needs.

The more integrated teenager may effectively participate in group activities or gangs. She may be sought after in a variety of social situations. Occasionally tomboyish, athletic abilities may be useful entrees to social acceptance. Coy and seductive behavior make her attractive to males and "popular" in high school and college. Aggression may be channeled into improved social relationships and academic and extracurricular activities. She will feel more comfortable in the company of men and may develop skills that will be useful for career goals. She may be attacted to drama or similar pursuits where her exhibitionistic needs can be satisfied. Interpersonal relationships may remain stable, though fluctuated with frequent flights, separations, and reunions.

Adult. The more primitive hysteric may marry early to an

insecure, dependent male who perceives her aggression as a sign of independence and capability. She, in turn, may develop a dependent, destructive role with her husband. They very quickly develop an isolated "parallel play" type of relationship where sexuality may be the major activity of common interest. However, their sexuality is usually unsatisfying and serves only a need for nurturance. The relationship often deteriorates, and as a consequence, the woman may develop psychosomatic complaints or depression, or begin extramarital affairs. Alcohol or drug abuse may increase. The woman may either turn to her husband with increasing dependence or passivity or may look outside the marriage to other men or, occasionally, to interests in club activities as a means of satisfying her dependent needs. She will achieve little in the way of academic or vocational success. She is viewed as emotionally unstable, demanding, and impulsive by her husband. Her relationship with children will be difficult and she will see them as demanding and nonrewarding.

The well-integrated hysteric, on the other hand, may develop considerable success in career goals and continue through to some academic success. Sexual contacts will persist as a way of achieving nurturance and attracting partners. Sexual satisfaction will be limited, however. Marriage may depend on her dependent-aggressive relationship with men, which may become prominent. She may look outside the marriage for more satisfaction, using either sexual or career avenues to achieve this. Clothes and cosmetics will become important ways to sustain physical attractiveness and achieve her exhibitionistic, egocentric goals. She may often be perceived as castrating and competitive by men. Exhibitionistic needs may be served through community organization and work. Physical complaints and psychosomatic problems may occur.

Middle age. The oral hysteric will develop more problems with alcohol or drug abuse, psychosomatic complaints, and depression as her sexual attractiveness fails. Chaotic relationships with men will continue in the same way. She may look older than her years. Exhibitionism and egocentricity tend to diminish as depression and other new psychopathology may appear. Chronic drug abuse, chronic depression, and suicide are not uncommon.

Better integrated hysterics will keenly feel the loss of beauty and sexual attractiveness. Exhibitionism, egocentricity, and aggressiveness may be served through success in career or volunteer work. Excessive use of cosmetics and redoubled energy in achieving attractiveness may occur. She may look outside the marriage for sexual contact or may find some satisfaction in her career. She and her husband may dimly recognize the distant, superficial relationship they have. She will experience difficulty with teenage children and may alternate between indulging and encouraging their sexual and aggressive behavior or becoming extremely moralistic, disciplining in a rigid arbitrary fashion. Depression and psychosomatic problems may emerge, and alcohol may be heavily used.

POSTULATED DYNAMICS

The hysteric experiences a period of early maternal deprivation. The more severe this is, the more the adult personality is seen as oral, dependent, infantile, pregenital, or reactive to the threat of narcissistic injury. Each potential hysteric is thus left with the need to generate additional nurturant sources throughout his subsequent development. This need becomes the mainspring for further developments and conflicts and is central to the adult personality. In the family, the availability of nurturance is often tied to sexual provocativeness, sickness, or childlike behavior alternating with adultlike behavior. Exhibitionism and manipulation are useful techniques to further satisfaction of these needs.

For the female child, the mothering person, having been unable to deliver sufficient nurturance during infancy, continues to be found wanting as the child grows older, and the little girl turns to the parent of the opposite sex. Hollender (1971) notes: "the crucial point developmentally is that young girls who become hysterical personalities turn to their fathers or mother's father as substitute mothers" (p. 22). A young girl then looks to father to supply the missing nurturance and can only extract it on the basis of her coy, seductive, flirtatious behavior which is, of course, rewarded with superficially focused interest—hardly an answer to her needs but better than nothing. As genital, sexual feelings and thoughts emerge, these must be repressed; however, the associated actions—for example, coy, seductive, flirtatious behavior—persists and is rewarded. This results in the split between behavior and feelings and thoughts—a characteristic which will continue and is critical.

The little girl wants mothering at two levels, in infancy as a nurturant source and again during the genital period as an identification model. Without a stable maternal resource for identification, the personality becomes that patchwork of behaviors rewarded by father, through sexualized interaction, and those acquired through mimicry of cultural stereotypes. Thus, a superficial, rigid, compartmentalized and incomplete identity or self-concept evolves. There is no integration or flexibility. The repertoire of behavior that is acquired is generated from the child's observation of social stereotypes and rewarded behaviors. Hollender (1971) suggests that the jet-set and movie colonies may provide the models. Subsequently, outside the home, such behaviors are reinforced by peers, fantasy, and further exposure to cultural stereotypes and cultural sources, for example, television, movies, and novels. Thus the social arena in some measure acts as a surrogate family providing models and reinforcements.

The male is faced with a somewhat similar situation. He also experiences the relative maternal deprivation during infancy, leaving him with the same felt need for nurturant sources. At the time of the oedipal struggle, he finds his father absent or unavailable as a role model. Consequently this leaves him with only his mother to relate to. She can now provide limited nurturance as a part of an eroticized overindulgent relationship.

Although mother has been unable to control and sustain a relationship with father, she now has a captive respondent in the child-man. She can reinforce those behaviors that she desires and extinguish those that are not needed. Again, since the boy has no adequate masculine role model to identify with, behaviors that develop are the results of the reinforcement from mother and mimicry of cultural stereotypes. They are a superficial patchwork of unrelated, poorly integrated actions; and since genital sexual feeling and thought must be repressed while sustaining the behaviors, affective and cognitive splitting results. Impulsive, pseudomasculine, hedonistic, manipulative behavior patterns may result depending on what behaviors mother rewards. Self-concept develops through the reinforced behavior patterns and interaction with mother, and the borrowed, romanticized behavior found among peers, gangs, and folk heroes on television and in movies. Such social stereotypes provide the basis then for a caricature of masculinity, with emphasis on the hypermasculine pattern, in an effort to deny the lack of firm masculine foundation and the early deprivation leading to dependency.

The child may either model his behavior after the parent of the opposite sex, producing a pseudomasculine female or pseudofeminine male, or he may develop a biologically appropriate but exaggerated pseudoadult behavior that is a caricature of the cultural norm for his or her biologic sex. As the child finds himself turning to the parent of the opposite sex for both nurturance and as a source of identification formation, a series of rather complex forces begin to operate. The male child, with no suitable father available, continues to relate to the mother, not only to capture the missed nurturance but also as a potential object for sex-role identity. The child is faced with an ever increasing ambivalence: On the one hand, he wishes to reestablish the passivity suitable for nurturance; on the other, he needs increasingly to deny passivity, particularly in the case of the male child, and to develop the assertive gender role consistent with social dictates. Reaction formation converts passivity to aggressivity as a mimicry of activity as well as an expression of frustration.

The female child, in contrast, has to give up the hope for nurturance from the mother and turn to her father; and then, in attempts to create a mothering individual out of father, she is constrained to develop a variety of attention-getting and seductive devices which largely assume the dimension of the "cute little girl." The child finds herself in an ambivalent relationship: on the one hand, she hopes to resurrect a relationship that will supply the nurturance so sorely missed earlier; on the other hand, she is catapulted to a pseudoadult role. Passivity must be denied through the use of reaction formation, and the opposite, aggressive behavior, is the outcome. The use of obsessive defenses at this stage is primarily related to dealing with feelings of passivity, and it generates aggressive and, at times, obstinate behavior patterns in the adult.

This latter stage of working through with the parent of the opposite sex, dealing with the ambivalence through reaction formations, and constructing an aggressive stance represents the best solution for the hysteric. Necessary for this resolution is the capacity for forming fairly solid object relations. Zetzel (1968) has pointed out that the true hysteric has sustained the capacity to form good honest relations with parents. This model can then be carried into therapy where it serves as the basis for the analytic process. To the extent the child falls short of this resolution, that is, never develops stable object relationships with the parent of either sex, oral issues dominate and the behavior is, at best, a mimicry of adult sexual role behavior. These individuals, the immature hysterics, do not have the capabilities necessary to greatly profit from insight-oriented psychotherapy or analysis.

SUMMARY

To summarize briefly, early psychoanalysts focused on the primitive urges and psychic conflicts that produced hysterical symptoms. They stressed the sexual rivalries and the fear of punishments associated with the oedipal complex. Later psychoanalysts pointed out the lack of adequate early mothering in individuals who develop hysterical symptoms. They placed additional emphasis on the importance of preoedipal issues, and also stressed that aggressive urges, as well as sexual urges, can produce hysterical symptoms.

Modern psychoanalysts broadened the earlier ideas of their colleagues as they further developed the concepts of character and ego psychology, and began to delineate the relationship between personality structure and symptom formation. Shapiro (1965) gave added depth to this perspective with his concept of neurotic style. Zetzel (1968) and Lazare (1971) identified important developmental and social forces involved in the formation of mature or infantile personality structures.

Keeping in mind the many theories regarding hysterical symptoms—social, affective, neurological, familial, and so on—it is our thesis that the concept of hysterical structure or hysterical personality provides us with the firmest clinical and conceptual basis. We understand hysterical personality to be a specific type of personality organization which utilizes repression of internal information and denial of external information as its major defense, tends to experience the world in a strongly emotional and biased way, and is not concerned with precise logic or clarity of thinking. We visualize hysterical structures as ranging from relatively mature, intact, and functional patterns to grossly immature structures with major deficits and limited ranges of function. We consider symptoms to be more or less an epiphenomena existing within the personality structure. The course of a symptom and its possible amelioration by psychoanalysis or psychotherapy is, as we see it, more dependent upon the underlying structure than upon the crisis that precipitated it.

Our review leads us to propose the following model and dynamics: Hysterical personality is associated with characteristics which arise from both pregenital and genital psychosexual levels. The more infantile personality organization arises as a result of inadequate mothering and deprivation during infancy and results in chaotic, extreme, and unstable behavior as an adult which is highly resistant to psychotherapeutic, psychoanalytic intervention. This is contrasted with the genital, or mature, hysterical personality organization, which has experienced less early deprivation, exhibits more intact object relationships, has experienced more success in vocational, educational, and social areas, and has symptoms amenable to the present armament of psychotherapeutic intervention.

We suggest that the central issues for the individual with a hysterical personality is the resolution of gender identity. We also suggest that this conflict is expressed through the lens of a personality structure which has been significantly cast and tinted by the relative amounts of early maternal deprivation experienced. The particular tinting of the lens may give a different coloration or manifestation to the adult behaviors, but the same central issues will identify the hysteric: aggression, emotionality, sexual problems, obstinancy, exhibitionism, egocentricity, sexual provocativeness, and dependency.

Early maternal deprivation places the child in a vulnerable position at the time of the oedipal struggle. The female child often seeks out the father as a substitute mother and may either identify with him (a pseudomasculine solution) or develop a culturally stereotyped feminine identity, drawing on cultural elements which are then reinforced in an eroticized relationship with the father (a pseudofeminine solution). The male has essentially the same problems. Upon entering the oedipal solution, he has already experienced moderate to severe early deprivation and, in addition, often finds his father unavailable or distant. He then again turns to the mother, who finds it easier to relate to the older child, and he may either identify with her (a pseudofeminine or effeminate homosexual solution) or he may draw from cultural stereotypes, the elements of which are reinforced by the mother, to develop a shaky, pseudomasculine identity. For both the male and the female child these identities are more a mimicry of cultural stereotypes, shaped through reinforcements by parents, than true identities obtained through the usual processes of introjection and identification. Thus, the succeeding personality is often rigid, fixed, and superficial and serves as a defense against the inner and earlier deprivation.

The common manifestations of the hysterical personality in the biologic male and female are related as mirror images, that is, exaggeration of feminine or masculine characteristics. In the female, we see as a common solution the prototype of the Southern belle, and in the male we often see the prototype of the exhibitionist gang member who is frequently, we feel, mistakenly diagnosed as sociopathic rather than hysterical.

Our hypotheses and speculations need to be explored and tested by further clinical observation and research. It would be important, for example, to correlate familial studies of Briquet's syndrome with the dynamics and psychological attributes observed by psychoanalysts. Further perceptual and personality research by those interested in cognitive styles would be most helpful. While it is certain that hysterical symptoms will continue, it is less certain, but hopeful, that we may be able to better understand and treat them. At this time, we suggest that the concept of hysterical personality, as we have proposed, is a useful platform from which to proceed.

REFERENCES

Abraham, K. (1912).*Selected Papers on Psychoanalysis.*New York: Basic Books.

Abse, W. D. (1959). Hysteria. In *American Handbook of Psychiatry*, ed. S. Arieti. New York: Basic Books.

American Psychiatric Association (1952). *Diagnostic and Statistical Manual of Mental Disorders (DSM I)*. Washington, D.C.

———(1968). *Diagnostic and Statistical Manuel of Mental Disorders (DSM II)*. Washington, D.C.

Arkonac, O., and Guze, S. (1963). A family study of hysteria. *New England Journal of Medicine* 268: 239-242.

Brady, J. P. (1967). Psychotherapy, learning theory and insight. *Archives of General Psychiatry* 16: 304.

Brady, J. P., and Lind, D. (1961). Experimental analysis of hysterical blindness. *Archives of General Psychiatry* 4: 331-339.

Breuer, J., and Freud, S. (1893-1895). Studies on hysteria. *Standard Edition* 2.

Bríquet, P. (1859). *Traité Clinique et Thérapeutique de l'Hysterie*. Paris: Balliere.

Buss, A. (1966). *Psychopathology*. New York: Wiley.

Cadoret, R. J., and King, L. J. (1974). *Psychiatry in Primary Care*. St. Louis: Mosby.

Chodoff, P., and Lyons, H. (1958). Hysteria, the hysterical personality, and "hysterical" conversion. *American Journal of Psychiatry* 114: 734-740.

Crocetti, G. M., and Lemkau, P. V. (1967). Schizophrenia II: epidemiology. In *Comprehensive Textbook of Psychiatry*, ed. Freedman and Kaplan. Baltimore: Williams and Wilkins.

Easser, B. R., and Lesser, S. R. (1965). Hysterical personality—a reevaluation. *Psychoanalytic Quarterly* 34: 389-405.

Erikson, E. H. (1950). *Childhood and Society*. New York: Norton.

Fenichel, O. (1945). *The Psychoanalytic Theory of Neurosis*. New York: Norton.

Foulks, E. F. (1972). *The Arctic Hysterias*. Washington, D.C.: American Anthropological Association.

Freeman, L. (1972). *The Story of Anna O*. New York: Walker.

Freud, A. (1936). *The Ego and the Mechanisms of Defense*. London: Hogarth Press.

Freud, S. (1888). Hysteria. *Standard Edition* 1: 39-60.

———(1893-1899). Early psycho-analytic publications. *Standard Edition* 3.

———(1901-1905). A case of hysteria, three essays on sexuality, and other works. *Standard Edition* 7.

———(1908). Character and anal eroticism. *Standard Edition* 9: 167-176.

Gedo, J. E., Sabshin, M., Sadow L., and Schlessing, N. (1964). "Studies on hysteria": a methodological evaluation. *Journal of the American Psychoanalytic Association* 12: 734.

Guze, S. (1975). The validity and significance of the clinical diagnosis of hysteria (Briquet's syndrome). *American Journal of Psychiatry* 132: 138-141.

Halleck, S. L. (1967). Hysterical personality—psychological, social and introgenic determinants. *Archives of General Psychiatry* 16: 750-757.

Hartmann, H. (1958). *Ego Psychology and the Problem of Adaptation.* New York: International Universities Press.

Hirsch, S. J., and Hollender, M. H. (1969). Hysterical psychoses: clarification of the concept. *American Journal of Psychiatry* 125: 909.

Hollender, M. H. (1971). Hysterical personality. *Comments on Contemporary Psychiatry* 1: 17-24.

Kernberg, O. (1967). Borderline personality organization. *Journal of the American Psychoanalytic Association* 15: 641-685.

Kline, D. F., and Davis, J. M. (1969). *Diagnosis and Drug Treatment of Psychiatric Disorders.* Baltimore: Waverly.

Kolb, L. C. (1973). *Noyes' Modern Clinical Psychiatry.* 8th ed. Philadelphia: W. B. Saunders.

LaBarre, W. (1969). *They Shall Take Up Serpents: Psychology of the Southern Snake Handling Cult.* New York: Schocken.

Langness, L. L. (1967). Hysterical psychosis—the cross-cultural evidence. *American Journal of Psychiatry* 124: 47-56.

Lazare, A. (1971). The hysterical character in psychoanalytic theory—evolution and confusion. *Archives of General Psychiatry* 25: 131-137.

Lazare, A., Klerman, G. L., and Armor, D. J. (1966). Oral, obsessive and hysterical personality patterns: an investigation of psycho-analytic concepts by means of factor analysis. *Archives of General Psychiatry* 14: 624-630.

———(1970). Oral, obsessive and hysterical personality patterns. *Journal of Psychiatric Research* 7: 275-290.

Lerner, H. E. (1974). The hysterical personality: a "woman's disease." *Comprehensive Psychiatry* 15: 157-164.

Linton, R. (1956). *Culture and Mental Disorders.* Springfield, Ill.: Charles C Thomas.

Ludwig, A. M. (1972). Hysteria: a neurobiologic theory. *Archives of General Psychiatry* 27: 771-786.

Luisada, P. V., Peele, R., and Pittard, E. A. (1974). The hysterical personality in men. *American Journal of Psychiatry* 131: 518-521.

MacKinnon, R. A., and Michels, R. R. (1971). *Psychiatric Interview in Clinical Practice.* Philadelphia: W. B. Saunders.

Malmquist, C. P. (1971). Hysteria in childhood. *Postgraduate Medicine* 50: 112-117.

Marmor, J. (1953). Orality in the hysterical personality. *Journal of the American Psychoanalytic Association* 1: 656-671.

Perley, J. M., and Guze, S. B. (1962). Hysteria—the stability and usefulness of clinical criteria. *New England Journal of Medicine* 266: 421-426.

Pollock, G. H. (1968). Bertha Pappenheim: addenda to her case history. *Journal of the American Psychoanalytic Association* 12: 734.

————(1973). The possible significance of childhood object loss in the Joseph Breuer-Bertha Pappenheim (Anna O.)-Sigmund Freud relationship: I, Josef Breuer. *Journal of the American Psychoanalytic Association* 16: 711.

Proctor, J. T. (1958). Hysteria in childhood. *American Journal of Orthopsychiatry* 28: 394-403.

Purtell, J. J., Robins, E., and Cohen, M. E. (1951). Observations on clinical aspects of hysteria—a quantitative study of fifty patients and one hundred and fifty-six control subjects. *Journal of the American Medical Association* 146: 902-909.

Rabkin, R. (1964). Conversion hysteria as social maladaptation. *Psychiatry* 27: 349-363.

Rangell, L. (1959). The nature of conversion. *Journal of the American Psychoanalytic Association* 17: 632-662.

Reich, W. (1933). *Character Analysis*. New York: Farrar, Straus, and Giroux.

Richman, J., and White, H. (1970). The family view of hysterical psychosis. *American Journal of Psychiatry* 127: 280-285.

Rock, N. (1971). Conversion reactors in childhood: a clinical study on childhood neuroses. *Journal of the American Academy of Child Psychiatry* 10: 65-93.

Schlessinger, N., Gedo, J. E., Miller, J., Pollock, G. H., Sabshin, M., and Sadow, L. (1967). The scientific style of Breuer and Freud in the origins of psychoanalysis. *Journal of the American Psychoanalytic Association* 15: 404.

Shapiro, D. (1965). *Neurotic Styles*. New York: Basic Books.

Skinner, B. F. (1953). *Science and Human Behavior*. New York: Macmillan.

Sperling, M. (1973). Conversion hysteria and conversion symptoms: a revision of classification and concepts. *Journal of the American Psychoanalytic Association* 21: 745-772.

Stampfl, T. G., and Lewis, P. J. (1967). Essentials of implosive therapy: a learning-theory-based psychodynamic behavioral therapy. *Journal of Abnormal Psychology* 72: 496-503.

Veith, I. (1965). *Hysteria: History of a Disease.* Chicago: University of Chicago Press.

Weingartner, H., and Faillace, L. A. (1971). Alcohol state-dependent learning in man. *The Journal of Nervous and Mental Diseases* 153: 365-406.

Wittels, F. (1930). The hysterical character. *Medical Review of Reviews* 36: 186.

Woerner, P. I., and Guze, S. B. (1968). A family and marital study of hysteria. *British Journal of Psychiatry* 114: 161-168.

Wolpe, J. (1969). *The Practice of Behavior Therapy.* New York: Pergamon.

Woodruff, R. A., Jr., Goodwin, D. W., and Guze, S. B. (1974). *Psychiatric Diagnosis.* New York: Oxford University Press.

Yates, A. J. (1970). *Behavior Therapy.* New York: Wiley.

Zetzel, E. R. (1968). So-called good hysteric. *International Journal of Psycho-Analysis* 49: 256.

CHAPTER 3

Epidemiology of Hysterical Phenomena: Evidence for a Psychosocial Theory

LYDIA TEMOSHOK, Ph.D.
C. CLIFFORD ATTKISSON, Ph.D.

"Hysteria is not a pathological phenomenon," the surrealists said more than forty years ago on that then-novel subject. "It is one of the supreme instruments of human expression." There may be a great deal of truth in that statement, as is often the case when subjects are viewed from artistic perspectives.

It is our thesis that hysterical phenomena are not so much manifestations of disease as forms of psychosocial adaptation and expression. While many writers on hysteria recognize the interdependence of psychological, social, and cultural systems, this implied etiological interdependence is rarely paralleled by actual methodology, description, or interpretation in studies of hysterical phenomena. Our interdisciplinary argument features the findings of such related behavioral sciences as psychiatry, psychiatric anthropology (Dubreuil and Wittkower 1976), cross-cultural psychiatry (Leighton and Murphy 1965), and social psychology.

Using a loosely phenomenological approach, we will consider the epidemiology of hysterical phenomena—its prevalence and incidence—and descriptive data of relevant diagnostic patterns. For the purposes of consensus we have ordered a rather wide range of hysterical phenomena into sanctioned diagnostic categories— hysterical neurosis (conversion and dissociative types), hysterical personality, etc.—and retained such labels as *hysterical psychosis*, and *hysterical contagion*, which have been used to refer to the more exotic varieties of hysteria.

Since it may not be readily apparent how a phenomenological-epidemiological discussion can illuminate etiological concerns, we offer the following examples. If a survey of articles concerning a diagnostic entity shows it to be equally prevalent among males and females, it is probably not advisable to entertain a psychodynamic theory of its etiology based on pregnancy conflicts, nor a physiological theory in terms of certain female hormones. Similarly, if a diagnostic entity occurs in three separate cultures at different historical intervals, it becomes clear that a single etiological hypothesis, limited to one culture and one epoch, may not be as useful as one incorporating common variables across time and space. In brief, we are adopting as an axiom Benedict's 1934 dictum that the diagnosis of psychiatric disorders cannot be made without regard to cultural environment.

While epidemiology can never entirely reproduce etiology, it is hoped that a careful consideration from a theoretically collaborative perspective, of the broadest possible spectrum of hysterical phenomena, both domestic and foreign, may yield greater understanding.

HYSTERICAL OR HISTRIONIC PERSONALITY

Traditional Descriptive Definitions

Soon after Wittels presented the first psychoanalytic description of the hysterical character in 1930, Reich (1933) offered one of the most complete behavioral descriptions of the type in women and men who demonstrated "an importunate sexual attitude . . . combined with a specific kind of *physical agility* exhibiting a distinct sexual nuance" (p. 204). The most recent authority, the *DSM II* (1968) diagnosis of hysterical personality states:

> These behavior patterns are characterized by excitability, emotional instability, over-reactivity, and self-dramatization. This self-dramatization is always attention-seeking and often seductive, whether or not the patient is aware of its purpose. These personalities are also immature, self-centered, often vain, and usually dependent on others. [p. 43]

Other sources such as Hinsie and Campbell (1970) have supplied their own lists of adjectives pertaining to the hysterical personality. The most popular behavioral description is that by Chodoff and Lyons (1958):

The hysterical personality is a term applicable to persons who are vain and egocentric, who display labile and excitable but shallow affectivity, whose dramatic, attention-seeking, and histrionic behavior may go to the extremes of lying and even pseudologia and phantastica, who are very conscious of sex, sexually provocative yet frigid, and who are dependently demanding in interpersonal situations. [p. 736]

Psychoanalytic Definitions

Phenomenological and psychoanalytic perspectives overlap in the definition of hysterical personality employed by the Menninger Clinic (as quoted in Berger 1971):

These individuals are characterized by extreme use of repression. Although accompanied by varying degrees of frigidity, usually classic conversion or dissociated symptoms are not prominent or are entirely absent. This reaction may manifest itself by flamboyant dramatizing or by generalized inhibition. In contrast to the infantile personality, the conflict in this reaction is on a phallic level.

Abraham (1921, 1924), Reich (1933), and Fenichel (1945) would essentially agree with this definition, which views the hysterical conflict to be at the phallic or oedipal level. Much recent psychoanalytic discussion has focused on whether the hysterical personality is one disorder, or has two distinct subtypes, genital (oedipal) and oral (preoedipal) in psychodynamic origin. Theories following Marmor (1953), which emphasize the oral fixation of hysterical personalities, are based on Wittels' (1930) and Freud's (1931) clinical observations of oral features in their cases.

Easser and Lesser (1965) argued that hysterical personalities differ with regard to object relations, mechanisms of defense, levels of fixation, and integration of the ego. They differentiated under the rubric *hysteroid* a group of patients who utilized the basic hysterical mechanism of emotion substitution, but who did so within a more infantile, dependent, borderline (or even psychotic) personality structure. The hysteroid was described as "sicker" in terms of exhibiting more extreme hysterical mannerisms, more erratic and less adaptive functioning, more ambivalent object relationships, a more disturbed family history indicating more serious maternal affect deprivation, and a more problem-strewn childhood and adolescence.

Along parallel lines, Zetzel (1968) distinguished two subtypes of the hysterical personality: (1) the *good* genital-level hysteric, whose main problem lies in developing and maintaining long-term heterosexual relationships and whose prognosis in psychoanalytic treatment is good, and (2) the *florid* hysteric, who does badly in therapy and who corresponds to Easser and Lesser's hysteroid patient in terms of preoedipally derived symptoms.

Abse (1974) introduced the term *hysteriform borderline personalities* to describe cases with "pronounced oral character traits" and an accompanying "severe narcissistic ego disorder" (p. 186), a description which seems nearly synonymous with Easser and Lesser's *hysteroid condition.* Finally, Tupin drew up tables which summarized the work of several authors in differentiating the personality traits, life history, and psychodynamics of "healthy (good or assertive)" versus "sick (bad or dependent)" hysterical personalities.

Berger (1971) commented that the division of hysterical personalities into two groups creates a problem in matching psychodynamic conceptualizations with labels. If the oral hysterics are so different psychodynamically from the true hysterics, he argued, then they shouldn't be subsumed under the hysteric label, unless there exists some connecting, underlying dynamic.

Through the perspective of object relations theory, Kernberg (1967) may offer a reconciliation. The hysterical personality would be placed on a continuum more toward the normal pole, which is exemplified by an individual with healthy, integrated, internalized object relations and an ability to form good interpersonal relationships. The hysteroid or florid hysteric would simply be moved farther down this continuum toward borderline and narcissistic character disorders.

Empirical-Descriptive Definitions

Applying the clinical-descriptive method well, Blinder (1966) studied the demographic and psychological characteristics of a heterogeneous sample of twenty-one women diagnosed as hysterical personalities. The sample was drawn equally from three locations—the University of California Medical Center in San Francisco, two London hospitals, and two hospitals in Copenhagen. Blinder pictured the hysterical personality as follows: Often the youngest child, she has been emotionally deprived in childhood by both mother and father. Her male relatives manifest a high incidence of sociopathic behavior. Her medical history is fraught with surgery, especially of a gynecological nature. She is sexually underdeveloped or inhibited and is paired with an inadequate and abusive husband; there is subsequently a high likelihood of separation and divorce. She has few genuine friendships and shows a striking defensive use of the mechanisms of denial.

Lazare, Klerman, and Armor (1966) derived their own list of seven traits for the hysterical personality from an eclectic selection of sources. In order to test the descriptive psychoanalytic concepts underlying the hysterical, the oral, and the obsessive personality constructs, they gave a twenty-trait self-rating form to ninety female outpatients and inpatients at Massachusetts General Hospital, and subjected the data to factor analysis. While the obsessive personality description emerged from this process almost identical with its factor, some of the predicted traits for the oral and the hysterical personality did not appear in their respective factors. For example, while *emotionality* was predicted and had a factor loading of .64, *aggression*—a type of emotionality not necessarily predicted for the hysterical personality had the highest loading of .70, and *oral aggression* had the third highest, .61. The predicted traits of *exhibitionism, egocentricity, sexual provocativeness,* and *dependence* were all represented in the factor with loadings ranging from .59 down to .40. Two predicted traits—*suggestibility* and *fear of sexuality* had negative or near-zero loadings. It is difficult to reconcile these latter results with such other conceptions of the hysterical personality as that of Lindberg and Lindegard (1963), who view the disorder *primarily* in terms of strong suggestibility and distractibility.

In any case, such empirical tests of descriptive content seem to represent a significant step toward a more scientifically based diagnostic system. Empirical tests can also provide support for clinical observations and etiological theories. For example, the traits of aggressivity and oral aggressivity in the study by Lazare et al. lend credence to the otherwise confounding observations of depressive features in the hysterical personality, and to its close relationship to preoedipal developmental factors.

Another attempt to verify a psychoanalytic formulation of hysteria was made by Prosen (1967), who questioned the conception, derived from Reich's 1933 theory of genital fixation, that hysterics are sexually frigid underneath a cloak of provocativeness. In a survey of the literature, Prosen found no direct relationship established between frigidity and the hysterical personality, and underlined this negative finding with material from two of his own clinical cases which revealed hypersexuality rather than frigidity, as well as "strong pregenital elements."

Perhaps because depressive symptoms seem inconsistent with the picture of emotional volatility and self-dramatization, such clinically significant features as orality, depression, and aggressivity are often ignored in descriptions allegedly made from behavioral observations. Depressive features in the hysterical personality *are*, however, assigned positive weight in articles by Prosen (1967), Guze (1967), Lazare and Klerman (1968), Bibb and Guze (1972), Slavney and McHugh (1974), and Luisada, Peele, and Pittard (1974). In the empirical-descriptive tradition, Luisada et al. composed an updated list of behavioral descriptors for both men and women which incorporates the connection with depression: (1) treatment initiated in late teens or early twenties, (2) a history of suicidal gesture, (3) underachievement in school or occupation, (4) sexual dissatisfaction, (5) interest in older mates, (6) overuse of alcohol or drugs, and (7) often, a tendency toward unreliability and lying.

In a study which encompassed a revised definition of the hysterical personality, Lazare and Klerman (1968) found hysterical features in 43 percent of a series of thirty-five hospitalized patients with depression.

One of the most recent empirical-descriptive studies was undertaken by Slavney and McHugh (1974), who contrasted a group of psychiatric inpatients diagnosed as hysterical personalities with a control inpatient group at the Cornell University Medical College's Department of Psychiatry at New York Hospital. They found that index patients differed from the control group (79 percent versus 32 percent, p <.001) mainly on the basis of frequent depression with or without previous suicide attempts. Other significant features for the patients with hysterical personality included previous suicide attempts, a perception of poor home atmosphere during childhood, and if married, an unhappy relationship. A paternal history of alcoholism was also a prominent feature (although not statistically significant) in the index patients. Differences between control and index cases were not found for several factors identified by Blinder (1966)—notably, sibling order, neurotic symptoms in childhood, attitude toward sex, history of abdominal surgery, and provocative or seductive manner. The possible significance of the discrepancies between these two studies and among other studies will be considered later.

In an even more recent empirical-descriptive study, which puts fuller emphasis on the empirical, Slavney and McHugh (1975) compared the MMPI mean scores of twenty-nine hysterical personality patients (diagnosed according to *DSM II* criteria) with those of twenty-nine paranoid schizophrenics and a psychiatrically heterogeneous control group. While index patients could be distinguished from paranoid schizophrenics on individual scales, depressed hysterical personalities had MMPI mean profiles essentially similar to depressed controls. This suggested to Slavney and McHugh either that (a) the index patients should have been additionally or differentially diagnosed as depressives, (b) the depressed controls may have been hysterical personalities, or (c) the MMPI was not as sensitive as diagnosticians in separating depressed hysterical personalities from other depressed patients. While we would agree with the authors in favoring the last alternative, there could be yet another interpretation of their findings: that depression is an inherent characteristic of the hysterical personality today, and that whatever makes an individual hysterical over and above these dynamics has not been adequately identified. Clearly, some realignment of the traditional description of hysterical personality must be made to accommodate the observations of oral and depressive features. Such studies as these are providing a much-needed empirical foundation upon which to construct new definitions.

Definitions Based on "Cognitive Style"

In a novel neurobiological theory, Ludwig (1972) attempted to account for some of the observable affect disturbances and cognitive stylistic features of hysteria by invoking Kretschmer's 1926 concept, the *sham death reflex* (1960), in which a posture of helplessness, with "hypnoid and stuporous" features, wards off attack. In this view, although the hysteric wards off psychological attack by seeming defenseless in an analogous immobilization reflex, the attendant alteration in consciousness results in blurred reality testing and in the attentional and cognitive dysfunctions normally observable in hysterics and not in a true hypnoid state.

Gelfman (1971) reviewed hysterical and depressive dynamics in an attempt to gain an understanding of how depressive features function in an hysterical personality. He championed Chodoff's position (1954) that the hysteric, in addition to repressing erotic impulses, represses hostile impulses in a manner similar to the depressive. Gelfman proposed that while the depressive then comes to view the world as an unkind place and/or himself as an inadequate actor in this world, suffering silently and passively with these perceptions, the hysteric aggressively acts out his or her rage at others through the typical hysterical manipulations.

This conceptualization supports Halleck's description (1967) of the social determinents which induce the American female to be indirectly aggressive through hysterical adaptation. Such behavior in a male, however, is viewed as a sign of illness or sexual deviancy (effeminacy, homosexuality). The more typical American male resorts to other means of expressing aggression—socially sanctioned career competition, or socially unsanctioned but sex-role-congruent sociopathic behavior.

Gelfman's and Halleck's conceptualization of the hysterical personality in terms of a differential *expression* of dynamics essentially similar to those of the depressive has much in common with other attempts to view mental disorders in terms of *neurotic style.*

Shapiro (1965) evolved the concept of neurotic style from the broader psychoanalytic concept of character by focusing upon how an individual functions in terms of ego operations, rather than in terms of motivation by libidinal forces. He characterized hysterical cognition, in general, as impressionistic—global, relatively diffuse, and lacking in sharpness of detail. In addition, Shapiro described the hysterical personality as highly suggestible, easily distracted, and often deficient in general factual knowledge. Although hysterics are generally mild mannered and well socialized, there is a tendency toward emotional outburst that they will disclaim really experiencing; it was something that "possessed" them. This passive awareness and external attribution is what is meant by the emotional shallowness of the hysterical personality. This mode of functioning favors the operation of repression as a defense mechanism. According to Shapiro, repression is "forgetting—the loss not of affect, but of *ideational* contents from consciousness, the failure of once-perceived contents to achieve the status of conscious memories" (p. 19).

It should be underlined that Shapiro has reversed the more common psychoanalytic interpretation. The standard line as exemplified in Schafer's statement that "excesssive reliance on this defense [repression] appears to hamper the development of broad intellectual, cultural interests, to impair the ability for independent and creative thinking, and to make for striking emotional lability and naivete" (1948, p. 32) implies that *because* of a pervasive deployment of the repressive defense, the hysterical personality demonstrates the characteristic hysterical mode of cognition.

Lerner's analysis (1974) of the hysterical personality is closer to Shapiro's in emphasizing that "the socialization of women leads to a style of personality and cognition that in its observable outcome is not dissimilar to the effect of repression" (p. 161). The too-frequent confusion, which Lerner pointed out, of typically socialized feminine behaviors with the diagnosis of hysteria must be kept in mind in any discussion of the epidemiology of the hysterical personality, especially with regard to differential prevalence rates between the sexes.

Epidemiology

Partly due to the lack of consensus about the definition of hysterical personality, there is a paucity of reliable epidemiological data. This state of affairs is illustrated by Moebius's dictum that "everyone is a little hysterical." Chodoff and Lyons in 1958 supposed that hysterical personality "is certainly diagnosed less frequently than formerly but to what extent this represents a real and to what an apparent, decline in its occurrence is less obvious" (p.736). Blinder (1966) agreed with the view that "only the more dramatic conversion symptoms have disappeared in the face of a sophisticated society's diminished tolerance for them" (p.234) and asserted that, in contrast, the hysterical *personality* is now "encountered with great frequency" (p. 235). More recent words on the subject were reported by Laplanche from a panel on "Hysteria Today":

> Hysteria is today less frequently a symptom condition and more often a character or personality disorder, nor do we see "pure" hysteria, either as a symptom or as a personality disorder. . . . An apparently hysterical personality may also manifest infantile, narcissistic, paranoid or schizoid traits. [1974, p. 459]

Rather than throw up our hands in hysterical despair at this perplexing and contradictory series of epidemiological opinions, we will strive to master the situation by citing articles with more empirical bases.

Age. Luisada et al. (1974) reported that age interacted with gender such that hysterical personality appeared more often in younger men, evidence which support the finding of a decline in male incidence with age in Lindberg and Lindegard's study (1963). The latter authors replicated their finding of a decline in male incidence in a clinical population with an independent series of 2,708 normal males (motorists) who cooperated in a medical-psychological survey.

Gender. The confounding of diagnostic bias with prevalence is dramatically illustrated in the diagnosis of hysterical personality. The prototypical free association to *hysterical personality* is a floridly histrionic woman, and indeed, most evocations of the concept resemble Chodoff and Lyon's well-known comment that the hysterical personality "is a picture of women in the words of men and . . . what the description sounds like amounts to a caricature of femininity" (1958, p. 739). These authors further argued that because the disorder was more commonly diagnosed in women, its description would be cast, naturally and pragmatically, in feminine terms—a prevalence-to-description causal route. On the other hand, Cameron (1963) attributed the more common diagnosis of hysterical personality in women to its continuity with typical feminine behaviors and characters

Wolowitz (1972) reiterated the theme of congruence between descriptions of hysterical and feminine characteristics, and extended this position to assert the "developmental appropriateness of an hysterical character in a nonpathological form in American women" (p. 307). The issue becomes, of course, what is meant by appropriate. It appears that Wolowitz means that, given the American proclivity toward sex role differentiation along the lines of emotional-expressive functions for females, and mastery-achievement for males, it is "comprehensible and almost predictable" (p. 313) that females would display more emotional responsivity and more desire for others' responsivity. With only a little exaggeration, these traits are recognizable as what people mean by the hysterical personality.

The majority of authors seem to agree with Reich (1933) and with Chodoff and Lyons' assertion (1958) that the hysterical personality in men is associated with passive, effeminate, or homosexual character traits. This description has been contested, however, by Malmquist (1971) and by Kolb, who suggested that the male hysterical personality is not outwardly feminine, but rather is a Don Juan character who defends against feelings of masculine inadequacy with "the need to deceive, outwit, and conquer" (p. 86). The emphasis on outwitting and deceiving to conquer is in accord with Halleck's psychosocial analysis (1967) that male hysterical personalities tend toward sociopathy, and by Blinder's finding (1966) of a high incidence of alcoholism and other forms of sociopathy in the male relatives of females with hysterical personalities. The association of male sociopathy and female *conversion* symptoms, which was discovered by Guze and his colleagues (Woerner and Guze 1968) is discussed in greater detail in the section on conversion hysteria.

A descriptive compromise between the Don Juan and effeminate types of expression of hysterical personality in males was achieved by Mackinnon and Michels (1971): "Some male patients with hysterical personalities have a prominent admixture of obsessive traits, whereas others show strong feminine identifications, as in grossly effeminate men or passive homosexuals." It might be expected that such a broadened definitional net would catch more males than would other definitions; indeed, these authors continued, "in certain other cultures or subcultures of our society, hysterical personalities are as common in males as in females" (p. 111).

There is disagreement in the field about the extent to which persons with hysterical personalities develop physical symptoms. Chodoff and Lyons (1958) found little association, whereas Lewis and Berman (1965) cited a frequent joint occurrence of the two disorders. These authors specified, however, that women more than men are liable to somatic illness, because this form of attention-seeking is more socially acceptable in women. Luisada et al. (1974) argued, however, to uphold Chodoff and Lyons' separation (1958) of hysterical personality and conversion hysteria, particularly on the basis of the recognition of serious interpersonal and social problems as paramount in hysterical personalities.

Because of the diagnostic controversy, it is almost impossible to make an estimate of differential prevalence or incidence of the hysterical personality between the sexes. At one extreme, Robins et al. (1952) suggested that hysteria in men is either very rare or nonexistent. Attempting to correct for diagnostic misunderstandings across more than twenty years, Lerner (1974) speculated that they must have been talking about the hysterical personality, since conversion and dissociative symptoms have always been observed with some frequency in males.

In reviewing all male patients officially labeled "hysterical personality" upon admittance to St. Elizabeths Hospital in Washington, D.C., since 1968, Luisada et al. (1974) found twenty-seven men who fitted the *DSM II* criteria, for a prevalence of roughly one per thousand diagnoses in this mixed population.

Lindberg and Lindegard (1963) employed a definition of strong suggestibility and distractability to describe a "hysteroid personality attitude" among operated and unoperated hospital patients. It should be noted that this seemingly idiosyncratic nomenclature could be due to translation from the Swedish, as their description generally coincides with many descriptions of the hysterical personality. Within their hospital sample, they reported the highest frequency (36.1 percent) of hysterical disorder in young males up to age twenty-nine, and a lower frequency (15.3 percent) for males over age forty-nine. By comparison, the frequency of the disorder among females remained at a constant 40-45 percent across all age groups, with the exception of the group over age forty-nine, which demonstrated a frequency of 27 percent. Within the female group, there was a significantly higher percentage of hysterical disorder in the operated group (surgical overtreatment group) than in the unoperated group, regardless of age; this higher percentage contrasted with no differences in the frequency of hysterical disorder among men in operated versus unoperated groups. Lindberg and Lindegard suggested that this difference might support a differential description of how males and females manifest a basic hysterical attitude.

The literature on the description and etiological theories of hysterical personality reveals a number of sources of confusion. One of these is the attempted division of hysterical personalities into "true" oedipally conflicted hysterics, and "hysteroid" or orally conflicted hysterics. Lazare (1971) said that these redefinitions amounted to separating an hysterical *character* disorder by recognition of its more pathological object relations, ego-syntonic maladaptive pattern, and more primitive libidinal orientation from a larger group of patients with hysterical personality traits. This diagnostic maneuver parallels the separation of the hysterical symptom from the larger group of conversion symptoms and seems to be a useful conceptual framework to apply in understanding a disunified field of theories and findings.

Another difficulty is the pervasive diagnostic tendency to describe hysterical personality in terms which overlap those for traditional feminine behaviors. Lerner (1974) concluded that "the challenge for diagnosticians is to refine their ability to evaluate . . . structural and genetic-dynamic considerations in a manner that will extricate them from the present confusion between hysteria and femininity" (p. 163).

An additional problem is how to interpret the aspects of orality and depression which have intruded into the more traditional definitions of the hysterical personality. Perhaps their introduction signifies an increasing diagnostic precision or conceptual clarity accrued over the years. On the other hand, it could indicate a genuine shift in the *nature* of the hysterical personality. This epidemiological-etiological question cannot be answered by the data and theories discussed up to this point. One method of finding out what something *is*, however, is to discover what it is *not;* and to this end, we will explore some adjacent hysterical phenomena in the following sections.

HYSTERICAL NEUROSIS, CONVERSION TYPE

Any discussion of the prevalence and incidence of hysterical conversion reactions must ultimately rest on sound nosological distinctions between conversion and adjacent phenomena. Definitional problems, however, are rampant in any discussion of hysteria, and no more so than in the arena of conversion reactions, where there is disarray not only among the defining variables themselves, but among diverse perspectives on these factors.

Definitions Based on Symptomatology

Conversion symptoms can occur across the spectrum of psychopathologies, from the hysteric to the catatonic schizophrenic. A number of writers (e.g., Guze 1967, W. C. Lewis 1974, A. Lewis 1975) have pointed out the wide range of outcomes associated with an initial diagnosis of hysteria used synonymously with conversion reaction. It would seem that a definition which focuses on conversion symptoms *per se* can not differentiate hysterical conversion reaction from conversion reaction due to other dynamics. This problem is illustrated by Fenichel's opening statement (1945) on conversion, that "symptomatic changes of physical functions occur which, unconsciously and in a distorted form, give expression to instinctual impulses that previously had been repressed" (p. 216). Similarly, Abse (1974), in his overview of conversion hysteria and dissociative syndromes, employed a basically symptomatic outline in categorizing various forms of hysteria; those for conversion reaction included, for example, convulsive hysteria, paralysis, involuntary movements, sensory disturbances, and affective disturbance. This form of description does not differ significantly from Fenichel's organization of his chapter on conversion: hysterical spells, monosymptomatic conversion, hysterical pains and identification, hysterical hallucination, hysterical motor disturbances, hysterical dream state, and hysterical disturbances of sensation. In a nod to psychodynamic considerations, Fenichel also separated these conversion symptoms, which he assigned to the realm of the oedipal complex, from such conversion symptoms as stuttering, psychogenic tic, and bronchial asthma, in which the unconscious impulses are said to be pregenital.

Empirical Approaches

Other writers, taking a more empirical stance toward a definition of conversion have shown that conversion reactions occur independently of hysterical personality or character disorders. Chodoff and Lyons (1958) found that three patients or 18 percent of a sample of seventeen with "unequivocal" conversion symptoms also satisfied the authors' criteria for the hysterical personality. Ziegler, Imboden, and Meyer (1960) stated that less than half of their conversion patients could be considered histrionic personalities. In McKegney's study (1967), two-thirds of the patients with conversion reaction "did not manifest serious character pathology" (p. 544), and therefore, by implication, were not histrionic personalities.

Within the borders of this empirical orientation, Eysenck's 1957 postulation of two fundamental dimensions of personality—neuroticism—psychoticism and introversion—extroversion—suggests the possibility of genetic predisposition. Eysenck proposed that individuals constitutionally prone to conversion symptoms are either psychopaths or individuals high in extroversion and neuroticism. This hypothesized association between delinquency or crime and conversion disorders for extroverted neurotics is somewhat supported by Guze's data (1964) on 13 male criminals. These men, who constituted 6 percent of a total sample of 223, demonstrated conversion symptoms such as paralysis, amnesia, aphonia, anesthesia, and blindness. Further, Guze found conversion symptoms in the criminal group associated with higher rates for other measures of delinquency and sociopathy (e.g., alcoholism, excessive fighting, frequent truency, running away, nonhonorable military discharge, poor work history, marital discord).

Psychodynamic Definitions

A third group, mainly psychoanalytic writers, invoke etiology and psychodynamics to distinguish conversion *reaction* from conversion *symptoms*. Rangell (1959) argued against the automatic, historically determined association between conversion and hysteria. In addition, he extended the meaning of the conversion process to cover a range of clinical syndromes and to refer back to any stage of libidinal or ego development. Rangell restricted the borders of this wider conception of conversion, however, to include only a displacement of energy under the pressure of defenses from psychic to somatic innervation and discharge; he thus avoided equating conversion with all psychophysiological reactions and other somatizations.

Sperling (1973) suggested that the term *conversion hysteria* should not be limited in its application to the voluntary neuromusculature or sensory perceptive systems. She further suggested that *all* conversions are *pregenital*, a conceptualization which contradicts Beres' recent delineation (reported by Laplanche 1974) of hysteria as an oedipal conflict with libidinal and aggressive components countered by repression and consequent symptomatic expression. In this sense, Sperling goes beyond even Marmor (1953), who emphasized that oedipal fixations in hysteria may be outgrowths of preoedipal, particularly oral, fixations. Since Sperling advocated "using as the differential diagnostic criteria the type of personality disorder and psychopathology of the individual patient" (p. 769-770), it is obvious this diagnostic definition does not parallel the definition of conversion favored by more empirical workers, who view conversion reaction as distint from personality disorder.

Briquet's Syndrome and the Criterion of Chronicity

Guze and his colleagues at Washington University, St. Louis, distinguished between a polysymptomatic conversion *disorder*, referred to as *Briquet's syndrome*, and a conversion symptom which implies hysterical neurosis, but not any specific etiology. The criterion of chronicity plays a large role in the Perley-Guze (1962) definition of Briquet's syndrome; this point is elaborated in the discussion of the section on Briquet's syndrome.

Incidence and Prevalence of Conversion

Some authors have argued against the notion of a decrease in the frequency of hysteria and suggested, instead, a change in the *form* of conversion reaction. Among 1,052 patients seen in formal consultation at the Yale-New Haven Medical Center from 1964-1966, 144 or 13.7 percent were diagnosed as manifesting a conversion reaction (McKegney 1967). This figure agrees with the findings of Ziegler, Imboden, and Meyer (1960) that conversion reaction patients constituted 13 percent of the patients seen by two of the authors at Johns Hopkins Hospital over a four-year period. In both reports, however, the conversion reactions were associated with other psychopathologies; overt depression was found in 22 percent of the McKegney sample of conversion patients, while 30 percent of the conversion patients in the Johns Hopkins series demonstrated "clinically evident features of depression" (p.908). It should be noted that the presence of depressive features in conversion reaction was significantly correlated ($p < .0001$) with age, with a mean of 46.9 years for this subgroup. In addition, another 14 percent of the Johns Hopkins sample manifested features of incipient schizophrenia.

Age. In terms of a differential description of childhood conversion reactions, compared with adult forms, Malmquist (1971) noted the presence in some children of *hysterogenic zones*, such as the joints and the epigastric area, especially the abdomen, as well as sensory disturbances, particularly in the visual realm. Motor manifestations included tics as the most prevalent disturbance. The conversion could also be manifested viscerally as vomiting, hiccups, urinary retention, etc., or vasomotorically in skin discolorations and stigmata. A rare case of stigmata in a ten-and-one-half-year-old, black, Baptist girl was reported by Early and Lifschutz (1974).

Bernstein (1969) commented upon a type of conversion reaction often seen in general hospitals—the adolescent girl with epileptiform seizures of psychogenic origin. These attacks resembled the hysterical convulsive attacks detected more frequently in Paris a century ago, but considered relatively rare today. (The exception of cross-cultural instances is discussed in the section on hysterical contagion.) As Bernstein explained the phenomenon in the context of three case examples of adolescent girls:

> Adolescence, with its many threats of instinctual flooding, its struggles for relatedness between individuals, along with great susceptibility to the environment and the youth culture of the moment, is a time of great turmoil, shifting of defenses, and experimentation with different styles of behavior. The path from conflict to symptoms is often more direct and visible. The hysterical crisis is an attempt to discharge intrapsychic conflict. . . . Their special medical situations permitted the temporary unseating of inner controls, and the patients grasped the opportunities to escape from intolerable situations, showing through their spells both their rage and their demand for help. [p. 34]

Conversion hysteria formerly was considered a disease with onset in adolescence. Proctor (1958) reported that 13 percent of the children seen at the North Carolina Child Psychiatric Center were diagnosed as conversion and/or dissociative reaction, and that 56 percent of this sample were males. The confluence of the two diagnoses here reflects, no doubt, the application of the old *DSM-I* classifications. Abse (1974) reported data from 1952-1958 at Chapel Hill that 22 out of 612 patients diagnosed with conversion reactions were under sixteen years of age. A significant number of the patients in the Zeigler et al. study (1960) were adolescents. The authors themselves do not give exact numbers for this group, but from data presented in the article, one could surmise that adolescents comprised a little over half of the sample.

In reviewing the medical literature on the epidemiology of conversion disorders, Rock (1971) found few more recent intensive studies of childhood conversion reactions than Proctor's observation of an apparently high incidence in latency-age children and adolescents. Using Zeigler's 1967 criteria for his own study of conversion cases at Walter Reed General Hospital in Washington, D.C. and at Tripler General Hospital in Honolulu, Rock diagnosed ten children as conversion reaction (sensory-motor or neuromotor disorder.) He concluded that conversion reactions in children are more frequent than is suggested by the literature and that the incidence of diagnosis depends on the physician's recognition of the symptoms as psychogenic. Since parents are more likely to take children to medical than to psychiatric facilities, conversion symptoms may go unrecognized or be misdiagnosed as physical ailments. This point recapitulates Szasz (1961), who suggested that those members of the lower classes who tend to consult medical rather than psychiatric specialists may have their psychiatric (conversion) symptoms misdiagnosed as physical.

At the University of Kentucky Medical Center in Lexington, Looff (1970) reported that of the one hundred children seen in psychiatric case consultations from 1964-1968, twenty-four had various psychophysiological disorders (physiological concomitants of prolonged, unresolved emotional stress), eight showed conversion reactions (which were restricted to disabilities in various sensory and voluntary motor systems), eight had combined conversion and psychophysiological symptoms, while the remaining sixty presented a mixed psychopathological picture. In contrast to other studies such as Chodoff and Lyons (1958), which concluded that conversion symptoms may occur in patients who do not demonstrate hysterical (histrionic) personalities, Looff found that all six girls in his conversion group exhibited "overdramatic, flamboyant, overlabile, overaffective, oversuggestive, coy and seductive behavior" (p. 324).

Gender. There is a disagreement about whether the prevalence of male conversion reactions is less than that for females, Chodoff (1974) stated that "conversion reactions occur at least as often in men as they do in women" (p. 1075), while Zeigler et al. (1960) found that 18 percent of a four-year patient series diagnosed at Johns Hopkins as conversion reaction were male. McKegney (1967) reported that males constituted 25 percent of the 144 conversion reaction patients diagnosed at Yale-New Haven Medical Center over a four-year period.

Weinstein, Eck, and Lyerly (1969) estimated that 25 to 30 percent of all male patients admitted to a Veterans Neuropsychiatric Hospital in Appalachia manifested classical conversion symptoms (hysterical paralysis and/or sensory loss) at some time during hospitalization. These authors postulated that a high incidence of conversion hysteria occurs in societies in which physical violence is an accepted, albeit stressful, form of communication. It should be noted, however, that since the population of patients in this study was male, this hypothesized association of conversion symptoms with violence, or at least with physical versus verbal expression, may exist only for males.

A similar dynamic may be useful in understanding the high incidence of classical conversion reactions among troops evacuated from fighting in Viet Nam to Clark Air Force Base Hospital in the Phillipines, as reported by Carden and Schramel (1966). In commenting upon his extensive experience with recruits suffering conversion reactions, Rabkin (1964) wrote that "short of improbable combat conditions, 'basic training' probably constituted the most intense and prolonged stress that these servicemen were apt to experience during their tour of duty" (p. 357). Since these recruits were not actually fighting, yet were still under stress, it is more likely that stress, rather than violence *per se* is the intervening variable in the conversion equation. That is, it seems that an association between violence and male conversion reactions may be subsumed under what we are advocating as a common etiology for conversion reactions across generations, classes, and cultures: unresolvable or inescapable stress which produces intrapsychic conflict and an attempt at adaptation through deployment of the conversion symptom. Compare the double-bind concept of Bateson et al. (1956) and Joseph Heller's *Catch 22*.

It is interesting in this context to consider Looff's finding (1970) that families of children with conversion reactions had difficulty verbally expressing conflicting feelings, affects (tenderness, rage, fear, longing, anxiety), or feelings about sexual issues. This somewhat substantiates the hypothesis advanced by Weinstein et al. (1969) that conversion reaction is associated with societies in which physical violence is an accepted form of communication. Szasz (1961) contributed a more basic structural interpretation: hysteria is a nondiscursive protolanguage, or body language, which emerges when direct verbal expression is not culturally accepted. Primarily nonverbal societies in which interpersonal conflicts are acted out *physically* could show a propensity (due perhaps to a combination of habit, social norms, and socialization) to act out intrapsychic conflicts, as well, in terms of *physical* illness.

Class. Hollingshead and Redlich (1958), in their classic study of the relationship between social class and mental disorder, found more diagnosed neurotics and fewer psychotics in the upper (I and II) than in the lower (IV and V) classes. This relationship was reversed, however, for *hysterical neurosis*, which occurred more frequently in the lower classes. That is, class IV neurotics presented more physically (versus verbally) expressed conversion symptoms, and class V patients were "unable to understand that their troubles [were] not physical illnesses" (p. 340).

In 1954, Chodoff observed that conversion hysteria was diagnosed less frequently, possibly because fewer neurological exams were conducted. He speculated that this could reflect the widening gulf between psychiatry and medicine, a decline of interest in Kraepelinian classification, and/or greater sophistication in diagnosing psychosomatic disorders. Chodoff also entertained the apparently contradictory hypothesis of an *actual* decline in the incidence of conversion hysteria which could be attributed in part to cultural change: "People are no longer as simple, unsophisticated, and uneducated as they used to be, and . . . are thus less prone to the development of the rather gross manifestations which sometimes characterize conversion hysteria, especially in the credulous and ignorant" (p. 76). Since Chodoff cited no data to support this conclusion, the reader may be more persuaded by Stephens and Kamp's finding (1962) that admission rates for hysteria at the Henry Phipps Psychiatric Clinic did not change significantly during the periods 1913 to 1920 and 1945 to 1960.

More recently, however, Chodoff (1974) has reversed to some degree his earlier position, rejecting the traditional psychoanalytic view that the condition has virtually disappeared, at least in its classical manifestations. He postulated that the disorder has simply changed its locale: "Conversion reactions are seen principally in the neurologic wards of general hospitals; among unsophisticated rural and urban populations; in military hospitals, especially in wartime; in settings where monetary compensation is an issue; and as a psychogenic embellishment of organic disease" (p. 1074). There is some modest support, in fact, for the premise that conversion symptoms are more common among unsophisticated rural and urban populations. Forbis and Janes (1965) observed a "marked incidence" of childhood conversion reactions in Arkansas, citing certain factors in the Bible Belt culture as predisposing to "excesses of repression" (p. 1223). Several other accounts which discuss conversion reactions in children concern southern or rural populations—North Carolina (Proctor 1958) and Kentucky (Looff 1970). Bart (1968) reported that women who entered the UCLA Neuropsychiatric Institute's neurology service, but whose complaints were later diagnosed as psychiatric, differed from women of similar age (forty to fifty-nine) who presented themselves to the psychiatric service with psychological reasons for their distress. The former group were usually of lower social status, rural in both birthplace and present residence, and poorly educated. Wittkower and Dubreuil (1968) reported that while the grosser, or classical, forms of hysteria are rare in Europe and the United States, they are common in developing coutries such as India, Lebanon, Egypt, and Tunesia.

Parenthesis on gender-culture interaction. Hysterical conversions were often diagnosed during the war years 1942-1945. Abse (1966) discussed his finding that Indian soldiers were more likely to manifest the disorder in terms of abdominal pains or convulsive attacks, while British soldiers showed nonconvulsive forms such as headaches. Fits occurred in 188 out of 370 cases of hysteria among Indian soldiers (51 percent), while they were predominating symptoms in only 7 out of 161 British hysteric cases (4 percent). Somatic conversion symptoms were probably reactions to the soldiers' conflict between not wanting to fight, yet being unwilling to consciously admit this. The form of such common symptoms as being unable to stand upright (astasia), or to walk (abasia), or to straighten the back (camptocormia) would, of course, make active duty impossible.

Interestingly, one of the few cross-cultural epidemiological studies of hysteria (Dube and Kumar 1974) reported that in northern India, the prevalence rate for conversion symptoms, where the most common form is a *convulsive fit*, is 8.9 per thousand. Females constituted 96.1 percent of all cases of hysteria. While the highest incidence was found in the age range fifteen to twenty-four, the highest prevalence fell between thirty-five and forty-four, and was especially observable in the higher castes, where, the authors hypothesize, there is "less opportunity for self-expression and independent activity." One might speculate from this latter report that Indian society, in terms of the sexual emancipation of its women, is at a level equivalent to that of nineteenth century Vienna. Further, the upper-class Viennese woman was probably more psychically as well as physically corseted than her lower-class counterpart, and the upper-class Indian woman could be seen as similarly restricted. Finally, since Indian culture (as well as nearly everyone in the nineteenth century and a large portion of the present American lower classes)finds manifestly mental symptoms less acceptable than does modern psychologically oriented Western society, it is not surprising that convulsive forms of hysteria predominated in Dube and Kumar's Indian sample.

Discussion: Sociological Considerations

Chodoff's statement (1954) that the "crude and gross manifestations" of hysteria are discovered particularly in "the credulous and ignorant" is not only insensitive and debasing, it is also founded on a tenuous assumption: just *how* do credulity and ignorance *cause* hysteria? A more humane, and at the same time, more intellectually satisfying sociological interpretation would view the etiology of the disorder as an attempt to resolve a *psychosocial* conflict, where the symptomatic expression is molded by the cultural context. Hysteria would, thus, decline in prevalence in those segments of society where (a) psychosocial conflict or stress is less, and (b) the cultural context does not sanction the classical forms of conversion reaction.

Another argument for the position that conversion symptoms are generated in response to an intrapsychic conflict which is engendered by certain social stresses and expressed in particular cultural contexts is provided by the historical record. This indicates a positive association of social class and hysteria in nineteenth century Europe, in contrast to the presently inverse relationship. Hollender (1972) cited the observation of some nineteenth century gynecologists who linked hysteria with affluence and indolence.

These physicians essentially stated that young women of the upper social class were trained from childhood to express themselves in a particular manner which included the hysterical mode. Symptoms might appear because they were poorly prepared to face the trials of adult life. . . . It was hardly surprising, therefore, that the affluent and indolent were more engaged in intrapsychic and interpersonal struggles and thus more prone to develop hysterical symptoms. It was also more acceptable for them to express themselves in this manner because such behavior was encouraged by the fashions of the time. The attention shown to them no doubt reinforced this mode of expression. Contrariwise, the lack of attention paid to similar symptoms in the poor probably tended to extinguish the hysterical mode in that class. [p. 312]

Szasz (1961) offered some socioeconomic reasons for conversion hysteria's present tendency to be an affliction of relatively uneducated, lower-class persons. For one thing, they are encountered least in the private offices of psychoanalysts and psychotherapists. They most often present in free or low-cost clinics or state hospitals. In such institutions, *physical* symptoms or unrecognized somatic conversion symptoms are tolerated and treated, but *psychiatric* complaints, if they are ever made, are less acceptable. Szasz argued further that hysteria is a "mixture of conflicting values and disparate games" (p. 262) whose goal is dominance and interpersonal control and whose strategies are predominately coercive, rather than self-helping or cooperative: "It is well-suited to children, uneducated people, the oppressed, and the fearful; in brief, to those who feel that their chances for self-realization and success on their own are poor. Thus, impersonation in general and lying in particular are employed as strategies for self-advancement" (p. 270). The implication here is that such strategies would be more common in lower-class persons than in upper-class persons who have more personal and institutional power.

BRIQUET'S SYNDROME

Since Perley and Guze introduced objective criteria for the diagnosis of hysteria in 1962, Guze and his colleagues at the

Department of Psychiatry, Washington University School of Medicine in St. Louis, have been pursuing a series of studies to clarify its diagnostic features. They use *hysteria* to indicate a syndrome originally described by Briquet in 1859 as a polysymptomatic disorder seen predominately in females, characterized by an onset before age thirty-five of recurrent or chronic medical problems.

The use of *syndrome* implies a uniform clinical picture and a consistency in the course of the disorder. One of the most irremediable problems with most diagnoses of hysteria has been the complex and heterogeneous picture at follow-up. A previously diagnosed hysteric might be found to suffer from an organic disease, schizophrenia, depression, or a personality disorder. This confusing state of the diagnostic art led Slater (1965) to conclude that there is nothing consistent in the medical condition of patients diagnosed as hysterics.

Thus, by comparison, it would seem admirable that a follow-up study by Perley and Guze (1962) found that 90 percent of the patients initially diagnosed as having hysteria on the basis of these authors' criteria maintained this diagnosis after six to eight years. The Perley-Guze diagnostic formula for selecting cases is (a) a complicated medical history with early onset (before age 35), (b) multiple somatic symptoms (at least twenty-five for a firm diagnosis) in nine of ten symptom areas, and (c) no other disorder which could explain some or all of the complaints.

Incidence and Prevalence

On the basis of a number of studies conducted by the St. Louis group (Perley and Guze 1962, Gatfield and Guze 1962, Farley, Woodruff, and Guze 1968, Woodruff, Clayton and Guze 1971), it is fairly obvious that the criteria for diagnosing hysteria, or Briquet's syndrome, represents significant progress in descriptive clinical psychiatry, in that the criteria selects a population homogeneous in prognosis, and describes a uniform clinical picture.

Woodruff (1967) applied the criteria in differentiating a syndrome independent of chronic medical illness for a sample of fifty women and found that 2 percent of this sample (that is, one woman) met all the criteria. Woodruff concluded that this 2 percent provided evidence for the validity of Briquet's syndrome "since the prevalence of hysteria in the general population is of approximately this magnitude" (p. 1118). One could debate this last statement on at least two grounds: (1) 1 to 2 percent prevalence for the general female population is not the same thing as 2 percent prevalence in a sample of women with medical illness, and (2) the 1 to 2 percent figure is not a solid fact against which the validity of hypotheses can be tested, since it was estimated on the basis of the clinical experience of the St. Louis group (this figure was reported in Arkonac and Guze 1963, but no data was cited) and on a study of one hundred postpartum women, *one* of whom met the full triad of diagnostic criteria (Farley et al. 1968).

In terms of sex differences, Woodruff et al. (1971) found that males apparently do not pass the homogeneous test required for confident assignment to Briquet's syndrome. Two men who seemed to meet their diagnostic criteria for a 1962 study developed, at follow-up, a brain tumor and schizophrenia, respectively. On the basis of other studies, Guze, Woodruff, and Clayton (1973) stated that no more than 2 or 3 percent of hysterics have been men. This figure suffers from the same vagueness as the previously cited 1 to 2 percent prevalence figure for hysteria in the female population. No actual data is cited, nor is it specified whether the authors used the strict Perley-Guze criteria or some other definition in arriving at this figure.

Kaminsky and Slavney (1976) noted from a study of the literature that most males are excluded from a diagnosis of hysteria when the prospect of possible compensation is found. Nevertheless, these authors described a male case who fully met the standards of Briquet's syndrome and who was an unlikely candidate for any "prospect of tangible reward accruing from illness"(p. 85).

Associated Variables

Guze, Allen and Grollmus (1962) suggested that hysteria may be significantly associated with some cases of *hyperemesis gravidarum* (vomiting during pregnancy serious enough to require hospitalization), but this accounted for only 13 percent of the reported series of patients.

Moving from the arena of obstetrics to criminology, Arkonac and Guze (1963) found, in a study of 172 relatives of 18 women diagnosed with Briquet's syndrome, that about 20 percent of the sisters of the index cases suffered from hysteria, while 33 percent of all male relatives presented histories of sociopathy and alcoholism. Woerner and Guze (1968) duplicated these findings, in essence, discovering, moreover, stormy marital histories and a striking prevalence (56 percent) of alcoholism and sociopathy in the husbands of fourteen index cases.

Cloninger and Guze (1970) found that sociopathy and hysteria were associated in the same woman for 26 percent of a group of convicted women felons, sociopathy *or* hysteria in 80 percent of the sample, sociopathy alone in 39 percent, and hysteria in 15 percent. Cloninger and Guze's 1975 study of forty-six families (first degree relatives) of convicted index women who were felons showed that sociopathic fathers had a highly significant proportion (78 percent) of hysteric daughters, compared with a control group of fathers where the proportion was 26 percent ($p < .001$). Further, the daughters of sociopathic fathers had a significantly higher prevalence (40 percent) of hysteria than a control group, where neither parent (11 percent), or only the mother (20 percent) was sociopathic or hysteric.

While the St. Louis investigators, in implying "pathogenic similarities" between sociopathy and hysteria, came the closest to saying anything about etiology, they did not clearly state whether these are genetic or psychosocial correlates. It is as least as likely, if not more parsimonious, to suggest that sociopathy and hysteria may be understood in psychosocial terms. That is, social stress may be resolved sociopathically in males, since such externalization is more traditionally accepted in American culture; on the other hand, equally stressed females possess more cultural maps for following the hysteric route. The finding of significant sociopathic and/or hysteric trends in the relatives of cases of Briquet's syndrome is less genetically impressive when one considers the plausible hypothesis that these families could be members of the especially stressed lower-class (a demographic variable which the St. Louis investigators could easily check), or simply members of an especially stressed family, which might well be the case when the mother or father is a convicted felon.

Discussion: Clinical and Experimental Relevance

There is no doubt that the St. Louis group has identified a diagnostically valid, uniform syndrome. There arises, however, what had been previously a subliminal issue: What is the phenomenological significance of this achievement? Woodruff et al. (1971) themselves emphasized that the strongest of the Perley-Guze criteria is the polysymptomatic nature of the illness, while the requirement that symptoms be medically unexplained seems an unnecessary distinction. Little or no data were presented regarding the applicability of the criteria to understanding the syndrome's etiology. Psychotherapeutic approaches and outcome data were also conspicuously neglected in all of the St. Louis reports. Perhaps the most serious flaw in their entire diagnostic enterprise is the tautology inherent in only selecting cases with an early onset and a history of recurrent or chronic medical problems, and their claiming they have discovered a *syndrome*. Such diagnostic consistency and constancy may be descriptively useful, but because it is built into their definition, it has little real predictive validity.

It might be instructive to compare another attempt at objective diagnosis—Reed's 1975 study of 120 inpatients who received a primary or consequent diagnosis of hysteria at St. Bartholomew's Hospital in London. On the basis of a three-year follow-up of 113 of these patients, Reed concluded that 13 percent demonstrated symptoms generally accepted as constituting hysteria: conversion, dissociative symptoms, *la belle indifférence*, and gain. Follow-up data suggested that the pattern of illness remains consistent for this group. Another 33 percent showed these symptoms, but also manifested such affective symptoms as depression and anxiety. Another group of 28 percent exhibited mainly affective symptoms and occasional hysteric symptomatology. Reed noted that many of these patients and some in the following fourth category had been originally diagnosed as hysterics because of their histrionic behavior. The fourth and fifth groups were found to suffer from schizophrenia, agorophobia, and actual organic illness, or disorders of disputed etiology.

The obvious question may be asked: Does the group of patients (13 percent of the total) who manifested true hysteria according to Reed correspond to the diagnostic syndrome advocated by Guze and his colleagues? While Reed's group of true hysterics was differentiated mainly by exclusion of diagnoses with depressive or anxious symptomatology, the criteria for Briquet's syndrome included depression, anxiety, and other affective symptoms in certain symptom groups. Reed argued that the consistency in the pattern of illness for the true hysteria group suggests the validity of a diagnosis in the absence of other symptoms on the basis of conversion/dissociative symptoms, *belle indifférence*, and primary or secondary gain. The diagnostic validity of Briquet's syndrome rests on an overlapping but clearly different set of uniform criteria. Clearly, diagnostic consistency is not enough to claim construct validity, as it results in two different phenomenological descriptions of hysteria. The purpose of this comparative exercise is to illustrate that other sets of objective-sounding criteria, which seem at least as rational, may be constructed for diagnosing hysteria, and that these might prove to be just as diagnostically stable as Briquet's syndrome.

Other misgivings about the St. Louis group's conception of hysteria center around its specificity, and thus, its limited application. Chodoff (1974) referred to the St. Louis group's "curious prejudice against conversion reactions, especially in men" (p. 1074). Kaminsky and Slavney (1976) found it biased against diagnosis of males because some of its featured criteria—pregnancy and menstrual complaints—are inapplicable to males and because "men generally report fewer symptoms than women" (p. 87), a response bias that must be compensated for at some point in any diagnostic system.

Given that the class and cultural context of hysteria has varied so considerably over its history, one might suspect that the Perley-Guze criteria are highly specific to a certain time (the 1960s and 1970s) and place (the United States). At least, one would feel more comfortable if the advocates of Briquet's syndrome could validate these criteria on a foreign sample. Further, its diagnostic usefulness seems drastically limited in terms of reference groups. For example, the syndrome makes diagnosis of males uncompensatingly stringent and, by its insistence on a long and complicated medical history, it practically excludes children and adolescents who may be just embarking down the conversion path. As an illustration of its restriction for use with adolescents, Kimble, William, and Agras (1975) reported that in teenagers they rarely found hysterical personality associated with a positive hysteria diagnosis according to the Perley-Guze criteria.

Meares and Horvath (1972) offered a simpler and more pragmatic diagnostic scheme. They assigned seventeen patients with conversion symptoms to chronic and acute groups on the basis of psychophysical and biographical criteria. These diagnoses appeared stable at a two-year follow-up. The authors suggested that the disorder designated as Briquet's syndrome or simply as hysteria by the St. Louis group "should perhaps be called 'chronic hysteria' to distinguish it from the transient disorder which might be called 'a conversion reaction' or 'acute hysteria'" (p. 653). This simpler bridge over the nomenclature gap seems to warrant further discussion and will be elaborated in later sections.

DISSOCIATIVE REACTIONS

A major change in the classification of hysterical phenomena was reflected in the *DSM II* (1968) separation of conversion and dissociative types of hysterical neuroses. The earlier association of the two categories, however, had already spread over much of the contemporary literature. The connection may reflect more than habit or resistance to change, since in many ways, the similarities between the two phenomena are as numerous as their differences.

Comparisons between Conversion and Dissociative Reactions

Both conversion and dissociative reactions are ubiquitous across a range of psychopathologies from the hysteric to the schizophrenic. While writers placing more emphasis on symptomatology would focus on the obvious differential *manifestations* of conversion versus dissociative reactions, psychodynamically oriented writers would be especially prone to associate the two on the basis of their similar dynamics, at least for uncontaminatedly hysterical patients. Cameron (1963) summarized the most obvious of these similarities as the pathological utilization of processes which exclude competing and contradictory tendencies:

> Both conversions and dissociations have their origin in a grossly defective function which fails to prevent eruption [sic] of unconscious derivatives into preconscious and conscious organizations when the patient is under unusual stress. The inevitable regression to more primitive levels, common to all the neuroses, leads both the conversion patient and the patient who dissociates to exaggerated and pathological processes of exclusion. Some segment of reality, internal or external, gets separated off from the rest of the personality organization. [p. 361]

Among the less obvious and more controversial *differences* between conversions and dissociations are the dynamic considerations centering around loss of function. For example, Cameron (1963) distinguished the circumscribed disturbance in conversion reaction, which leaves most of the personality intact, from the dissociative reaction, which may involve large segments of reality. He related this to the difference in the outcome of regression for the two disorders: "In dissociations the regression reactivates earlier and more primitive ego organizations than in phobias and conversion. It revives processes of primitive denial and ego-splitting which were used in infancy before mature repression had developed" (p. 362).

This argument would imply, by contrast, that conversions involve regression to a relatively *less* primitive phase—an assumption challenged by Marmor (1953), among others. Ultimately, Cameron seemed more impressed with symptomatic than with psychodynamic differences: "Even in the milder dissociative syndromes, such as *estrangement* and *depersonalization*, there are falsifications which are more like mild psychotic episodes than conversions. When it comes to dream-states, *massive amnesias*, *fugues*, and *multiple personalities*, the closeness to psychotic developments, and particularly to schizophrenia, becomes quite marked" (p. 337).

Dissociative States
Dreamlike dissociative states include what Cameron (1963) called trance or twilight states, psychogenic stupors, and somnambulism

or sleepwalking. Malmquist (1971) found that the twilight state, in which hallucinations occur, is common in childhood. On the other hand, according to Malmquist, children who sleepwalk tend to be intense, worried, and, in psychodynamic terms, burdened with overdeveloped superegos.

Cameron (1963) described three main varieties of *massive amnesia*: (1) massive amnesia without fugue, (2) massive amnesia with fugue, and (3) dissociated personality, which includes alternating double or multiple personalities. Abse (1974) considered the alterations of consciousness often associated with amnesia phenomena to be similar to, if not identical with, states of hypnotic trance. The classic works on fugue, such as Fisher (1945), and on multiple personality, such as Prince (1906, 1929), Wholey (1933), and Thigpen and Cleckley (1954, 1957) are sufficiently well known to exclude repetition here. While cases of multiple personality may be rare and becoming rarer, it is likely that most which have come to psychiatric attention have been written about; Abse (1966) found two hundred accounts in the literature. There are some indications of decreased incidence of the disorder, at least as this is reflected in published articles. Horton and Miller (1972) estimated that less than one hundred cases were reported in the last century and less than a dozen described in the last fifty years. Going back as far as 1807, Taylor and Martin (1944) admirably summarized and classified the seventy-six cases from published material "most available to the American Psychologist." This material presumably excluded reports in exotic languages.

Related Dissociative Phenomena

The tendency to classify with the psychoses certain phenomena considered elsewhere to be dissociative contributes to the overall confusion in hysterical classification. Psychotics may present dissociative symptoms, just as they may demonstrate various conversion reactions. Yet another illustration of ubiquitous nosological disarray is *depersonalization*. First described in 1872 and named in 1898-89, it was then viewed as a neuropathological disorder. Since, the term *depersonalization* has been used to refer not only to a nosological entity, but to various symptoms, and to a psychological defense in both neurotics and psychotics (Lehmann 1974).

Depersonalization as a *symptom* has been associated with epilepsy, drug states, encephalitis, manic depression, and schizophrenia; it has been observed in particularly stressed normals as well as in hysterics (Brauer, Harrow, and Tucker 1970). Again, reminiscent of the case with conversion reactions, a parallel development in classification is possibly also occurring around depersonalization phenomena. Just as Briquet's syndrome has gained strength as a diagnostic entity among the diverse forms of conversion, so persistent episodes of depersonalization are officially assigned a diagnostic niche in *DSM II* (1968) along with the neuroses.

Without focusing on symptomatology, other definitions regard depersonalization as a *defense*. Lehmann (1974) considered it a defense "against overwhelming affects based on developmental defects that may center on the separation-individuation phase" (p. 1223). Cattell and Cattell (1974) provided a more psychosocial variation on the theme. They viewed depersonalization as an ineffective defense in social isolation against double-binding parents and/or as a product of the anomie which, according to them, pervades contemporary America.

The British Medical Journal (1972) offered some finer distinctions within the depersonalization syndrome: *de-affectualization* is a sense of an inability to cry, worry, love, hate, etc., and *desomatization* includes changes in the experience of the size and shape of body parts. Cameron (1963) described a similar phenomenon under the rubric *somatic estrangement*.

Brauer et al. (1970) differentiated *depersonalization*, in which the person feels himself distant and detached from the world, from *derealization*, in which the person's immediate environment seems unreal to him. Cameron (1963) described an apparently synonymous disorder as *object estrangement*. Lehmann (1974) integrated the opinions of Mayer-Gross and Shorvon on this issue, concluding that derealization is usually considered to be part of a depersonalization experience, although not a necessary accompaniment.

Déjà vu, a false sense of familiarity with a place or person, may be viewed as the opposite of derealization, which is a false sense of *un*familiarity. In theorizing about the formal mechanism which could link the two phenomena, Siomopoulos (1972) incidentally provided support for Lower's position (1972) that depersonalization is characterized not by ego-splitting, but by splitting of affect:

> In derealization, a familiar affect is missing from a familiar object-affect whole. This is due to repression of pure affect viewed not as cathexis of an idea, but as a separate psychic structure. In déjà vu, the feeling of object familiarity is actually an awareness of a familiar affect constituting part of an object-affect whole. The phenomena of derealization and déjà vu appear to support the view that the affects are independent psychic structures following their own formal laws. [p. 88]

Epidemiology

The proceding discussion of the complexities surrounding the diagnoses of various dissociative phenomena should serve as preliminary warning that any assessment of incidence and prevalence cannot be taken at face value.

Perhaps the most comprehensive and up-to-date data on dissociative reactions were provided by Kirshner (1973). The incidence of "ego-alien behavior accompanied by varying degrees of amnesia" (a symptomatic definition) was 1.3 percent or 23 men out of 1,795 admissions to the Wright-Patterson Air Force Medical Center, from 1968-1970. The episodes appeared to be acute, and according to the authors, seven of them "could qualify as fugues." Seven civilian women patients (Air Force dependents) suffering from dissociative reaction were also studied. The diagnosis of hysterical character was more frequent for this small group. In addition, four of the seven women had histories suggesting conversion symptoms, compared to only one male patient. In the male dissociated series, there was a high incidence (65 percent) of legal difficulties, of which 26 percent were serious, compared with only 32 percent legal difficulties among a control group of twenty-five men, of which 26 percent were serious. Such factors as precipitating events, family background, and neurologic disease were not, on the whole, significant in distinguishing the dissociated patients from controls. The studies (described in the preceding section) conducted by the St. Louis investigators which found familial associations between sociopathy and hysteria may speak to the finding of legal difficulties in Kirshner's male series and the tendency toward conversion in the females.

In a study of 155 consecutive admissions to the Yale-New Haven Hospital, Tucker, Harrow, and Quinlan (1973) demonstrated a significant association of depersonalization with dysphoric affect and specific types of pathological thinking, as assessed by the Rorschach. These authors concluded that a certain core symptomatology, probably related to a chronic depressive character, may be present in various diagnostic groups of mental illness. Earlier in the paper, however, they had carefully qualified their association of depersonalization and depression, specifying that patients who scored high on depersonalization were not necessarily those with a primary depressive diagnosis. There was, however, a tendency (p < .10) for patients assessed as having secondary depressive features to score higher on depersonalization. These results somewhat corroborate the earlier findings of the same group (Brauer, Harrow, and Tucker 1970) that depersonalization was associated with younger patients and "strongly correlated with affective states and feelings, particularly depressive mood or low self-esteem but not specifically with depressive diagnoses" (p. 514).

Cross-cultural and Group Dissociative Phenomena

The psychoanalytic and psychiatric literature lacks cross-cultural epidemiological data, and especially descriptive data on dissociative reactions. In a brief section on group hysteria, Abse (1974) presented a potpourri of loosely-labeled descriptions which could be instances of hysterical conversion reactions, dissociative reactions (the Voodoo cult in Haiti), hysterical psychoses (*pibloktoq* and *whitico*), and even group dissociative reactions (glossolalia in North Carolina). At least one set of authors (Edwards and Angus, 1972) implied group dynamics, in addition to individual dynamics, in their conceptualization that depersonalization is influenced by suggestion and explodable into contagion.

The social-psychological perspective introduced yet another term to the list of depersonalization phenomena. Festinger, Pepitone, and Newcomb (1952) saw *deindividuation* as a state of affairs in which "individuals are not seen or paid attention to as individuals . . . and do not feel that they stand out as individuals" (p.

382). They hypothesized that when members of a group are deindividuated, such normally inhibited responses as hostile feelings or aggressive actions may be expressed. Wheeler (1966) showed that socially undesirable behavior could be spread by contagion, which reduced fear or restraint, possibly through the feeling of anonymity, which Wheeler equated with deindividuation. Cannavale, Scarr, and Pepitone (1970) clearly confirmed the association between deindividuation and "reduction in restraint"; they also demonstrated that deindividuation is primarily a group and not an individual response.

Group influence is central to Zimbardo's (1969) model of deindividuation. Systems of social and personal control typically create in the individual a sense of responsibility and a socially acceptable identity, but when attention to social and self-evaluation is diminished, as in certain group experiences or through hypnosis, behavior is liberated from these constraints and becomes more irrational and hedonistic. Zimbardo and Maslach (1971) observed a kind of hysterical contagion when hypnotic subjects in groups of three were told to experience "the expanded present." Zimbardo argued: "It should follow that subjects for whom the past (with its commitments and established 'face') is diminished as well as the future (with its apprehension over responsibility for being wrong or inappropriate), will be more persuadable and more likely to yield to situational pressures, as in mass hysteria" (p. 320).

The trance phenomenon of the !Kung Bushmen provides a cross-cultural example of an altered state of consciousness in a culturally sanctioned group context. Lee (1968) emphasized the high incidence of trance performers in the population; of 131 males, at least 60, and Lee would estimate about 50 percent, were active performers. While females were not actively involved in the "curing dance," they provided the musical backdrop which contributed to high emotional levels. The trance itself consisted of culturally stereotyped dance behaviors including intense concentration and hyperventilation. These, in turn, produced dizziness, spatial disorientation, hallucination, collapse, and muscular spasm in the "half death" phase. In the culmination of the trance, the performer moved among the spectators and participants. He concentrated especially on the sick, using the technique of "the laying on of hands" to cure. According to Lee, the increasing level of stimuli, emotional excitement, and hyperactivity in the !Kung Bushman trance performance also characterizes other forms of hyperalert or hyperkinetic trance states, such as those observed in religious revivals or possession cults.

The hungan, or spiritual leader of the church in Haiti, evidences a similar dissociative or trance state when he attempts to cure a patient of supernatural illness, believed by the natives to be caused by sorcery or voodoo. Kiev (1967) suggested that such treatments, which are often conducted as public religious ceremonies, provide an "opportunity for catharsis through empathy with the possessed and repression of hostile drives" (p. 474). Bourguignon (1973) posited a continuum of central nervous system arousal moving from hyper- to normal hypoarousal; from the waking state at the midpoint extend a range of tranquil states whose extreme hypoarousal point is the Yoga state of samādhi (p. 5).

Apparently, altered states of consciousness, whether of the hyper- or hypoarousal variety, are labeled mental disorders (fugue states, hysterical dissociative reactions, somnambulism, etc.) when they occur, seemingly idiosyncratically, in the Western world. On the other hand, such phenomena are referred to as *trance, possession cult*, etc. in non-Western societies.

It is our argument that the cultural context not only interprets such behaviors within the range of tolerated or even desirable behavior, but also molds their expression into a culturally determined pattern and may in many instances induce or influence their prevalence and incidence via the contagion process.

The cultural context may also contribute to the *etiology* of certain dissociated behaviors. For example, Greenbaum (1973) found that possession trance was more likely to occur in African societies which have a fixed internal status distinction, as between slaves and freemen, and a high degree of stratification or societal differentiation. Social change and societal stress have been postulated as precipitating factors for some forms of hysterical contagion, especially the cargo-cult movements discussed in a subsequent section. The cross-cultural prevalence of dissociated states may be rather high, judging from a five-year distribution study by Bourguignon (1968), in which 62 percent of a sample of 488 societies demonstrated some form of ritual which included hallucination.

Forms of dissociated or altered states of consciousness are found in the West in the snake-handling cults of the southern United States, discussed by La Barre (1962), and in glossolalia, specifically cited by Abse (1966) as a form of dissociative reaction. In an ethnographic treatment of the phenomenon of Pentecostal tongue-speaking, Goodman (1972) reported that glossolalia occurred across a wide range of cultures from a midwestern tent revival in Columbus, Ohio, circa 1966, to the Umbanda cult which emerged in Brazil in the 1930s. She emphasized that glossolalia always includes an altered state of consciousness.

American culture in the sixties and seventies, perhaps because of increased social conflict and psychosocial stress, may be engendering a greater incidence of group phenomena which incorporates dissociative features. Bourguignon (1973) commented on the increasing openness to the irrational and to altered states of consciousness in some sectors of contemporary American, citing the rise of drug-based hippie communes, Jesus freaks, the Krishna movement, Scientology, and the fascination with non-Western religions and philosophies. Further examples would include the popularity of the Don Juan series by anthropologist Carlos Casteneda, and the ameliorating academic respectability of topics in nonverbal behavior and the study of consciousness.

Discussion: Psychosocial Dynamics Linking Conversions and Dissociations

We may only speculate on the etiology of such developments along psychosocial lines. Relevant theories are discussed in subsequent sections, but the basic notion is that rapid social change and cultural confrontations are unsettling, socially seismological occurences which cause upheavals in the psychic landscape of individuals.

Such a perspective affects how we interpret the association of dissociative and conversion behaviors in a cross-cultural context and in group dissociative phenomena. The psychosocial perspective suggests that, phenomenologically and etiologically, these reactions may not be usefully distinguished from each other.

Abse (1966) focused on disorders in communication basic to such dissociative reactions as glossolalia, in which language loses its traditional secondary process meaning and is degraded to primary process significance. An analogous communicative distortion is at the root of conversion reactions, where word language regresses beyond even primitive speech to a body language whose meaning is dissociated from awareness. Further, just as conversion and dissociative reactions have been connected historically in clinical theory and practice, often on the basis of psychodynamic similarities, it is suggested that a common psychosocial etiology may prove to constitute a strong enough foundation to support another diagnostic merger.

HYSTERICAL CONTAGION

The selection of the term *hysterical contagion* is metaphorical and somewhat arbitrary, but it is intended to avoid certain terminological tangles and yet retain phenomenological usefulness. *Hysterical* is applied descriptively to highly emotional behavior which may include symptoms reminscent of those found in cases of clinical hysteria, while *contagion* suggests a rapid dissemination of this behavior. The best definition of hysterical contagion is offered by Kerckhoff and Back (1968):

A case of hysterical contagion . . . is one in which a set of experiences or behaviors which are heavily laden with the emotion of fear of a mysterious force are disseminated through a collectivity. The type of behavior that forms the manifest content of the case may vary widely from one example to the next, but all are indicative of fear, and all are inexplicable in terms of the usual standards of mechanical, chemical, or physiological causality. [p. 25]

Apparently synonymous phenomena include *mass hysteria* (Champion et al. 1963, Kagwa 1964, Pfeiffer 1964, Jacobs 1965, Ebrahim 1968, Faigel 1968, Muhangi 1973, Polk 1974, Stahl and

Lebedun 1974, Kirkpatrick 1975), *epidemic hysteria* or *hysterical epidemic* (Knight et al. 1965, Moss and McEvedy 1966, Friedman 1967, Helvie 1968, Sirois 1973), *group hysteria* (Olczak et al. 1971), *communicated hysteria* (Lyons and Potter 1970), *mass conversion reactions* (Levine et al. 1974), and at the sociological end of the spectrum, *behavioral contagion* (Wheeler 1966), and *collective delusion* (Medalia and Larsen 1958).

Attempts at Epidemiological Analysis

While the importance of group phenomena in the genesis of psychological problems has been recognized throughout history, most of the classical works on psychiatry and psychoanalysis have neglected to comment on hysterical contagion or have treated the phenomenon in an anecdotal manner. Because of this haphazard reporting, it is impossible to make epidemiological estimates. Sirois (1973) surveyed historical writings on the subject and classified much of the recent medical literature, concluding that hysterical epidemics reported currently are less numerous compared to those reported in similar articles appearing in the second half of the twentieth century in the French and German medical literature. There were few articles from 1900 to 1940, when attention was devoted to intrapsychic dynamics or neuropsychiatric aspects. There was a recrudescence of reported cases after the first modern description in 1943. While it is possible that this change reflected an increased incidence of hysterical contagion, Sirois attributed it more to the influence of the medical zeitgeist of the period 1900 to 1940 and to the recent interest in mystical, nonverbal, and nonrational phenomena (compare Glen 1970).

Sirois (1973) found twenty different episodes of epidemic hysteria between 1912 and 1972. Of these, thirteen occurred in schools, and the rest in factories, hospitals, and towns. Women were almost exclusively affected, except for two occurrences in Africa and one in Taiwan. While most of the victims were young, between the ages of ten and twenty, the episodes in Africa and some town incidents affected all age groups. The number of persons involved varied from ten to three hundred, but the majority of incidents affected groups of about thirty persons. The duration of the epidemics ranged from one day to six months.

In a slightly expanded version of his 1973 study, Sirois (1974) reported seventy-eight outbreaks of hysterical contagion in the world literature from 1912 to 1972; these included the twenty episodes reported earlier. Of this larger collection, thirty-four occurred in schools, seventeen in towns and rural areas, eight in factories and workshops, four in various institutions, and three in hospitals. On the basis of a pilot survey of 1800 schools in the Province of Quebec in 1973, Sirois estimated the *incidence* of hysterical outbreaks to be about 1 out of 900 to 1000 school settings.

Certain Malaysian figures are not included in Sirois's otherwise comprehensive review. Teoh and Yeoh (1973) reported that episodes of hysterical contagion occurred in twenty-nine schools in peninsular Malaysia between 1962 and 1971, while seventeen schools were involved in 1971 alone. Sirois excluded from consideration as *epidemic hysteria* those contagious processes institutionalized by the community. The most striking examples of such hysterical beliefs and behaviors are manifested in the widespread cargo-cult movements, of which more than ninety have been reported (Burton-Bradley, 1974).

Descriptive Classification. Sirois (1974) delineated three conditions for the analysis of hysterical outbreaks: (1) cases which manifested anxiety symptoms such as hyperventilation (the predominant symptom in literature reports), tachycardia, tremor, agitation, etc., (2) hysterical traits such as convulsions, paralysis, fainting, bizarre movements, and (3) other forms including epidemics of laughing or false conviction, depressive feelings, echolalia and echopraxia, transitory hallucinations, etc. Sirois (1973) classifed the epidemics according to their inception (common or individual source) and evolution (symptoms which appear rapidly in many people at once and produce an explosive epidemic versus cumulative transmission from one individual to another.) Most epidemics could be traced to an index case with subsequent dissemination, and Sirois speculated that other epidemics could also have been propagated by an individual source but that the brevity of the contagious process may have obscured this fact.

Sirois (1974) identified five epidemic profiles: (1) sudden onset with explosive development, (2) explosive onset but preceded by a prodromal stage with an identifiable index case, (3) cumulative outbreak, or chain reaction which usually appeared in closed institutionalized setting, (4) rebound outbreak, where there were two waves of symptomatic expression, and (5) large diffuse spread, as in some laughing, running, and panic epidemics.

Etiological Comments

The meticulous distinction among diverse forms of hysterical contagion does not resolve the principal question, Why are the episodes contagious? Sirois (1973) hypothesized that in conditions of social stress, the group can secure a state of individual satisfaction inaccessible outside this context. Behavior defined as sick is adopted as a solution because the instigating conflict can be neither mastered nor avoided, probably because of the individual's inability to mobilize more adaptive behavior. Sirois suggested another possibility: the activation of a conflict in the original case, then the release of conflicts which may be quite different for other members of the group, but which are expressed phenotypically in a similar manner as a communal reaction. Muhangi (1973) called this a "manifestation of serious mass anxiety" (p. 308).

Individual and Group Factors. In a field study of epidemic hysteria in a black high school, Knight et al. (1965) compared afflicted groups with controls to ascertain whether certain individual and group factors might serve as preconditions for the dissemination of hysterical behaviors. They found fewer individuals of average intelligence in the afflicted group, while "social factors were not especially suggestive, except that the hysteria group showed a slight tendency to have more broken homes" (p. 865). Olczak et al. (1971) investigated whether the victims of group conversion reactions were typified by an hysterical personality as indicated by the MMPI Hysteria Scale. Except for scores in the expected direction for females, the results concerning their general hypothesis were equivocal. Jacobs (1965) found that believers in the phantom slasher of Taipei tended to be mainly women and children from lower socioeconomical strata. According to this author, "these elements in society [are] most susceptible to hyper-suggestibility" (p. 326).

Moss and McEvedy (1966) found that on the Eysenck Personality Inventory, the neuroticism rather than the extroversion factor

seemed to discriminate between affected and nonaffected populations in an epidemic of overbreathing among British schoolgirls. The
results of psychological testing on girls involved in a 1972 outbreak
of epidemic hysteria in a Malay college (Teoh and Yeoh 1973) are
consistent with the findings of Moss and McEvedy (1966). The
severely affected group had a higher mean neuroticism score than
did the rest, while the mean extraversion scores were somewhat,
although not significantly, higher than for the other groups. Teoh
and Yeoh concluded from these results that individual girls who
developed *non-epidemic* hysterical conversion symptoms were
more likely to have hysterical personality structures. The association
did not hold for affected girls whose membership in a nuclear, but
deviant group seemed more determinative of susceptibility. For
these girls, the episode of hysteria was related, according to these
authors, "to strong social pressures placed upon the 'deviant'
affected girls to conform. . . . The outbreak of hysteria definitely
relieved personal and interpersonal tensions and presented for the
subjects a safety valve in a rigid society in transition" (p. 292-293).

Sociocultural factors. In a later study of this incident, Teoh,
Soewondo, and Sidharta (1975) attributed more causality to
sociocultural factors. They concluded that the affected girls were
feeling acutely the clash of traditional beliefs with contemporary
scientific knowledge and expressed their ambivalence and frustration through a hysterical process. This sociocultural explanation is in
line with Kerckoff and Back's study (1968). They observed that
although symptoms are first produced in socially isolated individuals, social ties are important in the consequent transmission of
hysterical behaviors. Wheeler (1966) contrasted behavioral contagion with such related social influence concepts as conformity,
imitation, social pressure, and social facilitation. Sirois (1973)
suggested that factors like cohesiveness or group isolation are as
important as individual personality variables. Most reports of
hysterical contagion concern closed groups such as schools or
prisons; the less isolated groups involve members of the same tribe
or hospital or groups with common cultural or occupational
conflicts which favor cohesion.

Chronic stress or a conflictual event is consistently associated with
all groups which manifest hysterical contagion. Structural strain is

the explanation most often cited by the more sociologically oriented writers. Smelser (1962) stated that for "any episode of collective behavior, we shall always find some kind of structural strain in the background" (p. 65). Structural strain is conceived of as a necessary but insufficient precondition for collective behaviors when institutionalized means of overcoming the strain are inadequate. To illustrate, structural strain was cited by Ebrahim (1968) as contributing to an outbreak of mass hysteria in African school children:

> The average African child has a strict upbringing with subservience to the all-powerful "elders." Exposure to new-world ideas which frequently challenge attitudes of these elders produces conflict in the child's mind. Escape from conflict may be sought through "illness." We believe that the basis for these epidemics is the emotional conflict aroused in children who are being brought up at home amidst traditional tribal conservatism, while being exposed in school to thoughts and ideas which challenge accepted beliefs. [p. 438]

Smelser (1962) cited the three components of a hysterical belief as (1) strain giving rise to an *unstructured* ambiguous stituation such as an abnormal or unexpected event or to *structured* ambiguous situations such as contemporary courtship and marriage, (2) anxiety involving a negative generalization (p. 89), and (3) redefinition of the situation in which the hysterical belief is adapted to reduce situational ambiguity by explaining past events, describing present ones, or predicting those in the future as manifestations of omnipotent forces, which to believers may seem to be the most logical explanation.

Reactive Movements

Such sociological explanations have been brought to bear upon the form of hysterical belief manifested in cargo cults. According to Burton-Bradley (1974), the cargo cult is a "specifically Melanesian form of adjustment related to the social change stemming from two cultures in contact" (p. 236). In this sense, a cargo cult includes goal-directed attempts to solve a real, not a psychological, problem. Of course, there is never a satisfactory solution, for the desired cargo never really arrives. One of the most famous examples of a crisis cargo cult was the Vailala Madness, which occurred in New Guinea after World War II and which was described by La Barre (1970) among others:

> The chief tenet of the cargo cult was that the ancestors and head relatives were to visit them soon in a large steamship loaded with gifts of tobacco, axes, calico, knives, foodstuffs, and the like. They were meanwhile to gather coconuts and sago to feast the ghostly crew, while the message was sent widely around. [p. 239]

Worsley (1968) stated that the hysterical behaviors demonstrated in most of the cults (mass possession, trances, fantasies, twitches, etc.) are less the result of any specific psychological characteristics of the Melanesians than "the product of the ambivalent attitudes and feelings of men torn between hatred of the White people who had destroyed the old way of life and who now dominated them by force, and the desire to obtain for themselves the possessions of these very Whites" (p. 44).

As a function of the white American culture's impact upon the Indian cultures of the United States, so-called nativistic movements developed (Linton 1943)—for example, the North American Ghost Dance movements of 1870 and 1890 (see La Barre 1970, for the most comprehensive treatment) and the Peyote cult (Slotkin 1965). Spindler (1968) called such cults reactive movements to suggest that they were basically reactions to the rapid social change occurring in the wake of a confrontation between divergent cultural systems. Spindler viewed the underlying features of both the Melanesian cargo cults and Menomini peyote cults as "the *search for identity* and the attempt to *reestablish cognitive control*" (p. 335).

Worsley (1968) applied the term *millenarian* to those movements which expect and prepare for a future period of supernatural bliss to be brought about by either supernatural or human intervention. Millenarian movements do not necessarily imply a culture clash, as do cargo cults; they are often fueled by internal, rather than intergroup, conflict and change. Talmon (1965) observed that most millenarian movements are (a) messianic, that is instigated, or more precisely, legitimized (according to Worsley 1968) by inspired, charismatic leaders or prophets, and (b) highly emotional, that is involving hysterical and paranoid phenomena through which emotional tension is expressed—twitching, shaking, convulsion, and often the deliberate shattering of sexual taboos. Many authors have commented upon the presence of millenarian features in the origins of those religions and political movements which involve a radical restructuring, rather than a gradual development, of beliefs.

The Psychosocial Stress Continuum and its Expression

Our argument is that the seemingly exotic phenomena associated with hysterical contagion and reactive movements anchor the sociocultural end of the same continuum as the so-called dissociated behaviors expressed on individual and interpersonal (or group) levels. The mechanism underlying all these phenomena, especially group and societal reactions, is hypothesized to be psychosocial stress engendered by cultural change and conflict. People are conditioned by their sociocultural groups to perceive, organize, and interpret the world according to certain patterns. When this habitual way of experiencing and thinking is threatened by new models, then the identities of individuals, as well as of communities and cultures, are threatened.

Whether such psychosocial stress is expressed at the individual, group, or societal level seems to depend on whether institutionalized means exist for reasserting identity. From this perspective, reactive movements may be viewed as active attempts to deal with a changing sociocultural environment either by adapting to it, trying to ressurect old identities (as in the Ghost Dance movement), or establishing new ones. Analogous behaviors at the group level (glossolalia and hysterical contagion) or at the individual level (conversion and dissociation) may still be interpreted as strivings for adaptation, although through a more basic process such as tension release.

Culturally *sanctioned* hysterical behaviors at the individual level, such as the !Kung Bushman trance performance, which establishes acceptable if unusual identities *within* the social group, should probably be considered sociocultural-level phenomena in order to distinguish them from the more pathogenic individual behaviors demonstrated in idiosyncratic dissociative reactions which are not culturally condoned, such as dissociated or multiple personality or hysterical psychosis.

HYSTERICAL PSYCHOSIS

In 1964, Hollender and Hirsch found very few references to hysterical psychosis in either the psychoanalytic or the psychiatric literature. They concluded, however, on the basis of a survey of six psychiatrists, that hysterical psychosis, which was a popular term during the early part of this century, is "still very much with us." Despite its lack of an official designation in *DSM II* (1968) and relative neglect in the literature, Hollender and Hirsch suggested that there "is even reason to believe that its popularity today is no less than it was half a century ago." (p. 1066).

Ten years later, Pankow (1974) nominated hysterical psychosis as one of those "unrewarding areas of psychiatry [which] attract the interest of neither practitioners nor theoreticians" (p. 408). A Frenchman, Pankow confirmed from colleagues in the United States that there was a rise in the incidence of hysterical psychosis, or *hysterica delusion*, which he differentiated from *hysterical crisis*. According to Pankow, while the hysterical symptom is linked with the patient's unconscious sexual desires in hysterical neurosis, access to the sexual sphere is blocked in hysterical psychosis by the psychotic process. Pankow distinguished hysterical delusion, which theoretically derives from disturbances in the *content* of the body image, from schizophrenic delusion, in which the *form* of the body image is disturbed, as well.

Hollender and Hirsch (1964) consider hysterical psychosis the most serious manifestation of hysterical process, with hysterical character at the opposite end of the scale.

Descriptively, hysterical psychosis is marked by a sudden and dramatic onset temporally related to a profoundly upsetting event or circumstance. Its manifestations include hallucinations, delusions, depersonalization and grossly unusual behavior. Thought disorders, when they occur, are usually sharply circumscribed and very transient. Affectivity, if altered, is changed in the direction of volatility and not flatness. The acute episode seldom lasts longer than one to three weeks, and the eruption is sealed off so that there is practically no residue. Hysterical psychosis is encountered most commonly in persons referred to as hysterical characters or personalities when faced by trying life situations or problems. [p. 1073]

Richman and White (1970) added to this conceptualization (acute onset, severe disturbance, and rapid recovery) several clinical observations indicative of a diagnosis of hysteria: (1) the absence of a schizophrenic thought disorder, (2) object relations which are differentiable quantitatively and qualitatively from those of the schizophrenic, and (3) the central importance of situational and interpersonal factors, in particular, the association of the illness with anxiety related to death, aggression, or actual object loss.

This latter point is elaborated by Martin (1971), who perceived hysterical psychosis as an extreme means of coping in hysterically predisposed women who "temporarily escape the disturbed symbiotic relationship in their marriage in preference to separation and individuation" (p. 748). This dynamic formulation could easily be applied to cases of dissociative neurosis.

Cross-cultural Syndromes

In view of the emphasis these authors place on the situational factors which precipitate an attack of hysterical psychosis, it is notable that cross-cultural reports of hysterical psychosis are more numerous than articles referring to American or European examples. Perhaps cross-cultural commentators, having an anthropological bent, are more situationally inclined, while clinicians surveying only their native culture have a better view of internal dynamics and might subsume equivalent examples of hysterical psychosis under depersonalization, etc. Although Hollender and Hirsch (1964) considered transient psychoses, such as the brief schizophrenias of soldiers in battle, under the rubric of hysterical psychosis, they were more cautious about assigning non-Western syndromes such as *whitico psychosis, amok, latah,* and *imu,* the same diagnostic label. Other authorities seem to imply the cultural idiosyncrasy of these non-Western psychiatric phenomena; Arieti's *American Handbook of Psychiatry,* for example, relegated them to a chapter on "exotic psychiatric syndromes" (Meth 1974). Langness (1967), however, maintained a less psychiatrically segregationist position by including non-Western manifestations as evidence for a syndrome of hysterical psychosis.

Whitiko psychosis. This disorder (also spelled *windigo*) occurs among the Cree and Ojibwa Indians of the northeastern United States and Canada, and has an equal incidence among males and females. According to Langness (1967), the *whitiko* victim believes himself possessed by the spirit of the *whitiko* monster and consequently develops distaste, even to the point of nausea, for his usual food and a compensating craving for the flesh of humans— often family members, whom he comes to perceive as edible animals. A cultural consideration renders the bizarre clinical symptoms at least understandable. Meth (1974) noted that cannibalism, recognized among the Eskimos as an extreme means of survival, may be interpreted as an attempt to solve a state of *psychic* crisis through symbolic (although sometimes gruesomely literal) enactment of a culturally determined solution of a *physical* crisis.

Amok. The term *amok* typically applies to Malayan cases, in which the victim would suddenly run berserk, killing several animals or people before being stopped or killed. According to Maguigad (1964), *amok* is derived from the Malay word *amoq*, which means engaging furiously in battle. This is not just an apt description of the contemporary amokers' state of murderous frenzy; it also refers, according to Murphy (1973) to the disorder's origins as a heroic, consciously chosen battle strategy, a point which will be referred to again. Linton (1956) reported a phenomenon occurring in the Amazon (specifically among the Tapirape, according to Linton's source); it is similar to *amok* in all respects, except that only pet animals, and not people, were subject to attack. Meth (1974) considered the Puerto Rican syndrome or *Mal de Pelea* akin to *amok*, though less extreme; Fernández-Marina referred only to the disorder's hyperkinetic episodes, without mention of killing. Meth (1974) cited allegedly parallel versions of *amok* in Melanesia, among the Bena Bena tribe of New Guinea, where it is called *negi negi* or *lulu*. Ackerknecht (1971) referred to previous reports in the literature of syndromes similar to *amok* in Siberia and India.

Considering the disorder's dynamic formulations, Maguigad

(1964) observed that the reaction occurs in persons who have repressed intense rage and that the experience is often accompanied by amnesia. The *amok* victim's experience of a vivid hallucinatory state combined with the factor of amnesia suggests a similarity to acute dissociative reactions. While Meth (1974) did not classify *amok* as an hysterical phenomenon, he employed terms evocative of hysterical dynamics:

> In other words, the *amok* patient externalized his desperate need to destroy the death-bringing inner conflict by killing other persons. The most violent cases of *amok* seem to occur in cultures which demand repression of hostility, as in Malaya, Bandung, and the Phillipines. [p. 731]

Latah and related disorders. Amok occurs almost exclusively in younger or middle-aged males (Kline 1963).In Malaya, a female version called *latah* chiefly afflicts middle-aged women. Yap (1952), has, however, in the most exhaustive acocunt of the disorder and related syndromes around the world, reported cases in children, adolescents, and the aged, as well. According to Meth (1974), syndromes similar to *latah* occur with equal frequency in men in other parts of the world: Siberia, Siam, Burma, the Phillipines, Madagascar, Nyasaland, Zaire, Somaliland, the southern part of the Sahara, and Tierra del Fuego.

The clinical picture of *latah* may be characterized by echolalia, coprolalia (in Indonesia, Kline [1963] noted the shouting of such phrases as "horse penis" and "cow vagina"; automatic obedience; its opposite (negativism); or echopraxia (behavioral mimicry). It seems to be triggered by something idiosyncratically disturbing to the individual, such as being tickled or pinched, or a loud noise. Murphy (1973) distinguished the startle pattern, which often involves coprolalia, from the imitative pattern. Yap (1952) attributed *latah*'s dynamics to sudden fright or psychological shock in "naive, underdeveloped or poorly endowed personalities" (p. 537) from the lower classes, with poorer education, and of rural rather than urban origin.

A Japanese form of the disease, *imu* or *inu* is precipitated by such creatures as snakes, snails, and caterpillars, which are considered frightening by the Ainu society. Along with such fear reactions, Wittkower and Dubreuil (1968) categorized *susto* or *magic fright*, found among Central and South American Indian tribes and non-Indians in the Andean highlands of Peru, Bolivia, and Columbia. This disorder is somewhat unique among hysterical psychoses in that it chiefly afflicts young children and infants, but only occasionally, adolescents or adults.

Linton (1956) related *latah* to *arctic hysteria* of the Asiatic type in terms of compulsive imitation (see Foulke 1972 for a full treatment). Another so-called arctic hysteria, *pibloktoq* (also spelled *piblokto* or *pibloktok*), is found in the Arctic east of St. Lawrence Island (Murphy and Leighton 1965). According to Langness (1967), this disorder afflicts both males and females, but more frequently females. After a period of irritability or withdrawal, the victim suddenly becomes excited and may tear off clothing, break furniture, shout obscenities, etc. until restrained by pursuers, at which point convulsive seizures and stuperous sleep or coma are common sequelae. Among the so-called copying manias, Meth (1974) included the Siberian *amurakh*, in which words or actions are mimicked, and *menerik*, a syndrome in which more extreme screaming and dancing fits are induced in Eskimos of both sexes.

Epidemiology

Murphy (1973) took the rather unusual tack of describing the epidemiology of *amok* historically as well as geographically. The first reference to *amok* in the written literature was by mid-sixteenth century, European travelers; they described groups of South Asians, who in battle would sacrifice their belongings, loved ones, and selves, rather than let these fall into the hands of the enemy. In the late 1700s and early 1800s, the term applied to a consciously mediated manifestation of murderous frenzy motivated in such persons as slaves or defeated soldiers by social frustration. Murphy cited Oxley's formal study of *amok* in mid-nineteenth century Singapore, to the effect that *amok* now afflicted ordinary workmen and appeared to be precipitated by somatic, rather than social, complaints. Unlike the soldiers and slaves of the previous century, *amok* victims denied identification with their acts and pleaded possession by the devil.

On the basis of Oxley's data, Murphy (1973) estimated that the yearly incidence of *amok* in the mid-nineteenth century was somewhere between 1 to 2 per 1000 adult males. From other studies, Murphy concluded that by the end of the nineteenth century, *amok* was regarded as more a psychiatric phenomenon, as illustrated by one observation of its occurrence in men of low intelligence and education who had recently moved from a rural setting to the city. Reports then indicated that *amok*, whose incidence had apparently increased through the mid-1800s, became rather rare by the turn of the century in several locations, especially where European doctors were practicing. Murphy's interpretation of reports from the 1920s and 1930s was that *amok* had again altered in character, this time from an acute, dissociative reaction to an episode in the course of a more chronic mental disorder.

As a statistical supplement to Murphy's excellent survey and analysis of the literature, we offer Teoh's chronicle (1972) of *amok* epidemiology in Malaysia, as it was reported in the English language *Straits Times Press*: For both rural and urban areas, there were twelve cases in the period 1935 to 1939, two from 1940 to 1944 (the war years), twenty-two from 1945 to 1949, twenty-six from 1950 to 1954, forty-two from 1955 to 1959, and forty-five from 1965 to 1970

The related *latah* syndrome presents a different history than *amok* in that there were no descriptions of it before the mid-nineteenth century, probably, according to Murphy, because it did not itself exist previously. The dramatic nature of the disorder certainly would have provoked medical or journalistic comment, whether or not the behavior received medical or psychiatric attribution. The incidence of *latah*, however, increased rapidly until the end of the nineteenth century, when it was common among the Amboinese, Javanese, and Malays, with almost as many male as female sufferers. Medical reports from the turn of the century indicated that *latah* knew no class distinctions, more often affected intellectually superior persons, and was unassociated with epilepsy, hysteria, or any chronic psychiatric process. Later papers around 1922 to 1924 observed a number of variations in this pattern: (1) a decreasing incidence in general, (2) an increase in the average age of victims to over forty, (3) an increase in the relative proportion of male victims in Malaysia above the previous nearly equal sex ratio, (4) a concentration of victims in the servant class, and (5) a greater association of *latah* with chronic mental disturbance.

Just as *amok* seemed to retreat into an epidemiological hibernation in the first half of the twentieth century before reemerging with greater strength, so *latah* seems also to be making a comeback. Murphy (1973) described the present picture of the syndrome in terms of a near 1 percent prevalence among rural Malays who have moved near the capital of Sarawak and among Javanese (mainly female) who have relocated from outlying villages to towns.

Psychosocial Etiology

Langness (1967) stressed the cultural specificity of these and related forms of hysterical psychosis in terms of (a) the culturally-defined stressful events which precipitate the illness, (b) the stereotypical behaviors during attacks which appear to be culturally patterned, and thus, learned, and (c) the predictable social response to the episodes.

In fact, social response to hysterical psychosis appears to determine the course of the disorder in several different cultures. Kline (1963) found that Indonesian *latah* appeared in hypersuggestable, hysterical-type personalities and that the attack lasted only as long as the woman was being teased; if the teasing lasted too long, however, the *latah* victim sometimes made efforts on her own to terminate the attack. Langness (1967) hypothesized that the tendency to tease and otherwise persecute *latah* victims even after attacks subsided contributes to an apparent chronicity in Malaysian and Japanese victims. Analogous episodes among the Bena Bena receive less public notoriety, allowing or encouraging the individual psychosis to be transient.

Langness (1967) noted parenthetically the factor of contagion in the instances of *Kuma* and *Huli*, which have been classified as forms of hysterical psychosis. These involve bizarre running and aggressive behaviors, and occur, respectively, in the New Guinea Highlands and Papua, in Oceania. According to Linton's 1956 observation, both the Old World variety of arctic hysteria and *latah* appear to be highly contagious: "If there are two or three individuals present who have this tendency and one of them is 'touched off,' the others promptly fall into the same state" (p. 115). Contagion would seem to be an important factor for such victims of hysterical psychoses; their only shared personality characteristics, according to Langness (1967) are "suggestibility, nonscientific modes of thinking, and perhaps an oversensitivity in responding to cues" (p. 151)—all characteristics applied by many accounts to the hysterical personality.

The *koro* (also known as *suo-yang*) syndrome of southeast Asia (particularly in the Malay Archipelago with its immigrants from southern China) is an example of what might be considered a contagious hysterical psychosis. In *koro*, the victim suddenly panics with the belief that his penis may retract into his abdomen, resulting in death. To prevent this, the patient may grip his penis with his hands and perhaps anchor it with a special wooden clasp, or, according to Meth (1974), he may induce his wife to practice fellatio, which seems to allay the phobia.

In a rare, Western report "The *koro* Pattern of Depersonalization in an American Schizophrenic Patient," Edwards (1970) emphasized the two components of the syndrome as (1) the belief in penis shrinkage, which observers of Western cases attribute to idiosyncratic psychopathology (p. 1172) and (2) the cultural, folk interpretation of that experience. Ngui (1969) reported on the 1967 *koro* epidemic in Singapore, which resulted in 536 cases. Of the interviewed cases, 8 were females who complained of retraction of the nipples or vulva. (Linton 1956 also described a female *koro* syndrome in Borneo). As in many reports of hysterical contagion, an event appeared to precipitate the epidemic. In this instance, there was an outbreak of swine fever, and 43.6 percent of the males attributed their condition to eating pork, while 50 percent remained noncommital about causal factors.

Hysterical Contagion as Hysterical Psychosis at the Group Level

One logical conclusion of the evidence presented is that so-called hysterical contagion is an example of hysterical psychosis at the group level. Contagion, in this view, would represent a *characteristic* of certain forms of hysterical psychosis, but would not delimit a separate category of hysteria. For example, the echolalia of the *latah* victim, who is subject to contagion, is strikingly similar to the glossolalia in a dissociative reaction heightened by group suggestion. Further, it is difficult to ignore the parallel phenomenology of acute dissociative reactions and hysterical psychosis, as defined by Richman and White (1970). For example, Bustamante's description (1967/1968) of cultural factors in hysterias with a schizophrenic clinical picture could be classified along with hysterical psychoses with little argument; the authors themselves relate these cases to dissociative reaction. The connection between (or confusion of, according to Goodman 1972) depersonalization phenomena such as glossolalia and hysterical contagion has been commented upon by Edwards and Angus (1972).

It seems to us, however, that *hysterical psychosis* is a label often affixed to foreign manifestations of dissociative phenomena (either literally foreign, or figuratively so in terms of the writer's difficulty in understanding underlying similarities). Further, just as dissociative phenomena occur at the group level in such forms as glossolalia, so hysterical psychosis transposed to the group scale becomes hysterical contagion. Murphy (1973) implied a common etiology linking *amok, latah,* and the cargo cults when he conceived of *amok* and *latah* "not as offshoots from Malayan cultural tradition but as transitional products of an interaction between that tradition and certain modernizing influences" (p. 48). This proposed relationship between social change and psychiatric symptom, in which an overall heightened suggestibility represents response to the demand to learn new customs, may be directly applied to an understanding of other psychiatric disorders through a combined epidemiological-etiological approach.

ANOREXIA NERVOSA: A POSTSCRIPT

Although some might accuse us of arbitrary oversimplification, evidence from a variety of sources could be marshaled to argue for inclusion of anorexia nervosa in a discussion of hysterical phenomena. Cameron (1963) considered the symptom of appetite loss in anorexia as an expression of unconscious body-metaphor conflict, and, therefore, a conversion reaction. Abse (1974) wrote that anorexia nervosa and subsequent physiological deterioration may follow an hysterical process. The St. Louis group (for example,

Woodruff et al. 1971) included anoretic symptoms—anorexia, weight loss, marked fluctuations in weight, food intolerances, and constipation—in group five of the nine symptom groups they apply as diagnostic criteria for Briquet's syndrome. The symptoms of vomiting and abdominal pain appear in their symptom-group six. Dysmenorrhea and amenorrhea, which often accompany anorexia are featured in their symptom-group seven. Indeed, amenorrhea is considered a prominant, even a major, sign of the illness by Halmi (1974), among others. Sexual indifference has also been noted in male anoretics (Beumont et al. 1972), and psychosexual immaturity has been observed in female victims (Crisp 1965). Other features of anorexia nervosa, particularly its predominant occurrence in adolescent females, suggests its relation to hysterical manifestations. The anoretic's denial of hunger, weakness, and weight loss recalls to a striking degree *la belle indifférence* of the classical hysteric.

Historically, anorexia nervosa has been diagnosed as either hysteria or obsessional neurosis, or a variant of severe depression or schizophrenia (Sours 1974). This confusing smorgasbord of labels and their underlying etiological hypotheses is reminiscent of our excursion into the literature on conversion disorders and suggests that anorexia nervosa, like conversion disorder, is probably not a specific nosological entity with a predictable outcome. It may be useful to consider anorexia and hysteria in the context of the following analogy: Genuine or *primary* anorexia nervosa (Bruch 1969) is to undifferentiated anorexia as Briquet's syndrome is to conversion symptoms. In light of this analogy, a brief discussion of anorexia nervosa may aid in the analysis of our main theme—the classification of hysterical phenomena.

Psychodynamically, the anoretic is like the hysteric who, according to such authors as Bruch (1965, 1969) and Crisp and Kalucy (1974), deploys massive repressive mechanisms. Other authors do not support this view that repression leads to splitting of the ego and to conceptual and perceptual disturbances. Shapiro (1965), for example, in his analysis of the hysterical character, did not interpret such cognitive characteristics as not knowing really what one thinks or feels as the *result* of repression; rather, he argued that such a mode of cognition merely favors a repressive defense.

As we interpret the underlying similarities, the anoretic and the hysteric are both generally less aware of or sensitive to sharply focused data. A similarly diffuse cognition of *internal* cues could account for the anoretic's seeming disregard of hunger, exhaustion, and emaciation, as well as for the conversion hysteric's proclivity to feel organic disorders in healthy body parts. This conceptualization could also be translated into the terms of Freud's (1900) discussion of the attenuation of attention cathexis, which impedes consciousness of both internal and external perception.

Epidemiology

Incidence. Some estimations of the average annual incidence of anorexia nervosa are provided by Kendell et al. (1973); they cited 1.6 per 100,000 population per year over a four-year period in northeast Scotland, .37 per 100,000 over a ten-year period in Monroe County, New York, and .66 per 100,000 over a seven-year period for the Camberwell area in southeast London. These figures are generally in agreement with Theander's overall incidence, in women only, of .24 per 100,000 inhabitants of southern Sweden per year over a thirty-year period (1970). The studies are not directly comparable, since his cases included only female inpatients, whereas the previously cited studies included both male and female outpatients from case registers.

Although many authors have noticed an apparent increase in incidence for anorexia nervosa, they have generally tempered this observation by cautioning that recent figures may be inflated by better case detection. Based on her own clinical experience, Bruch (1970) indicated an increase in cases from six patients between 1942 and 1954 to twelve between 1955 and 1959 and thirty-three between 1960 and 1967. Theander (1970) reported that in the final decade (1951 to 1960) of his thirty-year study, the incidence rose to .45 per 100,000; the overall average incidence was .24. Records from the files of the University of Iowa General and Psychopathic Hospitals from 1920 through 1972 (Halmi 1974) evidenced a rise in annual incidence from 1.3 cases (43 patients) seen at the University of Iowa General and Psychopathic Hospitals between 1920 and 1954 to 3 cases (51 patients) diagnosed from 1955 through 1971. Duddle (1973) found a statistically significant increase ($p < .001$) in the number of cases of anorexia nervosa presenting at the Manchester

University Student Health Center, from none between 1966 and 1968 to 13 between 1971 and 1972. Since there was no change in the patterns of other diagnoses, it seems unlikely that this is a diagnostic artifact.

Sex differences. Anorexia has always been conspicuously more frequent in females than in males. Halmi's survey (1974) included eighty-eight females and six males; the 6.3 percent for males corresponds to other reported figures. In an attempt to clear some of the diagnostic confusion surrounding anorexia nervosa in the male, Bruch (1971) distinguished genuine or *primary* anorexia nervosa from undifferentiated eating disturbances. Her observations from 1944 to 1969 on nine male patients (five in the primary group and four in the undifferentiated group) suggested, however, that diagnostic classification bore little relationship to the final outcome, since both groups manifested uniform symptoms of weight loss, severity of illness (there was one death in each group), and resistance to traditional treatments. Beumont et al. (1972) surveyed the world literature on anorexia nervosa in the male (one reference dates to 1767) and found eight-four papers reporting on two hundred and fifty male patients; the authors winnowed this down to twenty-five patients who were described adequately enough to warrant the designation "probably anorexia nervosa." Rowland's 1970 sample of thirty patients was 20 percent male—the highest percentage we found.

Age and other variables. From their own study of six male anoretic patients, Beumont et al. (1972) concluded that age of onset in the male—puberty, adolescence, or early adult life—corresponds to the age range in the female. It should be noted, however, that younger patients may be more likely to appear in studies which, like Halmi's (1974), include a pediatric age group. In her study of 94 hospital patients with anorexia nervosa, Halmi found an 8 percent incidence of onset before age ten. Rowland's review of thirty cases (1970) differentiated three age groups: a prepuberty group, which had a better prognosis, a teenage group (19-25), which tended to be the sickest and mainly psychotic, and those who were afflicted after age twenty-five, usually with less dramatic symptoms.

The observations of Beumont et al. (1972) on males also correspond to other reports on females when other aspects of the clinical picture are considered: previous obesity, abdominal discomfort on eating, induced vomiting, fear of obesity, obsession with food and body weight, retardation of puberty, and a generally healthy premorbid personality. These findings agree with descriptions of anorexia nervosa in the male offered by Bruch (1971) and Crisp and Toms (1972).

Demographic features. Kendell et al. (1973) reported not only that the incidence of anorexia nervosa has increased but that the disease is rare in blacks (a finding corroborated by Bruch 1970). There was a significant excess (p<.0001) in middle- to upper-class families, exclusively in the Camberwell area of London. While these data agree with Bruch's (1970) and with Theander's (1970) observations of strong upper-class predominance, Kendell et al. did *not* uncover a significant upper-class bias in their own reports on northeast Scotland or Monroe County, New York. The authors explained these differences and Theander's finding of a progressive rise in the proportion of patients from lower social groups, by hypothesizing that "anorexia nervosa is the product of culturally determined attitudes or behavior patterns, probably concerning food or sexuality, which were originally found only in middle-class families but are now becoming more evenly diffused throughout our society" (p. 203).

Rowland (1970) also failed to find an upper-class bias, although his sample was from a state hospital where more lower-class patients might be expected. The fact that 60 percent of his thirty patients were from the lowest income bracket indicates, at least, that the disorder is not unrepresented in that class. Conversely, the figures which indicate an overrepresentation of upper-class anorexia victims may reflect a sampling bias from private practice.

Etiological Considerations

According to Sours (1974), psychodynamic formulations for the syndrome have more recently emphasized early object relations instead of drive theories (which postulate ambivalence as a result of early fluctuations of oral deprivation and gratification and, in the pubescent girl, preoedipally derived regressive wishes which surface in an oral-anal mode of drive discharge). Sours pointed out that the characteristic features of an anoretic's developmental history stem from attachment to a domineering and controlling mother, whose influence interferes with separation and individuation in all phases of the daughter's development. The daughter's affect is suppressed and bound up somatically in the form of the anoretic pattern, including "falsification of exteroceptive and enteroceptive experiences" (p. 571).

This formulation, however, does not account for gender differences in apparent susceptibility to anorexia nervosa. These have been attributed to constitutional differences by Meyer (1971). He suggested that women are predisposed to oral reactions, since in his own studies of normal people under stress, it was revealed that women were liable to undereat or overeat four times more often than men, who had other ways of coping.

Duddle (1973) attributed a possible increase in cases of anorexia nervosa in a student population to increased nutrition in early childhood. He hypothesized that prolonged breast or bottle feeding leads to an imprinting on nutritional experience and to pubertal obesity, which then combine to precipitate anorexia nervosa in vulnerable personalities. This theory has several problems, not the least of which is how, then, to account for vulnerable personalities. Halmi (1974) reported significantly greater incidence of both low and high birth weights among anoretics than in the general population. She found no evidence that birth weights were associated with nutritional patterns in early childhood, although her study did discover a high incidence of feeding *problems* during infancy, as well as during preadolescence (25 percent) and adolescence (17 percent).

At the other end of the spectrum are sociological hypotheses, such as the suggestion by the German, von Baeyer (reported by Meyer 1971), that the recent rise in incidence for anorexia nervosa is related to the emancipation of women and the increasing number of professional women among mothers. It is unclear, however, *how* a working mother, or an emancipated woman, for that matter, induces anorexia nervosa in her offspring.

Conversion Hysteria and Anorexia Nervosa

Just as we interpret conversion reaction as an attempt to resolve a psychosocial conflict in which the symptomatic expression is molded by the sociocultural context, we could view anorexic symptoms in the light of conflict (whether generated by intrapsy-chic, interpersonal, and/or societal stresses) expressed in a cultural context which sanctions only certain manifestations of t is stress, and not others. Like hysterical phenomena, in general, the symptomatol-ogy of anorexia nervosa is shaped by certain cultural proclivities and sanctions internalized to some extent as individual attitudes, beliefs, or obsessions. The observations of Bruch (1969) regarding the cultural context of anorexia nervosa and obesity are applicable here:

> Western culture on the whole has been so hostile and derogatory toward obesity that even people with only a moderate degree of overweight face some problem in social relations. Adolescents, in particular, suffer from this negative social attitude; all of them are concerned about the adequacy of their physical development and are struggling for self-respect and a respected identity in the adult world. [p. 182-183]

Bruch cautioned that a cultural preoccupation with slimness is not enough to *cause* anorexia nervosa, but that it participates in its development in vulnerable personalities. Bruch (1975) spoke more specifically about the hypothesized nature of this vulnerability and related the anoretic's fixation on slimness to "extreme dependence on societal opinion and judgment" (p. 160). This externalized sensitivity itself may reflect a defect in self-identity traceable to disturbed family interaction patterns, which diffuse the boundaries of self and nonself, as Bruch elaborated:

> If responses to child-initiated clues are continuously inappropriate or contradictory, he will grow up without experiencing himself in control of his body and its function, lacking the conviction of living his own life. . . . Such individuals are perplexed when trying to differentiate between disturbances in the biological field and in emotional and interpersonal experiences. They are apt to misinter-pret discomfort in the self-body concept as externally induced.[p. 161]

This view is in accord with our own view that the sociocultural context *shapes* the form symptoms will take and may even add stress to an already vulnerable personality, but that intrapsychic conflicts, engendered perhaps by distorted early object relations and a cognitive-defensive style of coping with these conflicts, are probably always causally implicated.

The regression to childish attitudes, behaviors, styles of thinking, and sexuality is, of course, the pattern of the classical conversion hysteric. Bruch and others have argued that the conflicts of conversion hysteria and other neuroses are found in pseudo-anorexia nervosa, or psychoneurotic anorexia, but that the issue in primary anorexia nervosa is a struggle for control and a sense of identity. As male anoretics secm to fall into the pseudo-anorexia category more often than females, it might be suspected that pseudo and primary anorexia nervosa are really on the same continuum, differing mainly in the extent to which relative degrees of personality vulnerability, and psychosocial conflicts, are translated via sexually-patterned expression into the pathologic process.

Further support for the hypothesis that anorexia nervosa is on the same continuum as hysterical phenomena is provided when the sociological perspective is widened to include other societies. For example, the *susto* or *magic fright* of South America, which has been called hysterical psychosis, has many parallels with anorexia nervosa. Among these are its characteristic affliction of the young and its major symptoms—emaciation, loss of weight and strength, gastrointestinal disorders, generalized phobias, and depression. (Two symptoms which do not match the anorexic picture are rapid heart beat and intense anxiety.) Wittkower and Dubreuil's sociological interpretation of *susto* (1968) focused on the victim's panic engendered by arriving at an age-determined social role and feeling unable to fulfill it.

In the section on hysterical contagion, we discussed how, at the intergroup level, a clash of cultures often culminates in a frantic search for identity and cognitive control expressed as a reactive movement. Similarly, the cultural clash which occurs when a vulnerable South American child or an incipient anoretic faces discrepent social roles results in attempts to regain psychological equilibrium. Some societies have elaborate rites of passage which span the hiatus between life stages or social roles and often feature cathartic ceremonies to ease the transition by releasing tension.

These societies, we propose, would have fewer members who display hysterical phenomena at either the individual or group levels.

From this perspective, anorexia nervosa may be seen as an extreme form of adaptation to psychological gear shifting between life stages. The perceived lack of control over a changing social and sexual identity, which characterizes a stormy puberty, is likely to be felt by susceptible personalities as an overwhelming trauma. Such struggles for intrapsychic control are often repeated in the interpersonal arena, as in the often-noted primitive struggle for control between mother and anoretic daughter. In this sense, the anoretic's attempt to achieve dictatorial control over her body is both an *expression* of her need to gain control over all areas of her lifespace and an *attempted somatic solution* to intrapsychic and interpersonal loss of control and identity. The anoretic is solely in command of at least one thing—her thinness. The ritualistic behaviors of the anoretic, which have been interpreted by many writers as evidence of obsessive-compulsive characteristics, can be understood as part of this desperate set of maneuvers to gain control and to reestablish or maintain identity. Such rituals, we hypothesize, *function as hysterical processes*, analogous to the rituals of cargo cults and other reactive movements.

SUMMARY AND CONCLUSIONS

Our epidemiological approach to understanding the etiology of various hysterical phenomena has generally adhered to the method described by Dunham (1966): "The epidemiological investigator focuses upon his data for any clues that point to causative factors whether encompassed by biological, physiological, psychological, or sociological theory" (p. 3). It is almost axiomatic that when the end point is comprehension of psychiatric phenomena, this methodological route is especially strewn with obstacles. Among these are diagnosis and identification of dynamics, which we have attempted to avoid by assuming at the onset that diagnostic terms obscure more than they reveal and by relying more on phenomenological, descriptive data. Another major problem is that of the theoretical *source* of the data—medical, psychiatric or anthropological, directly or indirectly reported. Unfortunately, in the present paper we have had to rely on indirect sources from the literature, but this has also allowed us to gain perspective by permitting a wide sampling of diverse viewpoints.

From this wide perspective, we have been able to observe certain patterns in hysterical phenomena across time, place, form of expression, and diagnostic orientation. We will attempt to describe these patterns in terms of the intersection of two theories: (1) the elaboration of psychosocial stress as a product of social change (Murphy and Leighton 1965, Leighton 1974), and (2) the view that hysterical phenomena, whether they occur at the individual, group, or societal level, are forms of adaptation to psychosocial stress.

Murphy and Leighton (1965) regarded as the crucial points in a theory of psychosocial stress the *manner* in which cultural changes occur and *what this implies* for individuals within this culture. Cultural change *per se* is not the cause of psychosocial stress, according to these authors; rather, it is whether and how individuals adapt to this change. Adaptation in societies is usually accomplished through role structure, which means that cultural change often imposes more strain on certain roles than on others, or conversely, that certain roles, because of their rigidity or other limitations, are less adaptive to change and thus suffer more strain.

Such a conception of differential acculturation could account for some of the observed patterns of hysterical expression in different cultures and in subgroups within these cultures. For example, it could help explain the prevalence of hysterical conversion reactions among lower socioeconomic classes in the United States or, in the cross-cultural context, among people who have recently migrated from rural to more urban settings and experienced cultural change on an individual level. A compound theory of psychosocial stress and hysterical expression suggests why reactive movements and hysterical contagion are especially common in certain parts of the world, such as Malaysia, which have been experiencing particularly rapid social change.

Sex roles, which constitute one of the most important aspects of the role structure in a society, not only pattern the expression of adaptive behaviors (which include hysterical phenomena), but often differentially absorb the impact of cultural change. Such may

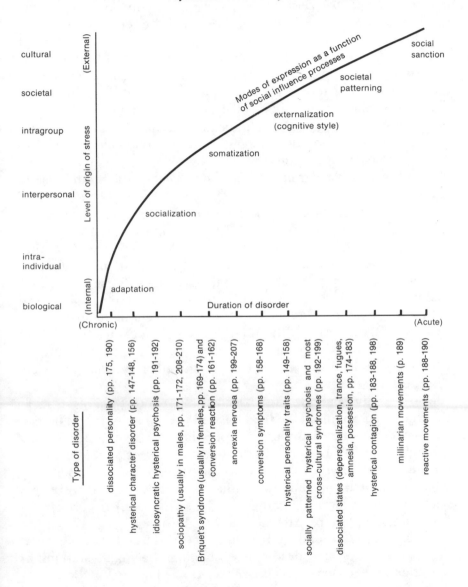

Figure 1: A Model of
Psychosocial Stress and Hysterical Expression

be the case with certain hysterical phenomena which appear with greater frequency among women—such as conversion hysteria in nineteenth century Europe or hysterical personality traits in the twentieth century. Although males may be equally prone to psychosocial stress in contemporary America, their way of expressing or adapting to this stress (various forms of soniopathy, for example), are usually not labeled hysterical. Our argument, in agreement with that of Blacker and Tupin in the previous chapter, is that these behaviors should be considered as hysterical phenomena on the basis of common psychosocial dynamics.

The approach to understanding hysterical phenomena which is being advocated here suggests a new system of categorization. To this end, we have diagrammed the theoretical thrust of our thesis in figure 1.

The horizontal dimension, duration of disorder reflects the proposal by Meares and Horvath (1972) that hysteria can be usefully considered in terms of chronicity versus acuteness. We believe that this reconceptualization of the more traditional distinct on of neurotic versus psychotic has several advantages. First, the various manifestations of hysterical phenomena align themselves more naturally along a chronic-acute than a psychotic-neurotic axis, where it is especially difficult to place *dissociative states* and *hysterical psychosis*. Secondly, an acute-chronic distinction more accurately reflects the untreated prognosis of various hystericel disorders.

At the individual level, the psychosocial context manifests itself through what Shapiro (1965) advocated as cognitive style. This can be viewed as the individual expression of psychosocial stress through socialized behavior patterns; the choice of pattern depends on one's sexual, age-level, or socioeconomic role and is tempered by genetic endowment and by conflicts encountered and responses learned in early familial interaction. (These topics are covered in the following chapters by Metcalf and by Horowitz.)

At the group, societal, end cultural levels, individual background variables are less important in explaining the manifestations of hysterical phenomena, as these higher-order factors function more in the *creation* of psychosocial stress and in its *shaping* of individual reaction to this stress. Thus, the further out one moves on the duration of disorder axis, the more likely hysterical phenomena are to be acute and have a social basis.

It should be noted that *hysterical psychosis* has two distinct locations in this scheme. One cross-cultural example of hysterical psychosis, *amok* (see Murphy 1973), has shifted in character with the passage of time from a disorder based on intragroup stress with a culturally patterned, and at times socially sanctioned, expression to being an episode within the more chronic psychiatric process of the narcissistically impaired hysterical personality. Thus, *amok* at the present time would be located more toward the chronic end of the duration-of-disorder dimension, and closer to the idiosyncratic manifestations of hysterical psychosis which are characteristic of Western cases.

The ordering of hysterical phenomena suggested in figure 1 appears to account for a number of findings in the literature, such as the lack of association between hysterical personality as a character disorder and hysterical contagion (indicated in figure 1 by the distance between these two disorders) and the correspondence between dissociative phenomena, which tend to be exacerbated or generated in a group context, and hysterical contagion (indicated by their contiguity in figure 1). Finally, this classification scheme provides a model for the distinction which many theorists are urging between *symptoms* and *character*. Thus, in figure 1, the three more characterological disorders—dissociated personality, hysterical character disorder, and idiosyncratic hysterical psychosis—are located at the chronic end of the duration-of-disorder dimension, and intersect at the intraindividual level of origin of stress. These disorders are separate from those which are more symptomatic in nature—e.g., Briquet's syndrome, conversion symptoms, and hysterical personality traits. This conceptualization would imply that conversion and dissociative symptoms share an etiological commonality across nosological boundaries. At the acute end of the spectrum, the more socially patterned phenomena are postulated to have an origin located outside of the "personality" and more in environmental interaction.

REFERENCES

Abraham, K.(1921). Contribution to a discussion on tic. In *Selected Papers on Psychoanalysis*. New York: Basic Books, 1966.

——— (1924). A short study of the development of the libido, viewed in the light of mental disorders. In *Selected Papers on Psychoanalysis*. New York: Basic Books, 1960.

Abse, D. W. (1966). *Hysteria and Related Mental Disorders: An Approach to Psychological Medicine*. Baltimore: Williams and Wilkins.

———(1974). Hysterical conversion and dissociative syndromes and the hysterical character. In *American Handbook of Psychiatry*, vol. 3, ed. S. Arieti and E. B. Brody. New York: Basic Books.

Ackerknecht, E. H. (1971). *Medicine and Ethnology: Selected Essays*. Ed. H. H. Walser and H. M. Koelbing. Baltimore: Johns Hopkins Press.

American Psychiatric Association (1952). *Diagnostic and Statistical Manual of Mental Disorders (DSM I)*. Washington, D.C.

——— (1968). *Diagnostic and Statistical Manual of Mental Disorders (DSM II)*. Washington, D.C.

Arkonac, O., and Guze, S. B. (1963). A family study of hysteria. *New England Journal of Medicine* 268: 239-242.

Bart, P. B. (1968). Social structure and vocabularies of discomfort: What happened to female hysteria? *Journal of Health and Social Behavior* 9: 188-193.

Bateson, G., Jackson, D. D., Haley, J., and Weakland, J. (1956). Toward a theory of schizophrenia. *Behavioral Science* 1: 241-264.

Benedict, R. (1934). *Patterns of Culture*. Boston: Houghton Mifflin.

Berger, D. M. (1971). Hysteria: in search of the animus. *Comprehensive Psychiatry* 12: 277-286.

Bernstein, N. R. (1969). Psychogenic seizures in adolescent girls. *Behavioral Neuropsychiatry* 1: 31-34.

Beumont, P. J. V., Beardwood, C. J., and Russell, G. F. M. (1972). The occurrence of the syndrome of anorexia nervosa in male subjects. *Psychological Medicine* 2:216-231.

Bibb, R. C., and Guze, S. B. (1972). Hysteria (Briquet's syndrome) in a psychiatric hospital: the significance of depression. *American Journal of Psychiatry* 128: 224-228.

Blinder, M. (1966). The hysterical personality. *Psychiatry* 29: 227-235.

Bourguignon, E. (1968). *A Cross-Cultural Study of Dissociational States*. Columbus: Ohio State University Press.

———, ed. (1973). *Religion, Altered States of Consciousness and Social Change*. Columbus: Ohio State University Press.

Boyer, L. B. (1964). Folk psychiatry of the Apaches of the Mascalero Indian Reservation. In *Magic, Faith, Healing: Studies in Primitive Psychiatry Today,* ed. A. Kiev. New York: Free Press.

Brauer, R., Harrow, M., and Tucker, G. J. (1970). Depersonalization phenomena in psychiatric patients. *British Journal of Psychiatry* 117: 509-515.

Bruch, H. (1965). Anoerxia nervosa and its differential diagnosis. *Journal of Nervous and Mental Diseases* 141: 555-556.

———(1969). Eating disorders in adolescence. *Proceedings of the American Psychopathological Association* 59: 181-196.

———(1970). Changing approaches to anorexia nervosa. In *Anorexia and Obesity,* ed. C. V. Rowland. International Psychiatry Clinics, vol. 7. Boston: Little, Brown.

———(1971). Anorexia nervosa in the male. *Psychosomatic Medicine* 33: 31-47.

———(1975). Obesity and anorexia nervosa: psychosocial aspects. *Australian and New Zealand Journal of Psychiatry* 9: 159-161

Burton-Bradley, B. G. (1974). Social change and psychosomatic response in Papua, New Guinea. *Psychotherapy and Psychosomatics* 23: 229-239.

Bustamante, J. A. (1967/1968). Cultural factors in hysterias with a schizophrenic clinical picture. *International Journal of Social Psychiatry* 14: 113-118.

Cameron, N. (1963). *Personality Development and Psychopathology: A Dynamic Approach.* Boston: Houghton Mifflin.

Cannavale, F. J., Scarr, H. A., and Pepitone, A. (1970). Deindividuation in the small group: further evidence. *Journal of Personality and Social Psychology* 16: 141-147.

Carden, N. L., and Schramel, D. J. (1966). Observations of conversion reactions seen in troops involved in the Viet Nam conflict. *American Journal of Psychiatry* 1: 21-31.

Cattell, J. P., and Cattell, J. S. (1974). Depersonalization: psychological and social perspectives. In *American Handbook of Psychiatry,* vol. 3, ed. S. Arieti. New York: Basic Books.

Champion, F. P., Taylor, R., Joseph, P. R., and Hedden, J. C. (1963). Mass hysteria associated with insect bites. *Journal of South Carolina Medical Association* 59: 351-353.

Chodoff, P. (1954). A re-examination of some aspects of conversion hysteria. *Psychiatry* 17: 75-81.

———(1974). The diagnosis of hysteria: an overview. *American Journal of Psychiatry* 131: 1073-1078.

Chodoff, P., and Lyons, H. (1958). Hysteria, the hysterical personality and "hysterical" conversion. *American Journal of Psychiatry* 114: 734-740.

Cloninger, C. R., and Guze, S. B. (1970). Psychiatric illness and female criminality: the role of sociopathy and hysteria in the antisocial woman. *American Journal of Psychiatry* 127: 303-311.

———(1975). Hysteria and parental psychiatric illness. *Psychological Medicine* 5: 27-31.

Crisp, A. H. (1965). Some aspects of the evolution, presentation, and follow-up of anorexia nervosa. *Proceedings of the Royal Society of Medicine* 58: 814-820.

Crisp, A. H., and Kalucy, R. S. (1974). Aspects of the perceptual disorder in anorexia nervosa. *British Journal of Medical Psychology* 47: 349-361.

Crisp, A. H., and Toms, D. A. (1972). Primary anorexia nervosa or weight phobia in the male: report on thirteen cases. *British Medical Journal* 1: 334-338.

Depersonalization syndromes (1972). *British Medical Journal* 4: 378.

DSM I and *II*. See American Psychiatric Association.

Dube, K. C., and Kumar, N. (1974). An epidemiological study of hysteria. *Journal of Biosocial Science* 6: 401-405.

Dubreuil, G. and Wittkower, E. D. (1976). Psychiatric anthropology: a historical perspective. *Psychiatry* 39: 130-141.

Duddle, M. (1973). An increase of anorexia nervosa in a university population. *British Journal of Psychiatry* 123: 711-712.

Dunham, H. W. (1966). Epidemiology of psychiatric disorders as a contribution to medical ecology. *Archives of General Psychiatry* 14: 1-19.

Early, L. F., and Lifschutz, J. E. (1974). A case of stigmata. *Archives of General Psychiatry* 30: 197-200.

Easser, B., and Lesser, S. (1965). The hysterical personality: a reevaluation. *Psychoanalytic Quarterly* 34: 390-405.

Ebrahim, G. J. (1968). Mass hysteria in school children: notes on 3 outbreaks in East Africa. *Clinical Pediatrics* 7: 437-438.

Edwards, J. G. (1970). The *koro* pattern of depersonalization in an American schizophrenic patient. *American Journal of Psychiatry* 126: 1171-1173.

Edwards, J. G., and Angus, J. W. S. (1972). Depersonalization. *British Journal of Psychiatry* 120: 242-244.

Eysenck, H. J. (1957). *The Dynamics of Anxiety and Hysteria: An Experimental Application of Modern Learning Theory to Psychiatry.* New York: Praeger.

Faigel, H. C. (1968). "The wandering womb": mass hysteria in school girls. *Clinical Pediatrics* 7: 377-383.

Farley, J., Woodruff, R. A., and Guze, S. B. (1968). The prevalence of hysteria and conversion symptoms. *British Journal of Psychiatry* 114: 1121-1125.

Fenichel, O. (1945). *The Psychoanalytic Theory of Neurosis*. New York: Norton.

Festinger, L., Pepitone, A., and Newcomb, T. (1952). Some consequences of deindividuation in a group. *Journal of Abnormal and Social Psychology* 47: 382-389.

Fisher, C. (1945). Amnesic states in war neuroses: the psychogenesis of fugues. *Psychoanalytic Quarterly* 14: 437-468.

Forbis, O. L., and Janes, R. H., Jr. (1965). Hysteria in childhood. *Southern Medical Journal* 58: 1221-1225.

Foulks, E. F. (1972). *The Arctic Hysterias*. Washington, D.C.: American Anthropological Association.

Freud, S. (1900) The interpretation of dreams. *Standard Edition* 4/5: 1-630.

———(1931). Libidinal types. *Standard Edition* 21: 215-222.

Friedman, T. (1967). Methodological considerations and research needs in the study of epidemic hysteria. *American Journal of Public Health* 57: 2009-2011.

Gatfield, P. D., and Guze, S. B. (1962). Prognosis and differential diagnosis of conversion reactions. *Diseases of the Nervous System* 23: 623-631.

Gelfman, M. (1971). Dynamics of the correlations between hysteria and depression. *American Journal of Psychotherapy* 25: 83-92.

Glenn, M. L. (1970). Religious conversion and the mystical experience. *Psychiatric Quarterly* 44: 636-651.

Goodman, F. D. (1972). *Speaking in Tongues: A Cross-Cultural Study of Glossolalia*. Chicago: University of Chicago Press.

Greenbaum, L. (1973). Societal correlates of possession trance in sub-Sahara Africa. In *Religion, Altered States of Consciousness and Social Change*, ed. E. Bourguignon, Columbus: Ohio State University Press.

Guze, S. B. (1964). Conversion symptoms in criminals. *American Journal of Psychiatry* 121: 580-583.

———(1967). The diagnosis of hysteria: what are we trying to do? *American Journal of Psychiatry* 124: 491-498.

Guze, S. B., Allen, D. H., and Grollmus, J. M. (1962). The prevalence of Hyperemesis Gravidarum: a study of 162 psychiatric and 98 medical patients. *American Journal of Obstetrics and Gynecology* 84: 1859-1864.

Guze, S. B., Woodruff, R. A., and Clayton, P. J. (1973). Sex, age, and the diagnosis of hysteria (Briquet's syndrome). *American Journal of Psychiatry* 129: 745-748.

Halleck, S. (1967). Hysterical personality traits—psychological, social, and iatrogenic determinants. *Archives of General Psychiatry* 16: 750-757.

Halmi, K. A. (1974). Anorexia nervosa: demographic and clinical features in 94 cases. *Psychosomatic Medicine* 361:18-26.

Helvie, C. O. (1968). An epidemic of hysteria in a high school. *The Journal of School Health* 38: 505-508.

Hinsie, L., and Campbell, P. (1970). *Psychiatric Dictionary.* 4th ed. New York: Oxford.

Hollender, M. H. (1972). Conversion hysteria: a post-Freudian reinterpretation of nineteenth century psycho-social data. *Archives of General Psychiatry* 26: 311-314.

Hollender, M. H., and Hirsch, S. J. (1964). Hysterical psychosis. *American Journal of Psychiatry* 120: 1066-1074.

Hollingshead, A. B., and Redlich, F. C. (1958). *Social Class and Mental Illness.* New York: Wiley.

Horton, P., and Miller, D. (1972). The etiology of multiple personality. *Comprehensive Psychiatry* 13: 151-159.

Jacobs, N. (1965). The phantom slasher of Taipei: mass hysteria in a non-Western society. *Social Problems* 12: 318-322.

Kagwa, B. H. (1964). The problem of mass hysteria in East Africa. *East African Medical Journal* 31: 561-566.

Kaminsky, M. J., and Slavney, P. R. (1976). Methodology and personality in Briquet's syndrome: a reappraisal. *American Journal of Psychiatry* 133: 85-88.

Kendell, R. E., Hall, D. J., Hailey, A., and Babigian, H. M. (1973). The epidemiology of anorexia nervosa. *Psychological Medicine* 3: 200-203.

Kerckhoff, A. C., and Back, K. W. (1968). *The June Bug: A Study of Hysterical Contagion.* New York: Appleton-Century-Crofts.

Kernberg, O. (1967). Borderline personality organization. *Journal of the American Psychoanalytic Association* 15: 641-685.

Kiev, A. (1967). Psychotherapy in Haitian Voodoo. *American Journal of Psychotherapy* 21: 469-476.

Kimble, R., William, J. G., and Agras, S. (1975). A comparison of two methods of diagnosing hysteria. *American Journal of Psychiatry* 132: 1197-1199.

Kirkpatrick, R. G. (1975). Collective consciousness and mass hysteria: collective behavior and anti-pornography crusades in Durkheimian perspective. *Human Relations* 28: 63-84.

Kirshner, L. A. (1973). Dissociative reactions: an historical review and clinical study. *Acta Psychiatrica Scandanavica* 49: 698-711.

Kline, M. S. (1963). Psychiatry in Indonesia. *American Journal of Psychiatry* 119: 809-815.

Knight, J. A., Friedman, T. I., and Sulianti, J. (1965). Epidemic hysteria; a field study. *American Journal of Public Health* 55: 858-865.
Kolb, L. C. (1968). *Noyes' Modern Clinical Psychiatry.* 7th ed. Philadelphia: W. B. Saunders.
Kretschmer, E. (1960). *Hysteria, Reflex, and Instinct.* Trans. V. Baskin and W. Baskin. New York: Philosophical Library.
La Barre, W. (1962). *They Shall Take Up Serpents.* Minneapolis: Minnesota University Press.
———(1970). *The Ghost Dance: The Origins of Religion.* Garden City: Doubleday.
Langness, L. L. (1967). Hysterical psychosis—the cross-cultural evidence. *American Journal of Psychiatry* 124: 143-151.
Laplanche, J. (1974). Panel on 'hysteria today.' *International Journal of Psycho-analysis* 55: 459-469.
Lazare, A. (1971). The hysterical character in psychoanalytic theory—evolution and confusion. *Archives of General Psychiatry* 25: 131-137.
Lazare, A., and Klerman, G. L, (1968). Hysteria and depression: the frequency and significance of hysterical personality features in hospitalized depressed women. *American Journal of Psychiatry* 124: 48-56.
Lazare, A., Klerman, G. L., and Armor, D. J. (1966). Oral, obsessive and hysterical personality patterns. *Archives of General Psychiatry* 14: 624-630.
Lee, R. B. (1968). The sociology of !Kung Bushman trance performances. In *Trance and Possession States,* ed. R. Prince. Montreal: R. M. Burke Memorial Society.
Lehmann, L. S. (1974). Depersonalization. *American Journal of Psychiatry* 131: 1221-1224.
Leighton, A. H. (1974). Social disintegration and mental disorder. In *American Handbook of Psychiatry,* vol. 2, ed. S. Arieti. New York: Basic Books.
Leighton, A. H., and Murphy, T. M. (1965). Cross-cultural psychiatry. In *Approaches to Cross-Cultural Psychiatry,* ed. T. M. Murphy and A. H. Leighton. Ithaca: Cornell University Press.
Lerner, H. E. (1974). The hysterical personality: a "woman's disease." *Comprehensive Psychiatry* 15: 157-164.
Levine, R. J., Romm, F. J., Sexton, D. J., Wood, B. T., and Kaiser, J. (1974). Outbreak of psychosomatic illness at a rural elementary school. *Lancet* 11: 1500-1503.
Lewis, A. (1975). The survival of hysteria. *Psychologial Medicine* 5: 9-12.

Lewis, W. C. (1974). Hysteria: The consultant's dilemma. *Archives of General Psychiatry* 30: 145-151.

Lewis, W. C., and Berman, M. (1965). Studies of conversion hysteria. *Archives of General Psychiatry* 13: 275-282.

Lindberg, B. J., and Lindegard, B. (1963). Studies of the hysteroid personality attitude. *Acta Psychiatrica Scandanavica* 39: 170-180.

Linton, R. (1943). Natavistic movements. *American Anthropologist* 45: 230-240.

———(1956). *Culture and Mental Disorders.* Springfield: Charles C Thomas.

Looff, D. D. (1970). Psychophysiologic and conversion reactions in children. *Journal of the American Academy of Child Psychiatry* 9: 318-331.

Lower, R. B. (1972). Affect changes in depersonalization. *Psychoanalytical Review* 59: 565-577.

Ludwig, A. M. (1972). Hysteria: a neurobiological theory. *Archives of General Psychiatry* 27: 771-777.

Luisada, P., and Peele, R., and Pittard, E. (1974). The hysterical personality in men. *American Journal of Psychiatry* 131: 518-522.

Lyons, H. A., and Potter, P. E. (1970). Communicated hysteria—an episode in a secondary school. *Journal of the Irish Medical Association* 63: 377-379.

McKegney, F. P. (1967). The incidence and characteristics of patients with conversion reactions I: a general hospital consultation service sample. *American Journal of Psychiatry* 124: 542-545.

Mackinnon, R. A., and Michels, R. (1971). *The Psychiatric Interview in Clinical Practice.* Philadelphia: W. B. Saunders.

Maguigad, E. L. (1964). Psychiatry in the Phillipines. *American Journal of Psychiatry* 121: 21-25.

Malmquist, C. P. (1971). Hysteria in childhood. *Postgraduate Medicine* 50: 112-117.

Margetts, E. L. (1976). The semantics of hysteria continued. *American Journal of Psychiatry* 133: 103.

Marmor, J. (1953). Orality in the hysterical personality. *Journal of the American Psychoanalytic Association* 1: 656-671.

Martin, P. A. (1971). Dynamic considerations of the hysterical psychosis. *American Journal of Psychiatry* 128: 745-748.

Meares, R., and Horvath, T. (1972). "Acute" and "chronic" hysteria. *British Journal of Psychiatry* 121: 653-657.

Medalia, N. Z., and Larsen, O. (1958). Diffusion and belief in a collective delusion: the Seattle windshield pitting epidemic. *American Sociological Review* 23: 180-186.

Meth, J. M. (1974). Exotic psychiatric syndromes. In *American Handbook of Psychiatry*, vol. 3, ed. S. Arieti and E. B. Brody. New York: Basic Books.

Meyer, J. E. (1971). Anorexia nervosa of adolescence: the central syndrome of the anorexia nervosa group. *British Journal of Psychiatry* 118: 539-542.

Moss, P. D., and McEvedy, C. P. (1966). An epidemic of overbreathing among school girls. *British Medical Journal* 2: 1295-1300.

Muhangi, J. R. (1973). A preliminary report on "mass hysteria" in an Ankole school in Uganda. *East African Medical Journal* 50: 304-308.

Murphy, H. B. M. (1973). History and the evolution of syndromes: the striking case of *latah* and *amok*. In *Psychopathology: Contributions from the Social, Behavioral, and Biological Sciences*, ed. M. Hammer, K. Salzinger, and S. Sutton. New York: Wiley.

Murphy, J. M., and Leighton, A. H. (1965). Native conceptions of psychiatric disorder. In *Approaches to Cross-Cultural Psychiatry*, ed. J. M. Murphy and A. H. Leighton. Ithaca: Cornell University Press.

Ngui, P. W. (1969). The *koro* epidemic in Singapore. *Australia and New Zealand Journal of Psychiatry* 3: 263-266.

Olczak, P. V., Donnerstein, E., Hershberger, T. J., and Kahn, I. (1971). Group hysteria and the MMPI. *Psychological Reports* 28: 413-414.

Pankow, G. W. (1974). The body image in hysterical psychosis. *International Journal of Psycho-analysis* 55: 407-414.

Perley, M. J., and Guze, S. B. (1962). Hysteria—the stability and usefulness of clinical criteria. *The New England Journal of Medicine* 266: 421-426.

Pfeiffer, P. H. (1964). Mass hysteria masquerading as food poisoning. *Journal of the Maine Medical Association* 55: 27.

Polk, L. D. (1974). Mass hysteria in an elementary school. *Clinical Pediatrics* 13: 1013-1014.

Prince, M. (1906). *The Dissociation of a Personality*. New York: Longmans, Green.

———(1929). *Clinical and Experimental Studies in Personality*. Cambridge, Mass.: Sci-Art Publishers.

Proctor, J. T. (1958). Hysteria in childhood. *American Journal of Orthopsychiatry* 28: 394-407.

Prosen, H. (1967). Sexuality in females with "hysteria." *American Journal of Psychiatry* 124: 687-692.

Rabkin, R. (1964). Conversion hysteria as social maladaptation. *Psychiatry* 27: 349-363.

Rangell, L. (1959). The nature of conversion. *Journal of the American Psychoanalytic Association* 7: 632-662.

Reed, J. L. (1975). The diagnosis of "hysteria." *Psychological Medicine* 5: 13-17.

Reich, W. (1933). *Character Analysis*. New York: Farrar, Straus and Giroux, 1972.

Richman, J., and White, H. A. (1970). A family view of hysterical psychosis. *American Journal of Psychiatry* 127: 280-285.

Robins, E., Purtell, J., Cohen, M., and Mandel, E. (1952). "Hysteria" in men. *New England Journal of Medicine* 246: 677-

Rock, N. L. (1971). Conversion reactions in childhood: a clinical study on childhood neuroses. *Journal of the American Academy of Child Psychiatry* 10: 65-93.

Rowland, C. R., Jr. (1970). Anorexia nervosa: a survey of the literature and review of 30 cases. *Anorexia and Obesity*, vol. 7, ed. C. R. Rowland. Boston: Little, Brown.

Schafer, R. (1948). *Clinical Application of Psychological Tests*. New York: International Universities Press.

Shapiro, D. (1965). *Neurotic Styles*. New York: Basic Books.

Siomopoulus, V. (1972). Derealization and deja vu: formal mechanisms. *American Journal of Psychotherapy* 26: 84-89.

Sirois, F. (1973). Les épidémies d'hystérie: Revue de la Littérature, réflexions sur le problème de la contagion psychopathologique. *L'Union Medicale du Canada* 102: 1906-1915.

Sirois, F. (1974). Epidemic hysteria. *Acta Psychiatrica Scandanavica (Suppl.)* 252: 11-46.

Slater, E. (1965). Diagnosis of hysteria. *British Medical Journal* 1: 395-399.

Slavney, P. R., and McHugh, P. R. (1974). The hysterical personality. *Archives of General Psychiatry* 30: 325-332.

———(1975). The hysterical personality: an attempt at validation with the MMPI. *Archives of General Psychiatry* 32: 186-190.

Slotkin, J. S. (1965). The peyote way. In *Reader in Comparative Religion: An Anthropological Approach*, ed. W. A. Lessa and E. Z. Vogt. New York: Harper.

Smelser, N. (1962). *Theory of Collective Behavior*. New York: Free Press.

Sours, J. A. (1974). The anorexia nervosa syndrome. *International Journal of Psycho-Analysis* 55: 567-576.

Sperling, M. (1973). Conversion hysteria and conversion symptoms: a revision of classifications and concepts. *Journal of the American Psychoanalytic Association* 21: 745-772.

Spindler, G. D. (1968). Psychocultural adaptation. In *The Study of Personality: An Interdisciplinary Appraisal*, ed. E. Norbeck, New York: Holt, Rinehart and Winston.

Stahl, S. M., and Lebedun, M. (1974). Mystery gas: an analysis of mass hysteria. *Journal of Health and Social Behavior* 15: 44-50.

Stephens, J. H., and Kamp, M. (1962). On some aspects of hysteria: a clinical study. *Journal of Nervous and Mental Disease* 134: 305.

Szasz, T. S. (1961). *The Myth of Mental Illness: Foundations of a Theory of Personal Conduct.* New York: Hoeber-Harper.

Talmon, Y. (1965). Pursuit of the millennium: the relation between religions and social change. In *Reader in Comparative Religion: An Anthropological Approach,* ed. W. A. Lessa and E. Z. Vogt, New York: Harper.

Taylor, W. S., and Martin, M. F. (1944). Multiple personality. *Journal of Abnormal and Social Psychology* 39: 281-300.

Teoh, J. I. (1972). The changing psychopathology of *amok. Psychiatry* 35: 345-351.

Teoh, J. I., Soewondo, S., and Sidharta, M. (1975). Epidemic hysteria in Malaysian schools: an illustrative episode. *Psychiatry* 38: 258-268.

Teoh, J. I., and Yeoh, K. (1973). Cultural conflict and transition: epidemic hysteria and social sanction. *Australian and New Zealand Journal of Psychiatry* 7: 283-293.

Theander, S. (1970). Anorexia nervosa. *Acta Psychiatrica Scandanavica (Suppl.)* 214: 1-194.

Thigpen, C. H., and Cleckley, H. (1954). A case of multiple personality. *Journal of Abnormal and Social Psychology* 49: 135-151.

————(1957). *The Three Faces of Eve.* New York: McGraw-Hill.

Tucker, G. H., Harrow, M., and Quinlan, D. (1973). Depersonalization, dysphoria, and thought disturbance. *American Journal of Psychiatry* 130: 702-706.

Tupin, J. P. (1974). Hysterical and cyclothymic personalities. In *Personality Disorders: Diagnosis and Management,* ed., J. R. Lion, pp. 70-84. Baltimore: Williams and Wilkins.

Weinstein, E. A., Eck, R. A., and Lyerly, O. G. (1969). Conversion hysteria in Appalachia. *Psychiatry* 32: 334-341.

Wheeler, L. (1966). Toward a theory of behavioral contagion. *Psychological Review* 73: 179-192.

Wholey, C. C. (1933). A case of multiple personality. *American Journal of Psychiatry* 89: 653-688.

Wittels, F. (1930). The hysterical character. *Medical Review of Reviews* 36: 186-190.

Wittkower, E. D., and Dubreuil, G. (1968). Cultural factors in mental illness. In *The Study of Personality: An Interdisciplinary Appraisal,* ed. E. Norbeck. New York: Holt, Rinehart and Winston.

Woerner, P. I., and Guze, S. B. (1968). A family and marital study of hysteria. *British Journal of Psychiatry* 114: 161-168.

Wolowitz, H. M. (1972) Hysterical character and feminine identity. In *Readings in the Psychology of Women*, ed. J. M. Bardwick. New York: Harper.

Woodruff, R. A. (1967). Hysteria: an evaluation of objective diagnostic criteria by the study of women with chronic medical illness. *British Journal of Psychiatry* 114: 1115-1119.

Woodruff, R. A., Clayton, P. J., and Guze, S. B. (1971). Hysteria: studies of diagnosis, outcome, and prevalence. *Journal of the American Medical Association* 215: 425-428.

Worsley, P. (1968). *The Trumpet Shall Sound*. New York: Shocken.

Yap, P. M. (1952). The *latah* reaction: its pathodynamics and nosological position. *Journal of Mental Science* 98: 515-564.

Zetzel, E. (1968). The so-called good hysteric. *International Journal of Psycho-analysis* 49: 256-260.

Ziegler, D. K. (1967). Neurological disease and hysteria: the differential diagnosis. *International Journal of Neuropsychiatry* 3: 388-396.

Ziegler, F. F., Imboden, J. B., and Meyer, E. (1960). Contemporary conversion reactions: a clinical study. *American Journal of Psychiatry* 116: 901-910.

Zimbardo, P. G. (1969). The human choice: individuation, reason, and order vs. deindividuation, impulse, and chaos. *Nebraska Symposium on Motivation* 17: 237-307.

Zimbardo, P. G., and Maslach, C. (1971). Liberating behavior from time-bound control: expanding the present through hypnosis. *Journal of Applied Social Psychology* 1: 305-323.

CHAPTER 4

Childhood: From Process To Structure

AUBREY METCALF, M.D.

One fruitful avenue toward understanding the problems of adults has been the study of similar conditions in childhood, where the antecedents of later disorder can often be delineated. With matters hysterical, of course, there are plenty of examples of conversion phenomena in childhood and some of what appears to be hysteria proper. These are the discrete and sometimes striking symptom complexes and behaviors that make the hysterical disorders so provocative in both children and adults. But, is there a personality type, a style of thinking and acting, that underlies and gives rise to these symptoms in children as in adults? If there is a hysterical character disorder in adults, is there also then a hysterical character disorder in children, and does the former often or always proceed from the latter?

It seems prudent to say from the outset that observation and treatment of children indicates that what is ordinarily meant by character disorder does not occur in children. That is, the stable and predictable configuration of inadequate or pathological thought and behavior which is the hallmark of character disorder in the adult cannot ordinarily be ascribed to the child of preschool and grammar school age. As a matter of fact, many of the traits associated with hysterical personality are a part of normal development in children.

Yet the issue is by no means so easily set aside. Everyone knows that even small children have characteristic ways of responding that are predictable. Many children have "styles" that can be recognized through their series of developmental stages, even if the manifest behavior is different. The question persists then in modified form; can a hysterical style of behavior be identified in childhood, does it predispose to hysterical character later in life and, if so, how does it come about?

It is beyond the scope of this chapter to review personality theory, of which the understanding of hysterical phenomena and the roots of the hysterical character are but a part. The aim here is to examine the milieu, intrapsychic and interpersonal, within which a child may develop a hysterical style of behavior. In attempting to do this it is inevitable that the laws governing the formation of all personality types will be invoked.

THE ORIGINS OF ADULT CHARACTER DISORDER

Before considering the question of hysterical personality in children, it will be well to begin on more familiar ground through a consideration of the problems met in understanding adult character disorders. It is inevitable, in the psychotherapy of many adults, for the therapist to become aware that the patient has a characteristic manner of thinking, feeling, and behaving which, although inefficient and sometimes downright destructive, seems relatively free from intrapsychic conflict in the usual sense. It is as if the patient no longer is aware of conflict, or had effectively become inured to it. These ways of feeling and behaving seem, to the observer, to have an enduring, almost automatic feel, as if whatever nascent conflict and pathologic learning originally produced them had precipitated into a smoothly functioning set of behavioral systems, a solid psychic structure, which is much less susceptible to insight and change than more current neurotic problems. This is especially true for many of those patients who are finally classed, somewhat despairingly at times, as hysterical characters.

We make the assumption that the rather inflexible personality structure we see in these adult patients was once more supple, more apparently conflictful and ambivalent, and thus more amenable to resolution than it appears to be in the present. Projecting backward through our patient's life, we infer that there was a time when the patient had the potential to develop alternative routes of behavior and feeling. We may even isolate, through meticulous and repeated recollections and insights in therapy, those periods in the patient's life where specific environmental conditions interacted with specific intrapsychic states to produce specific sequelae. Dynamic theories of psychopathology have been built on these retrospective reconstructions, and in therapy there are few alternative ways to proceed. But when we use these theories for anterospective prediction the result is much less convincing. Freud (1920) was alive to this problem when he wrote:

> So long as we trace development from its final outcome backwards, the chain of events appears continuous and we feel we have gained in insight which is completely satisfactory and even exhaustive. But if we proceed the reverse way, if we start from the premises inferred from the analysis and try to follow these up to the final result, then we no longer get the impression of an inevitable sequence of events which could not have been otherwise determined. We notice at once that there might have been another result, and that we might have been just as well able to understand and explain the latter. . . .Hence the chain of causation can always be recognized with certainty if we follow the line of analysis, whereas to predict. . .is impossible. [p. 167]

Everyone believes that early interpersonal experience is of the greatest importance in development, but scientific data is difficult to gather. The most glaring lack in theoretical formulations about the hysterical character is a firsthand study of the interpersonal relationships of the yet-to-become-hysterical patient while he or she is still a child. Aside from gross neglect and abuse, those more subtle factors which we suspect to underlie many psychological maldevelopments—behaviors reflecting unconscious ambivalence toward the child, narcissistic projections onto the child, symbiosis with the child, and so forth—are often not obvious to superficial examination and checklist questioning. Nothing in cumulative therapeutic work with children and their parents is more secure than the fact that unconscious parental attitudes are effectively communicated to the child (including the necessity that they remain unconscious) and that through thousands of interactions, the child is inaugurated as a family participant with his or her unique role to play in the interactions and peculiar style of the family. These facts are, nevertheless, hard to prove. Since these roles and styles are beyond the conscious recognition of the persons involved, they are unlikely to be reported, even if the examiners know what they're looking for; and unless the interactions of the family are witnessed in person, direct retrieval of the matrix that brings this about is lost.

What we are usually faced with in treatment of adults is the need to understand the antecedents of personality deriving from complicated emotional events in a child through that child's memory resudues twenty or thirty years later. This attempt is, of course, open to the gravest scientific criticism (Garmezy 1974) and yet it has been and continues to be the main source of internal data illuminating the formation of personality, healthy and pathological. It is certainly a frequent experience in long-term psychotherapy and psychoanalysis that as emotional conflict recedes with treatment, events and persons from the patient's past become more clearly dimensional and humanly understandable than when first reported in diagnostic evaluation and early treatment. One might imagine that in the most serious disorders of childhood, studied while the patient is still a child, reconstruction of the etiological conditions might be clearer. This is not the case. Walker and Szurek (1973) describe serious drawbacks in using even well observed and recorded retrospective data from parents on the early childhood development of their psychotic child as far as drawing warranted scientific statements from them is concerned. What they found is that prolonged therapeutic work prepared only *some* parents for remembering painful events, feelings, and conflict states of possible significance in the evolution of their child's disorder.

What is lacking are well designed *prospective* studies that include sufficient objective observations of the child and family on the one hand and internal, clinical data from each on the other. From this, valid correlations could be made of the intrapsychic and the interpersonal roots of personality and pathology and their interrelationships. Until such time as these studies are made, explanations of the origins of personality must remain tentative.

Progress in theoretical formulations. As far as the origins of hysterical personality are concerned, one thing has become certain as time has gone on; issues once apparently settled simply and elegantly by early writers, such as the relationship between hysteria and conversion, seem now to be much more complicated. In working backward from adult patients with hysterical disorders Freud, Reich, and Fenechel found an incomplete oedipal resolution in persons who were otherwise relatively well developed. They felt the manifestations of the illness indicated that the patient's personality was fixated at the phallic stage. This formulation held sway for many years.

Beginning with a paper by Marmor (1953), reviewed in the previous chapter, the literature reflected the common experience that the preoedipal history of most patients with hysterical symptoms revealed intense frustration of oral needs and that there was a marked tendency for oral features to predominate in these hysterical symptoms. Adding weight to the argument, Marmor pointed to the relationship of hysteria to addiction and to schizophrenia, both of which seem associated with early pathology. It became clear that for many patients with hysterical symptoms problems originating in a phase of development much earlier than the oedipal must play a part. In the ensuing debate, conversion was recognized by many as an expression of forbidden wishes in symbolic form, or via body language, or as a way to escape life-threatening stress, at almost any age or stage of development and in almost any pathological personality configuration (Rangell 1959, Ludwig 1972).

Lazare (1971) has reviewed the psychoanalytic theory of the hysterical character and finds a number of more recent writers in agreement that the group of patients with hysterical traits and oedipal symptoms include a broad spectrum from those with serious pregenital problems to those with conflicts only at the phallic level. These poles differ in regard to object relations, mechanisms of defense, levels of fixation and integration, and the maturity of the synthetic functions of the ego. These patients may share traits in common, but they are more apt to be exaggerated in the "sicker," that is, the more immature, orally fixated group. Thus the sicker patients show more blatant and infantile hysterical symptoms than the healthier ones do.

This way of looking at the continuum of personality forms is helpful when used to consider childhood personality as well. Its use is made easier by virtue of the fact that the life experience of the latency child does not provide for the development of the skill or the complexity of repetoire that an adult would possess in seeking the very same immature goals. For this reason children are more direct and simple in their behavior and more transparent in their aims than an adult would ordinarily be. A child seeking a relatively oedipal relationship with an adult through sexualized behavior will act in a strikingly different manner from a child sexualizing her attempts to elicit more regressive satisfactions. For example, a sensitive adult observer might be shocked by his own beginning erotic response to a seductive advance by a child who had achieved the phallic stage of libidinal development. That same observer is not likely to be moved by the blatant sexual provocations of a youngster whose behavior stems from earlier phases.

The level of personality development may be more apparent in children. This distinction usually is not so easily seen in the two types of adult hysteric. The more immature adult still may command rather sophisticated behavior that initially belies its regressive source.

The idea of oral pathology as the basis of hysterical symptoms is natural to our understanding that more primitive patterns of behavior are learned first and most thoroughly, especially those learned in relation to the first attachment figure. Such behavior is resorted to automatically later, when more mature behavior is opposed or otherwise fails to achieve its goal. The normal child, in contradistinction to the normal adult, quickly retreats to these earlier behavioral systems on being stressed or disappointed. The firmly put-to-bed toddler may comfort himself by sucking his thumb after his mother leaves. He may throw a tantrum when a toy is snatched away by another child. Above all, he is egocentric and naturally sees the world strictly as it relates to him. This tendency does not make the child an oral character. Such classification only makes sense when immature traits in an older child or adult predominate where the stage of physical and social maturity calls for more adaptive abilities. The critical feature is the phase-appropriateness and effectiveness of ego functions and the mechanisms of defense.

CULTURE AND CHARACTER PATHOLOGY

The diagnosis of character pathology is always a relative matter in which culture plays a very prominent part. The description of the influence of culture on the formation of character is a whole discipline in itself and cannot be adequately reviewed here. It rests, however, on the same hypothesis that underlies our grasp of how the mother, and later the family, influence the developing infant. The early cultural anthropologists, guided by psychoanalytic theory, found that Freud's thesis that sexual development determined character was inadequate to the data. Their material required an interpersonal theory in addition. Just as it seemed evident that the varieties of maternal response affected the direction taken by the drive derivatives in infancy, so it seemed to Fromme and Horney that cultural influences, brought to the child by the family and the subgroup, guided the development of behavior in all parts of personality, including the sexual. Opler (1969) points out that the struggle which produces character is not just between libidinal wishes and some sort of internal ego-control principle, but between actual living persons, the child and his models—mother, family, and subgroup. Erickson (1963) has attempted an elaborate extrapolation of the psychosexual theory of development to take into account the influences of culture.

That culture may incline toward hysterical symptomatology and character seems evident from the study of some social structures. An example of this is the hysterical style of the male children in some Latin cultures where both fathers and mothers dote on the son's machismo. What may serve well enough in a Central American hamlet or an ethnic subgroup in the ghetto may not be sufficient for the interpersonal requirements of a modern large city. What works on the playground or in certain families may not be up to the complications met with later in life. Youngsters developing the hysterical role do not often become patients because they are either acting like their parents or acting out for their parents and culture, and are thus not seen as disordered. Indeed, they are not disordered from a cultural point of view unless their symptoms are too discordant with the social group or their own functioning. For example, LaBarre and LaBarre (1965) report a well-studied and followed case of cultural conditioning in a twelve-year-old prepubertal child raised in the Bible Belt of the South. In this case the conditioning eventually led to hysterical blindness. Here the matter must be left in favor of pursuing a further inquiry into the development of hysterical pathology in any one child.

A GENERIC DEFINITION OF CHARACTER PATHOLOGY

Bearing in mind the influence of the family and of society on personality formation, a generic definition of character pathology may be attempted. Character pathology exists when the individual has developed few alternative strategies to adapt to environmental demands despite the fact that the environment does not prevent such development. It exists where resilience of ego functions under stress is lacking and most especially where the patterns of adaptation are themselves sources of conflict with the environment. Such might be true, say, of the man who resorts repeatedly to picking a fight when some barroom opinion of his meets effective rebuttal.

A character disorder can be inferred only when less effective and more regressive behavior consistently occurs where the interpersonal and social situation calls for—and would permit—more effective and mature behavior. This situation is much less frequently the case in childhood than in adult life because of the impressive effect of the personal relationships the child has with his care-givers.

In analogy to the example given above, when a frustrated child strikes another child the behavior of the adults is definitive in bringing about reinforcement, suppression, or evolution of alternatives to this form of action. If the parent encourages or demands that the child fight, there will be a strong impetus for this social response to occur and persist even when the situation calls for and would permit more sophisticated arbitration. The development of more mature behavior is hampered by the general unsatisfactory nature of an aggressive response, which itself brings on further frustration and provokes further regression and a sense of ineffectuality. If, on the other hand, suppression of the self-assertive impulse is required, without indication of how the situation could be better handled, and especially when there is the strong implication that to assert oneself is bad, then the stage is set for submissive behavior with internalization of a conflictful and guilty self-attitude. In either case, the child is effectively held back from the elaboration of conflict-free behavioral systems which bring satisfaction; and if the situation goes on long enough beyond those epigenetic phases of childhood where learning more adaptive behavior is appropriate, then it becomes more and more difficult to change and will appear more and more like the character pathology described in adults.

At this point it is well to remember that the impression of the presence of character disorder in childhood is gained through the reports of the parents and other care-givers who often are unaware of how their own attitudes and behaviors have constrained the child. Many children brought to evaluation for behavior disorders are seen by the adults with whom they live as incorrigibly maladapted and set in their ways, free from remorse or anxiety, and, in short, evidencing a character disorder. Yet many of these same children, when provided with a group or foster home environment where there is strong, unconflicted (therapeutic) encouragement to behave more appropriately, will rapidly resume their forward development. Since only a small percentage of children are removed from their home environment and put into such ideal care-giving situations, the potential resilience of childhood is not often so clearly demonstrated. But the fact that it does happen in those few children ideally placed is strong evidence that the inflexible character disorders seen in adult life do not often have their counterpart before adolescence. This underscores the nascency of the personality traits common to childhood and implies that the whole understanding of the child's personality must include the consideration of the intercurrent, as-yet-not-internalized parental influence. When such intractability as seen in adults does occur in childhood, as with autism and childhood schizophrenia, we cannot escape the conviction that these are youngsters who have sustained more serious or prolonged injury or deficiency of attachment in the early phases of life. Their treatment presents the same difficulties as does the treatment of the "sick" or oral hysterical characters in adult life. The symptomatology of these youngsters may be tinged with pseudosexuality, but the basic problems appear to rest on faulty and inadequate early attachments. This hypothesis needs much further consideration and research.

HYSTERIA IN CHILDHOOD

The relationship between manifest symptoms of hysteria, paralyses, blindness, paresthesias, and the like and the preexisting character type is even more unclear in childhood than it is in adult life. Children of all ages and personality types seem more amenable to suggestion and hypnosis than are adults, and this is also likely to hold for conversion reactions as well, but statistical evidence is lacking. There are as yet few studies of the personality structure of children who have shown even overt hysteria in one form or another, although there is no dearth of reports on striking symptoms of this kind in children (Sheffield 1898). Robins (1966) showed that girls diagnosed as having hysteria during their childhood were only slightly more susceptible to falling ill with hysteria (not hysterical personality) in adult life than were others. None of the boys with hysteria in childhood had such symptoms when they grew up. What concerns us here is not the overt hysteria, which apparently can occur in children and adults of all personality types, but whether something like adult hysterical personality can be identified in childhood.

True hysterical and pseudohysterical personality in childhood. Very little has been written about the matrix out of which hysterical personality grows. Indeed, a sharp differentiation of hysterical psychoneurosis from hysterical personality in childhood is nowhere in evidence. The Group for the Advancement of Psychiatry report (1966) on classification of childhood disorders does not list hysterical psychoneurosis at all; recognizing the transience of the child's intercurrent development, the report rightly steers clear of character classifications. It provides "hysterical personality disorder" as a diagnostic category instead.

In one sense, it might be said that there can be no such thing in childhood as a mild hysterical personality since the cardinal features of the adult disorder, egocentrism and urgent attention-seeking behavior, are not as inappropriate in the school-aged child as they are in the adult.[1] Those girls and boys who have good ego development and the characteristics "healthy" or "good" hysterical traits are often popular and successful through the grade school years and come into neurotic problems only if during their adolescence they fail to learn more adaptive social responses that take others' needs into account. Those unusual children whose traits are reminiscent of the highly disturbed, or "oral" adult hysterical characters, as described by Zetzel (1968), Easser and Lesser (1965), and others reviewed in the previous chapter, are much more easily seen to be infantile in their provocative sexual play, their aggressive cuteness, and their childish demands for attention.

In such comparisons it is important to separate the internal state of the very disturbed adult hysteric, with the characteristic infantile fixations and oral orientation, and the pseudohysteric child, even though their behavior patterns appear similar. The adult has reached a stage of personality coalescence which is difficult or impossible to alter with psychoanalytic techniques. The child, so long as he or she is still a child, may remain behaviorly fixated at an immature level, but is still responding to the constrictive and selectively shaping influences within the family that have not yet been substantially internalized. Such a child remains suspended in a nascent state, exhibiting those behaviors that fit him into his environment and either not learning or inhibiting those alternative behaviors that would lead to, and indicate, further growth. As long as a child has not had serious difficulties with his primary attachments in infancy, he will retain the capacity to rapidly develop appropriate behavior well into the teen years when given the liberty and encouragement to do so.

The mother-child attachment bond. The qualification implied in the last sentence above points to the association of serious psychopathology in childhood or adult life with injuries and deficiencies in the mother-child attachment in the first year of life. Such inadequacies seem to be able to distort or even prevent normal development. Evidence is accruing that early oral deprivations, that is, deprivations of adequate social attachment to mother or caregiver, are associated with the functional psychoses of childhood and with sociopathy, addiction, and schizophrenia in later life.

It is becoming clearer now, from a number of sources in addition to psychoanalytical theories, that at an early time in infancy a child needs one, or at most a few human figures on which to focus an attachment, a social bond; it's through this relationship that the early forms of integrated behavior evolve. The subsequent stages of psychological development are then nurtured, and in part elicited and determined, by this interpersonal experience. In the absence or serious distortion of this essential bonding, severe malformations or arrests of psychic development can occur—even death. But if even a minimally adequate attachment is formed, personality development goes forward, rooted in the biological inclinations of the child, in its temperament and special sensitivities, in its natural energy and alertness. Instinctual drives express themselves in behavioral fragments and then systems, more or less prompted by intrinsic patterns common to the species and met by the reciprocal encouragement or discouragement of the attachment figures. From these interactions, then, patterns of behavior emerge and are shaped by the interpersonal responses. The child's experience, coupled with his ability to conceptualize reality, will characterize how he perceives the world and deals with what he perceives. These patterns, the beginnings of personality, are also labile and regress easily; above all they are dependent on the reciprocal reinforcement continuously available from the attachment figures.

Speculation about how the influence of the attachment bond effects future personality is irresistible, even though scientific evidence is hard to come by. Nevertheless, anyone who has seen the Brody and Axelrad films (1967,1968) of the relationship of feeding behavior and emerging personality in infants or the Robertson's films (1969) on separation from the mother in infancy will be convinced of the association. Along this line of thought there is very recent and provocative experimental evidence that by one year of age deficiencies of attachment may result in the child's averting its gaze from the mother on reunion after a brief separation, as if in aloof anger and rejection (Main 1977). These same children, tested again at age two, showed abnormalities of interaction with a friendly stranger, even when their mothers were present. Ainsworth (1973) has a group of young children with whom she is able to demonstrate three general types of attachment by the age of one year: (1) secure, (2) insecure, and (3) unattached. The aversion of gaze shown by Main occurs in the insecure group and persists in the unattached group.

It would be too tidy to expect to find that adult psychopathology neatly issues from the latter two groups, the more neurotic from the insecure group and the more severe and infantile types from the unattached group. Nevertheless, it would be surprising if the serious emotional disorders of later life were not found to cluster in the unattached group grown up, since maldevelopment in the oral phase is so often identified ?s the substrate from which later, more serious, behavioral pathology emerges. Because the traits under consideration here require substantial object relationships in order to occur at all, very early attachment deficiencies of the third variety seem unlikely to play a prominent part in the development of hysterical personality. It seems entirely possible, however, to correlate some of the striking characteristics of hysterical style with behaviors that are prominent in some of those infants in the insecure group. The insatiable attention-seeking of the hysteric may have some of its origin in the partially frustrated attachment behavior of signaling to the mother. The partial frustration has the paradoxical effect of increasing the behavior rather than extinguishing it. A close study of analogous behaviors in the insecure group might reveal a number of hysterical antecedents inaugurated by these unconscious, partial frustrations by the mother coupled with encouragement to continue the attention-seeking.

THE BIOLOGICAL SUBSTRATE OF PERSONALITY

Any psychological theory that attempts to understand and explain manifest behavior, thinking and feeling begins this explanation in the biological substrate or infrastructure of the personality and its interaction with external stimuli. It has been traditional to think of behavior as the result of specific, constitutional factors interacting with specific environmental factors to produce specific, predictable behavior. Such thinking underlies all dynamic explanations of behavior and is the basis of what is knows as "psychic determinism." Darwin, in 1859, in the chapter on "Instinct" in *The Origin of Species*, notes that each species is endowed with its own peculiar repertoire of behavior just as it is endowed with its anatomy and that instincts (by which he meant instinctual behavior) are as important as corporeal structures in the welfare of each species. But how was it to be explained that when a child of a certain age was exposed to a seemingly standard experience he always behaved in a nonfunctional way, whereas an older child exposed to the same experience evolved functional responses? The epigenetic theory, borrowed from embryology, was the answer. For certain experiences to have meaning, to become part of the functional repertoire, certain prior developments must have taken place. Each current substrate of personality had in turn antecedent structure and experience which brought it about (through assimilation and accommodation, in the words of Piaget) back to the biological potential of the gametes.

It has been the special province of psychoanalytic theory to explain the origins of behavior and the unfolding of personality on the basis of inferred instinctual drives and their derivatives. Insofar as the drives represent biological forces finding psychological representation in the psychic apparatus they are constitutional. Ethological theory, in approaching the same issue, holds that the behavioral systems which culminate in the focused attachment of the infant to its primary care-giver around the age of six months begin as discrete, fixed-action patterns which are present at birth and are sensitive to a broad range of environmental stimuli. These behaviors are constitutional. Nevertheless, so much experience with the world is necessary, so much epigenetic development must occur in those first six months before the child establishes a true object relationship, before it is able to focus its attachment on the figure of its mother, that even these more biologically determined sources of behavior are changed all out of recognition. They are so potentiated, shaped, and determined by environmental events that they come to constitute a type of learning.

In physical ontogeny we see that the organism unfolds properly only if timely and appropriate environmental conditions and stimulations are present, especially during the sensitive periods of rapid growth. In psychological ontogeny, an analogous situation obtains. Innate patterns of perception, fixed-action behaviors, and affectual predispositions are provided in the germ plasm and achieve their ordinary potential for development when they are met with phase-specific interactional and emotional experiences, as would be expectable in the environment within which the species evolved. For mankind, these experiences are exceedingly complicated after the first two or three months of life, when the interaction between the growing child and his care-giver becomes predominantly a social event.

All during this process the infant experiences its social interactions with the care-giver through its physical sensibilities (those visual, tactile, auditory modalities which have a predominantly intaking vector), and its focus is on bodily parts and vague internal satisfactions. Thus the drives achieve psychic representation in terms of the physical interactions through which they are experienced. The inner picture of what one is grows, apparently *de novo*, in each child as the precipitate of physical experiences with the social partner. Since the infant in the first few months is ignorant of the survival necessity for the relationship with its care-giver or even of its essentially "social" nature, its psychic representations will be of the physical needs and their satisfactions. This is the hallmark of the primary process. That the productions of children, psychotic experiences, and the recollections of adults in psychoanalytic treatment so often are rendered in terms of these bodily satisfactions or frustrations is testimony to the fact that the psychic representation of these early impressions colors the experience of subsequent development throughout life.

THE ROOTS OF CHARACTER

The sources of character may be organized under two broad categories: the constitutional and the environmental. The constitutional sources produce their influence through the gene chemistry, which finds its expression in the configuration of the body and the structure of the nervous system, including the hormonal arrangements which also influence appearance and behavior. The environmental sources are those effects and experiences which meet the organism where it is in its development and shape it through all manner of learning, thereby contributing to the epigenetic ontogeny for good or ill. We have spoken some here about the biological substrates of behavior and personality, and we will consider these specifically, if briefly, when dealing with the sources of hysterical personality. But before entering into a discussion of the learned factors in hysterical personality in children it would be well to outline three categories of learning which emerge successively in infancy and which apply to the formation of every personality type: (1) the intrinsic direction taken by the drives, (2) the overt parental example, and (3) the shaping effect on the child's behavior of interpersonal affects and signals, conscious and unconscious.

The drives. To the extent that in any one individual the direction taken by the drives is affected by the environment, this direction can be considered the earliest and most biologically linked learning process and is most influential in determining the direction and style of the first behaviors. It is the basis for the attachment behaviors of the infant becoming focused on one primary figure and thus is the origin of eventual true object relations.

The newborn begins by preferring certain general visual configurations over other configurations and seems more attuned to a female voice than to a male voice. Later the infant will attend more to the human face—any face presented straight on—and still later it will prefer its mother's face. After attachment to the primary object is complete, somewhere between the sixth and the twelfth month in home-raised infants, it is difficult to interrupt this attachment and reestablish it with another primary object. This progressive narrowing of attachment to a few specific figures has the quality of imprinting, the behavior described originally by Lorenz in ducklings, and has recently had its most thorough exposition for humans by John Bowlby (1969).

Overt parental example. The second type of learning is not present at birth, but it shortly begins to be obvious. It gradually becomes the most important source of all personality traits: the example of behavior that the child observes in those around him. This learning begins in simple mirroring of fragments of adult and sibling behavior before any attachment or true object relationship is apparent. Certain body movements, especially those to do with the mouth, face, and head, have a tendency to reflect similar movements in the care-givers. Headbobbing and mouth opening, lip smacking and tongue play are a few of the early mimicry behaviors that anyone familiar with infants will recognize. Later, more complete series of actions will be mimicked as the child willfully imitates and identifies with the behavior and thought processes of one or both parents. The peekaboo, pattycake, and verbal babytalk games of the first six months of life are common examples. Further on, the toddler will begin to show whole blocks of rather complex imitations derived from close observation of his parents without grasping the purpose of these behaviors. "Shifting gears" while in the child's car seat is such a behavior. This incorporation illustrates not only the increasing mastery of the physical body but also the progress of the internalization of the child's idea of the meaning of the parents' behavior, their motivations and their thought processes. The cat will be petted or its tail pulled, teddies will be punished or rewarded, and all manner of adult everyday activity will appear in miniature, especially while the adult is actually doing that activity.

Shaping effects of parental intervention. The third type of learning situation relevant here is one that becomes progressively more important as the object relationships mature. Although it may begin as early as the third month, it reaches its greates intensity after the age of two, when the child begins to grasp his mother's intentions, her plans, and especially her affects in relation to his own impulses and feelings. These perceptions of parental overt and covert inhibitions and reinforcements will cause the child to shape his behavior, to some extent, to conform to these parental interventions, including the acting out of parental unconscious impulses by the child. One common example is the eighteen-month-old whose mother subtly encourages him to hit her, trample on her feet, and pull her hair, reflecting her attitude about herself and/or her wish to do that to others. A little later, when cognitive functioning is more mature, the child's impulses and his attitude toward these impulses will be revealed in his play dialogue, which will be a reflection of how he perceives his mother's feelings. For a two and a half-year-old runabout, the making and serving of imaginary tea will show this imitation: who gets served first, what is said, the distribution of praise and correction, and so forth. At first, one may see clearly the youngster's thoughts played out, as yet still externalized and not yet imbued with qualities of goodness or badness. A little later the bad will be firmly suppressed from play and then from consciousness altogether. The tea party of the three- and four-year-old will more often be quite proper and correct, as the avenues for behavior and for admission of impulses to consciousness are increasingly controlled by the child himself, especially if all the while these attitudes are supported by consistent parental behavior.

The communication between the mother and the child is thus seen to the template for the communication within the child's mind between instinctual derivatives emerging into awareness and what is permitted in mental representation. Any necessity imposed on the child—or assumed by him to be expected—to distort or ward off certain tabooed impulses will provide the child with the cognitive signposts indicating what must be repressed, denied, or projected.

Of course, the three categories of learning spoken of here do not exhaust the list of possibilities, but they do cover those that have to do with interpersonal relationships and attachments, without which, certainly, no significant psychological development will occur.

ANALOGY WITH RADIATION OF SPECIES

After the initial attachments are secure and the child enters the active, run-about phase, between eighteen and thirty-six months, new behaviors seem to stream out and diversify much like radiations of variety in a species that has come to occupy a favorable ecological niche. Like the favorable environment, which tolerates these radiations, some parents allow much experimentation, guiding and shaping behavior only when appropriate to the child's best interests and those demands of society that the parents feel are justified. In healthy families these guidelines change with the stages of development so that both behavioral and emotional growth keep pace with the chronological age of the child. For example, father might stay close to his daughter at play when she is eighteen months old in order to see to it that she doesn't attempt activities that her coordination could not handle. The same protection at age three would tend to give the child the idea that she is fragile or uncoordinated, in need of protection.

The analogy to the radiation of species can be carried one step further in that parents who provide the milieu within which hysterical traits occur in their children are like those stringent, negative-feedback environments within which the alternative radiations are severely restricted. As long as these stringent conditions apply, the species remains static in its physical structure and behavioral adaptation to its strict environment. The capacity for radiation remains, however, latently waiting for more favorable conditions. With a child, the latent capacity to develop is present

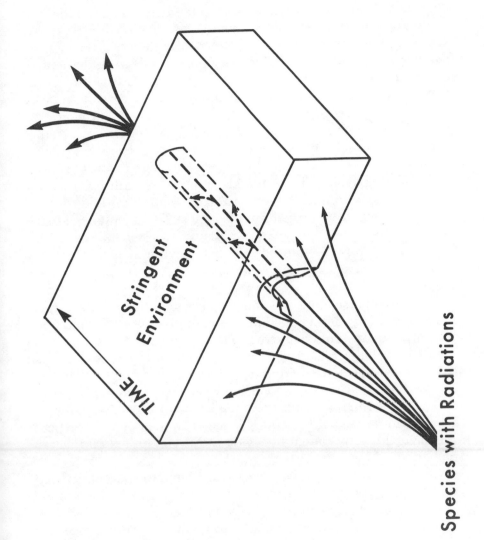

FIGURE 1

also, but it is inversely proportional to the length of time that the restriction is in effect. If the environment provided by the parents is static and thus increasingly inappropriate as the child reaches the oedipal period and beyond, then the capacity to learn and originate new and more adequate behavioral systems decreases. If this continues through the usual personality thaw and reorganization of the period of adolescent conflicts, an internal structure of personality is formed and operates with little regard for external feedback and may be relatively impervious to outside obstruction or encouragement to change. In short, a character disorder results.

This analogy may be illustrated, in an oversimplified way, by seeing the environment as a template, superimposed on the radiating forms of the organism. As long as the negative feedback operates, the animal species rapidly conforms and thereafter remains the same—adapted to that environment. When the restriction is lifted, the organism radiates new forms again (see figure 1).

This is, of course, only one dimension of the situation. Reciprocal interaction between the child and its care-giver affects them both. The infant's constitutional givens play an important role, potentiated by the adult's preexisting attitudes about these givens. The child helps shape his own environment. An upset, irritable infant may invoke feelings of guilt and helplessness in its mother, and her behavior then may contribute to the tension rather than relieve it. Some rigid parents, if they once conceive of their child as difficult, see the child's subsequent behavior as difficult no matter what the child does.

In the evolution of the behavior of any child the parents (society, the physical world and so on) provide the template. If this template is static and restrictive, it will resemble the ethological analogy, except that if the restriction goes on too long, the capacity to generate change is reduced. In the hypothetical ideal situation the templates laid down by the parental and societal environments would have wide apertures and would shift with the necessities of the successive developmental stages so that by the time evolving personality becomes a structure after adolescence, there would be considerable adaptedness as well as adaptability already present (see figure 2).

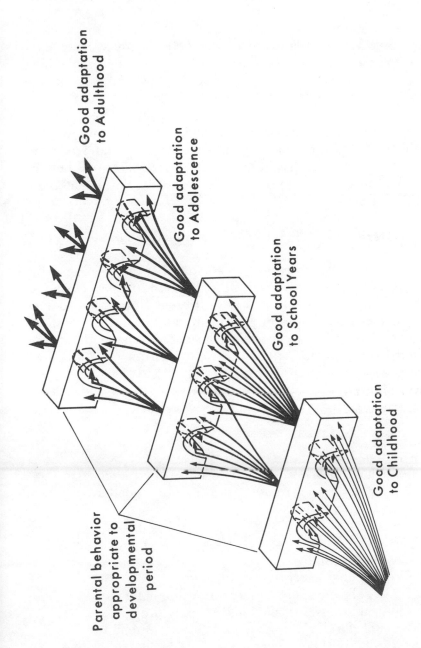

Parental behavior appropriate to developmental period

Good adaptation to Adulthood

Good adaptation to Adolescence

Good adaptation to School Years

Good adaptation to Childhood

FIGURE 2

Clinical experience testifies to the potential for growth in children when pathological templates are lifted, whether through psychotherapeutic intervention with the child and his parents, favorable shifts in his environment, or the naturally healthy impetus of the developmental thrust, especially in adolescence.

It is important to bear in mind that the analogy to species radiation discussed here relates only to the behavior that one can observe. What the child's intrapsychic constellations are can be inferred from the child's play, through psychological testing, through psychotherapy or analysis in childhood, and to some extent through all these modalities in adult life.

THE ROOTS OF HYSTERICAL PERSONALITY

There seems to be no reason to assume that the sources of the hysterical personality disorder in childhood or the hysterical character disorder in adulthood are different from those sources which produce other types of personality and character. Some of these general sources have just been considered. What remains to be indicated here are some specific areas which may be of special importance in the evolution of hysterical traits and of later hysterical psychopathology. These involve both constitutional and learned factors, a number of which will be discussed below according to this outline:

Constitutional
    Congenital temperament as determined by the genes
    Behaviors fixed or strongly determined by gender or
        hormonal influence
Learned Factors
    Constitutional givens which affect environmental response
        Gender of child
        Physical characteristics of the child
        Early behavioral characteristics of the child
        Physical illnesses of the child in early life
    Effects of parental conflicts and anxiety on child's
        developing behavior
    Effects of inappropriate libidinization of the parent/child
        relationship

Constitutional or inherited factors. We still know almost as little as ever about the possible predispositional factors in *any* character trait, to say nothing of interpersonal styles as epigenetically evolved and complicated as those under examination here. What may be inherited is a general tendency, an inclination, to develop certain types of behavior rather than others. It seems plausible that there may be a congenital activity type or inborn temperament, such as described by Thomas and others (1963), which influences the direction and quality of the initial interaction between mother and child. For example, a child who was especially alert and responsive might draw an early overstimulation in certain families and for this reason become unduly attuned to outside stimuli, an often noted characteristic of hysterical personality. Such correlations of apparent congenital temperament and hysterical traits depend on the solidity of the hypothesis of congenital temperament, a proposition by no means firmly established.

The greater frequency of hysterical traits in women than in men continues to be provocative but thus far seems most satisfactorily explained by reference to cultural influences, since dependency, egocentrism, and the like are more often tolerated or even encouraged in girls than in boys. Blacker and Tupin consider this issue in detail in chapter 2. The part played in the evolution of typical "feminine" or "masculine" behaviors by the influence of sex-linked substrates in the genes or the effects of sexual hormones before birth or at pubescence is suspected, but as yet little is known about this in humans. Whether these factors further influence the presence or absence of more pathological "hysterical" traits is entirely unknown.

Constitutional givens and environmental response. There are important factors in the constitution of the infant which are givens at birth but which stimulate parental responses which then affect what that child learns. The most striking of these is the gender of the child. Whether it is a girl or a boy, has blue eyes or brown, is assertive or passive—all these variables will tend to elicit different responses from the parents in line with their hopes, fears, identifications, and preconceptions. These responses feed back into the child's developing behavioral systems in a way that shapes the direction taken by his own responses, and later his attitude about himself.

Those who deal with newborns and infants often hear parents attribute qualities to their children that are not at all obvious to others. Boys are commonly seen as tough, aggressive, and destined for success in sports; girls are often described as sweet, shy, and in need of their father's protection, even though the children in question may be of identical size and behavior to an objective observer.

Physical illness. The child who develops hysterical traits starts life, as all others do, with the basics described above, but he may experience early in life special events which predispose to these traits. Beginning with Schilder (1939), many authors point to the occasion of physical illness in infancy or childhood, with its focus on the body, as fundamental for later hysterical symptomatology. Abse (1974) points out that often the parents are neglectful when the child is healthy and then remorsefully attentive when the child is sick *or distressed* (Abse's emphasis). Such a primary focus on the body might be another impetus toward seeking attention to, and through, the physical modalities.

The issue of parental misemphasis on real bodily illness or special attention to only transient or insignificant infirmities needs statistical confirmation but appears to be central at least to those hysterics who somatize. This point recollects Freud's description of Schreber's paranoid delusions, which seemed to take their origins from actual bizarre behavior toward him in his childhood by his father.

Just how much the somatic disabilities of infancy—colic, exema, and (later) asthma—are intrinsic failures of physiological balance and how much they are the individual infant's unique somatic response to a poor object relationship is not well understood. Spitz (1965), in his consideration of the psychotoxic factors in these illnesses in the first year of life, attempted to delineate the special conditions that exist between the mother and the child which produce the various symptoms. Although this specificity has not been confirmed by later studies, it is well known in both adult and child psychiatry that specific illnesses or physical traits in a child affect parents, and that parents may dwell on, or develop phobias of, these attributes of their child. Again, whether such a focus predisposes the child to hysterical preoccupations with the body later in life can only be settled by anterospective studies.

Parental conflicts and anxiety. A second important source of pathological learning in children showing hysterical traits is the inhibiting effect of the anxiety provoked in the child when he becomes aware he is acting in a way which causes anxiety in the parent. If the child is insecurely attached and seeking the reassurance of parental attention and approval, the recognition of parental anxiety will be a stimulus for the child to retreat to commonly successful maneuvers to attain this reassurance. These behaviors will mark one pole of the unconscious conflict of the parent. The child remains relatively fixed at certain immature behavioral levels due to this reciprocity between his behavior and what the parent wishes unconsciously. This direction may even be opposite to what the parent says and believes he or she wants.

For an example we can return to the eighteen-month-old who ends up stepping all over his mother and pulling her hair while mother is trying to talk to her friend. The child sees mother's attention fixed on someone else and attempts to elicit reassuring signals that mother is attending to him also. Mother may be anxious that her child make a good impression, but she also may have pressing needs of her own to relate to the friend. This anxiety is communicated to the child by ambivalent attachment signals from mother which are unsatisfying. Mother continues to look at her friend, her flow of speech gets faster and more tense, and she mechanically handles the child in a way which excludes the youngster from the main channel of exchange between the two adults. The mother is fearful that her own needs will not be met if the child intervenes. At this point the child becomes aggressive in his attempts to get on mother's lap and in that effort steps on his mother's feet and shoves his way in. Mother responds by giving her full attention then to the child, rewarding the regressive behavior and consolidating the cycle.

Millon (1969) suggests that the hysterically inclined child, whom he refers to as the "active-dependent" personality type, may have had many different care-takers in infancy who supplied him with intense, short-lived stimulus gratifications that came at irregular intervals. He notes that irregular schedules of reinforcement establish deeply ingrained habits that are highly resistant to extinction. He feels that the persistent yet erratic dependency behaviors of this type of personality may reflect a pathological form of intense stimulus-seeking traceable to highly charged, varied, and irregular stimulus reinforcements associated with early attachment learning.

Encouragement to look to others for fulfillment and help. A predominant constellation in the early life of a child with hysterical traits (or such an adult, on recollection of her childhood) is the overt encouragement to expect and demand help, guidance, and the good things of life while covertly signaling that these are beyond the child's competence and can only be supplied by the parent. In this regard, the parent treats the child as he or she would have liked to have been treated as a child that is indulged. When the child responds by inhibiting her own alternatives of action and conforming to the behavior indicated, the parent is flattered by the attention and gives it in return; but the parent is consciously disappointed and disapproving, as was the mother in the last example: she says no, but takes it.

The child's healthy emotional development is inhibited by innumerable repetitions of these double instructions by parents whose fixed and inappropriate expectations neither adapt to the child's immature level of understanding nor shift with the advance of the child's capacities. Even if the developmental thrust carries the child further in specific age-appropriate behaviors, as it often does, these islands of reciprocal social expectation remain as points toward which the child and the parents, orient and to which they habitually regress. These points will be among the main features when a child is finally brought for psychiatric evaluation, usually for symptoms other than the hysterical behavior.

It is common, for example, for the child to be seen as physically delicate. While overtly emphasizing the importance of physical conditioning or sports, the parents, who themselves may be active, give the child the message that she must not become proficient or competitive, but rather remain weak and in need of help. This is again a projection of the parents' own yearnings. It seems clear that, in such circumstances, part of the hysterical propensity to repression is brought about by the necessity to square the inconsistency of the two parental messages by acting on the covert one without being aware there ever was such a message. The use of repression in the child seems a reflection of the importance to the parents that these yearning of their own for attention and help remain firmly repressed. With such families it is not so much rejection that causes a feeling of insecurity in the child as the capricious alternation of approval and disgust which keeps the child hoping to please but never sure of what will please, and thus more dependent on outside direction.

The suppression of anger and assertiveness. Sperling (1973), describing in detail an adult patient, reminds us of the importance of the mother in the evolution of hysterical personality and conversion. Indeed, she sees the basic conflicts of the hysterical diathesis as originating in the mother-child relationship. She emphasizes how certain mothers, caught in unconscious conflict, do not permit expressions of anger and assertiveness, or even anxiety, in the child but encourage dependency and passivity instead. At the same time, the mother does not expect the child to be able to cope with anxiety-provoking situations without her help. The child becomes aware that anger and assertiveness threaten the already insecure relationship with mother and thus learns that these responses must be firmly and early repressed from consciousness. The submissive behavior, in addition to its attention-getting value, is also motivated by a reaction formation against the warded-off anger and frustration. There is quite a difference between a mother who says don't express it so strongly or don't do it that way and the mother who says, in effect, don't express it at all, or, don't even think it. It is the displaced and "immature" acting up, the reactive self-isolation and the autoerotic activity that finally brings such a youngster to the attention of a child psychiatrist, as is the case with the first clinical example to be described presently.

Inappropriate sexualization of the parent/child relationship. Children whose parents have been physically overstimulating—especially when the parents infantilize the child as a projection of themselves—may elicit the early and intense development in the child of sensuality, which may divert him from other exploratory interests if it continues at high levels beyond the first year or so. Since this inappropriate sensuality is connected with the social interactions that are the vehicle for its transmission, this may lead in later life to the need to maintain a similarly high level of egocentric and sexually oriented interactions typical of the hysterical personality. Since such interactions serve a stereotyped function for the parents that is referable only to their own unconscious preoccupations, these interactions are not fitted to the child's changing need for social reciprocity. Stimulation of this kind may not even be simply what the child actually wishes and reaches out for, but may have a teasing, incomplete quality that keeps him coming back for more but not often getting the truly satisfying maternal behaviors that he seeks. Beyond this, clinical evidence indicates that in many cases there are multiple sources of stimulation, and satisfying play occurs only at irregular intervals without enough consistency for the child to focus on one figure.

When the sensual stimulation is specifically sexual or contains pronounced sexual features, and especially if the adult involved is conflicted about such behavior and represses the awareness of the sexual elements, the situation predisposes to a hysterical outcome. The closer the physical interaction approaches actual sexual stimulation, the more likely it is that the child will respond by a strong surge of participation, accompanied by complete repression of the awareness of his own interest: again, the typical hysterical result. The younger the child, the more he or she will experience the interaction as an attachment, an intaking experience—essentially oral. The paradigm is the intense focus of attention of the infant on its attachment figure. The seduced child is schooled to respond to the intensely stimulating sexualized attention but is to forget the parent's invitation to gain pleasure by these means. What is left is an overinvestment of the bodily functions at the expense of other learning.

It is as yet unknown how often seduced and sexually misused children become hysterics. It seems most likely that the earlier the abuse occurs the more the child will show serious character malformation reminiscent of oral stage pathology, not only because of the premature stimulation of sexual behaviors, but because of the grosser nature of the adults' misuse of the child for their own purposes and the likelihood that such parents will be significantly abusive and deficient in other ways as well. As far as seductions of older children are concerned, we know that Freud had to retreat on his conviction that his patients had fallen ill of neuroses because of actual parental seduction. Nevertheless, it seems likely that children and adults with sexualized, hysterical traits have actually experienced unconsciously sexualized behavior at the hands of their parents, if not actual physical seduction.

HYSTERICAL TYPES IN CHILDHOOD

Out of the spectrum of children between age six and thirteen who appear to have hysterical traits three representative types can be isolated to serve as descriptive of the whole group.

The first and most mature of these types is a youngster who would almost never be seen as disordered since he or she rarely presents any disturbance or distress within the family during latency. Such children are like early editions of the "good" or "healthy" hysteric as described by Lazare (1971). There is a predominance of oedipal over oral conflicts and, if the youngster in question is a girl, she will be focused on her relationship with her father, which will be colorfully romanticized. She might have some difficulties in mastering the cognitive part of schoolwork because of her tendency to overgeneralize, her lack of acute attention to detail, and her deficiency in analytical ability, but she would more than make up for this socially by animation and attentiveness to others. Her social skills, which are apt to be precocious, equip her to make her way well with peers and teachers alike. She may be quite artistic. In her background we would expect to find a relatively intact family group, good attachment as an infant, intense and emotional relationships with her father and brothers, and a depreciated relationship with her mother, whom she would see as drab and uninteresting compared to herself. Such a well-developed and interesting child and family is diagnosable, in theory at least, if she and her parents become sufficiently well known to the psychiatric observer. This is unlikely to happen in childhood but may come to pass when such a child seeks psychotherapy or analysis in her adult life. Just what percentage of children of this type actually become ill with hysterical character disorder as adults is not known, but the hypothesis presented here holds they would not. Rather they would show neurotic traits.

The other two types of children with hysterical traits comprise those who are most commonly brought to pediatricians and child psychiatrists for evaluation and treatment. They have occasioned some disequilibrium within the family, or have provoked such negative response outside the family that help is sought. These children and their parents are quickly seen to be more disordered than the first type of child described above and cluster in either a second, less seriously disturbed group, or a third, more seriously disturbed group. The less seriously disturbed group resembles the more disturbed in *reported* behavior, but they can be told apart at some point in the diagnostic process. The prognosis for the two poles of the pathological continuum they represent are significantly different. Often, differentiation can reliably be made only through assessment of the relative impoverishment of the child's ego development and the relative level and rigidity of the parents' personality by means of a course of psychotherapeutic evaluation of each family member.

Common complaints in both pathological types. General complaints about children in both categories are the following. Although they tend to be outgoing, engaging and charming initially, they are often soon seen as irritating and intrusive, impulsive, and more "selfish" than even the norm for their age. They are more than usually emotional, but in a superficial way, yielding quickly to indications that others have different feelings by abruptly changing their tack. This trait gives them a fickle and capricious quality which loses comrades as fast as their gregarious and shallow friendliness gains them. Above all, such youngsters seek approval and attention, as if they were trying to fill themselves up. This has a pronounced intaking quality which accounts for the striking pregenital impression these children make on the observer, despite whatever overt sexual behaviors they may be mimicking. They have learned that their satisfactions are dependent on others, and that this satisfaction is variable and may be withdrawn at any time. Therefore they press for more now. They crave stimulation and excitement and seek it through interpersonal contacts, often with much younger children who are liable to give them respectful attention but who may not yet be able to demand reciprocation. Genital exposure and confused sexual play that is mixed with aggressive components are frequently among the presenting complaints. Such children are uneasy in the give and take with peers; they are labile in their emotions and either erupt in inappropriate and sometimes bizarre piques or retreat from the field.

One of the most impressive traits of these children is that they have an uncanny sensitivity to the moods and unexpressed thoughts of the adults with thom they have a relationship. They search the adult's face for clues and act on what they imagine is there. With those they know well, they are often accurate, especially in the recognition of unconscious motivations. With others, they are quite often inaccurate since their conclusions spring from their confused and misleading ideas strongly colored by their excitable interest in all bodily orifices and functions. If the unconscious attention of the adult is focused on the same eroticized topics, such a youngster will not fail to become excited. They give the impression of being used to receiving some sort of positive response from adults in this regard and become confused or frightened when it is not forthcoming, as in the first playroom sessions. Their pseudosexual provocations, both with adults and peers, seem to result not in satisfactions but in a heightening of diffuse tension and excitement which is then discharged in tantrums and aggressive motor behavior, often self-hurtful. This brings on further guilt and feelings of worthlessness, another round of ingratiating obsequiousness and an attempt to obey to rules. These attempts are fragile and fail, often because of a breakthrough of negativism, resulting in further punishment.

Sexual behavior. The sexuality of the hysterical personality in childhood is deceptive. The overly "feminine" or seductive traits are only superficially sexual; they really express the identifications with the orally seductive parent as a means of retrieving or maintaining love or the acting out of hostile manipulations. The hysterical child is seldom seeking a sexual partner but is absorbing the eroticized positive or negative attention of the parent. If the mother herself is hysterical or infantilizing in her encouragement or competition with her pretty child, any fixation of the child in this style is easy to understand. If the mother, herself, neurotically restricted and repressed, identifies with the child's eroticized behavior, the youngster will express these impulses for her if not spared by the influence of a firm, mature father.

Alternatively, a little girl who is deprived of adequate mothering may turn to an abnormally close tie with her father. If this relationship becomes sexualized, because of father's conflicts, the child learns this technique and uses it to earn dependent gratifications from future father figures at the cost of submission and passivity. The relationship remains superficial because at the point it is elicited it is based on the young child's inability to love in a mature way, that is, to seek the other person's best interests as well as her own. Hysterical personality can have its beginning when the little girl manages to turn her father into a substitute mother (Hollender 1971).

If it's the father who inaugurates the overmothering, he sees his daughter (or, as is sometimes the case, his son) as weak and young. These are essentially projections onto her of his own oral neediness. In his solicitous attitude toward her, including his special interest in her body, he is almost literally taking care of himself as a small child. If he leads her into petting games, thinking of her as a less threatening sexual partner than her mother, her flirtatiousness will reflect this skin erotization. Perhaps the strongest, most persuasive setting for the development of hysterical personality in childhood is the combination of both such parents, as shown by the first family presented below in the clinical reports.

Learning skills. The ego abilities of these patients vary. Some youngsters operate well in school, where the reciprocal distorting interpersonal cues may be absent. Most suffer truncation of their cognitive development, with the inevitable limiting of learning skills and learning. Their tense, sexualized play testifies to the anxiety attached to seeing and hearing, an anxiety which contributes to their impressionistic style. They are so busy acting on their sexual and aggressive theories and then forgetting the actions that they have little time or interest in the mastery of learning. If this occurs early in life, during the third and fourth year especially, instrumental skills can be so poorly acquired that the child may develop special learning disabilities which add to and complicate the youngster's emotional problems (Anthony 1961).

The mechanisms of defense. In differentiating between the less and the more seriously disturbed youngsters with hysterical traits, an assessment of their current and habitual defense systems is in order. The hysterical style is born not only in the need, for example, to ward off libidinal impulses from awareness (which might be accomplished by any number of defensive styles) but in the use of particular mechanisms and not others. How are these likely to arise?

The earliest defensive systems evolve to preserve homeostasis in the biological drives, to master reality, and to handle object anxiety. They become more elaborate and specific as they develop in concert with appropriate shifts in parental expectations. The level of defense increases in complexity as maturation proceeds, the more sophisticated systems evolving in an epigenetic way from the less mature previous stages. The child elaborates her defensive structure in collaboration with her mother, incorporating and identifying with gross segments of her mother's overt behavior and unconscious conflicts. Through thousands of interactions overt and covert, blatant and subtle, the mother's cognitive style and habitual ways of cognitive processing shape and determine to a major degree the daughter's selection of certain defenses over others. Later, in the context of the playroom session, or in psychotherapy as an adult, the child's defenses will again be displayed in characteristic types of resistance to the treatment and avoidance or distortion of topics introduced by the therapist as well as those that emerge from within the patient. When these observations of the child can be put together with an assessment of the level of parental defensive functioning, a clearer understanding of the cause and likely prognosis of the child's pathology is possible.

Although it may be that the first type of child described in this section—the healthiest—generates her style for the most part as an intrapsychic defense against the purely biological drives of the oedipal period, it is certainly obvious from clinical work that the two categories of children with more serious pathology are heavily influenced in their maldevelopment by their interaction with their mother and also sometimes with their father. In the first family to be described, the mother, abetted strongly by the father, acted out her libidinal wishes through encouragement of her daughter's sexualized behavior while supressing expressions of anger and assertiveness in her. This appeared to lead toward the elaboration of relatively mature defenses in the child such as repression of the awareness of the sexual elements in her behavior and reaction formation and intellectualization to handle the self-assertive impulses and her anger at frustration. In the second case described, we will see that the child had to act out the mother's eroticized aggressive impulses and continued to use more primitive and immature defenses such as schizoid fantasy, where she retreated to mental images and playroom scenes of great violence and sadism.

The descriptions here are not of the mechanisms of defense per se, which are evanescent, waxing and waning in complex interaction with each other as glimpsed during a psychoanalytic hour or playroom session. They are, rather, what the observer can see that can be recorded: the defensive behavior, the characteristic style of the child, from which the various mechanisms of defense can be inferred.

In Vaillant's excellent paper on the hierarchy of defenses (1971), he identifies four progressive levels of defense structure: (1) the narcissistic defenses, (2) the immature defenses, (3) the neurotic defenses, (4) the mature defenses. The two categories of latency children showing hysterical traits tend to cluster their defensive systems in either of the middle two of these four levels.

Although the healthier children of the two pathological types show immature defenses some of the time, or when under severe stress, they mostly have recourse to the neurotic types, especially "forgetting," that is repression and dissociation (neurotic denial). "I don't know" is likely to be the first answer that comes to their lips on being questioned on practically any topic. This is not simply a ploy to avoid self-incrimination but often a fact, for memories are frequently not accessible to them, and when they are, they are vague and impressionistic. The earlier this defense forms the more impoverished the actual fund of information retained in memory will be, again increasing the child's dependence on the outside world for signs of self-worth. Identification, taking on as one's own the behaviors of the parents, provides a global method of coping without integrating. This results in a poor sense of self and a tendency to variable response and a cognitive style unequal to intellectual pursuits despite excellent endowment (Shapiro 1965). Reaction formation and displacement are also characteristic of the more developed hysterical types in childhood and serve to assist repression in the conflicts over unacceptable instinctual impulses, especially those having to do with getting and giving, as in oral and phallic periods.

In contrast, conflicts around rage and issues of power and dominance, so much more pressing for the less developed of the children, are not always well handled by repression. Some combination under the general category of intellectualization may be required: isolation, rationalization, ritual, undoing, and magical thinking. For the more immature child, whose parents are unable to present appropriate models or responses and expectations, more immature defenses such as projection, hypochondriasis, passive aggression, and especially schizoid fantasy are much more usual. Such a child is not defending because of conflicts over sexual thoughts and impulses but in response to the parental expectations that the child be a protagonist in scenes from the parents' unconscious fantasies—fantasies that are almost always a sadistic distortion of narcissistic struggles for survival with objects from the parents' past. In these situations neurotic repression, usually evolved later to handle oedipal impulses, is prematurely and malignantly evoked to furnish out the child's inadequate repertoire of defenses, and this causes a tendency to repress all intrapsychic life rather than just the forbidden libidinal impulses, as in other types of pathology.

Prognosis. Briefly, children falling into the less disturbed portion of this group have had adequate attachments in early life (often the girl is attached more prominently to her father than to her mother), but for their own reasons mother or father or both continue to treat the child as if she were much younger than she is. This may continue even though she shows more mature behavior elsewhere than in their presence. The parental expectations are communicated in the behavior they encourage or inhibit, and they usually demonstrate in their own personality style the basics of the traits the child has picked up, by osmosis as it were, from the earliest years. Close aquaintance with these children reveals that they have achieved some or even many developmental landmarks but are treated by their parents as if they were much less capable than they are.

If such a situation were recognized early enough in the life of the child, treatment of one or both parents alone would likely be sufficient to prevent fixation in the child.[2] Once the cluster of traits develops fully, the youngster's future development will depend on the natural course of her parents' disorder and the opportunity for the influence of other significant adults including psychotherapists. A certain portion of such children probably recover with positive experiences during adolescence. Starr (1953) holds that in many cases of hysteria and anxiety neuroses in childhood the impact of pathological parental attitudes and traits not only acted as determining factors in the genesis of the problem but were *current* elements which kept the child's illness active at the point of diagnosis.

The prognostically less hopeful portion of this group will have had poorer relationships with their mothers and a more blatant hysterical style. They are less amenable to therapy. The disorder in their parents is more severe and resistant to therapy also, even if the parents were willing patients, which they are not. At times, only a trial of treatment will differentiate between the more seriously ill child, with her immature defenses and intense parental stimulation, and the less disordered child, with her defenses dominated by repression but with greater development concealed behind her symptoms. While it may be that the more developed child can be successfully treated alone, therapy for the parents is a great adjunct to accurate diagnosis and good outcome and may be virtually the only chance, short of residential placement, for the sicker child (Szurek, Johnson and Falstein 1942, Szurek 1954).

The hypothesis advanced here is that the more mature child with hysterical traits who does not get treatment or otherwise escape the fixating environment will form the major portion of that group from which the hysterical characters emerge in later life. Further, the sicker, less developed child who does not get treatment will not achieve even that level of function but will instead comprise the group from which the more disabling personality forms emerge, the grossly immature and impulsive characters, the infantile characters, and perhaps the addictive and sociopathic characters as well. Thus in later life these more disturbed children with hysterical traits would not ordinarily be identified as hysterical personalities.

TESTING THE THEORY

These theoretical statements will now be illustrated by clinical illustrations derived from the evaluation and long-term treatment of two families, each with a child who manifested hysterical traits. One family has a child with a milder disturbance; the other contains a child with more severe developmental impairment. What we know about the etiology of the hysterical personality, or any personality, is considerably less than the sum of the assertions catalogued here. Even if these assertions are too dogmatic in tone, it is hoped that the complexity of the examples to follow will temper this tone and indicate that explanations cannot be reduced to simple cause and effect.

Therapy with a family in the favorable group. Anne C. was nine years old when brought to psychiatric evaluation for what her mother described as "something wrong from the beginning." She had a problem minding, was consistently immature, oppositional, and "forever doing things she's too old to be doing." This included being forgetful, impulsive, emotional and having special interest in "bathroom" topics. The request for help came at that time because Ann was getting worse in her behavior and performance despite one year of a special school for remediation of "auditory dyslexia." The parents disagreed over whether Ann's behavior was her problem or whether it was due to their faulty discipline. They accused first themselves and then each other alternatingly. They were alarmed at the apparently sexual way Ann and her five-year-old brother would continually hold wrestling matches with each other, rolling on the floor together clutching each other's genital areas and getting more and more excited until they had to be sent to their separate rooms. Ann was a consciously wanted first child whose gestation and delivery were unremarkable. Her mother never considered nursing, so Ann was bottle fed. She had colic and was quite irritable from the first, "never went to sleep without crying" and "cried every night from twelve to four," which didn't stop until she was a year old. The home was so tense that the pediatrician prescribed a tranquilizer for both mother and child and recommended a vacation away from her. The parents did take a nine-day holiday away from Ann when she was nine months old, leaving her in the care of a nanny. This prolonged separation at a crucial phase of attachment may have played a part in Ann's vulnerability to regression.

Ann was a picky eater, but her developmental landmarks were achieved early and she was large for her age. Her parents showed many snapshots of her in infancy which indicated Ann had no problems with social smiling or positive response to her family. During her second and third year she had trouble with moving her bowels and required suppositories and laxatives. This culminated in the formation of a fissure which was not diagnosed for some time. Ann was always afraid to move her bowels and used to run around excitedly before a movement. Otherwise her health was good.

By Ann's third birthday she was dressing herself and tying her shoes. During this year her brother was born. Her father mentioned he felt she always considered her brother an interloper. When she entered nursery school at age three, she was a watcher not a joiner. The school kept her with younger children even though she was the largest of them. They didn't feel she was ready when it was time for kindergarten.

During the first and second grade she had a very hard time handling herself with the other children and was pushed about despite her size. She was tutored at home during one summer, but she never would do her homework and couldn't learn the flash cards. She loved to color and draw for fun, but it was not until the end of kindergarten that she was able to draw representationally. Her mother thought of her as helter-skelter, running, laughing and acting in a very immature way but did not think much of this since "all her friends are also that way—immature and giddy." These friends tended to be a year or more younger than she.

Ann's father, Mr. C., a highly paid partner in a moderately large and successful firm, originally called to ask for help in protecting his children from his wife's bad influence, claiming they differed greatly on how to handle the children. He said his wife wouldn't come in, but she appeared with him on the first visit, during which he described their differences in a very accusatory manner.

In the course of conjoint and individual psychotherapy with the parents, it became evident that there was a great deal of sensual contact between Ann and her father which Ann had experienced as very exciting (she spontaneously told of this herself. in the playroom). He frequently bathed both the children and carefully dried them after the bath. It seemed clear from the context within which this was reported that neither parent was conscious of the frustration and tension engendered in the sexually stimulating play between Ann and her father and between her and her brother. In an early playroom session she told of how exciting it was for her to be caught in the trap of her grandfather's legs and how much fun it was for her to ride horsey on his foot. She was eager to know whether the therapist tickled his children and described how much she enjoyed it when her father tickled her until she "couldn't stand it." Her capacity for regressive attention-getting and the physical nature of this behavior was well illustrated by an episode which occurred early in treatment. Her brother messed his pants in a slight bout of diarrhea. When Ann saw her father was affectionately bathing him and telling him it was all right, Ann pushed out some formed stool into her own pants as she stood watching them. Her mother was furious, feeling that the child was old enough to know better.

In subsequent individual sessions with the father the topic of his children seldom came up. He was aware that this concern about the children and his wife's behavior was, in part, a rationalization for his own return to treatment. He had been in psychotherapy twice before in the last ten years and was in psychoanalysis for more than a year up until nine months before the beginning of the present treatment. This information emerged well after treatment had begun. He said he had quit the analysis because he wasn't getting anywhere.

Mr. C. quickly showed himself an obsessive person, riddled with guilt about his strong sexual and aggressive impulses (not actions) and filled with resentment at what he felt amounted to his being deprived of what he deserved from those around him. The theme of his competition with his brother was prominent. Behind his repetitive thoughts and fantasies was a great deal of hostility covered by a smile. He was afraid of destroying others with his brightness and success and therefore dissembled the brightness and undercut the success by an excessively deferential manner, which he immediately applied in his treatment. He hoped to enlist the sympathy and help of the therapist in diagnosing his wife as the cause of all the family's problems. This attitude yielded intermittently to an awareness, to his chagrin, that his own behavior with her and the children played a prominent part in the situation.

Mrs. C. was a strikingly intense, very slim woman who, without being aware of it, communicated great physical tension in the way she moved and held her body and flexed the muscles of her neck as she talked. In her individual sessions she indicated her concern about her awareness that she did not love Ann in the same way she loved her boy, David. She described Ann as a very great responsibility who yielded little gratification in return. She was obviously trying to do her best to care for her daughter and had been doing so for years, but within her very rigid and organized program she recognized that her child was not flourishing.

Mrs. C. liked to iron and did a good deal of it. She was passionately insistent on arranging her schedule so that she could swim two miles twice a week "to work off my aggressions," she said. She often could not fall asleep after a full day of activities and regularly took a mild tranquilizer for this just after her ritual shower at night. Much of her early sessions were taken up with descriptions of how Ann failed to change her school ctothes into play clothes or jumped on the bed or put toys in the wrong place. She was irritated that Ann needed so much attention, and she feared she might be too "analytical" and "organized" for the child's good. In sexual matters she gave the initial impression of being a prude. She was willing to come for psychotherapy, her first such experience, if the therapist thought it might help her daughter.

The psychologist who examined Ann early in the child's treatment concluded that her intellectual functioning was clearly limited and on an overall basis fell to a below-average level. In some areas, particularly but not exclusively those affected by school achievement, her functioning was even poorer, although on three of the ten Wechsler Intelligence Scale for Children subtests her score did reach the average level. Ann's perceptual-motor problems were varied and substantial. It was felt that there was an approximate two-year lag in the development of perceptual-motor skills, which seemed great enough to produce the obvious impairment in Ann's academic skills. Ann was seen to have a substantial emotional disturbance and to be highly immature. She was quite anxious, almost openly so in affective interaction with others in the projective testing. She indicated strong interest in others but found interaction threatening and tended to turn away toward fantasy to escape the threat. The psychologist's findings suggested that her relationships with both adults and peers had the quality of an open wish to be loved and accepted, but she sustained feelings of being inadequate and undeserving and was preoccupied with sensual impulses. Action on these impulses failed to bring satisfaction, causing instead frustration and anger and a turning toward confused fantasy. The fantasies were not satisfying enough to prevent her continued attempts to achieve more satisfying relationships; but instead of achieving these, she seemed to be in the process of developing hysterical personality patterns. Psychotherapy was strongly recommended.

Treatment began with twice-weekly playroom sessions for Ann and one weekly conjoint and one weekly individual session for each of her parents. In the first several months of playroom treatment Ann displayed the phenomena of an immature childhood hysterical style in a striking way. She was always cheerful and smiling and usually brought a number of things from home, dolls and cuddly bears. She searched the therapist's face and appearance for signs of change and continually tried to guess his thoughts and reactions to her—how many children does he have, does he ever get angry with them, could she see his angry face, and the like. Later, a good many comments about his breath, his hair, and his moustache made it clear she was acutely aware of his physical nearness. This attention did not have a seductive or even an endearing quality but was delivered inappropriately and with a heightening of tension that was deflected but not relieved by attempts at interpretive comment.

The playroom hours were almost always active and physical, scattered and labile; and for this reason it was often difficult to see associations between the conjoined activities. Inquiry along this line produced the child's ever ready "I don't know." Often the main theme of a session would be either some sexualized activity between the Barbie dolls, usually two preteen girl dolls and a rather busty woman doll, or formless aggressive fights between the wolf and the alligator handpuppets alternately held by each participant. The impoverishment of her fantasy was impressive. Handpuppet play always had a very elementary story line, without plot, elaboration, or variation; just straight biting, to the tune of the therapist's growling. With the dolls she would say, for example, "You want to see something?" and then pull up the mature doll's blouse to expose her breasts, after which there was usually a good deal of aggressive spanking and reproaching by the older doll of the two child dolls and also some (very French) kissing and making up by the dolls. With the pingpong-ball guns she added no embellishment, no sallies or retreats; just peppering away at point-blank range, followed perhaps by, "Do you ever get angry at a child in here?"

Ann's performance of physical activities such as throwing and catching, darts, and other endeavors was grossly poor although her fine motor movements were normal. Suggestions on how she might do the activity better resulted usually in deterioration in her performance. Nevertheless she would, perhaps the next hour, request the instructions again and then be able to follow through on them, as if she was freer to use and learn when she herself requested the help. Later in the first year of treatment she wanted very much to learn how to use a yo-yo and practiced until she mastered the rudiments of that skill.

Ann's worst behavioral deteriorations would come at points where she found herself behind in a game or unable to solve an addition problem in keeping score or unable to understand a move in checkers. She would impulsively condemn herself, become agitated and want to quit the game. She several times reached the point of saying "I don't want to come here any more" as an expression of her frustration. She had difficulty waiting for her turn in board games or card games and often just took one turn after another, oblivious of the therapist.

Ann maintained an interest in the physical bodies of her dolls but was flustered and confused when specifics were involved, as if the details were cloudy in her mind. In trying to tell a story about a sick cousin in the hospital she couldn't clarify what she wanted to ask about the tubes going into his body. She retreated into violent sexual play with the dolls when she was uneasy about the therapist's questions after a bout of stealing candybars from the school's treat box. There were many repetitions of the bad mother theme, with the mother punishing the children and the children retaliating. These sequences were frightening to her, and if the therapist said something like "Sometimes a girl can get pretty angry at her mother," she would ask when the hour would be up. Once when she was ordering the therapist around, she said "Pretend you never will be mad at me."

The early conjoint sessions with the parents concentrated mostly on ways of dealing with Ann, and there were frequent discussions of the handling of the sexualized physical play between the two children and between the children and their father. This led to effective techniques for separating the children at those times and for diminishing the father's sexualized bodily care. Both parents acknowledged in the course of time that they recognized in themselves an element of inappropriate sensual enjoyment in the physical handling of the children. As soon as this came to open discussion in the treatment, the problems of Ann's sexualized behavior at home greatly diminished, and her preoccupation with the Barbie dolls and fighting handpuppets in the playroom gave way to activities more characteristic of latency.

After this the conjoint sessions turned to the parents' relationship with each other. When the C.'s began to address themselves to their own problems their treatment and found more effective methods of handling their children to their satisfaction, it had the effect of lifting their static and distorted constrictions, and this released their daughter from the reciprocal stimuli that had kept her from adequate development. She then rapidly moved toward a more normal pattern for her age. She began to be more interested in games of skill and in improving her technique in the various physical activities of the playroom. She watched the therapist's face less and persevered when failing. More form and content entered her fantasy play at the same time that the aggressively sexualized and assaultive elements diminished. She began to cast the therapist in more elaborate oedipal roles appropriate to her age: having him, as her father, rescue her with an ambulance, cooking for him, caring for him while mother was away and speculations, such as, "Maybe I'll marry you." There were glowing reports from the school that her comprehension and performance there had improved greatly as had her social relationships with peers.

After eight months of twice-weekly treatment Ann was so improved that her sessions were reduced to one per week and the conjoint treatment to one per month so that the parents, by that time both deeply engaged in their own treatment, could go to two individual sessions per week each. Both were working in a way that they might have, had they sought individual treatment for themselves, and both were making significant progress. This was especially true of Mrs. C., whose rituals had decreased to the extent that she had time to begin preparation for entry into a postgraduate professional school. She said, "For the first time in my life I feel like a real mother."

After a year of treatment, a repetition of psychological testing showed six subtests of the WISC in the average range, and there was no longer any question that Ann's potential intelligence was average. Her skill deficiencies in learning had clarified themselves to difficulty with maintenance of directionality, with sequencing, with rotational errors, and with integration of parts into whole. With this specificity an improved special program was mounted at her school to focus on these deficiencies. She was still emotionally disturbed and immature but seemed to be integrating her inner experience more adequately and was not so overwhelmed by her anxieties. She was expected to do well in further psychotherapy.

From material developed in the treatment of her parents over sixteen months time, it was possible to identify some of the factors that played a part in the development of Ann's hysterical style. Ann's father identifed with her against her mother, whose strict ways of doing things annoyed him as his own father's rules had in the past. In his attempt to defend her and oppose his wife, he interfered with her adaptation, communicating to her his feeling that she was weak and incapable. He also identified with her in this weakness and incapacity for he felt that way about himself in his competition with his brother. This led him to indulge her in those ways he himself wished to be indulged, that is, to be attended to physically in every possible way. These attentions excited Ann but also elicited anxiety and repression in her since she was dimly aware of his own conflictful feelings. It seemed possible that this stimulation-repression cycle started early in life, affecting her curiosity and her retention of the details that she was learning at the time thus contributing to her failure to learn the instrumental perceptual-motor skills during the nursery school years.

For her part, Mrs. C. recognized in Ann the pretty, father's favorite child that she herself had been in the preschool years. She saw her as a rival for her husband's affection and was angry at her for the load of responsibility she represented. At the same time, she felt sorry for her as Ann fell behind in maturation, and she felt guilty for whatever part she might have played in that, just as she was guilty about her own behavior toward her brother, to whom she felt superior and who was a failure in her father's eyes. Her mother's evaluation of her was clear to Ann and undermined her self-respect. Mrs. C.'s guilt motivated part of her toleration of Ann's immaturity, but this indulgence alternated with repressive rules in all areas and a sharp, almost fanatical, stickling on details of dress and demeanor. Although at the point of beginning treatment Mrs. C. presented almost a classic obsessional personality she had quite obviously retreated to this position from a well developed hysterical style herself in latency. A good many of Ann's outbursts at home had elements in them that her mother could recognize as her own. She held herself responsible for Ann's deficiencies, as she had blamed herself for her brother's problems. When she clarified some of these things and managed to begin handling situations with the children at home better, she felt less guilty and more of a mother.

Ann is an example of a child whose development was held back substantially by the static interaction dictated by her parents' unconscious conflicts and projections, which prevented them from providing for her needs. When these constrictive templates were lifted in psychotherapy, the child quickly began catching up to what would be expected from a girl her age.

Therapy with a family in the less favorable group. Cathy B. was six years old when she was brought to the child psychiatric clinic for evaluation of her excitable, argumentative, and manipulative behavior for which her mother found difficulty setting limits. Also, she had developed a tendency to be flirtatious and coquettish with her mother's boyfriends in the past and was now approaching her stepfather by stroking and whispering profanity in his ear and by touching his genitals through his clothing. Her mother felt jealous but helpless to intervene.

An extended clinical evaluation through work with all family members indicated that Cathy had grown up in a disturbed and disrupted environment and that her symptoms appeared to be reactions to problems within and between the adults with whom she lived. She did not appear markedly disturbed, but there was concern that the direction of her development augered for future personality disorder of the hysterical type. The family accepted the offer of individual therapy. This treatment went on for three years with a succession of psychiatric residents on six-month rotation in children's psychiatry. Each family member saw the same therapist for once-weekly individual sessions.

Cathy's stepfather, Mr. R., was twenty-six when the treatment began. He spent his time as a potter and volunteer "art therapist." He had been unable to find a suitable direction for himself after graduating in philosophy from a small college and was contemplating attending theology school. He did begin this training during the period of his therapy but dropped out after a short time. He contributed to the family's income, but his wife's business provided the largest share.

Initially, Mr. R. was concerned that the evaluation might have a negative effect on his own mental stability, and reluctance to be in treatment characterized much of his contact with the clinic. Twice he temporarily discontinued his treatment before finally saying he would come only once a month to talk about Cathy. In the last year of treatment he and his wife had become interested in self-improvement through the Gurdjieff system, and when the episode occurred that precipitated the family's withdrawal from treatment, he expected to help Cathy through involvement in that method.

During this therapy hours Mr. R. was concerned about both his anger at, and his sexual feelings for, Cathy, and his inadequate handling of these by detachment and immobility. He was conflicted about his role as a limit setter and disciplinarian and worried about his wife's demanding dependency and his own passivity. Although he made some changes, especially after the birth of his own daughter, he responded poorly to changes in therapists, and it was felt he was of little help to Cathy or her mother in their interpersonal struggles. Of the three, he made the least progress in treatment. Intellectualization was his primary defense, and he appeared to be intermittently psychotic in this thinking.

Mrs. R., also twenty-six at the time of the evaluation, was much more voluble and dramatic than her husband. Her personality was scarcely more stable than his, but she supported the family, later another child, her half-sister, and an unwelcome friend of her husband's through an increasingly successful photography studio. Mrs. R. was the only child of her parent's marriage, which ended in divorce when she was three years old and after much physical and verbal abuse between her parents. She recalled that during this marriage, her father, an alcoholic, would take her with him when visiting his girlfriends. Her mother was a vain, self-absorbed person whom she could remember sitting before a mirror for long periods admiring her breasts, combing her hair and trying on clothes. Mrs. R. felt her own most successful portraits and model posings were of a type that would have complimented her mother's appearance. Their relationship was that of "bickering sisters," and Mrs. R. recalled feeling lonely and unloved, often being left at home after school and in the evenings by both parents. After her mother remarried, Mrs. R. remembers hearing her mother and stepfather's loud and rough sexual play through the bedroom wall.

Mrs. R. married after one year of junior college to John B., and Cathy was born eleven months later, when her mother and father were twenty. Mrs. R. reported that the marriage went downhill from the beginning, but the couple stayed together, nursed her mother in her last illness and moved to the Bay Area of California, where they both occupied themselves with work and Mrs. R.

quickly became quite successful. There was another pregnancy, not very much wanted even in the beginning, and it ended in a stillbirth. After this, when Cathy was about four years old, the parents separated for good, and she and her mother moved to a nearby metropolis where Mrs. R. began a frantic dating spree ("fifty men in six months"). She said she enjoyed controlling these relationships by her teasing and coquettish behavior. Cathy watched her mother with these dates, including sexual embraces, and would herself seek attention by being boisterous, putting herself between her mother and the dates, and by imitating her mother's flirtatious and sexual approaches to men. About a year before seeking help for Cathy, Mrs. R. met and began to live with Mr. R., who became her second husband as soon as her divorce was final.

Mrs. R. participated actively in the evaluation and subsequent treatment but in a flighty and disorganized way so that she managed to avoid talking about specific incidents or emotions most of the time. Her inital diagnosis was hysterical personality, but further aquaintance prompted a more ominous formulation. Her investment in the treatment was more intense than that of her husband, and her work was more useful to her, but it also fell short of major success. During the therapeutic work she gave birth to another daughter, in the hope that by having a child of his own her husband would feel more real involvement in their marriage; yet at the same time she began to have an affair with one of her work associates and described him as the first person with whom she felt sexually fulfilled.

Major issues in Mrs. R.'s therapy were a yearning to be cared for, fear of being neglected, and anger at men. She was quite fearful of expressing these angry feelings lest they end relationships, but she was aware she often acted bossy and guileful. As a mother she was self-critical for neglecting her children, but at the same time she envied them their child status and identified their needs as her own. It was clear her inability to set limits on Cathy's misbehavior was due to her own vicarious pleasure in observing the acts. She behaved toward Cathy as if Cathy were a peer with whom she could bicker, as she had done with her mother. She was teasingly provocative with two of her male therapists, and both of them observed that her coy approaches at times were a vehicle for anger rather than positive feelings. Her attitude toward her treatment was consistently that of questioning and challenging the therapists on their personal life, tastes and styles, habits and beliefs. There were constant doubts of the therapist's competency, implicit criticisms and dissatisfaction, advice seeking and postures of helplessness. She brought in a wealth of material, dreams and associations, but veered away from affect-laden issues, seeming to lose the details when asked for particulars. She had rapid fluctuations in emotion, but usually she was not consciously experiencing the emotion even as she expressed it. A thorough working transference developed only partially, and that with only one therapist. During the last six months of treatment, her husband had stopped coming in regularly and she herself began to find reasons for not attending her sessions. When the fee was reassessed upward because of the increasing success of her business, she felt great anger, betrayal, and a sense of being punished. The culminative resistances could not be resolved, and the family dropped out of treatment.

Despite the fact that very little progress was made in the therapy of her mother and stepfather, both of whom had been described by several therapists as borderline (the stepfather at one point being called "psychoticlike"), Cathy's intellectual and learning abilities and her immediate emotional relationship to the therapist seemed to indicate that whatever the chaos at that point in her life, her early attachment and development had been adequate. Her parents were not yet estranged in the first year of her life, both were attending junior college, and there was apparently some support from the grandparents. It may be that Cathy was attended during that time much as she herself later attended the dolls in the playroom—adequately. Her mother must have identified with the parental role sufficiently because Cathy's first two years of development seem to have been relatively normal.

Difficulties arose when the parents returned to the Midwest to nurse Mrs. R's mother through to her death from cancer. Cathy was two. It was known from her treatment that Mrs. R. felt that her mother didn't give her the "right kind of attention," and it may be that whatever support there was there evaporated during the grandmother's last illness.

In spite of these difficulties Cathy seemed capable and normal at age three in nursery school when the parents moved to the Bay Area. There was then another pregnancy and a deterioration in the parent's relationship which was hastened by the unwanted child, born dead. This was followed by the separation and divorce during Cathy's fourth year of life. From what was subsequently revealed in the playroom, it appears that it was during this fourth and fifth year that Cathy began the behavior which revealed conflicts to which she so easily returned later during stress and disappointment. Certainly after age two she was picking up on her mother's cognitive style, and it seems likely that this took on the trappings of the hostile erotization of her mother's relationships with men and of arguments and competition with women. There was evidence that Mrs. R. used her daughter as a peer with whom to argue, act up through, and manipulate. At that point Mrs. R. appears to have regressed and become promiscuous, and Cathy and she began to be rivals for the attention of the men callers. Just at the time that Cathy's cognitive structure was being shaped, and her own sexual-sensual feelings were able to focus on a father image in the callers, her mother's own conflicts here were being expressed as hostile behavior in the guise of seductions. Cathy had to share her mother's attention with the men, for which she was angry, while at the same time competing with her mother for the attention she craved from the same men.

It became clear in Mrs. R.'s treatment that she felt very inadequate, neglected by her own mother, inferior to men, incomplete as compared to them, and angry at them, expressing the anger in hostile seductiveness which accomplished three purposes at once: to control, punish, and attract attention. The "many dates" stopped with her remarriage when Cathy was five and a half, but the competitiveness between mother and daughter for the new husband continued. He was essentially paralyzed by Cathy's seductiveness, attracted by it and uneasy. Her mother felt "envy" but couldn't intervene.

When evaluated at age six, Cathy was active, voluble like her mother, and expressed immediately in the playroom a rich fantasy life concerned with the interpersonal relationships that characterized her chaotic family life. It was not difficult to correlate the playroom scenes with the happenings in her family life as reported by her parents. At the point of initial evaluation she was preoccupied with the idea of brothers, and that children must intervene to regulate the violent life of the adults. (Her mother had asked during the evaluation, "Is the child forced to be an adult if the adults in the family act like children?") Psychological testing found her bright, normal, with castration fears, but not very disturbed as yet in her development.

In the playroom treatment there were early aggressive attacks on the dolls, biting and stabbing predominating. Much of this was directed toward the genitals of the human dolls. She was consistently destructive toward the genitals of the male figures. If the dolls were made to have intercourse they bit each other's heads off afterward. It appeared here that she was resonating with her mother's hostile use of seduction themes. Over time they were amenable to a reenactment, with a different outcome, in the playroom. She did not repeat a feint at the therapist's genitals in that early period after he had responded firmly and calmly. Not long after this, tender and caring themes emerged that were intermixed with destructivity.

During this period it seemed her oedipal inclinations were being contaminated by the underlying acting out of her mother's hostility toward men, and her own frustrated needs for fatherly attention without sexuality, both pregenital strivings. Her own father was distant and unavailable; her stepfather was aroused and paralyzed. Only the therapist remained for any adequate working through of these mixtures of needs and impulses. The success of the therapist's efforts was measurable in the caring themes and psychiatrist idealizations which appeared later in treatment. Cathy seemed to be sorting out two major inclinations in her relationship to the male therapists: tenderness and aggression. When the therapist calmly turned away first her attack on his genitals and a later, more seductive, invitation, she began to take care of him with proper tea parties and the loving care of babies, in which he was involved in a fatherly way. But before this type of play emerged, there was messiness in the playroom, disorderly fingerpainting and water play, and an attempt to forcibly feed the therapist. Normal oedipal themes could not emerge before the pathological preoedipal strivings, so abetted by her home environment, could be worked through.

With this disturbed family there were, of course, many intersecting and conflicting themes to be winnowed in assessing how this particular youngster developed her hysterical style. There is, for example, the event of the stillborn brother, which Cathy was reported to have accused her mother of killing, and the birth of a sister subsequent to the beginning of treatment. When she was seven, a wierd boarder stayed with the family for some months and caused a great deal of problems, the father ambivalently admiring him and the mother hating him but not able to evict him. Cathy regressed during this time to playing out fantasies of mayhem and murder culminating in a scheme to cut off the boarder's penis. Such ideas were apparently provoked or encouraged by Cathy finding a wooden dildo around the house.

Despite the lack of progress in her parents, the themes across the three years of psychotherapy reflected substantial advance in Cathy's cognitive and psychological development. It seemed clear this was the direct result of playroom work. That the concomitant therapy with the parents had a sparing effect that intermittently lifted the static and inappropriate interactions between the child and her parents was inferred but difficult to document. Nevertheless, Cathy remained vulnerable to rapid regression under stress (such as her sister's birth or the boarder) to those sadistically "sexual" and hostile behaviors that characterized her when she first came to the clinic.

This family showed an impressive interweaving of the sexual behaviors with aggressive and hateful impulses in both mother and child and suggests one avenue through which hysterical styles with less favorable prognoses arise. It seemed that through therapy Cathy moved through her oedipal phase into latency, but retained her vulnerability to regression. Had she not had this help, it appears she would have been in great danger of developing a very inadequate personality. Taking her parents' immature personalities into account, Cathy's prognosis, despite her progress, must still be guarded.

It remains to summarize the points to which clinical inference and theoretical abstraction have brought the concept of hysterical personality in childhood.

If one were to use only the *Diagnostic and Statistical Manual II* to assess the presence or absence of a hysterical personality in a child between three and seven or eight, few children would escape that diagnosis. Clearly, such classifications are too inclusive for use with most children who show hysterical traits. The state of development of the child, his or her age, and the relative balance of ego structure as compared to psychosexual and psychosocial maturity are of crucial importance. The quality and quantity of interpersonal relationships, especially with parents, play a part in the manifest behavior that is characteristic of the child. How long that influence has been present, how rigid or flexible, static or progressive it is will figure in the result and must be taken into account in diagnosis.

In adult personality disorder, the traits described appear relatively fixed, as if they are characteristic emissions of an internal cognitive structure. In children, however, character is determined by the appropriateness of their interpersonal environment in relation to their age and social milieu and is in constant flux toward maturity due to the impetus of biological givens. The degree to which this impetus realizes its aim will be determined by the quality of the interaction of the growing child with the parenting persons and especially by the length of time inappropriate interactions persist. In general, the earlier a deficiency appears in the reciprocity of the first attachments, the more serious the subsequent maladjustment.

The labels appended to patients are abstractions designed to facilitate our thinking and understanding and therefore our treatment. They do not fully describe any disease state, nor do they indicate the balance between strengths and weaknesses even in adulthood, to say nothing of childhood. To identify a child as having a hysterical character disorder then would be such a gross oversimplification as to operate more as a hindrance than a help. Fuller understanding of the parent-child interactions and a psychotherapeutic acquaintance with the inner life of all three will often reveal the framework from which pathological and protopathological traits in the child emerge. These traits are shaped and sometimes elicited by parental attitudes, conscious and unconscious, which are a reflection of the parents' own immature intrapsychic life and are more than the child can tolerate without distortion and constriction.

At this state of the art it might be too much to expect to discover and treat incipient hysterical personality in the nascent state in school-aged children with very great frequency. The most that can be said is that a large group of children with commonly recognized hysterical traits can be identified. It is proposed here that if we remove those children who are showing these traits because they are normal for their age and if sufficient data can be obtained through evaluation and treatment of the remaining children and their parents, two poles or subgroups can be differentiated. The children in the more mature group are in danger of fixating at the level of symptomatology which if unchanged by therapy or other environmental factors will later be called hysterical character. With treatment of these children, or their parents, or both, the prognosis is good. The other pole consists of a subgroup of children who are less developed, have more disturbed parents, and are at risk for a variety of disabling personality disorders of later life only one of which is the so-called sick hysterical personality. This group does not often reach effective treatment and the prognosis must be guarded.

What holds here must also hold for the formation of personality and personality pathology of all sorts. The scientific validation of this proposal will have to wait for psychoanalytically informed, long-term observation of many children and their parents in psychotherapy and in their own environments. This is a prospect not likely to be realized soon.

NOTES

1. Henry Rosner (1975) has briefly reported the successful analysis of a six-year-old girl whose sexual symptoms were so intense that he felt she already had a serious character deformity of the hysterical type. Treatment had been precipitated when she developed acute regressive symptoms subsequent to being denied access to her three-and-one-half-year-old brother when he went to the toilet. Her mother reported that *for about two years* (emphasis added) this child had accompanied her younger brother into the bathroom and was overheard telling him: "I'll rub it and then you will be able to make." Unfortunately, Rosner mentions little information about the parents beyond this provocative piece of data.

2. Zelda Wolpe (1953) reports the treatment of the father of a four-and-one-half-year-old girl with functional blindness of three years duration.

The father's therapy and the therapist's influence on the rest of the family through the father, resulted in the relief of this symptom in the child.

REFERENCES

Abse, W. (1974). Hysteria within the context of the family. *Journal of Operational Psychiatry* 6: 31-42.

Ainsworth, M. (1973). The development of infant-mother attachment. In *Review of Child Development Research No. 3*, ed. B. Caldwell and H. Ricciuti, pp. 1-94.

Anthony, E. (1961). Learning difficulties in childhood: report of a panel. *Journal of the American Psychoanalytic Association* 9: 124-134.

Bowlby, J. (1969). *Attachment and Loss. Vol. I: Attachment*. New York: Basic Books.

Briquet, P. (1854). *Traité Clinique et Thérapeutique de l'Hystérie*. Paris: Ballière.

Brody, S., and Axelrad, S. (1967). *Mother-Infant Interaction No. 1: at Six Weeks*. A film.

———(1968). *Mother-Infant Interaction No. 2: at Six Months*. A film.

Easser, B. and Lesser, S. (1965). Hysterical personality: a reevaluation. *Psychoanalytic Quarterly* 34: 390-405.

Erikson, E. (1963). *Childhood and Society*. 2nd ed. New York: Norton.

Freud, S. (1920). The psychogenesis of a case of homosexuality in a woman. *Standard Edition* 18: 146-172.

Garmezy, N. (1974). Children at risk: the search for the antecedents of schizophrenia, part I. *Schizophrenia Bulletin*, No. 8, pp. 14-90. National Institute of Mental Health.

Group for the Advancement of Psychiatry (1966). Report of the committee on child psychiatry. In *The Psychopathological Disorders of Childhood*. New York: Scribner.

Hollender, M. (1971). The hysterical personality. *Comments on Contemporary Psychiatry* 1: 17-24.

La Barre, M., and La Barre, W. (1965). The worm in the honeysuckle. *Social Casework* 46: 399-413.

Lazare, A. (1971). The hysterical character in psychoanalytic theory: evolution and confusion. *Archives of General Psychiatry* 25: 131-137.

Ludwig, A. (1972). Hysteria: a neurobiological theory. *Archives of General Psychiatry* 27: 771-777.

Main, M. (1977). Analysis of a peculiar form of reunion behavior seen in some day-care children: its history and sequelae in children who are home reared. In *Social Development in Day Care*, ed. R. Webb. Baltimore: John Hopkins Press.

Marmor, J. (1953). Orality in the hysterical personality. *Journal of the American Psychiatric Association* 1: 656-671.

Millon, T. (1969). *Modern Psychopathology*. Philadelphia: W. B. Saunders.

Opler, M. (1969). Culture and child rearing. In *Modern Perspective in International Child Psychiatry*, ed. J. Howells, pp. 309-320. Edinburgh: Oliver and Boyd.

Rangell, L. (1959). The nature of conversion. *Journal of the American Psychoanalytic Association* 17: 632-662.

Robertson, J., and Robertson, J. (1969). *John, 17 Months: Nine Days in a Residential Nursery*. A film. London: Tavistock Research Center.

Robins, L. (1966). Childhood behavior predicting later diagnosis. In *Deviant Children Grown Up*, pp. 135-158. Baltimore: Williams and Wilkins.

Rosner, H. (1975). Clinical and diagnostic considerations in the analysis of a five-year-old hysteric. *Journal of the American Psychiatric Association* 23: 507-534.

Shapiro, D. (1965). *Neurotic Styles*. New York: Basic Books.

Sheffield, H. (1898). Childhood as it occurs in the United States of America. *New York Medical Journal* 68: 412-416, 433-436.

Schilder, P. (1939). The concept of hysteria. *American Journal of Psychoanalysis* 95: 1389-1413.

Sperling, M. (1973). Conversion hysteria and conversion symptoms: a revision of classification and concepts. *Journal of the American Psychoanalytic Association* 21: 745-771.

Spitz, R. (1965). *The First Year of Life*. New York: International Universities Press.

Starr, P. H. (1953). Some observations on the diagnostic aspects of childhood hysteria. *The Nervous Child* 10: 231.

Szurek, S., (1954). Concerning sexual disorders of parents and children. *Journal of Nervous and Mental Diseases* 120: 369-378.

Szurek, S., Johnson, A., and Falstein, E. (1942). Collaborative psychiatric therapy of parent-child problems. *American Journal of Orthopsychiatry* 12: 511-516.

Thomas, A., Chess, S., Birch, H., Herzig, M., and Korn, S. (1963). *Behavioral Individuality in Early Childhood*. New York: New York University Press.

Vaillant, G. (1971). Theoretical hierarchy of adaptive ego mechanisms. *Archives of General Psychiatry* 24: 107-118.

Walker, J., and Szurek, S. (1973). Early childhood development of psychotic children: a study of anamnestic methods. In *Clinical Studies in Childhood Psychoses*, ed. S. Szurek and I. Berlin. New York: Brunner/Mazel.

Wolpe, Z. (1953). Psychogenic visual disturbance in a four-year-old child. *The Nervous Child* 10: 314-325.

Zetzel, E. (1968). The so-called good hysteric. *International Journal of Psycho-Analysis* 49: 256-260.

CHAPTER 5

Basic Treatment Issues

DAVID W. ALLEN, M.D.

An average treatable case of hysterical personality will often go through phases. The initial phase is one of presentation of self and complaints in a particular light, often one that is an appeal for attention. This is followed quickly, once a therapeutic attachment is established, by a period of regression in which unresolved conflicts and childhood fixations are manifested within the therapeutic relationship itself. Ideally, this phase overlaps with a period of working through, the therapeutic antidote to the multiply determined nature of the patient's state at onset of treatment. Finally, termination encompasses the difficult task of separation, itself a phase of important work on self development for the hysterical personality.

This chapter will focus on major themes during these phases, especially on initial problems. Since the extended and complete treatment of a single case will be described in thorough detail in chapter 6, a broad view will be given here through the use of case vignettes. As described in chapter 2, hysterical symptoms were not synonymous with hysterical personality. Nonetheless, persons who do fall within this typology often present for treatment with a conversion or dissociative symptom, and so treatment of such complaints will be included.

The techniques of psychotherapy cover such a wide gamut that any discussion must be circumscribed by boundaries. The approach

This chapter has been prepared with the assistance of Sarah Peele and the editorial help of JoAnn DiLorenzo. The quotation from Allen and Houston, Psychiatry 22:41-49, 1959 by the William Alanson White Psychiatric Foundation, is reprinted by permission.

here is that of brief or extended treatment guided by psychoanalytic theory, using the basic ground rules of psychodynamic psychotherapy (Abse 1974). The main patient type under consideration is the hysterical personality who has developed a separated, although conflicted, self-representation and who has advanced, in terms of capacity for relationship, to at least the beginning of genital aims and conflict configurations. For the more severely impaired hysterical personality, who has not advanced developmentally from pregenital levels of character formation, the addition of techniques for treatment of narcissistic and borderline character disorders would be appropriate (Giovaccini 1975, Kernberg 1970, 1974, Kohut 1971).

THE MOST COMMON TREATMENT THEMES

Running through the chronicle of hysteria treatment are several colorful themes. One is that the nature of symptom onset, and even the cure, may be quite dramatic. The course is often variable and associated with difficulties in differential diagnosis. Another important theme, although often expressed only vaguely or intuitively, is that sexual and aggressive impulses were repressed and yet returned in a distorted expression through somatic or behavioral symptoms. Finally, there is the theme of the conflicting emotions aroused by hysterics in those who treat them. Many of these themes are illustrated in the following case example.

An athetoid teen-ager. A young psychiatric resident was called in consultation to see a pretty sixteen-year-old farm girl who had been referred to the university hospital with the diagnosis of a possible rheumatic fever athetosis. About two weeks prior to admission she had developed a rhythmic, slow, writhing movement of her right shoulder which continued in spasms almost unabated day and night. Since the onset the patient had hardly slept and had very little to eat and drink. When the resident first saw her, she was lying in bed, and every few seconds made a kind of twitching shrug with her right shoulder. In spite of this symptom and the fact that she looked rather dehydrated and pale, her demeanor was quite bland and calm. The history was of a sudden onset without apparent cause. There was no history of fever or cardiac symptoms other than somewhat elevated pulse rate, and no history of joint pain.

The past medical history was not remarkable and neither was the initial family history except for the fact that her family belonged to a strict fundamentalist Protestant sect. Mental status examination indicated no loss of contact with reality or other evidence of psychosis. Except for the symptom as described, her physical examination and a careful neurologic examination revealed no abnormalities, nor did routine lab work and testing of sedimentation rate. The resident, proud of his neurologic and medical acumen, was troubled that despite repeated questioning, the patient, although apparently cooperative, was totally unable to recall any possible traumatic emotional situation connected with the onset.

The resident presented the case to his superior, a psychoanalyst, who insisted that in addition to the motor symptoms without evidence of physical lesion, and despite the patient's calm mental attitude, the resident should be able to demonstrate other positive psychological findings before diagnosing a conversion reaction. There should be a stress of onset, with efforts to ward off some unacceptable impulse and a fantasy which had partially escaped repression and returned to the consciousness in the form of the symptom. The psychoanalyst insisted that the writhing and twitching of the patient's shoulder in some way symbolized the conflict, and that the patient's inability to relate the symptom to any emotional stress was evidence of the resistance in her own mind— the manifestation of a defense against anxiety.

When plagued by the resident for more tangible help, the analyst said that undoubtedly through hypnosis or Amytal interviews the patient's symptom could be relieved temporarily and relevant history obtained. But he suggested that it would be more therapeutic to enlist the patient's conscious cooperation in recovering the memory and fantasy, and that this could be done from available clues. Her shrugging might represent, for example, he said, a warding off of a wished-for and feared incestuous impulse such as a caress from her father. She might have been sleeping in the same bed with him, with her right shoulder up, and imagining his hand on her shoulder.

The resident thought his consultant's hypothesis almost bizarre. But he returned to the patient and asked her to describe the sleeping arrangements in her home. Without hesitation she said that her grandparents had come to visit shortly before the onset of her symptoms and that she had had to move into the bedroom with her parents. Further questioning quickly elicited the fact that she slept next to her father, facing the wall, on her left side, with her right shoulder up. During the night she had had to crawl over her father to get out of bed in order to visit the outhouse. And it was upon her return to bed, just as she was starting to fall asleep, that the uncontrollable twitching of her right shoulder had begun.

I shall not go into futher detail on this case except to say that I was the resident, not the psychoanalyst. And the very day the patient talked about the bedroom, her shoulder twitching began to diminish, and in another day or two she was completely free of it.

INITIAL PHASE

Approaching the Presenting Symptoms
The hysterical symptom should not be assaulted by direct interpretation. One of Freud's early cases is instructive on this point.

The mother of a hysterical girl confided to me [Freud] the homosexual experience which had greatly contributed to the fixation of the girl's attacks. The mother had herself surprised the scene; but the patient had completely forgotten it, though it occurred when she was approaching puberty. [Freud 1913, pp. 141-142]

Freud learned then that "every time I repeated her mother's story to the girl she reacted with a hysterical attack, and after this she forgot the story once more" (p. 141). Clearly, there was stiffened resistance against knowledge being forced upon the patient. The patient finally simulated feeble-mindedness and developed a complete loss of memory in order to protect herself against the conscious knowledge of the incident. (pp. 141-142)

While perhaps extreme in demonstrating the forcefulness of resistances, the case is certainly not atypical of the ineffectiveness of an attempted direct attack on a firmly placed symptom, especially when the symptom has a strong function in the patient's psychic economy. Any attempt to remove a patient's hysterical symptom by direct reasoning tends to produce a negative result. It is just as futile to attempt to rid the hysteric of his symptom by explaining to him the functional nature of his reaction as it is to attempt to reason away the paranoid's delusions. To approach treatment along the expected lines of layman logic only strengthens the patient's symptoms and intensifies his negative feelings toward therapy and the therapist. The patient's defensive system is a reaction to his inner anxiety, and his anxiety is heightened and his defenses further excited by threats of external attack. His resistances are stiffened even if he is able to agree with the therapist's evidence and reasoning. The patient's symptom is impregnable from the front, as it were, and only a well-prepared and well-timed flank attack or encirclement will relieve it.

The usefulness and effectiveness of the oblique approach is more apparent in long-term therapy, but to a degree it applies in even the briefest psychotherapy, as the following case illustrates. In even an hour's time, information was collected and rapport developed; and interpretation did not directly assault the symptom but dealt with it gently through the roots of the underlying dilemma. This is not to say that there need be any concealment of the therapist's intent to try to understand the patient and of his wish to have the patient's active cooperation in the process—quite the contrary. Nor is it to say that appropriate questions may not be asked, clarifications requested, or juxtapositions of information made.

A premedical student. A premedical student appears in the emergency room with a history of acute onset of feelings of a mass in his throat, sensations of gagging, and uncontrolled vomiting for forty-eight hours. He is given parenteral thorazine, and the retching stops, but he continues to complain of the feeling of the mass in his throat and experiences distressing gagging sensations.

In consultation I discover that the onset of symptoms began a few hours after he had been to the dental clinic, where a male friend of his, a few years older, had done the dental work on him, his hands and instruments in the patient's mouth. A brief review of his background revealed that since childhood the patient had been highly industrious, helping a competent mother run a family business. The father was affectionate, but passive and ineffectual. The patient felt that he himself carried the family aspirations. I ask the patient to describe the mass in his throat. He says that it is a greasy mass and indicates with his hand that its dimensions are about six inches long and one and a half inches in diameter. My tentative formulation to myself is that the young man defends against passive tendencies and oral dependent longings by his characteristic independence and industriousness. Further, I feel that the patient has probably had difficulty in attaining a comfortable masculine identification. In childhood he might have wished for a closer relationship with a strong and capable father. All of these factors probably conspired to produce a latent homosexual conflict which became acute at the time of his oral-physical contact with his friend the dentist.

What should the psychiatrist's intervention be? Should he reassure the patient? Prescribe more thorazine? Tell him that he needs long-term psychiatric treatment? Offer him a genetic-dynamic formulation of his case? Or interpret the phallic symbolism of the mass in his throat by suddenly thrusting a large hot dog in his face, as Lionel Blitzsten is once alleged to have done with a woman opera singer with aphonia? Blitzsten caused the singer to scream and thereby relieved her loss of voice (Orr 1961, p. 46). She developed this hysterical symptom shortly after her first experience with fellatio, and Blitzsten's rather dramatic action interpretation was an attempt to relieve her acute aphonia a few hours before she was scheduled to sing an important role. This kind of dramatic action interpretation had the advantage of surprise in connection with an acute symptom in which the symbolic meaning seemed almost flagrantly preconscious and easily relatable to the recent memory of fellatio. But it was a gimmicky treatment, and while it may have a place in the technique of certain peculiarly gifted therapists such as Blitzsten presumably was, it was risky and is generally to be avoided.

The problem with the premedical student is to do neither too little nor too much within the context of the rapport the psychiatrist has built up in the hour of the interview. I said to the patient, "It sounds as if you've always been a pretty independent guy and it's difficult for you to accept help even from a friend and colleague." In my opinion, this statement touched on the essential issues, and at any rate it was quite acceptable to the patient, who smiled and agreed and, in a short while, announced that the lump in his throat was beginning to go away. If at some subsequent time he requires further psychotherapy, he at least has had a helpful, nonthreatening introduction to it.

Since direct assault on symptoms is often contraindicated, it follows that one must work on underlying causes. In such an approach the relationship established between patient and therapist becomes a key concern for alteration of the pathological situation. For in the transference phenomena that usually emerge, the core problems that underlie symptom formation and characteristic maladaptations can be gradually explored.

Transference

Hysterical patients make contact immediately, and it is a reparative contact they seek. Their anxiety and acting out against deeper involvements derive from fears and fixations going back to earliest object relations. The narcissism of the hysterical personality bespeaks an impairment in the earliest experiences of loving and being loved and in the conditioned expectations arising out of these body experiences with self and others. These early impairments interfere with normal gender-identity development and result in the compensatory, intensified pseudosexuality described in the previous chapters.

For the beginning therapist, such patients give the clearest and most accessible evidence of transference. The dynamics are less obscure than in most other kinds of patients. The crux of the treatment of the hysterical personality *is* the transference. If we give wrong interpretations, we can correct them in the light of later information. If we miss opportunities to interpret, they will occur again and again. But if we mishandle the transference, the treatment is in trouble. *Mishandling the transference or failing to establish a therapeutic alliance is almost the only vital mistake,* and it is exceedingly difficult to repair. The history of handling the transference is virtually the history of the evolvement of the treatment of hysteria which became systematically understandable only with the advent of psychoanalysis.

Transference was a stumbling block for Freud's colleague Breuer and a stepping-stone for Freud (Jones 1953). When Breuer treated Anna O., she had developed a museum of symptoms—paralyses, contractures, anesthesias—after much physical contact in nursing her dying father. A highly intelligent and attractive young woman, she first pointed out the value of cathartic talking, but she became very attached to Breuer, and his consuming interest in her began to make Mrs. Breuer jealous. When the patient developed a phantom pregnancy, Breuer was profoundly shocked, but managed to calm her and then fled in a cold sweat. The patient's accusation that he was the father of the child was too much for Breuer. He broke off treatment and left the next morning with his wife for Venice. Ten years later, when he called on Freud in consultation on a case of hysteria and Freud pointed out evidence of a developing pregnancy fantasy by the patient, Breuer, without saying a word, picked up his hat and cane and left the house (pp. 224-226).

In reviewing the history of the treatment of hysteria, certain principles—approaching the symptom through its underlying causes, and attending to the proper management of the transference—become clear. An adequate theoretical basis for consistent, understandable, repeatable, and teachable application of the therapeutic principles became possible with Freud. Prior to that, treatment results were more a matter of chance and the personality of the therapist.

Countertransference

Now, with three-quarters of a century of psychoanalytic treatment of hysteria behind us, we have little excuse for not knowing the principles of treating hysteria and the limitations of the method. Practical experiences of many analysts and therapists are available to supplement the direct practical experience of the individual therapist.

In the treatment of hysterical personality, the therapist should not avoid the eroticized transference. He should allow it to develop, and in time, like the hostile transference, the therapist should analyze it. But the therapist must guard against possible eroticized and hostile countertransferences in himself. A brief review of such counter-transferences may help alert the beginning therapist to this issue, and provide an interesting reminder to the experienced clinician.

Before Freud was born, a young English physician in the early 1800's, Robert Brudenell Carter, described by Veith (1970), developed a method of treating hysterics that was essentially free-associative and cathartic in that he encouraged the patient to "fill the outline" (p. 207). Carter cautioned against suggesting motives to the patient. He clearly understood much about overdetermination and sexual and narcissistic factors. What he apparently did not understand—even intuitively—was the transference. And he had countertransference problems. As Veith (1970) notes, "Underlying his perceptiveness one senses an antipathy towards his hysterical patients, perhaps the expression of his youthful impatience with the whims and foibles of women and their 'moral obliquity' " (p. 209). Perhaps it was his antipathy to hysterics as much as the lack of recognition of his work by the Victorian generation that led Carter to discontinue treating hysterics and become an eye surgeon (pp. 199-209).

Both Breuer and Carter had countertransference reactions to patients, which made it difficult for them to work with the patient's transference. And when the inquisitors of the Middle Ages and Puritan New England imputed secret sensuous pleasures and practices to the hysterics of their times, they were probably having countertransference reactions as well. The harsh treatment rendered by those judges says almost as much for their own suffering as for that of their victims.

In the past, however, nonexploitive, intuitive psychotherapists whose personal maturity has immunized them against countertransference entanglements have often been able to be helpful to hysterical patients. William Osler (Schneck 1963) wrote of S. Weir Mitchell's ability to be helpful to hysterics. Emaciated, nervous, full of whims and fancies, the patient was unable to digest any food unless she lay upon her back with her eyes shut. Standing at the foot of her bed, Mitchell felt that every suggestion he made as to treatment had been "forestalled." Every physician had urged her to exercise, to keep on her feet, to get about.

M. [Mitchell] on the inspiration of the moment told her to remain in bed. She took food better but found that on attempting to get up she was so weak that she could scarcely stand from lack of exercise. M. says he felt that he had run up against a stone wall. About this time he had seen on several occasions a quack named Lyons, who professed to cure, by passes and rubbings, a confirmed ataxic in such a way that he could get about for an hour or more at a time. The idea occurred to him to substitute for exercise the movements of the muscles caused by rubbings and friction and . . . [after giving several lessons to an aide] he instructed her to rub Mrs. S. for a certain time each day. The improvement began to be noticed and to the rubbing was added the electrical stimulation of the muscle also substituted for the active movement. The food was taken more freely, she gained in flesh and gradually recovered and was sent to her home. . . . The improvement persisted; she has since borne several more children and has been the soul of many enterprises in her native town. An incident, postpartum so to speak, was a letter from Mrs. S.'s mother, a wealthy New England woman, a speaker at temperance meetings, full of 'isms, etc. She wrote to Dr. M. to say that bodily comfort and ease, health and enjoyment might be dearly bought if at the price of eternal peace. For he had recommended her daughter to take champagne and to have a maid to assist her in her toilette. The former she considered not only unnecessary but hurtful, the latter quite superfluous, as any well-instructed New England husband was quite capable of helping his wife in her toilette. [Schneck 1973, p. 85]

It will be obvious here that Mitchell's encouragement of libidinal gratification, his permission of regression, and his countering of an overly severe superego influence are understandable in the psychoanalytic view. He is not put off by any feelings of "moral obliquity"; he does not dislike his patient. He is her ally against her inner enemy.

Often negative to psychoanalysis, Mitchell is like Freud in his empathy for his patient's humanity and in his intuitive understanding of the depth of her needs (see Veith's discussion in chapter 1 of this volume and Vieth 1970). And how interesting that he notes and reports on the reproach of the patient's mother to him in a way that connects the patient's difficulties with the mother's attitudes. But he does not reproach the mother either.

Beginning Treatment and the Emergence of the Transference

The general principles of psychotherapy apply in the treatment of the patient with a hysterical personality, but clinical experience teaches us that there are a number of rather predictable kinds of therapeutic difficulty and opportunity which are likely to be encountered in various phases of treatment. It is important during the initial phase that the therapist not act in ways which will make the resolution of the later phases of treatment more difficult or impossible. Freud's (1912) advice on this is still most pertinent:

> "Young and eager psycho-analysts will no doubt be tempted to bring their own individuality freely into the discussion, in order to carry the patient along with them and lift him over the barriers of his own narrow personality. . . . The doctor should be opaque to his patients and, like a mirror, should show them nothing but what is shown to him" (pp. 117, 118).

This advice has too often been misinterpreted to mean coldness and passivity. Its meaning is more simple and direct: it is not useful in overcoming patient resistance to give glimpses of one's own problems or intimate information about one's life, for it is the patient with a hysterical personality who is most likely to demand and provoke a therapist to revealing his own problems. The patient may feel alone in exposing his thought in treatment, find it unfair and feel that trust in the intimacy calls for similar revelations by the therapist. This feeling of unfairness is further evidence of the working of the unconscious resistances to understanding by the patient of his anxiety about regression into conflictual areas of childhood thought and feeling. He feels vulnerable, but exactly to what he does not know.

If the therapist adopts a familiar attitude with the patient, it may induce earlier revelations of certain consciously suppressed information, but the initial gain is lost later a thousandfold in the impediments the familiarity places in the way of the development of a clearly delineated transference which can be seen and felt by the therapist and interpreted and made conscious to the patient. If the therapist is to find the role the patient tends to project on to him and use it to clarify the patient's reactions, then he must not interfere with the process of the patient's attributions by bringing his own life into the patient's treatment.

The therapist stands at the interface of the patient's unconscious fantasy world and his real world. The therapist needs to be able to demonstrate that what the patient attaches to him is the last part of a long thread winding back through the patient's life to childhood.

Sometimes, out of anxiety about self-revelation, the patient seeks to reverse the roles of patient and therapist. He wants to know all about the therapist's thoughts and life as a prerequisite to revealing himself, or because he thinks the therapist more interesting, or because he thinks of the therapist as a model to pattern himself after. Often, indeed, such patients feel they had a defective parent model in childhood. That attitude, then, is already a forcible manifestation of the transference as the patient seeks to reexperience and remake his childhood and past. He is already searching for the defects in the therapist which *he knows* must be there as he seeks to recreate the relationship with the parent imago.

In analysis and in extensive psychoanalytic uncovering psychotherapy, an attitude by the therapist that is too intimate and self-revealing is incorrect technique. In psychotherapy, however, the therapist has more leeway for self-revelation when the goal is for limited and immediate symptom relief and he does not contemplate more extensive working through of character defenses and cognitive style. More than ever, in such instances, the therapist must know what he is doing and what he is sacrificing for an immediate gain.

The Therapeutic Alliance

Establishing a relationship with the patient, collecting information about him, organizing the information, and using it to communicate what may be useful to the patient are appropriate tasks for the therapist. The establishment of the therapeutic role within the relationship is a matter of utmost priority. The therapist asks himself—and in various ways he asks the patient—what's wrong? Why now? And how did it come about? The therapist attempts to understand those critical areas of human life having to do with stress reactions and character development: the patient's object relations, past and present; the patient's relationship to himself—his body and self-image, his identity; and the patient's concepts and values and how he experiences them.

As clinical data begins to accumulate, answers will reveal that the hysterical personality has strong narcissistic needs and seeks constant reassurance of worth, admiration, and love. And the hysteric is exquisitely sensitive to even the faintest sign of rejection. In part, the hysterical personality seems to need constant narcissistic gratification in order to maintain ego integrity and to reduce the anxiety constantly generated by a gender-identity confusion underlying the compensatory pseudosexuality.

Lacking constant narcissistic supplies and a sense of union or merging with the therapist, the hysteric experiences anxiety, frustration, and anger. He becomes demanding, ashamed, and guilty. In turn, confidence in his own integrity and worth diminishes. He then seeks reassurance that by destructive impulses and global rage he has not harmed the therapist as a potential supplier for his narcissistic needs. The patient may then increase his demands for favors and special recognition. He requires extra time at the end of the session or on the telephone, or he may ask for prescriptions for sedatives or tranquilizers.

Reacting sexually or aggressively in an attempt to define his gender identity, the hysteric tries to force the therapist to have more "real" contact with him. He thereby hopes to gratify and counteract his unconscious fantasies of omnipotence and helplessness. These inward dilemmas of omnipotence and helplessness and longings for merging and separateness manifest themselves in the relationship with the therapist, often in the form of demanding total gratification or nothing. It is as if the patient is saying, "Either you give me everything or I break off treatment; and if you give me everything it will destroy us." And now there is a dilemma and an opportunity for the therapist. In fact, the therapist knows the dilemma is coming and waits for it to develop so he can make an emotionally meaningful interpretation.

If the therapist attempts to gratify the patient's demands, they become endless. Then the patient's feelings of omnipotence increase, he manipulates the therapist at will, and he feels guilty and frightened of loss of control. Any effective therapy ends. Many a beginning therapist has been usefully if painfully instructed by the experience of going this destructive route with a patient. On the other hand, if the therapist takes a harsh stand or a punitive or critical attitude and refuses any concession, the patient may not be able to tolerate the deprivation or rejection and the resulting engulfing anxiety and rage. The patient may be unable to continue in treatment and will break off or react with stubborn uncooperativeness or an ultimatum. And the same new therapist who was painfully instructed about permissiveness often fills out his experience in this opposite direction.

The splitting tendency of the patient, manifesting and externalizing itself in the relationship with the therapist, is the therapist's opportunity. His only way out is also the way out for the patient. The therapist must maintain a neutral, steady therapeutic attitude without either indulgent gratification or retaliation. He reminds the patient of the therapeutic task, and he focuses on the patient's feelings of frustration, anxiety, and anger. As the patient is able to express these feelings verbally, it becomes possible to examine and interpret the patient's underlying fantasies of power and impotence, belief in his power to destroy and rescue, feelings of worthlessness, and need to be rescued. Often the female hysteric, whom we do see more commonly in the treatment than the male hysteric, seems to be demanding rescue by a magic, powerful parent figure.

The therapist must avoid being drawn into the patient's cycle of acting out, gratification, shame or guilt, self-punishment, suffering, guilt relief, and more acting out to obtain graticiation. He must avoid participating in the cycle while he helps the patient examine and understand it. In so doing, he helps the patient to have a learning experience of delaying action and of tolerating some deprivation and frustration, thus finding better forms of gratification.

A word is in order here about how the patient comes to treatment or the manner in which the patient is referred since these events make the beginning and the continuation of treatment more or less difficult. Sometimes a patient has been evaluated by a good psychiatrist or psychoanalyst, has been thought to be analyzable, and has been prepared for analysis or intensive psychotherapy through consultation with the referring doctor. In such a case the patient has a general knowledge of what to expect in terms of time, frequency, continuity, cost, and the nature of the treatment. I usually take this patient, at least on a trial basis, right into analysis or psychoanalytic psychotherapy. I do this even if the patient has a history of repeated and intense but rather superficial personal relationships outside of therapy and even if he has seen a number of previous therapists and at some point has broken off treatment with them.

However, if the patient does not come to me referred in the most appropriate manner or is self-referred but has a history of brief and broken-off relationships, including disrupted therapy with previous therapists, I generally undertake a kind of transitional therapy. I do this either for the purpose of making an adequate referral to another therapist for more definitive work or with the idea of possibly preparing the patient for more extensive therapy with me. Either way, I probably tell the patient something like the following: "Well, this pattern of your breaking off relationships at some point seems to be pretty clear, and I suppose the same thing will, in time, threaten to happen to us if we are going to be working together. You understand, of course, that either of us will be free to discontinue treatment at any time. But I want to call to your attention that it might be important to understand, if we can, what it is that drives you to that pattern of repeatedly breaking off your relationships, why it's necessary for you to do that. Anyway, I just want you to know that in time, the pattern is almost certain to come into the treatment here. And when it does, do you think you might wish to consider taking the opportunity to see what the breaking off could be guarding against, rather than just automatically or reflexively reenacting the same pattern?" Some such statement, made initially, may help later to gain the patient's conscious cooperation when the dilemma of the transference develops.

MIDDLE PHASE

Work on Gender Identification

In time, it can become possible to examine the patient's sense of gender-identity confusion, the absence of inner certainty and integrity, and the core fantasies of merging and destruction, of being destroyed or made whole or perfect by some sort of unification and splitting or rebirth experience. The manifestations of all these fantasies in the treatment relationship and other relationships need to be examined and related to their beginnings in early object experiences. Then the patient can be helped to see what kinds and degrees of gratification are realistically possible for him and what is realistically possible in therapy.

During this phase a romantic or erotic transference may develop. The patient believes he or she is in love with the therapist and as a resistance to working this through may insist on a "real" relationship with the therapist. If the patient resists interpretations and tests the therapist with threats to quit, it may be necessary to confront them quite directly. For example, one may say: "Here we are again at the breaking-off point. We can see that we are on the horns of a dilemma. You say that you love me and that it is real. But if we were to have a romantic relationship, however gratifying it might be, it would certainly go the way of previous relationships in your life and you would be no better off than before. On the other hand, if I don't go along with you on such a "real relationship," and if I insist that we need to analyze what's happening, you can always feel hurt or angry and use that to break off treatment. That too will defeat us. We can see that it's a damned-either-way thing unless we manage to understand it and work it through."

These situations occur in both heterosexual and homosexual pairing of patient to therapist. For example a male patient with an essentially hysterical character makeup, including hypermasculinity or pseudomasculinity, will also have a pattern of moving on in his personal and occupational relationships when intimacy-engendered tensions build up. In some ways they are more difficult to treat when the therapist is a man. He may not only be frightened off by the welling up of homosexual undertones in the relationship with a male therapist but by the intensely threatening dependency aspect of the relationship. He feels a strength in making demands but a weakness in asking for help or even in accepting it. The male stereotype calls for independence, assertiveness, and concealment of tenderness with other males. Hence the urge to flee treatment if these threatening feelings begin to arise with a therapist. Dependency and sentiment are more acceptable in the female stereotype and hence do not so sharply threaten the early treatment relationship.

Society, incidentally, tends to treat men who have a hysterical personality differently from the way it treats women with this style of behavior, particularly if the acting out tends to infringe on legal constraints. Society is more punitive to the male hysteric. An attractive young woman hysteric who runs up charge accounts or bounces checks is never held as accountable nor is her social reputation as damaged as the male hysteric who may rather rapidly become embroiled in legal entanglements which further impair his social adaptation and which may even result in his being labeled sociopathic. As Blacker and Tupin have pointed out in chapter 2 however, it is more accurately a pseudosociopathy.

Working Through Interpersonal Dilemmas

Attractive, provocative, manipulative, young hysterical women are often difficult for young male psychiatric residents to treat. Houston and I (Allen and Houston 1959) wrote of our experience in a training clinic working with some of these patients and young male therapists. We described typical clinical situations and countertransference problems and demonstrate how, by setting limits and sometimes by working with spouses or families, hysterical personalities can be effectively treated.

The following case, taken from that study, illustrates the development of the relationship and adequate data gathering before attempting significant interpretations of the patient's interpersonal dilemmas as they begin to be double binds for the therapist. The reader will note that the interpretive approach with this hysterical character is through the defense against feeling, although the patient acts as though she is free to feel and consciously believes that she is. The interpretations are within the cognitive style of the patient and enable the patient to reestablish thought connections which in turn make her acting out understandable, less automatic, and more under voluntary control.

A dismissed student. A young woman had repeatedly been involved in various kinds of activities which in effect harmed both herself and her family. Both of her parents had already been in treatment for reasons of their own, but had in the course of their therapy come to recognize their daughter's need for help. She had been sexually promiscuous, had had an illegal abortion, had been dismissed from a well-known women's college because of getting drunk, and had been involved in a number of serious automobile accidents with a group of young hot-rod enthusiasts.

Often she came into the office dressed in a very provocative manner, and several times she came directly from the beach in her bathing suit or from the tennis courts in shorts.

After a time the therapist was able to point out to the patient that her acting out occurred at times when she felt tense, and always after a period of external pressure had passed—for instance, following school examinations. The patient acknowledged this and said that at these times she had the feeling of wanting "to rebel, do something different, kick over the traces." At this point she was not aware that this wish concealed an underlying fear of losing control of herself, which, in turn, covered a guilty wish for abandoned behavior. The acting out thus served as a counterphobic defense against the fear and at the same time provided a displaced discharge for the original warded-off impulse. The patient emphasized that she believed in individual freedom, was against stereotyped thinking, and admired the expression of natural feelings.

In connection with a bit of the patient's acting-out behavior, the therapist suggested that the patient actually was not free to choose her course of action, that she had to act out in a rebellious way. The patient at first insisted that she did not *have* to, that she *wanted* to. But the therapist said, "It may seem that way to you, but I think you might agree that you are at least unable to control what you will want to do— that is, you are unable to want to put off acting at these times of tension." The patient demurred, saying that the therapist was simply trying to lay a semantic trap for her. The therapist said, "If you feel that I am trying to trap you, it seems that you imagine that the problems we are trying to understand are between us rather than within you. You are aware that you distrust me, but apparently you are not aware that you distrust yourself."

At a later session she gleefully confronted the therapist with the fact that she had not acted out in a period of tension according to the pattern the therapist had anticipated. The therapist agreed that the patient had indeed been able to refrain from action, but pointed out that she was able to do so not for the sake of understanding the tension, but in order to rebel against the therapist—to prove him wrong. The patient grudgingly admitted that such was indeed the motive.

Later, both the therapist and the patient came to see how the patient was engaged in a complicated sequence of mental gymnastics, trying to anticipate the therapist's unspoken predictions about her acting out, and then doing the opposite. The therapist remarked that her behavior in these respects was not free but was in fact controlled by what she imagined he expected of her. The patient again grudgingly agreed. Later the therapist pointed out that the patient used her mental image of his approval or disapproval as reason to do what she herself wanted to do to discharge tension. She used either the therapist's imagined approval to support what she wanted to do, or his imagined disapproval as justification to rebel and do what she wanted to do. Her use of the imagined support or prohibition alleviated the guilt associated with hitherto unconscious fantasies. After this interpretation was examined repeatedly by the patient, her acting out diminished, but she expressed much anger verbally against the therapist and against her parents.

The result of all this psychological maneuvering was that the patient got into a position where she could explore her relationship to her parents—particularly her reactions to what she felt were their repeated violations of her trust in them. Ultimately it became clear that the patient had a great deal of conflict about closeness to anyone—fear of it and desire for it—because of her early disappointing experiences with her parents. She was able to work this conflict through in her relationship with the therapist. As the therapy proceeded, her acting out gradually stopped; she became more successful in her university work; and her relationships improved at home and with her peers. [Allen and Houston 1959, p. 47]

The Recurrent Danger of Countertransference

In clinical fact, all of us are driven irresistibly to repeat our childhood, and it is helpful to know this and to know in what ways our childhood drives us. One of the great recurring difficulties in doing psychotherapy occurs when there is a blind overlap of the transferences which both patient and therapist bring to treatment. Then overidentification occurs, and the therapist is unable to interpret correctly. And then he is in serious jeopardy of acting out with or against the patient. In either event, the reaction is utterly destructive to therapy. It is not just certain therapists who have a tendency toward nontherapeutic involvement with hysterics. People other than therapists sometimes also have an affinity for distressing relationships with hysterics, as in the following case.

A creative businessman. An intelligent, intuitive, and creative businessman whose work is on the fringes of the entertainment industry comes to treatment. He is quite consciously manipulative and to some extent his manipulativeness and his own acting-out tendencies have contributed to the success of his work. He is pragmatically honest in his business dealings and very effective in maintaining harmony in his business organization, largely because of his sensitivity to the feelings of others. This man, however, is driven irresistibly to relationships with beautiful, intelligent women with hysterical personalities. And he has been married to a succession of them. Each time tensions build up, there is a lack of mutual reciprocal nurturing; he becomes wildly distressed and angry with his wife; he breaks off the relationship to go with another woman who is already, literally, in the offing.

It may come as no surprise that this patient's mother—beautiful, intelligent, hysterical—ran away with another man when the patient was at the end of his oedipal period, leaving him with his father and grandparents. Incidentally, this man is not postmaritally vindictive with these women and often finds a place for them in his business organization, where he maintains a friendship and in a sense takes care of them as he does his mother, who is some distance away.

One can imagine the difficulties in treatment if this man were the psychiatrist, psychologist, or social worker treating a hysterical woman and if he had not been well trained and well analyzed. Probably the best that could happen would be that out of ethical considerations he would refer her to another therapist—while he prepared to marry her.

Let us pause to reconsider four treatment guidelines. First, don't make an initial interpretative attack directly on the patient's symptom. Second, cultivate a good working alliance with the patient, a positive relationship, before making interpretations. Third, allow clinical data to accumulate until conclusions seem almost obvious, before even tentatively pointing them out. It would follow that usually no attempt should be made to deprive the patient of secondary gain attending a symptom or behavior pattern until there is enough understanding of the primary gain, that is, the forces that initially converged to produce the symptom or character trait. When this is understood, it is sometimes possible in the context of psychotherapy to suggest better and more direct gratification of conflicting needs. And finally, the fourth rule, a rule that is simpler to state than to apply, establish and maintain the relationship with the patient and the manner of working so as to maximize analyzing throughout the whole treatment and to minimize any reality basis for the patient's conscious expectations of any other form of gratification, such as acting out together.

Tailoring Treatment to the Hysteric's Thinking Style

The bland affect of the hysteric in the acute conversion reaction is one indication of the effectiveness with which the mental mechanism of repression can work: repression blanks out anxiety and the anxiety-producing ideas. In the hysterical personality, there seems to be an excess of affect; but it is also pseudoaffect, an as-if feeling, which in part functions to screen out the intensity of threatening feeling. This pseudoaffect may counterphobically permit partial gratification.

With the obsessional, in contrast, small amounts of anxiety are permitted into consciousness but are kept within manageable limits by the mechanisms of isolation of affect—doing and undoing, reversal, reaction formation, and regression. In contrast with the narcissism, sensitivity, and emotionality of the hysterical personality, the obsessive-compulsive seems emotionally blunted. In the obsessive, the forgetting or repressing is mostly limited to dissolving the feeling connections between memories and ideas, leaving the ideas isolated but conscious. However, conclusions with appropriate feeling tone may not be drawn even though anxiety and other distressing affects are avoided. The obsessive-compulsive consciousness focuses on, dwells on, certain thoughts and lines of thinking, and in so doing excludes certain feelings and other thoughts leading to threatening or unbearable feelings.

In short, the hysteric has repressed or dissolved the ideational connections between *feelings* to defend against certain affects; the obsessive-compulsive has repressed or dissolved the feeling connections between *ideas* to defend against certain threatening affects. Curiously, these two styles of thinking, though, in a sense opposites, are not mutually exclusive and to some extent can coexist in the same person. And there is a sense in which the obsessive-compulsive and hysteric are similar in that the obsessive-compulsive dwells on the *thought* content without appropriate conclusion of thought and feelings; and the hysterical personality dwells on *feeling* without appropriate conclusion of feeling and thought.

In the anxiety-hysteric or phobic person, anxiety may be intense but it is limited to the phobic situation or stimulus. The phobic is to an extent intermediate between the hysteric and the obsessive-compulsive and shows some elements of the thinking styles of both the hysteric and the obsessive.

Shapiro (1965) writes of the factual memories of obsessive-compulsives. He believes the obsessive's thinking provides material on which the recollection must be drawn. He contrasts this to the hysteric's thinking style in terms of apperception, apprehension, data gathering, and recall:

> [The hysteric's thinking is] global, relatively diffuse, and lacking in sharpness, particularly in sharp detail. In a word, it is *impressionistic*. In contrast to the active, intense, and sharply focused attention of the obsessive-compulsive, hysterical cognition seems relatively lacking in sharp focus of attention; in contrast to the compulsive's active and prolonged searching for detail, the hysterical person tends cognitively to respond quickly and is highly susceptible to what is immediately impressive, striking, or merely obvious. [pp. 111-112]

Shapiro believes that the lack of detail and definition in hysterical cognition is neither the result of the mental mechanism of repression nor of the exclusion of specific ideational or emotional contents from consciousness; rather, he thinks that it is a form of cognition in itself, a form that results in vagueness or diffuseness rather than explicit exclusion (p. 113).

We can look at the hysteric's lack of sharp definition and thought content in another way, one that has implications for therapy. To the extent that the hysteric still unconsciously seeks to reestablish the nurturant child-mother relationship, there is an expectation, an unconscious demand, for an intuitive, primarily nonverbal, global understanding from others. Hysterics seem forever surprised at not being understood; they seem to feel that of course others know what they are feeling and that if their needs are misinterpreted or not met, it is out of some sort of lack of love, rejection, or even hostile perversity by the others. When, for instance, a female hysteric and male obsessive-compulsive are in a close relationship like marriage, the hysteric often seems amazed and offended at the failure of her husband to apprehend her feeling state. And the obsessive-compulsive in that marriage just as often seems astonished at the wife's failure to comprehend what seems to him logically obvious in his linear style of thinking.

One of the frequently experienced misunderstandings with hysterics is that manifestations of need for elements of preverbal closeness, such as the wish to be held or cuddled, are reacted to by the other person as an overture for genital sexuality. "I just want to be held and kissed, but my husband always gets turned on and wants to have sex," a female hysteric may complain.

I have described some of the similar ties and differences in the ways hysterics and obsessive-compulsives react that affect the strategy and tactics of therapy with them. Every experienced therapist knows that narcissism, libido, mental mechanisms of defense, phase-specific learning, object loss, and many other perspectives can all be used to scrutinize the healthy and unhealthy elements of mental life. One such perspective which I have found useful in understanding the hysteric's thinking style is that of scopophilic-exhibitionistic conflict.

Much of the hypercathexes of these looking-showing factors can occur in the phallic-oedipal period, which is critical and familiar in contributing to the hysterical constellation. But how does a therapist use a perspective such as the scopophilic-exhibitionistic to understand the hysteric's cognitive style in a clinically useful way? Let us examine a case of late-onset hysteria where the patient's rather typical emotionality and the vagueness of thought content were gradually understandable as defenses against fears of intimate seeing and being seen. The treatment in fact pivoted in this case on scopophilic-exhibitionistic genetic-dynamic factors. How these factors were conditioned in the patient's early life, how they were constantly being played out again and again in the patient's daily life and in the transference, and how they affected the treatment technique can be seen in the following account. Clarification of these problems was to be an essential ingredient in the treatment process.

In this case, as in all cases, the principles of overdetermination and multiple functioning are operative. The relevant factors, as in all cases, need not immediately dance right up and introduce themselves to the therapist, although they are in there dancing. It is their interconnections that are elusive. We must be open to seeing these elusive interconnections in order to fit the treatment to the hysteric's thinking style.

The matron and the trembling hand. An intelligent, attractive, gentle-looking, fifty-year-old woman with a high school education came to treatment with a complaint of her right hand trembling when she attempted to sign her name in public. She had a fear of signing her name in any sort of public situation—filling out a questionnaire, signing a check, and so on. She also had a fear of going to see doctors and was afraid of hospitals although she had done volunteer work in them. She complained of anxiety and depression for many previous years, but especially in the preceding two, and more recently after a visit to see her son, daughter-in-law, and grandchild on the East Coast. On that visit her mother had returned West with her. Her mother suffered from Parkinsonism with considerable trembling of her hands.

The patient was afraid that her own symptoms had something to do with the menopause because her menstrual flow had been scanty and irregular during the previous year. She reported feeling more tense and irritable for several days before menstruation.

When she came to treatment the patient wondered whether anyone had ever had a similar symptom or fear of her hand trembling. She thought that maybe it could not be understood and that maybe she could not be helped. Her internist had attempted to reassure her about her nervousness. He had told her she did not need to see a psychiatrist. Her gynecologist, however, had encouraged her to seek psychiatric treatment.

Family and past history revealed that the patient had grown up in the southeastern United States, as had her husband. She was the middle of five children. The oldest brother had been killed during World War II. The next oldest brother was somewhat alcoholic. A younger brother was married and apparently had a stable life. The patient's sister, four years younger than the patient, had committed suicide after giving birth to a second child, a girl.

The patient said her mother had had a "hard life." The mother's father had been an alcoholic and the mother's early life was very insecure. The patient's mother had had Parkinsonism for a good many years and she too was afraid of going out in public. At the time the patient initially came to see me, she was attempting to do everything for her mother's visit that was possible, but she was finding that she felt nervous being with her mother so much.

The patient's father was described as distant but hard working. He had become a heavy drinker after his oldest son was killed. The patient's paternal grandfather had died when the patient's father was a young man, leaving him without much education but with a crippled brother, a dominating mother, and a farm. The patient's father worked mostly as a construction worker and carpenter and was considered very "good with his hands." in various kinds of skilled labor. The patient said that she had never been able to talk to her father, that he was a very silent man, seldom speaking except when he was drinking, and that she was troubled by the estrangement between her parents. Her mother said there was nothing good about the patient's father at all. And yet the patient loved both of them.

The paternal grandfather had been the head of a school, and he left a large library which remained in the family, although the patient was never allowed to read the books. Early in treatment the patient hesitantly scanned the bookshelves in my office and asked if I could recommend something for her to read that would help her. I replied that, offhand, I did not know of anything that would necessarily be of much help to her. "The main thing that I think you'll find helpful is just to talk to me about whatever is on your mind while you're here," I said. "It's not necessary to do any homework." "If I read something I feel like it might help me understand better," she said, "but I've heard that sometimes it's not a good idea, that it can interfere with treatment. Do you think I shouldn't read about psychiatric things?" "Well, there are pros and cons on that," I replied. "I guess reading *can* be used in ways to avoid understanding oneself, but it does seem to help people sometimes, too. Why can't you just feel free to read whatever you'd like and we'll see how it goes?"

The patient's paternal grandmother lived with the family while the patient was growing up. The grandmother tended to give a great deal of unasked-for advice. The patient, however, spoke of her grandmother as having had "kind hands." The grandmother was a midwife and knew about sexual matters but the patient did not feel she could discuss such things with her. (The grandmother had had an illegitimate child, although it was never clear as to when this had happened.)

Another of the grandmother's children, the patient's crippled uncle, about five years older than the patient, also lived with the family while she was growing up. The uncle apparently had a Pott's disease kyphosis from tuberculosis of the spine. He was never sent to school, and he may have been somewhat mentally retarded. When he approached puberty, he began sleeping with the grandmother, displacing the patient from that comforting position.

The patient knew her husband in high school, where she had been elected a beauty queen. He grew up in a tenant farmer's family. The patient was fond of her husband's parents, especially of the husband's father, who had died about a year and a half before the patient came into treatment. After World War II her husband had worked his way through the state university and had done well. The patient believed that the frequent moves she and her husband had had to make in the course of his career had done much to cause her to feel insecure. Her husband was a vice-president of an industrial firm with interests all over the country, and he had been something of a troubleshooter for them.

The patient looked younger than her stated years. She had a kind of little-girl manner about her, often smiling in a "cute" way. And she dressed somewhat like a young girl, often wearing little white boots, rather frilly clothes—all a bit out of keeping with her years. Often, too, she wore a dark outer garment such as a dark dress or dark slacks and sweater, while underneath she wore a white blouse. With the white boots she suggested a total whiteness underneath the dark outer layer of clothing.

There was also a feeling of gentleness and kindliness about this patient. In fact, by all accounts, she was a gentle and kind mother to her son, who was getting along well with his wife and two children. He lived in the area where the patient had grown up; and he worked the family farm although he had a master's degree and had done work in educational counseling. The patient and her husband had raised her sister's daughter after the sister's suicide. Both the patient and the patient's husband were fond of this niece who had been almost like a daughter. And they were distressed that she had married a man who had a drinking problem and was abusive to her. The niece lived in the Midwest and occasionally came to visit the patient.

In addition to the hand trembling that brought the patient to treatment, she had other fears of being looked at. She was something of an artist but was afraid to show her work. The past history indicated that she had always been somewhat fearful in public situations, was afraid in school of being called on to read aloud or recite in class, and was often afraid to go to school for fear of being put on the spot in the classroom. In the second grade, after her family had moved from the farm in connection with her father's construction work, the patient did not know the way home from school; she remembered vividly one incident when she cried, being ashamed to tell the teacher she did not know her way home. She often pretended to be sick in order to avoid having to go to school.

The patient also had anxiety about looking at people closely or looking at things. In the office with me it was apparent that she was even fearful of looking very directly at me or of looking around the office. For a long time she did not realize the office had a second exit door.

While it did not come out in the first interview it evolved ultimately that the patient was fearful of having her husband of more than thirty years see her in the nude. She had refused to have sexual relations with him except in the dark. She wore underclothing under her nightgown or pajamas when she went to bed, and in fact wore heavy underclothing at all times in order to be protected against being seen. Her mother, incidentally, was not afraid of wearing sheer nightgowns. The patient had never examined her own genitals with the aid of a mirror. In foreplay she permitted her husband to touch only her breasts, never her clitoris or genitals. On one occasion after several months of treatment she asked me whether I thought her husband's buying magazines like *Playboy*, *Oui*, and *Penthouse*, which showed nude women, had anything to do with her refusal to let him see her undressed.

The patient's husband, incidentally, was supportive of her continuing treatment. Several times he came and talked with me, both with the patient and separately, because he was concerned that the patient seemed to be increasing her consumption of alcohol in the evening. Because of the history of alcoholism both in her family and in his, he was afraid she might be becoming an alcoholic.

The patient's husband was totally unaware of her having any sexual difficulties except for the fact that she had not been willing to have intercourse with him in the light. In the past she had not been able to achieve orgasm, although she had regularly feigned it. The husband felt the patient was satisfied with their sexual life together. She did not feel that this was the case, however.

In describing how to fit treatment to a hysteric's thinking style, it is relevant to know that this patient made a point of keeping scrapbooks for persons she cared about—her son, her niece, and others. Periodically she presented these scrapbooks of photographs and memorabilia to them. In the course of her work with me she developed a kind of scrapbook for me in the sense of bringing me clippings, sending me scores of pages of notes, and bringing in written notes. It was through showing me these scrapbook pieces that the patient was able to reveal some things that had been difficult for her to speak about in more direct ways.

For some time after beginning treatment and the taking of the initial history, the patient found it difficult to talk with me. She became increasingly apprehensive about keeping her appointments and felt she did not know what to talk about. She often wanted me to direct her as to what she should say. I pointed out that in the nature of treatment I needed to be relatively quiet and that although this was part of what bothered her, as had her father's silence, she was also made anxious by feeling on the spot to reveal herself. The patient often brought in the notes I have mentioned and referred to them or read them aloud in order to be able to have something to talk about. And sometimes the notes she sent between times were about being sorry that she had not been able to talk more freely.

At first, I saw this patient only once or twice a week for several months. Because of her difficulty in looking at me or in having me look at her, the patient *wanted* to use the couch. We talked about it for a while, and then I saw her four times a week in more or less full analytic treatment with the patient using the couch and attempting to report her associations freely.

After the patient had been in treatment for about one year, she learned I had written *The Fear of Looking* (1974), and she wanted to read it. I did not discourage her but asked, "Why can't you read whatever you wish, including my book? Is there some connection with not being allowed to read your father's books?" "Maybe so," she replied. "I never thought of that." She was clearly pleased at the idea of reading the book. She was much relieved in reading it to discover that other people shared her anxieties about looking and being looked at and as a result of having read the book, she seemed more confident that there were possibilities of working out her difficulties in treatment. Also as a result of having read the book, she decided that one of the ways of helping herself overcome her difficulties was to abandon the use of the couch and to resume sitting in the chair opposite me and to force herself to look at me.

To show herself and me that she was looking at me acutely, she would often make reference to some article of my clothing, usually my tie—describing the color of it or alluding to the fact that I was wearing a bright yellow striped tie—or the like. The patient, incidentally, made her husband's ties for him, and they were usually of bright colors. She began to paint more. According to her husband her paintings were quite good, but she refused to allow them to be exhibited or to allow her husband to show them to any except close friends. Most of them she kept hidden at home.

Early in treatment this patient tended to gloss over specifics and to talk in generalities. Sometimes she would dismiss my request for detailed information with, "Oh, you know what I mean; we don't need to go into that." Partly this wish to gloss and evade grew from feelings of shame and guilt. As treatment progressed, however, her interest in understanding and the value she saw for understanding by going into details helped override her sense of shame. Her style of talking, if not of cognition, was observably altered.

Over the years there were many reasons why the patient felt ashamed of her family and background in spite of her love for the various members of the family. She was ashamed of the father's drinking, of the grandmother's illegitimate child, of her crippled uncle. As an adult she was ashamed of sexual acting out on the part of her sister and of the sister's suicide. She was also ashamed of her brother's alcoholism. And she was ashamed of having sexual impulses of her own toward men other than her husband.

As the patient gradually worked over various aspects of her shame about herself and her family, new information came to light. One of the significant things that evolved was an early childhood memory which the patient dated as occurring shortly after the birth of her sister—when the patient was four years old. At that time the new baby was sleeping in the bed with the patient's mother and the patient was sleeping in the father's bed in the same bedroom. The father apparently had been drinking and during the night the patient recalled that she awoke to find the father fondling her genitals. The patient made a moaning sound and pushed his hand away. She was sure that he was awake and conscious of what he was doing, but neither she nor the father ever acknowledged what had occurred. The patient never disclosed the incident to her mother, but she was always fearful of sleeping with her father after that.

The patient remembered another sexually traumatic incident which occurred when she was about eight or nine. The crippled uncle attempted to have intercourse with her in the presence of her brothers, who were encouraging the uncle to make the attempt. The uncle got on top of her but made no genital penetration. The patient was terribly ashamed of this incident and again remembered being unable to tell her parents about it, although apparently the mother had some inkling of what had happened since she spoke to the patient of having to keep an eye on the uncle because of his tendency to exhibit himself sexually and to molest small girls.

Slowly it became possible to link up the patient's fear of signing her name in public and a fear of being good with her hands to her frequent previous statements about her father being good with his hands—meaning in a manually skilled way—and the childhood traumatic sexual incident with him. These disclosures, however, did not altogether alleviate the patient's anxieties. In fact when I first linked them up, the patient was made so anxious she felt extremely faint in getting up from the couch and felt it necessary to sit for several minutes in the waiting room before she could recover enough sense of strength and equilibrium to walk the several blocks to her home.

While the patient went through a period of some erotic transference attachment to me, she got over that. She was finally able to have a true orgasm in intercourse with her husband. The first time orgasm occurred she was frightened enough to exclaim, "Oh, I'm going to have a heart attack!" But she began to feel more comfortable about that too, and she was pleased at the results of treatment, although for a long time she was still quite anxious about some elements of showing herself more freely to me through her talking.

I hope the reader will agree with me that while this patient is primarily classifiable as a hysteric, the scopophilic-exhibitionistic factors were active determinants in the course of treatment. Crucial as determinants of her psychopathology and cognitive style, these looking-showing conflicts were also determinants in the development and handling of the transference. The case illustrates one way a therapist can tailor the treatment to fit the thinking style of the hysteric.

An Aside on the Right and Left Cerebral Hemispheres.

Of theoretical interest, and tending to support contrasting thinking styles for the hysterics and the obsessive-compulsive are the studies of the right and left cerebral hemisphere functions (Galin 1974). It would seem that the thinking styles described for the hysteric and for the obsessive-compulsive in many ways correspond respectively to the thinking functions of the right and left cerebral hemispheres of the brain that have been reported by some investigators. When the corpus callosum, the great tract connecting the two cerebral hemispheres, is transected, it becomes possible to demonstrate the separate functions of each hemisphere: the right is global, holistic, impressionistic, and aesthetic in its apperception; the left deals in details, verbal memory, logic, discrete recall, linearity, and time sequence (Callaway 1975). Both these left-right hemisphere modes of functioning have obvious adaptive value, and each complements the other. One is tempted to speculate that when a clearly defined hysteric or obsessive-compulsive style of thinking exists, it may have resulted from a suppression or repression of the functions of the complementary cerebral hemisphere or that the functions of the complementing hemisphere were not fully activated at some critical time in a specific maturational period.

Among hysterics and obsessive-compulsives of comparable levels of intelligence, it seems to me more common to find the hysterics lacking in mathematical ability and the obsessive-compulsive quite able in mathematics (at least in arithmetic calculations). Obsessive-compulsives may be good at bridge and routine money matters; the hysteric, rarely. But the hysteric is often better at such activities as acting, art, and interior decorating.

Thinking Style—Continued

The so-called vagueness or emptiness of the hysteric's thinking is apparent but is not the whole story by any means. For example, I treated a very creative woman artist who had a hysterical style in talking, dressing, and behavior. And she clearly had a degree of gender-identity confusion. For this patient, making art forms equaled remaking her body image. She had even had a plastic surgeon remodel her breasts, making them smaller to fulfill an unconscious wish to be more like her brother. In her usual talk, this artist reacted in global terms, often impressionistically, or with seeming vagueness. But in fact she had much specific information and ability to deal with detail both visual and otherwise.

As repressions are lifted in the course of therapy with hysterics it is often even more apparent that details of events do indeed register with the patient but are immediately pushed from consciousness with only a kind of blurred afterimage available in symbolic outline.

Consider the following familiar example. A therapist is a couple of minutes late in starting an appointment. The patient shows a definite negative response. She is uncharacteristically silent or slow to start talking. She reports feeling "down," but she does not consciously relate her reaction to the narcissistic hurt of the therapist's lateness. Asked if she were possibly reacting to the therapist's lateness, she says that she did not notice he was late. Almost always she gives a large real-life reason for her depressed mood or asserts she doesn't know why she feels down. But in any event, she implies that the therapist is not as important a part of her life as might be inferred by his question about her reaction to his lateness. While her denial or lack of awareness can be either a narcissistic protection or a counterstrike at the therapist or both, it is clear that the detail registers and the patient reacts, albeit in a rather totalistic way, as though the therapist's lateness constituted a major rejection.

To better to understand how you treat the hysteric, it is important to recognize both the contrast and the similarity between the hysteric and the obsessive-compulsive.

I oversimplify to assert that we teach the hysteric to think and the obsessive to feel. To put it another way, the obsessive-compulsive has to rediscover the feeling links between thoughts, and the hysteric needs to relearn the thought connections between feelings. In treatment the obsessive-compulsive tends to intellectualize without feeling and the hysteric seems to emotionalize without thinking clearly. The hysteric is in a sense phobic about thinking, and the compulsive phobic about feeling. But I wish to emphasize that with the hysteric and the obsessive-compulsive, what is ultimately being defended against by their mental mechanisms and by their styles, is feeling. The therapist must treat the feeling part, must help the patients work through the defenses and reexperience the warded off ideas. In treating hysterics, however, you first have to point out that they really do not feel as much as they seem to be feeling. The woman hysteric may be frigid and does not feel sexually, but in other areas she also does not feel as much as she seems to be feeling. Just as her sexuality is a kind of acted sexuality, a role-played sexuality, her anger is often a kind of acted anger. The problem with this patient is to help her learn how to think better about certain situations. To do this, the therapist might first point out that her anger is a kind of as-if feeling. It is a pseudofeeling, an acted feeling, and that is one of the reasons this patient is called histrionic or theatrical—because she is acting and not fully feeling what seems to be felt. In the acting there is a defense against the very feeling that is portrayed, and that defense is what the therapist must first point out. The therapist directs attention toward what the hysteric is having trouble feeling.

The obsessive-compulsive, who seems to think so logically and linearly, up to a point, and has such a good factual and technical memory, is also having trouble with feelings and is defending against feeling. He has trouble making decisions and yet may be dogmatic in defense against his uncertainties. He constantly reverses and undoes things he says. For example, he will compliment the therapist and then immediately have to take it back or revise it. Or, he attacks the therapist and says something derogatory, and then must take it back: "Sometimes I think you're full of crap. But most of the time what you say makes sense." You see the immediate reversal and taking back. The reason for this reversal is that the obsessive-compulsive defends against certain feelings that he senses would evolve if he continued that line of thinking. This reversing mechanism serves to let through only a little anxiety, a little feeling, and maintains a control with which he is constantly struggling. He is both afraid of losing control and yet wishes to let go.

With the obsessive-compulsive you bring his attention to this mental mechanism of defense, of doing and undoing; you invite him to continue the line of thinking he is prone to shut off. You direct his attention first to what he is having trouble thinking. If he is attacking and you have called this mechanism to his attention, you may be able to say, "Now, at any moment, you are automatically going to feel like taking all that back." To some extent this forces him to go on a bit further than he ordinarily would. He begins to loosen up his constricted switching back and forth and goes further in each direction. As he goes back and forth further and further, he *feels* a bit more of what he has been guarding against.

So en route to teaching the hysteric to think and the obsessive-compulsive to feel, the therapist first teaches the hysteric to *feel more* and the obsessive-compulsive to *think further*.

To summarize, both the hysteric and the obsessive-compulsive defend against feeling by the use of their characteristic mental mechanisms of defense and thinking styles. The therapist must help the patients work through the defenses and reexperience the warded-off defended feelings before their styles of perceiving and thinking can change.

The hysteric and the obsessive-compulsive deal with words differently. If the hysteric says something about being "irritated" and you reply with the word "anger" it will not bother him. An obsessive-compulsive on the other hand, often makes excessively sharp distinctions between related words and is sometimes pedantic about it. For example, I have a patient who says, "I didn't say *angry*. I said I was *irritated*." I say, "Aren't these things pretty closely connected?" "No," he says, "they're very different. I certainly was not angry. I was irritated, not angry," he emphasizes. "Well, granted there's a difference between irritated and angry, and you've emphasized the difference, isn't it mainly a difference of degree? Aren't they related—at least second cousins maybe?"

If the patient's resistances are so strong that he treats all this with grim seriousness, further irritation, or intellectualizing, you generally let it go and press no further on the connection at this time. And here the therapist must bear in mind that it is in communicating with the patient through the patient's cognitive style that the therapist can be most effective. It is of little use to ask the hysteric at the outset to think in a manner almost utterly foreign to him. And it's just as useless to ask the obsessive-compulsive to feel feelings he cannot sense.

Therefore, the first therapeutic step, as I've mentioned before, is for the hysteric to feel more fully and for the obsessive-compulsive to think more logically. The initial interpretations are in these directions. To the hysteric, for example, you say "You are really not feeling that so intensely." To the obsessive-compulsive, you may say, "If you extend that line of thinking without taking it back or counterbalancing it, where might it lead?" A patient is usually unconscious of his thinking style without an outside observer to make him aware of it. It works the same way with characteristics of a culture—members of the culture are unconscious of their life styles when a basis for comparison is lacking.

THE TERMINATION PHASE

By the termination phase, the patient will have worked through many of his core neurotic conflicts in the context of the transference, in the examination and alteration of his current interpersonal relationships, and in the review of his life story. Because of his need for attention, he will have tested the therapeutic situation in many different ways and have experienced turbulent emotional episodes as his unconscious aims to recapitulate the past and obtain "this time" a more satisfactory outcome are frustrated. But he will have found some gratification in the treatment situation itself, in the undivided attention and concern of the therapist.

As separation from the therapist and the therapy situation is contemplated, there will be repetition of many of the earlier themes in the context of giving up the gratification of being in treatment. At this point, the hysterical personality will often reveal aspects of fantasies of rescue and nurture that have remained previously veiled. Especially prominent may be fantasies of relationships beyond the treatment conclusion. Only during this phase may residual symptoms be relinquished, especially symptoms that were maintained because of the fantasy of a particular kind of secondary gain. For example, the patient may have a covert wish for indefinite continuation of treatment, and only in the termination phase is it possible to examine and resolve the desperate need for an enduring, sustaining relationship.

All the dilemmas of how to relate to other persons, to gain attention, to fulfill an authentic sexual role will be reviewed now in relation to the important issues of transience of relationship. The patient may wish to continue a transference as a defense against the risks of a real relationship outside of the therapeutic situation, as illustrated in the following case example of a course of treatment (for other details of this case see Allen 1974, pp. 93-97).

A student nurse. An intelligent, attractive, foreign-born student nurse sought psychiatric treatment near the end of her training. She complained of feeling mixed up, depressed, anxious, and of a compulsion to overeat and then to gag herself to vomit. These symptoms had begun several months before when she was kissed by a young doctor, at which time instead of feeling pleasurably aroused sexually, she felt as if she were going to be smothered. She felt gagging and nausea. These symptoms had occurred repeatedly after that when kissed by other men. She was a virgin and felt herself unable to work out a relationship with a man. The patient also felt threatened by a demanding, older nurse supervisor. Although this patient's immediate presenting symptom was hysterical gagging, she also had phobic and obsessive-compulsive traits; her personality pattern, however, most nearly fitted that of the hysterical personality.

An only child, the patient's past history revealed many personality resources and adaptive strengths, including the ability to develop enduring friendships. In latency, her parents had divorced after a marriage stormy with physical and verbal fighting. The principal traumas for the patient appeared to have been in the oedipal period. There were overdetermining factors regarding things oral and anal: early feeding problems, struggle with the mother about food, the mother angrily trying to cram homework papers into the patient's mouth on one occasion, and a tonsillectomy without anesthesia as a small child. The patient had been given laxatives and enemas, and she feared assault from both ends. Her father was an artist and fencer. In childhood she had had a disturbing fantasy, later repressed, of his raping her anally.

The patient was taken into traditional psychoanalysis, and over a period of about three years she worked through anxieties about her relationships with men and women and became entirely free of symptoms. She was able to experience sexual feelings directly in appropriate situations and angry feelings in situations calling for anger without, in either case, being overwhelmed by anxiety or anxiety-induced symptoms. She has remained free of symptoms for many years and is married and the mother of two children.

One of the chief problems in the course of a somewhat stormy transference neurosis was not only the interweaving of attempts to fence or fight with the analyst and seduce him, but the patient's use of the transference relationship as a resistance to working out any real-life relationship with men, even though to do so had been her purpose in entering analysis. For example, she would say, "Oh, I know we can't get married now. I know your rules. But after analysis. . . ." This attitude required repeated interpretation of her defense against the real-life relationship with a suitable man.

There are defenses against defenses and reversals against reversals, and these days when many patients in analysis or analytically oriented psychotherapy know something of analytic theory, they are also quick to interpret their reactions to the therapist as transference reactions, and they seek to *dismiss* them on that account. When the patient dismisses a reaction to the therapist as transference, interpretation must be upward rather than downward: that is, the therapist must remind the patient that to call the reaction to the therapist "transference" is to avert anxiety about real and immediate feelings toward the therapist. After adequate working through, the underlying true transference feelings can become apparent and interpretable.

The student nurse went through just this sequence of getting to the underlying transference feelings. As erotic feelings toward the analyst began to develop, she was quick to discount them as transference feelings. She seemed never, however, to doubt the validity of whatever negative feelings occurred in the course of treatment. But in time it became easy to demonstrate to the patient the childhood paradigms for her anger. When it finally became clear to the patient that there would be no real-life romantic relationship with the analyst, she felt betrayed by him as she had felt betrayed by both of her parents. For a time she then attempted to defer working out her relationships with men on the grounds that the analyst was a perfect example of how no man could ever be trusted.

During the middle phase of the analysis these themes were worked through, with gains in her concept of self and in her repertoire of possible relationships with others. They were to repeat themselves later when, with improvement, the theme of completing the treatment contract occurred.

During the final phase of the analysis the transference theme of needing the analyst for a real relationship intensified, and the content of the patient's associations became heavily oral. Thoughts of food and intellectual imbibing were common. She went through rapidly shifting periods of a sort of sweet verbal sucking at me and wishing to prolong a kind of dreamy hanging on to the analytic nipple, and bitter, biting comments at me as though I were an ungiving dried-up breast. There were fantasies of suckling at my penis. Sometimes, too, there was a kind of spitting back of unwanted interpretations as if thrusting away an intrusive nipple, an overfeeding mother.

These periods were experienced with less of a peremptory and needy quality as the termination point approached. She reproached herself for these wishes, but in a mild manner, and exhorted herself to become independent of analysis and the analyst. She expressed realistic satisfaction with the progress she had made, sadness that fantastic goals had not been achieved and nostalgia that analysis could not become a way of life.

CONCLUDING REMARKS

If characterologic substrata are to be worked with to any worthwhile extent, it may be important *not* to attempt to relieve the symptom or presenting complaint promptly since it is the patient's disturbance that is at first the prime motivation for continuing treatment. Premature correct interpretations of the meaning of a symptom may strengthen the defenses and drive the patient from treatment but to the extent that they also may produce some immediate symptom relief these premature interpretations thus deprive the patient of motivation for more fundamental working through.

Perhaps because of changes in our society, including more widespread understanding of some kinds of symptoms as stress reactions as well as more liberal and informed attitudes toward sexuality, the kinds of hysterical symptoms have shifted over the years. The acute, naive, symbolizing conversion symptom is rarely seen nowadays except in the lower socioeconomic and less educated groups and among religious groups which are both constrictive and intensely emotional. But the hysterical character or histrionic personality has continued to be prominent. This too will undoubtedly change in manifestation with the times.

In a sense, the hysterical style *is* the symptom. Nowadays it is often very close to being the presenting symptom itself. More often, though, the presenting symptom is still a result of some immediate effect of the patient's cognitive and behavioral style. Not infrequently the patient comes to treatment acutely depressed or acutely anxious *and* with a more global complaint of an ungratifying, distressing life which the patient has begun to see falls into repetitive patterns despite conscious attempts to avert them.

It is small wonder that the patient can by voluntary effort alone modify his behavior so slightly when we consider the cumulative conditioning of his lifetime, the more or less fixed forms of imprintlike learning in the early years of his psychosexual maturation, and underlying gender-identity confusion. Similarly, it may seem folly for the therapist to attempt to help the patient toward a massive reordering of his thinking style. Indeed massive reordering cannot be an immediate goal and gratification for either therapist or patient in the day-to-day work of psychotherapy.

Instead, gratifications for the therapist are in the easy use of his curiosity, in understanding, and in the craftsmanship of finding and freeing from automaticity what might be called patients' learned reflexes—reactions just below consciousness which can be made conscious with the help of the therapist. Apart from any symptom relief there is also gratification for the patient in the process of therapy itself, in satisfying his curiosity, in the enjoyment of self understanding, and in increased self esteem.

An essential part of the craftsmanship in therapy is to communicate within the cognitive style of the patient with full respect for the patient's feelings and values. The hysterical thinking style is not inferior as far as it goes, but the hysterical style needs the complementary advantages of detailed, linear, "left-hemisphere thinking" as well. In a sense, the hysteric does need to learn how to think and what to connect in thinking, just as the obsessive-compulsive needs to learn how to feel and what to connect in feeling. The therapist has to start from where the patient is, not from where the therapist or others think the patient should be; and if this is not done the patient will shut off cooperative disclosure of himself and therapy will be thwarted. Therapy is a special threat to the patient when his thinking style is considered the symptom because the style is identified with the self, and to change the style, as it were, threatens annihilation of the self rather than removal of an ego-alien symptom.

No one wants to lose a sense of self, yet that is, in fact, what a change of cognitive style threatens. Because losing something can be so threatening, it is useful and indeed more accurate for both the therapist and the patient to be aware that analyzing and understanding a conflict or a complex does not necessarily mean giving it up or losing it, but rather means being able through understanding to make the involved forces work for the person rather than work unconsciously to his detriment.

Irrespective of a voiced wish for sudden "cure," people do not like a sudden leaving of familiar experience. A patient once said to me, "A vicious circle is a kind of structure—and if it's a familiar one it can become a kind of home—like a project or a cause or a good workout. . . . I guess I can always count on my neurosis." Faced with change, people often need a transitional object and time for the transitional experience. They need a psychologic bridge from the old to the new. And sometimes they need a companion and a chance to try out the new on a small scale and retreat again and again to familiar psychologic territory before separation from the old and before individuation into a newly extended self. Sometimes, almost as a rule, new ways of reacting involve resuming old interrupted ways of reacting.

Reformation in thought and feeling and an affirmative yielding to change, or at least a passive acceptance of change, precede new actions. Just to take the steps and make the choices of what to talk about without direction from the therapist seems frightening to many patients. Thus, early in treatment I may have to tell the patient:"I think you will find that you can trust your thoughts to lead us to whatever we need to know. I hope to demonstrate that to you. In this sort of work we can't always tell in advance what may be most important to know. And, anyway, it's not up to either you or me to decide in advance. We just have to accept what comes and let it fit itself into the picture. In time something will begin to repeat and connect, and if you just talk frankly about whatever comes to mind while you're here, sooner or later the important things will become clear to us." Dogma or authoritative direction provides instant familiarity or a kind of portable comforting something. But in the end dogma is the enemy of human freedom, flexibility, change, and growth. And it is death to the intellect.

In concluding, I would like to emphasize that while one obviously must fit the treatment to the patient, it is generally helpful to adopt the attitude that, so far as possible, the patient must be a coequal investigator with the therapist. The therapist, generally, should avoid giving advice and should arouse the patient's own powers of initiative. The therapist should be wary of overidentifying with the patient. He should give the patient ample opportunity to tell his own story unimpeded by interruptions; and the therapist should not be hasty to interpret. In fact, he will be most effective if he focuses on the patient's difficulties in full disclosure and waits to interpret the patient's dilemmas of contradictory and conflicting feelings.

And most effective of all are the interpretations of transference that the therapist can meaningfully make only if he waits for dilemmas to be felt in the damned-either-way responses the patient unconsciously tends to evoke in him. Under these conditions, the abreactive effect is greatest. The patient does the maximum and optimal mastering work for himself, and the transference manifestations and the transference neurosis become the most illuminating. Therapeutic interventions become both easier and more cogent.

Under the conditions of waiting for the damned-either-way response the therapist can best find the roles he is playing in the patient's projections. He can best demonstrate to the patient that the patient is actively reliving his past in the treatment and in present-day conflicts of id, ego, superego, and external reality. Figuratively, the therapist holds the string at the juncture of the real world and the labyrinthine world of the patient's unconscious and past. The therapist allows the patient to unwind that string regressively throughout its long length into earliest childhood. And when the patient comes forward again the therapist gives him back his string and the map of his labyrinth. Generally no effort should be made to force the pace of the unraveling. The patient needs to explore in his own time and pace in order to master. And the patient's feeling forced to yield to the therapist does not usually bring a sense of inner freedom. Only when the patient is stuck does the therapist need to clear the way a little with interpretation or give a little push with an inquiry.

When an attractive young hysterical patient suddenly turns over on the couch and says, "But that's enough about me, Doctor, let's talk about you," the therapist has an opportunity to interpret. The patient has a right to keep the analytic situation and the analyst free for fantasy, and it is the analyst's responsibility to guard that right. He should interpret her wish to know about him as a fear of having him know about her and a fear of knowing more about herself. Thus to the patient he might well say, "I think you'll agree that my life doesn't belong in your treatment. But perhaps you're anxious about having us *both* know *your* thoughts."

The therapeutic situation offers ample opportunity for mobilizing scopophilic-exhibitionistic anxiety for both the patient and the therapist, expecially with hysterical patients. Nowhere else in life does anyone tell another *all* his thoughts. Years of work in supervising psychiatrists in training convinces me that one of the sources of the beginning therapist's anxieties is an inhibited scopophilia. The doctor's need to act, to advise, to prescribe, to do something, to tell about himself is often a kind of exhibitionistic and narcissistic defense against anxieties associated with quiet and thorough observation. The ability to defer action in favor of benign curiosity is, however, a necessary prerequisite for real diagnostic understanding in depth.

Finally, in all of his interventions with the patient the therapist must bear in mind that the patient too has a difficult task, that he is in a situation making him particularly vulnerable to intensifications of shame and guilt. Whatever is said to the patient the therapist should phrase tactfully in a way to cause the least injury to self esteem while doing the necessary therapeutic work. Hopefully, the patient can get to the point where he not only realizes that he doesn't have to hide himself but where he discovers that he no longer wishes to hide.

REFERENCES

Abse, W. D. (1974). Hysterical conversion and dissociative syndromes and the hysterical character. In *American Handbook of Psychiatry*, vol. 3, ed. S. Arieti and E. B. Brody. New York: Basic Books.

Allen, D. W. (1974). *The Fear of Looking: Scopophilic-Exhibitionistic Conflicts*. Charlottesville: University Press of Virginia.

Allen, D. W., and Houston, M. (1959). The management of hysteroid acting-out patients in a training clinic. *Psychiatry* 22:41-49.

Callaway, E. (1975). Psychiatry today. *The Western Journal of Medicine* 122:349-354.

Freud, S. (1912). Recommendations to physicians practising psycho-analysis. *Standard Edition* 12:109-120.

———(1913). On beginning the treatment. *Standard Edition* 12:121-144.

Galin, D. (1974). Implications for psychiatry of left and right cerebral specialization. *Archives of General Psychiatry* 31:572-583.

Giovacchini, P.(1975). *Psychoanalysis of Character Disorders.* New York: Jason Aronson.

Jones, E. (1953). *The Life and Work of Sigmund Freud.* Vol. 1. New York: Basic Books.

Kernberg, O. (1970). Factors in the psychoanalytic treatment of narcissistic personalities. *Journal of the American Psychoanalytic Association* 18:51-85.

———(1974). Further contributions to the treatment of narcissistic personalities. *International Journal of Psycho-Analysis* 55:215-240.

Kohut, H. (1971). *Analysis of the Self.* New York: International Universities Press.

Orr, D. W. (1961). Lionel Blitzsten, the teacher. In *N. Lionel Blitzsten, M.D.: Psychoanalyst, Teacher, Friend 1893-1952.* New York: International Universities Press (private distribution only).

Schneck, J. M. (1963). Historical notes: William Osler, S. Weir Mitchell, and the origin of the "rest cure." *American Journal of Psychiatry* 119:894-895.

Shapiro, D. (1965). *Neurotic Styles.* New York: Basic Books.

Veith, I. (1970). *Hysteria: The History of a Disease.* Chicago: University of Chicago Press.

CHAPTER 6

Structure and the Processes of Change

MARDI J. HOROWITZ, M.D.

Hysterical personality is described in terms of behavioral traits, and these patterns in turn are based on a person's style of information processing and his basic schemata of self and the world. Modification of character requires change in ways of thinking and change of inner maps as well as the learning of new behavioral repertoires. This chapter examines hysterical personality in terms of the processes of such change.

Cognitive style and cognitive structure are individual, and the delineation of patterns and changes requires individual description within such a typology as hysterical personality. No person fits a type perfectly, but a representative patient can provide this kind of individualized analysis. The patient to be described in this chapter changed during psychoanalysis, and the story of this change allows us to examine the matrix of past history, current patterns of relationships and immediate enactments in the therapy situation as they pertain to cognitive structure. If the cognitive process and structure of a person with a hysterical personality is understood thoroughly enough through examination of the extensive information available from a psychoanalysis, then the clarity gained should allow eventual development of interventions that produce change in briefer forms of treatment.

This article appears in different form in the *International Review of Psycho-Analysis* 4: 23-49 and is used with their permission.

The central issues are those described in earlier chapters. In terms of cognitive style, there is a need to examine the use of repression and denial and to understand how these defenses are modified with character change. In terms of self-constructs, the development of a pseudofeminine or pseudomasculine self-image and the evolution of a more mature self-image is central. In terms of relationships, the focus would be on change from stereotyped reenactments (of dyads and triads within the fantasy, for instance) to attachments based on current real attributes.

Each trait is composed of multiple part processes. Change takes place at the level of these multiple processes and therefore requires detailed examination. For example, repression must be examined not globally as an accomplishment but in terms of the several cognitive operations that go into warding off constellations of ideas and emotions.

The purpose, then, of this chapter is the analysis of change in a person with hysterical personality during the course of a psychoanalysis. The method is the use of the extensive information gained in this form of treatment to examine the patterns of a person with this typology as these patterns are highlighted by their change. This analysis of the changes and the change process will add the cognitive and object-relations points of view of contemporary psychodynamics to classical metapsychological formulations.

The strategy of approach involves a series of steps. First, the current life problems of a person with a hysterical personality (though not a "perfect" one) will be described. To give an overview of the outcome, the state of these problems at the onset and at the end of treatment will be compared. Then background history will enlarge the picture. The story will continue by describing the history of the psychoanalysis. Then the changes in the person will be formulated from the traditional metapsychological points of view. With such models in mind, it will be possible to reexamine hysterical traits from another vantage point: two aspects of ego psychology closer to clinical data than are the usual metapsychological discussions. These aspects of ego psychology are the cognitive point of view, which examines changes in style of thought, emotion, and defensive process and clarifies changes in inner models of the relationships of self and others.

A REPRESENTATIVE CASE

Presenting Complaints and Identifying Information

Miss Smith was twenty-five when she came for treatment. Slender and well-formed, she had striking black hair and a pale, attractive face. During the first few interviews she dressed in a glamorous fashion, although not quite within any current style. She comported herself in a poised, sophisticated manner, but this seemed strained, as if it were a facade. Behind many evocative social gestures and conversational gambits she seemed uneasy and tense. Labile emotional expressions, unintentional "seductiveness," and covert cues to elicit rescue were observed.

She said she had come because she felt depressed and unsure about how to continue her life. She had come at the suggestion of a mental health professional who had seen her in consultation because she was depressed. After making these statements she feigned excessive uncertainty as to why she had come, as an attempt to elicit reassurance, advice, and direction.

She identified the immediate precipitant of her malaise as a recent separation from a lover. But her depressed feelings were not simply reactive grief within a mourning process. She recognized that this separation was part of a recurrent pattern of failure to develop enduring attachments to either men or women. She felt defective, unlovable, and incapable of loving or friendship. In addition to an inability to be relaxed and intimate, she could not achieve orgastic climax in sexual intercourse.

When treatment began, Miss Smith was entering a final year of internship before obtaining a credential as a dietician. This apprenticeship was progressing poorly. Some days instead of going to work, she stayed in her bed at the boardinghouse where she lived. She sometimes felt too dizzy, lightheaded, and apathetic to get up in the morning, and was uncertain of whether her illness was physical or psychological. Phobias, dissociative episodes, lightheadedness, dizzy spells, and various genito-urinary and gastrointestinal symptoms episodically occurred, but doctors found nothing physically amiss. At times she felt elated and entered into almost frantic activity, but dejection quickly recurred.

During evaluation, she reported another motive for treatment and

TABLE 1

SIGNS AND SYMPTOMS AT ONSET AND TERMINATION OF TREATMENT

Reported as Initial Complaints or Present Early in Analysis	State at Termination of Analysis
1. Generally depressed with episodes of hypomanic elation	1. No depression or hypomania Specifically sad at times, happy at times
2. Anorgasmic	2. Capable of orgasm
3. Unable to love men	3. Able to love men
4. Friendless	4. Makes and keeps friends
5. Apathetic	5. Capable of sustained action
6. Childless	6. Unchanged
7. Episodic dizziness, anxiety attacks and physical complaints	7. Generally absent (has potential for recurrence when under stress); sharp reduction in physical complaints
8. Low self-esteem	8. Markedly improved
9. Phobias present	9. Phobias absent

reason for depression. Her older sister had recently had her second baby. Even if she were to be cured of sexual inhibitions and inability to love, she could not marry and bear children in time to "catch up."

Most of the complaints present at the onset of analysis were relieved by the time analysis was completed. To provide an overview, the state of various signs and symptoms is listed for both time periods in table 1. The plan to prepare this chapter was discussed with the patient more than a year after termination. The symptomatic improvements present when treatment terminated had persisted. She had advanced in a rewarding career and felt successful in what she did. She was unmarried but was able to relate tenderly and orgastically to men. She felt that "analysis was the best thing [she] had ever done and that it was astounding in view of how [she] was before and after." She found that problems came up in everyday life but she was coping well with them.

Patient's Background

Throughout her analysis, Miss Smith consistently represented her mother as rigid and moralistic. Her family found the mother devoted but joyless and often depressed. Deeply involved with an orthodox church, she served on its committee on pornography, and was concerned throughout life with social propriety. Her origin as the child of lower middle class parents meant that her marriage to Mr. Smith, son of a once prominent Chicago family, indicated upward mobility. She was initially as proud of the match as she was later ashamed by Mr. Smith's eventual vocational and social failures.

Mrs. Smith was trained in a semi-professional skill. After her first child, a daughter, was born, she stayed home as housewife and mother. The patient was born two years later, to be followed in two more years by a third daughter. This third child had mild congenital deformities and was also susceptible to viral diseases and allergies. Reconstruction and family stories suggest that the mother had an untreated depressive episode after this last pregnancy. Her own problems and the infirmities of her youngest baby kept Mrs. Smith from returning to work although the family income was meager. During this period of maternal depression and preoccupation with a sickly younger sibling, the patient turned to her father for mothering, with inconsistent results. (The frequency of this situation in the background of persons who develop hysterical personalities was discussed by Blacker and Tupin in chapter 2.) Later, she also turned to her older sister for mothering, and this too had its good as well as frustrating aspects. When the children entered school, Mrs. Smith returned to work at a large military base where, because of her great work productivity, efficiency, and self-effacing nature, she rapidly attained semiexecutive responsibility. Her success there provided a central gratification in her life, although she also felt used by the male military officers who took credit for her work.

The first daughter and older sister was lively and spunky throughout her early growth period. She began promiscuous sexual activities early in adolescence while continuing average work in school. The patient, the second child, was quieter, more intelligent and well-behaved, and more successful in school. The third child and younger sister was sickly, less intelligent than the other two, and received a great deal of nursing care from the mother.

Miss Smith recollects her mother's subsequent obesity as coarse and unappealing. Mrs. Smith also had, as a regular activity, the task of reviewing magazines for obscene content so that they might be banned by the church. She hid these magazines in her lingerie drawer, an open secret in the family. The proud moralistic stance of the mother seems to have been brittle for she sometimes wept uncontrollably over conflicts within the family. At such times she felt helpless and complained of being unappreciated. She also felt insecure in public. For example, when the need arose to return a purchase at a department store, she would have the two older girls, when they were adolescents, do it for her.

Mr. Smith was unusual. All of his daughters regarded him as a failure and a sexual pervert, but also knew him to be intelligent, artistically gifted, and capable of enthusiasm. One of his greatest eccentricities was nudism. He insisted upon practicing his nudity around the house, including taking his breakfast while naked. He assumed the function of waking each daughter, and while undressed, would lie on their beds, above the covers, until they arose. During early adolescence this so embarrassed and upset the patient that she begged her mother to make him stop. Her mother would cry and claim that she was helpless.

In Miss Smith's recollections her father most often appears as selfish and immature. But he was also recollected later in the analysis as affectionate, lively, and endearing. He drew well and would amuse the children with cartoons. He sometimes took the patient for a ride in the car, thrilling her by turns at high speed. However, even ideal images of her father had their disappointing side. When he was obviously and repeatedly cheated by mechanics and used-car dealers, his aura of expertise with cars was demolished.

Mr. Smith had graduated from a major university with honors in art history. He then found an unusually good job as assistant curator of an art museum but was let go at the end of one year. After a sequence of further false starts he became a pigment tester for a line of paints, going from factory to factory to assure quality control. The salary was low; he was regarded as a failure by more successful friends and relatives, and he counterphobically flaunted his blue collar status at social and family gatherings.

While the father overtly chided his oldest daughter for her sexual behavior, he was covertly interested and teased her for the details of sexual encounters. Later, when Miss Smith was in college, he wanted to visit her in order to flirt with her roommate. There were other episodes of his flirtations with women, such as waitresses. These were pathetic longings without romantic action or real intent. He demonstrated an almost ludicrous pseudomasculinity. This pseudosexuality is similar to that discussed in the earlier chapter by Blacker and Tupin. While he ridiculed the smut committee, he surreptitiously read the pornographic material from his wife's drawer. At times he masturbated so that sounds could be overheard, or left his fly unzipped in public. Like his flirtatiousness, these exhibitionistic traits were limited, for he was never apprehended in a flagrant act. Together, the parents set a familial standard of both denial and rationalization of such behaviors within the verbal communication of the family network.

Anger, anxiety, and guilt over erotic events characterized Miss Smith's childhood. A few repetitive memories from the analysis illustrate these events. When she was about four or five years old, her older sister encouraged her to strip before a group of boys nine to thirteen years old. Upon removing her panties she was roundly laughed at. Some years later, a boy she had especially admired from afar asked her to his room. He showed her an obscene photograph, and she rushed out. Striptease was a perennially favored game of the oldest sister, and the three girls often played it together.

She commenced menstruation when she was nine years old. She was surprised at the blood, having had no educative preparation for menarche. Her sister, who was eleven, was quite supportive, although her own periods had not yet begun. When the mother came home she assumed the menses to be painful and put the patient to bed. Her older sister reached menarche shortly thereafter. Unlike the patient, she began growing breasts and pubic hair. The patient assumed her own breasts would never grow, and her sister encouraged her in this belief.

This older sister went on to flagrant promiscuous activities which the parents deplored but did not stop. The patient remained a quiet and withdrawn adolescent, devoted to religion and books. She daydreamed about boys but was afraid of them. She went to the earliest mass to avoid the shame of being seen with her family, since she felt the congregation looked down on them as social inferiors. In church, she imagined herself recognized as especially good and spiritual and relished the eventual damnation of her older sister. It would be she who would be rescued by an ideal lover, she who would marry and have children she would love and bring up properly.

Miss Smith was sent to a religious prep school and boarded there. She felt miserably homesick, but was only allowed home on occasional weekends. She hoped that her spiritual goodness would result in recognition from peers and teachers, and was disappointed. The socially prominent girls, who told stories of their various sexual adventures with boys, were better groomed and dressed and more appealing to teachers.

All three sisters had little social poise. Role models at home made ideal identifications difficult. The older sister learned by experience. Her early sexual exploits suggested a pseudofeminine role, but she was able to gradually learn a more appropriate gender identity during adolescent sexuality. She matured gradually into an interesting and vivacious person. She dated a series of men, then married one whom the patient felt to be outstanding. This marriage proved sound, and the sister continued to develop into a warm and compassionate woman. The failure of damnation of this sister for her earlier promiscuity was the central cause of the patient's later alteration in religious beliefs. Meanwhile, the younger sister was plagued by difficulties. She lived at home after graduation from high school, held marginal jobs, and had an impoverished social life.

While drastically limited in social activities, Miss Smith did well academically in private school and was accepted into a good college. Wealth in the father's family, withheld from him personally, provided a trust fund for her education and later life. Her mother suggested that she major in economics since it could lead to a glamorous life in the world of finance. Not knowing what else to do, she followed this suggestion. During the first years she felt insecure and somewhat fraudulent when she got good grades. Neither of the other sisters was able to complete college, but Miss Smith could not stabilize her feelings of superiority or knowledgeability.

Dramatically, one day in church shortly after her twentieth birthday, she decided that God did not exist and that her restraint from sexual activity was wasted. With a sense of anger, but no particular plan, she allowed herself to be seduced by a man she admired who was president of her church group. She then fantasied they were engaged. When he married someone else, she was surprised and dismayed. Only then did she begin to masturbate, with accompanying feelings of guilt and anxiety.

On completion of college she obtained an unusually good position in a banking corporation, where, in addition to other advantages, her work had the romantic component of travel. She did satisfactory work but felt that she was only pretending to be capable. Contacts with coworkers frightened her. She gradually assumed a facade of poise and glamour, and entered into two affairs. In the first, she was clearly used and then dropped. In the second, she seemed to find the love she sought. Although she supported the young man financially, he appeared to be "on the way up." Again, while nothing had been said, she assumed they were engaged. When he walked out on her, she felt bitter and depressed.

At this point of crisis, Miss Smith was determined to reorganize herself. She recognized her continued lack of pleasure in sexual intercourse. She felt fraudulent at work. She decided to change her position and to learn actively about sex. She selected nutrition as a field and entered graduate school with the aim of becoming a dietician in a large medical center. While she did not seek out particular men, she entered into whatever affairs happenstance provided; they were uniformly unsatisfying and brief.

Attractive, personable, and successful young men were too overwhelming. Instead she tended to meet either older men or younger men who were ineligible for marriage. Courtship rituals with their slow explorations were also too anxiety provoking. Undressing together, especially slowly, was particularly threatening. She preferred to short circuit courtship rituals and tests, to get into bed as quickly as possible, feeling that the relationship could be more friendly and "less frantic" after intercourse.

The men she became involved with fell into two distinct patterns in a personal heirarchy. Men of "lower" status might be successful financially but were either much less physically attractive or much older than she. Men of "higher" status were younger and as good looking as she was, but were ineligible and hence tolerable because of some other feature.

In the affairs with younger men she generally felt herself to be a used and abused person. She would submit rapidly to intercourse, then expect to be taken out, especially to good restaurants, and shown off as a desirable companion. Instead, she would be driven directly home. Sometimes she would lend the lover money, clean his apartment, or perform some submissive task. She was unable to reveal, much less assert or insist upon, her own desires and need for dignity. Her one aggressive move was to reveal her frigidity, usually at some later point in the relationship. This challenge sometimes made men increase their efforts to get her to achieve a climax. They were never successful.

Older or lower status men would fall in love with her, treat her tenderly, give her gifts. Then the glamorous, free, uninhibited swinger role that she initially played in every affair would rapidly deteriorate. She began to feel apathetic and deadened in their presence. The only remaining excitement was in deciding when and how she would reveal these feelings and stop seeing them. To avoid hurting them the affair might be protracted with futile attempts on their part to be of more interest. These attempts would ultimately fail.

She would eventually challenge each man's virility by revelations of his inability to bring her to orgasm. Every affair ended in disaster. Either she was hurt, or she hurt some man. Her hopes for marriage and children grew dim. Sexual freedom and sensual pleasure did not come with sexual experience. Her graduate work entered the phase of internship, and this began to go poorly as her inability to get along easily with other people interfered with her performance.

When a final affair collapsed, which had seemed unusually promising for marriage, she felt painfully depressed and aware of a lack of progress in any area of her life. Someone she knew had been greatly helped by psychotherapy, and she decided to consult the same therapist. The extent of her difficulties, together with her strong motivation and intelligence, prompted a referral for consideration of psychoanalysis.

Initial Clinical Observations and Formulations

The first interviews followed a pattern similar to her relationships with men. Initially, she appeared as glamorous, animated, talkative, and provocative. Under the facade of poise however, she seemed tense, frightened, and sad. She changed topics readily, became passive and wanted direction. Her statements contained vague descriptors such as "it," "you know," and "something." She was easily distracted, responded with labile moods, was seductive without awareness, sought attention, and delivered her history in a global and impressionistic, rather than a detailed, manner. She often trailed off in the middle of an idea, saying, "I don't know."

Initial formulations were drawn after the first few interviews. She felt exploited in relationships with "higher" status, more sadistic men. Her goal was not gratification of masochistic aims so much as it was to make a prepayment of suffering which would magically entitle her to the later gratification of being rescued. The idealized father figure who would rescue her was either the same man, now transformed into positive aims by his guilt at having injured her, or another man aroused by her despair.

In the relationships with "lower" status males she was able to ward off a defective self-image because they fulfilled the role of an inferior person. For example, an older lover would rhapsodize to her about her youthful beauty. She then rejected him for being of an

inappropriate age for her. She would, however, be racked by guilt
for having hurt him. The failure of men to arouse her was used as
proof that she could not be excited and thus would never lose
control and perform acts that were taboo (symbolically incestuous).
In this role position, the power and danger of men was reversed into
a pathetic, ridiculous impotence. She was not defective, but strong
beyond their weak efforts; a heroine destined for some more
romantic lover, as in the tale of Sleeping Beauty.

In the history of her sparse relationships with women there was
also a pattern. With them she was as pseudodaughterly as she was
pseudosexual with men. Initially, she was compliant and overhelp-
ful. When women came to rely upon her, she would then either
withdraw out of anger at not getting enough in return or wrest
power from them in the form of job responsibilities or the approval
of superiors (usually male). If and when she won a victory, she
would give up because she felt unable to carry it off to some point of
completion. In general, she was afraid of continued attachment to
any competent, effective, active person of either sex.

These patterns with men and women seemed to be an
unconscious attempt to reconstruct her family situation in adult life,
much as it was schematically organized in her mind during early
development. She had not given up the hope of union with her
father or the hope of nurturative and care-taking rescue by an
idealized father-mother. She had, however, accomplished many of
the tasks of earlier developmental periods. While she had a
defective sense of self, she had separated her self-concept from her
representations of others: she had gone beyond the symbiotic phase
of ego development with relative success.

Her main defenses were repression and denial. The mental
contents warded off by these maneuvers were related to sexual
strivings, aggressive impulses, the threat of desertion and isolation.
Anxiety, fear, depression, and guilt were activated by the particular
aims and object connections of these themes. But the detailed
dynamics were not evident at this early period. Because of her
neurotic character structure, her strong motivation, and her
intelligence, analysis was considered the treatment of choice.

To continue the historical line, the analysis will be described first
in sequence. Later, the treatment process will be reconstructed in
terms of modifications of cognitive style and object relationships.

First Year

As mentioned previously, she presented herself as vivacious, earnest, intelligent, and compliant during the evaluation hours. She asked many questions, asked for direction, and requested little favors such as telephone usage, carfare, and time changes. Then, after a decision for a trial of analysis, her grooming became much less meticulous, her demeanor more childlike and anxious, her periods of silence became more frequent, and she wanted to be instructed or prodded on how to continue.

This inital series of hours was used by her to test the analyst's response to provocations. When he was neither too reactive to attention-getting devices nor too responsive to demands for support, she began talking of current difficulties at work and in a new love affair. This most recent affair was begun impulsively, coinciding with the onset of treatment, and it was seen later as a defensive maneuver to prevent a positive transference. She had read about analysis, and felt she was expected to fall in love with her therapist. She thought this preposterous, an indication of the eccentric ideas the therapist probably held, and the last thing that would ever happen—however much the analyst might try to evoke such feelings.

In any topical context she continued to test the analyst, to see if he would respond erratically when she was provocative, comfort her when she was upset, or pursue her when she was distant. This pattern was repetitive, at increasingly clearer levels of awareness, throughout most of the treatment period. After weeks of these episodes, she entered the room late and distraught. Obviously shaken, she stood dramatically against the door and announced that she had come only to say goodbye, that she could not go on with analysis because, among other things, she could not tolerate lying on the couch.

She agreed to talk this over and spent several sessions sitting in a chair. The constant neutrality and "coolness" of the analyst reassured her, but she complained bitterly that she needed tranquilizers and directive counseling from a "real person." She continued analysis, resumed use of the couch, but her depression increased. She spent mornings in bed and avoided her internship duties. She then had to take a leave of absence from school to avert being officially dropped, began three affairs at once, and risked pregnancy. She had stopped birth control pills because of side effects but was too frightened of gynecologists to request a diaphragm.

During the analytic hours she demanded and pleaded for help. She found it hard to verbalize her ideas and feelings and wanted the analyst to disclose his personal weaknesses so that she would know it was all right to reveal hers. She reported many other kinds of treatment in which therapists were more revealing, kinder, more giving, faster, and better. She admitted that she consciously withheld information and reports of current events. The analyst's response to these various maneuvers was to clarify what she was saying, largely by repetition. For example, with transference issues he might say, "You want me to do something more active to help you" or "You don't think you can stand it if I just keep listening and telling you what I think is going on." With outside issues, the analyst attempted to clarify patterns of interaction and cause and effect. Again, the style involved short repetitions of what she had said and occasional requests for more detail.

Some additional flavor of the analytic process may be provided by a process note of a typical, not especially "good" or "bad" hour, five months into treatment.

Process note. She arrived on time (she had frequently been late). Although she spoke in her usual disjointed way, with trailing off, frequent "I don't knows," and unconnected phrases, she seemed to express a guarded enthusiasm. She described an observation she had made about herself at the end of the previous hour. She noticed that she had rushed out of the room without looking at me at the end of the hour and that she felt nervous at the time. It was as I had said previously: she was scared when she felt intimate, telling of her feelings during the hours. She had also felt humiliated when I said the hour was up and had wanted to get out before I noticed her feelings.

That night she had a dream. She was in my office and was giving permission for some sort of operation. Then I changed into her employer who, in the dream, was cast as a doctor discussing something with another doctor. He was going to operate on her eye with a laser beam, without knowing how she felt about it. She emphasized, by repetition, the importance of her fear that the doctors did not know how frightened she was.

Her associations to laser beams were of superhuman power, superman and his X-ray vision, and "something that might get into her and destroy her." Doctors were persons who were impersonal, powerful, greedy, and did what they wanted. My only comment concerned one element in the dream that had to do with the dangers of vision; now that she felt committed to the analysis she was afraid of insight, of the light analysis might shed on her problems.

She admitted that she was frightened of the analysis now that it seemed possible to her. She added associations to a memory of being in a doctor's office with her mother. It was a regular appointment of her mother's, and there was a fat woman who was there frequently. She used to fantasy that the fat woman came to get sexual pleasure, that she was excited by and enjoyed examinations. I asked what kind of examinations, and she said the doctor was a gynecologist.

She went on to say that she sometimes fantasies that she is her mother and imagines having operations that would be unpleasant and painful. I said she spoke of these painful operations as if they had a delicious quality. She was startled, paused, then said this reminded her that she had recently gone to the dentist. He injected Novocain into her gums which became numb, and she felt good. Then she realized her tooth would actually be pulled and she became nervous and cried. He was kind and she felt very close to him. She always feels very close to doctors after some such procedure. She usually tells herself this is because the anxiety is over. But maybe it is because there is a sexual component to the relationship. She then saw this as one of my ideas and denied it.

The next topic was a story about her not wanting a new male friend to know she had sexual feelings toward him because he was married. I said that she was afraid of knowing, herself, that she had sexual feelings. She was silent, then blurted out that she had planned before the hour to say what she had said up to this point but didn't want to go any further. I said she was frightened of the idea of letting her thoughts come spontaneously. While that was what she was saying, she seemed startled to hear me say it and interpreted the remark as if it were a directive that she must free associate. She wondered how long it usually took analytic patients to learn to free associate. She liked the idea that it was taking her unusually long and that she was a difficult patient because that would show that she has great personal integrity.

In subsequent hours Miss Smith revealed indirect sexual fantasies of the analyst in dreams and daydreams, but denied their implications. She developed a phobia of walking on the street near the office, with a specific theme of fear of being seen by the analyst. This phobia generalized to a fear of riding buses because people might look at her and feel disgust, knowing that she was going to see an analyst whom she, they would presume, loved madly and foolishly.

She continued to insist that she badly needed sexual advice, support, and warmth, but was not getting it. Her wishes that she be counseled in sexual technique closely paralleled her most frequently used masturbation fantasy. In that fantary, she imagined a woman lying on an examining table. A nurse told her that the doctor was examining the woman and that the procedure was done for medical reasons, was quite safe, and had nothing to do with sex. It was implied that later the doctor would gradually and carefully explain all kinds of details about sexual intercourse. The doctor, in the visual images of the fantasy, was scarcely present and the woman was only vaguely herself.

In spite of her demands to be given more, she reacted in an almost startled manner to many statements by the analyst. She episodically insisted that his clarifications were forcing her to go too far. The analyst and psychoanalysis were alternately boring and weird, orthodox and decadent, pushing her too fast and not helping at all. Nonetheless, towards the end of the year, she was working rather hard on clarifying many important life patterns and getting a first approximation of their meanings. A turning point, perhaps equal in importance to her not leaving analysis when frightened, was her rejection of a marriage proposal made by a wealthy, attractive young man who would have taken her away to another country. The proposal reenacted one of her favorite fantasies, and her reluctance to accept it signaled recognition of the deep-seated and, thus far, unresolved nature of her characterological problems.

She began to accept confrontations and clarifications about her global denials, childlike establishment of simple rules (a form of rationalization), and abrupt cessation of topics. As her life patterns became clear, they seemed very sad to her and she became depressed. A one-month vacation by the analyst deepened this depression. She stated she had made the wrong choice when she decided to continue analysis and might go crazy during the free interval.

She berated the returning analyst for deserting her. At the same time she began to bring up pertinent memories from childhood in which she had experienced similar feelings from maternal deprivations. Her envy of her older sister who was able to "get away" from the family, and of her younger sister who received special care within the family also emerged. Her angry wishes that this older sister be punished for her sexual activities were associated with her hitherto unconscious guilt over her own sexual acts. The wish to be like her sick younger sister and deserve special and continuous attention also emerged and was connected to similar feelings of yearning for attention from the analyst. Her wishes emerged clearly in a dream. She had gone crazy, and the analyst was thus forced to take care of her "properly" by bringing her to live in his home-sanitorium. The scene was of a white columned mansion, surrounded by tranquil lawns, with therapy conducted beside a swimming pool. Special among a group of woman patients, she would lie along the diving board as if asleep, and receive tender care.

Second Year

The anniversary of one year of analysis led to a renewed period of depression. She had heard that special patients finished in one year and she was disappointed. She reacted by setting a termination date one year hence. She found it intolerable to think of analysis lasting any longer than that. She made increased efforts at self-observation and at free association. Guarded enthusiasm about understanding herself and gaining control of her behavior led to an increasingly evident transference neurosis in which she tried to ward off sexual interest, anxiety, and guilt.

Various arousing and traumatic childhood memories were

reported, such as her fearful fascination as she was allowed to watch her father shave off his pubic hair. She expected the analyst to be enthused by such revelations because they would prove his eccentric psychoanalytic theories. While she discounted the meaning of such memories, she both feared and expected that they would lead to fervid cooperation on analytic work, lyrical excitement, and then a carried-away sexual transport by both parties during the treatment hour.

Trying out these ideas in relatively clear language without such results gave her an increased sense of safety. With a lessened fear of intimacy, and also as a resistance to the transference, she became closer to one of two concurrent male friends. Her exploitation and rescue fantasies were clarified. While trying out greater freedom she developed anxiety attacks when with her male friend or enroute to the treatment hours.

Once again preoccupied with the analysis and analyst, she decided to give up her male friends until she was cured of her sexual inhibitions. She masturbated more and began work on her recurrent masturbation fantasies. She recognized her inhibitions against representing men, penises, or vaginas even in her private fantasies. Then the woman nurse figure became a primary sexual object. Although she was afraid of becoming a homosexual, she threatened the analyst by stating her intentions to experiment with homosexuality if he did not hurry and cure her frigidity with men. Her main homosexual fantasies were a wish to stare at large breasts, and sexualized wishes for nurturance at the breast.

When the threat of homosexuality did not evoke a nonanalytic response from the therapist, and while under pressure from the clarification and interpretation of the transference meanings of these threats, she again carried her testing of the analytic situation to an extreme. She engaged in behavior that carried the risk of being assaulted by men. She started several new affairs, and then threatened suicide during the depression that resulted when these impulsive relationships ended badly.

The analyst responded with tactful and limited interpretations, avoiding interventions of rescue or rejection which she tried to provoke. She seemed to develop an increased sense of the analyst as a safe and stable person; there was reduction in her use of denial and repression, and turbulent acting out also diminished. Sexual fantasies about the analyst were spoken of clearly and linked to childhood memories of relationships with her father. The emotional responses were more fully developed and were experienced as tolerable levels of anxiety, depression, and guilt, rather than as emotional storms.

Third Year

The third year could be summarized as a working through of various constellations of ideas and feelings toward her father and mother as repeated in transference neuroses. While interpretation of resistances remained a prominent technique, her responses were different. Instead of denial and repression, she changed her defensive operations. She used dreams, free associations, and recollections well, accepted and helped with reconstructions, and experienced and reported bodily sensations and feeling states as they fluctuated during the hour. Instead of global depressions she felt sad and disappointed about specific facets of her life.

In general, she moved from a passive to an active stance. She had been working as a secretary after dropping out of her graduate training. She was now able to get a paramedical job on the basis of her partial training as a dietician and reapply to school.

With continued work on her defective body image, avoidance of ideas about sex, inhibitions of arousal, and fear of altered consciousness during intercourse, she began to enjoy sexual activities with men. Her first orgasm occurred during mutual masturbation; she then had an orgasm during intercourse. There were still difficulties, however, and fuller erotic experiences were not achieved until after a termination date was set some time later.

With increased freedom in heterosexual activities and fantasies, her free-floating anxiety attacks changed into phobic forms. For example, after experimenting with fellatio for the first time she feared that an ordinary facial pimple was a syphilitic canker. Her aggressive and castrating impulses toward men also emerged into clear representational expression. She wanted to control the man's penis, or at least govern in an exaggerated way when it would or would not enter her body. Without such control she feared her body would be hurt.

This fear of being hurt was reasonable in view of her childlike body image. As she was able to think and communicate more clearly, she could reveal that her self-image did not include a vaginal opening. During intercourse she had been numb in the pelvic area, although genital feelings were possible when she was alone and masturbated. Now she was able to explore herself and use words to label genital parts. The "nonexistent area" in her body image went through stages; first of cloacal chaos in which her vagina and rectum were imagined as coalesced, and then a sense of a separate, inadequate but discrete vagina about two inches in maximum length.

Not suprisingly, preganancy fantasies emerged in dreams, then in daydreams and reverie. Her masturbation fantasies evolved in a series of increasingly mature forms. First she imagined herself as a vague child-woman, then as a man, being the one in control and telling a virgin about both pelvic examinations and the sex act. Next, repreating the homosexual phase of the previous year, she imagined herself as a woman doing things to another woman, and finally herself as a woman being fondled by a very gentle, reassuring man.

This work led to intensification of the sexualized transference neurosis. She became frightened by her emotional experiences during therapy hours. She fantasied that she would cry so much she could never stop, or else that the anlayst would be so moved that the love affair would at last become irresistible. Alternate exhibitionistic and voyeuristic impulses were clarified and related to her phobias and to various recalled experiences with both parents.

Fourth Year

A mixture of yearning, frustration, hostility, and disgust toward her mother had emerged episodically throughout the analysis, and at this point poignant emotional memories about her occupied center stage. Entwined with these memories were her envy of both sisters, the jealousy and the thwarted competitive urges toward her older sister, and resentment for the attentive ministrations received by the younger sister. She worked through several patterns of relationships between herself and other women, both historically and in the present, as well as those mirrored currently in the analytic situation.

In one of these configurations she was the poor, passive, helpless victim of the hostility and lack of concern from her mother, the analyst, or an older woman. At other times she remained a hapless victim, but the other person was not so much an aggressor as simply insufficient. An idealized masculine rescuer was, in a life script on the order of that described by Berne (1961), supposed to find and care for her at this point. When she was a child of about four or five her father did fulfill this role, taking her for car rides to cheer her up. Her ideal version of him was later displaced by disillusionment but remained as a configuration of hope for another hero. In another configuration, she at last unleashed the destructive reactions to her disappointments. To her great surprise, embarrassment, anxiety, guilt, and pleasure, she was able to tongue lash the analyst. She had fantasies of shooting him and of blowing up his car, and feared visiting her parents because she would tear the lid off their hypocrisies and denials. Once again, the analysis was a dangerous provocation and could be responsible for any mayhem she might commit.

As she was able to tolerate the experience of strong feelings without a sense of losing control, the various representations of herself in relation to members of her family were described, reviewed, and reconsidered with increasing clarity. Using her adult mind, she was able to compare memories and fantasies with one another. Compartmentalization of good and bad images of each important person was reduced, and she had feelings of "realization" about people. For example, she was deeply moved by being able to remember her father as having both good and bad qualities. He was interesting, sincere, esthetic, even powerful at times while also neurotic, infantile, perverse, seductive, and unreliable.

Her self-representations had also changed as therapy progressed, but now these changes were more clearly delineated. There was a period of conscious alteration in her sense of her body and her identity. She had fantasies and dreams of the analyst's wife, a woman she had never heard of or seen, but presumed existed. The wife was imagined variously as her mother, sisters, and ego ideal. First the wife was imagined as an idealized and flamboyant mistress-type named "Titsy." She also fantasied the wife as sickly or fat, and herself as a yearned-for substitute. Then the wife image in dreams changed to a mature, attractive, concerned woman who spoke kindly to her. In one of the patient's dreams she had come to the analyst's home. Uneasy about how appropriate the visit might be, she was told by the wife that it was alright, and they then talked sociably together. Miss Smith identified in a comparatively deliberate way with these idealized projections. She allowed herself to continue complaining about her own mother, to feel sad that her mother would never change, and again, to fantasy being the child of the analyst and his wife.

During this period Miss Smith changed her style of grooming and dress to one that seemed somehow to "fit" her personality. She experienced guilt at entering a different status, one higher than her mother, especially as she was now able to meet and get to know men of the professional class. Finally, she had feelings of "reality" about her mother, was able to accept her parent's limitations, and to give up some of her own feelings of contemptuous superiority. During the first part of the analysis she had been remote from her parents. During the third year she had visited them and returned disappointed. In view of her own altered impressions of them and her feelings of control, she had expected a magical change in them that would make them capable of more intimate relationships with her. Now, when she visited them again, she felt that she could accept them as they were. She no longer felt the need to accuse them nor was she disappointed by the limitations still imposed on her relationships with them.

Her sexual fantasies continued to shift, and she felt more open toward both the physical and emotional components of relating to men. She also began to have experiences of "reality" which were simply keen perceptions with knowledge of what was going on. She felt as if her body parts and those of her sexual partner were real, and this surprised her. She recognized a residual fear of enthusiasm in sex and linked this to her fear of enthusiasm in the analysis. Resistance was generally absent, and major interpretive efforts seemed unnecessary as the work progressed by itself, as it were.

She felt in control of her life, effective, able to think and feel, to work out her own solutions to everday life problems. Ideas of transience, life ending in death, aging, and menopause occurred and filled her with sadness. Then she discussed ideas of terminating the analysis. After several emergences and avoidances of this idea, a termination date a half a year off was agreed upon. She then experienced this date setting as an unfair trick and as a loss of interest on the part of the analyst. The ending was ill-timed, she felt, because, while her symptoms were gone and her life was in control, she had neither married and had a child nor embarked securely on her profession. A series of transferênce repetitions occurred in which the analyst was compared to the uncaring mother. Gratified by his fine performance in curing her, the analyst now no longer cared what she might or might not do, and planned to get rid of her before giving everything. On the other hand, he was also like the tricky, eccentric father. The termination was a way to confront her with her residual problems, or perhaps a device that would lead to a postanalytic love tryst. These reactions were readily translated into words and understanding, with toleration and working through of related emotions and memories. At the end, she felt a little sad that she had lost some interest in the analysis, and was very grateful for the results of the work. She had occasional fears of relapse, but according to the follow-up mentioned earlier, these fears were unfounded.

THE PROCESSES OF CHANGE

The clinical inferences about Miss Smith can now be reviewed in terms of basic patterns both before and at the end of treatment. Changes will be considered first in terms of the customary methapsychological points of view (Rapaport and Gill 1958), then in terms of the cognitive point of view. Discussing the six metapsychological points of view one by one leads to such redundancy that they have been combined into three compatible pairs: the developmental and adaptational, the structural and topographic, and the economic and dynamic points of view.

Development and Adaptation

In the hierarchical model of metapsychology suggested by Gedo and Goldberg (1973), Miss Smith would be seen as beginning the analysis in Phase IV, that is, the stage of psychosexual and psychosocial development in which the main hazards are moral anxiety over incestuous and agressive object-related strivings. Her principle defenses, repression and denial, developed because of a cognitive preparedness for such modes at that developmental stage plus the family practice of utilizing these defenses in communication.

Her characerological development was also colored by an ambivalent attachment to her mother. She yearned for maternal care as might be exemplified by cuddling and radiant mutuality of interest. She got less than she wanted and was reactively angry, but did not surrender hope of affectionate rapprochement.

By her oedipal period of childhood development, Miss Smith had successfully differentiated herself from her mother, and she had a gender identification as female. But precursors of adult female sexuality, such as flirtatiousness and display, were warded off. A self image as an attractive female was not integrated. Instead she felt partially defective. Her childlike and defective self-schema was not revised because everyday forms of sexual self images and representations were warded off. In general, this was done to avoid the threat of guilt and anxiety over sexual excitement and fear of sexual assault if she were to be provocative. With analysis, these warding-off maneuvers were interpreted, clarified, and counteracted by intentional acts of thought and behavior. The childlike and defective self-schemata were reprocessed in terms of conscious experience of current self-images and representations. She was graudually able to integrate female genitalia into her self-schemata, leading to increased confidence in her capacity for sexual relations.

In addition to this progression toward completion of the genital phase of psychosexual development, Miss Smith had persistent conflicts unresolved in the oral phase as outlined in earlier chapters and suggested by Marmor (1953), Easser and Lesser (1965), and Zetzel (1970). Strong yearnings to be nurtured, literally and symbolically, were associated unconsciously with a magical belief that someone always suffered when such desires were present.

Either she would suck dry and deplete her mother, as her mother virtually told her she had done, or she would be deliberately neglected as unworthy of concern. These oral-aggressive components of this constellation and feelings extended into a blurred anal-sadistic dimension in which she wanted to let go of her feelings but feared a disastrous loss of control. If she knew she was angry with her mother or any other nurturative-frustrating figure, then she would lose control and have a destructive temper tantrum. The fear of loss of sphincter control also colored her sexual experiments since she had explicit fearful fantasies of bowel or bladder mishaps if enthusiastic sexual responses were to occur.

Analytic work instigated the conscious processing of these variegated and blurred-together themes. She was able to differentiate sexual strivings from wishes to be held and comforted. Her impulsivity in sexual relationships was attenuated once she could seek what she wanted at any particular time without confusions of aim and could accept partial gratification. She came to recognize when she was enraged over frustration and how she warded off the emergence of such anger.

Her oedipal fantasies were integrated with an unusual frequency of real life events. Her father was sexually provocative in his exhibitionism, and there was a real impairment in the mother-father relationship. Any fantasy she might entertain in conscious awareness was difficult to isolate from memories of expectations of real occurrences.

Her self- and object-schemata at the onset of analysis concretized an internalized version of these familial patterns into a set of stereotyped roles. These roles, to be described later in detail, were imposed compulsively on every relationship. Real experiences were held at such great distance by nonappraisal of meanings and by general denial. These stereotypes were perpetuated rather than revised. Hence all men were alternately tricky, exciting, and dangerously self-seeking or else they were devalued, disgusting, or depressing. During analysis these stereotypes were compared with current self- and object-images with appropriate and gradual revision. As a result of improved recognition of real possibilities, she developed a more appropriate and extensive repertoire of potential roles. This helped her to act differently, to understand people better, and to obtain social reinforcement for her improvement.

The overstimulating oedipal father and the hostile, withholding, "bad" pregenital mother had been warded off from conscious and emotional experience but had at the same time operated as perpetual stereotypes for "role-casting" others in her interpersonal relationships. Nonrecognition was necessary because both stereotypes led to relationships in which she was exquisitely vulnerable to reactive anxiety and guilt. The analytic situation allowed her to first test the analyst by her various transference *behaviors*. When he was neither excessively nice nor excessively mean, it became safe to begin to *experience* the maternal transference; just as when the analyst was neither too provocative nor too remote or "selfish," she could begin to experience the paternal transference. With transference experience came childhood memories linked to the particular feeling state as well as acting out of the configurations in extraanalytic current relationships. The combination of childhood memories, transference experience, and a certain amount of "playing out" in real life led to greater freedom to express childlike emotions and to alter the stereotyped self-object schemata. Maturation was evident in her surrender of both her pregenital and her oedipal demands upon the world and in her simultaneous experience of less fear of retribution. These changes will be reviewed in greater detail in the final section of this chapter when revision of self- and object-schemata and role relationships are discussed.

Structural and Topographic Points of View

Before analysis, Miss Smith operated in a constricted way. Ego functions most severely affected were attention deployment, conscious thought, memory, and fantasy. Her experience of emotion was inhibited. She feared any strong feelings and reacted to them as if they were instrusive and uncontrollable forces. Overgeneralization of associations led her to react to her peers as if they were like her parents. Taboos against sexual and aggressive strivings were primitive and led to a strong predisposition toward guilt. Like the primary impulses, ideas that would evoke guilty feelings were repressed and yet occasionally intruded into conscious awareness. Because of the general use of repression and denial, she seldom knew exactly what she wished and could not plan effective action toward gratification. Instead, there was episodic emotional experience, especially anxiety, without clear relationship of the feelings to ideational representations.

Conscious experiences had to be avoided not only because of the guilty responses that might occur but because thoughts were equated with actions. This posture was based on her own fears of loss of control and the religious attitude that harboring certain thoughts could be sinful. These attitudes were reexamined during analysis, and she learned to qualify differences between thought and action. As she became able to experience thought in areas of conflict, she was able to review and rework the various attitudes that contributed to conflict.

This review process had many facets, not the least of which was the development of an integrated set of ego ideals. At the onset of analysis she had little sense of an authentic autonomous self. She preferred the "swinger" self-representation to the depressed, neurotic, and childlike self-representation that seemed the only alternative. Either role was in conflict with values that were not integrated into the self-schemata but rather functioned as introjects of mother and father. When she experienced herself as a sexually active swinger, she was vulnerable to internal experiences of an introject of her rule-bound, sin-preoccupied mother. This sense of another person reprimanding her was a form of self-criticism for being corrupt and evil. When she experienced herself as a "good" woman who worked responsibly to do her duty, then an equivalent introject associated with her father excoriated her for being a passive victim: dead, inhibited, uninteresting, and stupidly compliant. In either instance, the values seemed to have their own activity, separate from her self-schemata.

In the course of the analysis she realized the extent to which the various value systems were components of her self-schemata. She could reexamine her standards and revise attitudes that she did not feel were rational or in accord with her growing sense of adult morality. As a way of regulating life choices she began to adhere to a set of principles actively avowed by the self rather than by punishment-oriented fears.

At first, the acquisition of new cognitive skills and the modification of old cognitive habits occurred because of the positive relationship with the therapist. This relationship was based on both the therapeutic alliance with its components of realistic hope and trust and the positive transference with its component fantasies of love and attention. The strength of the introjected therapist, part real and part fantasy, counteracted the strength of parental introjects because he was the immediate potential source of rewards and punishments. The power of ideas attributed to the therapist, such as the acceptability of thinking the unthinkable, gained ascendancy over equivalent ideas about criticisms attributed to parents and God. Later, as transference fantasies were relinquished, she tended to identify with the therapist's neutral, objective, rational, thoughtful, reality-attentive, patient, and nonjudgmental operations. Thus she learned to conceptualize clearly where she once had been globally vague. The learning occurred both by the trial-and-error discovery that clarity helped her to feel in control and by the automatic learning that goes with valuing and identifying with another person.

Dynamic and Economic Points of View

As described in previous sections, two clusters of warded-off mental contents and typical defensive operations characterized her dynamics. One cluster was oedipal in configuration. The second was concerned with pregenital ambivalence centered on her mother. In the oedipal cluster of impulse-defense configurations, sexual strivings toward her father conflicted with (1) taboos against incest, (2) fear of competitive maternal retaliation, and (3) fear of loss of control and sexual assault. Secondary themes in this cluster included destructive wishes against mother and father with reactive guilt. The destructive wishes against her father included a desire to wrest from him masculine power and independence. The destructive wishes against her mother included a desire to take adult female genitalia and child bearing capacities away from her and to assume the mother's role in the family. Destructive wishes also concerned her sisters. If she could rid the family of them, she could occupy their positions.

This complex of oedipal themes was particularly difficult to work through during childhood because she was not dealing with her own unconscious fantasy. Her father's real sexual displays added danger. If she were exhibitionistic herself or voyeuristically interested in him, then he might lose control. Her principal method of warding off these threats was inhibition of sensation, thought, and action. Total inhibition maintained emotional states within tolerable limits. But the relative strength of strivings and external stimulation exceeded her capacity for complete avoidance. Under threat of a partial failure in repressive maneuvers, she experienced instrusive attacks of anxiety and guilt which she saw as dangerous lapses of control, even if ideation remained unclear. To reduce the threat, secondary defenses such as displacement were instituted, resulting in the formation of symptoms such as phobias and hypochondriasis.

The change process involved revising the impulse-defense configuration for this cluster of themes. The first step was confrontation, enabling her to recognize the extensiveness of denial as a defensive maneuver. Awareness led to control and altered the balance of forces between defensive and impulsive aims. Conscious thought increased, and she found herself able to tolerate clarity. For example, as she tested out the analyst in the transference situation, she found him safely nonreactive to her provocations. This sense of safety along with attention to her tendency to deny ideationally what she was doing behaviorally led to awareness that she was acting out exhibitionistic and voyeuristic fantasies. These current behavioral strivings were then conceptualized. Once conceptualized, the ideas and feelings could be linked associatively with childhood memories, hitherto repressed in large part, of her felt emotions and response to her father's behavior. The segregation of memory fragments decreased, allowing a coherent story to emerge.

As a further example of repression, a specific memory can be considered. At the onset of treatment, she remembered her father lying nude on her bed. The memory was not in this sense repressed. As the analysis progressed, she recalled and reexperienced her visual curiosity about the movement of his semierect penis, a detail of the memory that had been repressed. She was able to reexperience her feelings of revulsion and anger at her mother for not making her father stop behaving in this way. The connection of the feelings for her mother with the memory of her father helped integrate the experience into a holistic framework of memory. She realized how similar these feelings were to her currently active desires to see the analyst's car, his wife, and his body. As the associational connections were worked through, the need to ward off these desires by denial and repression lessened, and she could then allow herself to dream of them without great humiliation, guilt, and anxiety. This trial of clear thinking about a subject in the comparative safety of the treatment situation trained her and convinced her of the acceptability of thinking about conflictive ideas in current everday life. Through such processes she learned to change her cognitive style.

Once defensive maneuvers were less mandatory, there was a general decrease in tension, and she could bend her capacities to other efforts. As memories and fantasies could be reviewed in conscious secondary-process thought, primary-process associations and appraisals became less powerful as determinants of action plans. For example, she could get to know the qualities of a new male acquaintance by checking and rechecking her perceptions and appraisals, rather than by entering into a role relationship based on primitive stereotypes.

The second main cluster of warded-off contents we have already labeled as pregenital. It included an unconscious evaluation of herself as insufficiently nurtured as a child, and led to arousal of depression and rage. These emotions were averted by repression, denial, rationalization, fantasy distortion of reality, and reaction formation. She could also use undoing, although not to the extent found in obsessional personalities. When anxiety and guilt provoked by the first cluster of sexual themes emerged in the analysis she would shift the organization of her experience to the second culster of deprivation themes. These deprivation themes evoked a mood that oscillated betweeen resigned helplessness and a kind of angry sadness, and tended to reduce sexual excitation.

THE COGNITIVE POINT OF VIEW: A SUBDIVISION OF THE PSYCHOLOGY OF EGO FUNCTIONS

The modification of defenses as they occur in the form of resistances is essential if transference neuroses are to evolve, be examined, and be resolved. In the following section the focus is first on the thought, emotion, and control processes by which defenses are accomplished and on the alterations of these processes in the course of treatment. The next focus is on how modification of defensive styles permits both revision and development of core schemata of self and other, a cognitive structural change related to behavior pattern change. An emphasis on new learning will be added to the familiar concepts of insight, working through, and conflict resolution.

Patterns of Cognition and How They Changed

Miss Smith manifested many of the characteristics accorded the prototype of the hysterical personality. As discussed in earlier chapters, Shapiro (1965) has given a penetrating analysis of how these traits are mediated by particular cognitive styles. Along with other leading theorists of cognitive controls, Shapiro emphasizes the impressionistic distortions of incoming perceptual stimuli, the rapid and short-circuited appraisal of meanings, and the limited categories and availability of memory as central aspects of thought in the hysterical personality (see also Gardner et al 1959, Klein et al. 1962).

For the description of shifts in the neurotic cognitive style of Miss Smith, it is desirable to clearly describe segments of the cognitive process, from perception to decisive completion of a train of thought. Then the change in each segment can be discussed in terms of the treatment process and final outcome. To prevent excessive segmentalization, four areas for discussion have been selected: perceptual attention, representation, association, and resolution of incongruities.

Perceptual Attention

Miss Smith habitually deployed her attention in a global manner. Her descriptions of events were vague, impressionistic, and left the listener with little sense of the context or order of events. It is possible that this trait might have been a style of communication, but as the analyst empathized and entered deeply into the patient's experience, it seemed that vagueness extended to her perceptions as well and was not just an inhibited form of speech. She described events that occurred within the analytic hour in the same way; and when asked about the quality of her experience, she confirmed these inferences. At the same time, details of the environment that might relate to her current wishful and fearful expectancies were hyperattended. This is a general characteristic of object-seeking attention and thought organization in an hysterical personality (Fairbairn 1954, Wisdom 1961, Myerson 1969). That is, details of the environment symbolically relevant to such concerns were discovered rapidly but were not accurately appraised.

For example, during a period of heightened sexualized transference feelings, she had frequent illusions that men she saw walking on the street were the analyst. She recognized peripheral cues quickly but retained the illusory recognition until the men passed quite close to her. She was alert to another person's interests and could mold her self-presentation to fit. Details were disproportionate, overemphasized, and combined with generalities about facets of an interpersonal situation. While she was quick to note the surface attitudes of another person, she seemed unaware of her own acts, of what was revealed by her facial expression or bodily gestures. She might move her head coquettishly or swing her legs, and not realize that she was doing this. Such imprecision of perception seemed to be due to a too-rapid construction of images, an overreadiness toward conclusion, an overusage of expectancy schemata. Perceptual rechecking, which would have counteracted a rapid illusion such as seeing the analyst in the street, was seldom utilized; thus errors of assumption and extended illusions occurred,

During analysis, the defensive reasons for not recognizing her own actions were interpreted. It was paradoxical but possible to call her vagueness of perception to her attention. The interventions led her to conscious efforts to counteract her automatic, nonconscious tendencies. She slowly learned to notice details, observe her own acts, and gather clues about her own motivational states and those of others. This learning was made possible by her increased tolerance for emotional responses to the incoming information. Increased awareness led to all other changes in information processing just as, transactively, the changes in how she processed information produced a wider repertoire of expectancy schemata and increased perception. These styles and changes are summarized in table 2.

TABLE 2
PATTERNS AND CHANGE IN PERCEPTUAL ATTENTION

Style
———

1. On wholes rather than details
2. On person's interests and surface attitude toward her
3. Selective inattention to own acts
4. Dominated by stimuli relevant to immediate internal fantasies (either wishful or fearful)

Change During Treatment
————————————

Learned to attend to details, own acts, context of interpersonal situation, clues to motives of self and other.

Representation

Information can gain expression in lexical, image (in various sensory systems), and enactive (bodily) modes of representation (Horowitz 1972). Any person's style can be discussed in terms of his habitual usage of and translations among the three styles. In an "ideal" person, representation in one mode could be readily translated into other forms of representation. Such cross-modal expression gives breadth and depth to meaning. Miss Smith habitually used enactive and image modes for conflicted mental contents; she tended to inhibit translation of such information into words. Her enactive representations included body movements indicative of sexual interest. As mentioned in the previous section, her awareness of these expressions was quite limited. She did not know she behaved provocatively and could not label her posture, gesture, or facial expression with specific words describing meaning.

Representation of images derived through perception was also affected by a particular style. As already indicated, schemata of expectancy had relative dominion. These expectations could force a perceptual sampling of external reality into a template configured by what Knapp (1974) would call her long-standing interpersonal fantasies. The dynamic themes of looking and being seen, sexual interest, guilt, anxiety, and anger provided many such templates. More specifically, self- and object-dyads, centered on herself as waif and on an object as rescuer or aggressor, provided a prefiguration for appraisal of new information. The results were representations that composited sets of information from within and without but that were heavily slanted in favor of internal contributions.

These contributing factors to a given representation were scrutinized carefully in multiple episodes of microanalysis as each conflicting experience was reviewed in the analyses (see Horowitz 1974). The verbal nature of the analytic situation, the prevailing demand for translation of experience into words, led to details of report beyond her personal tendency to vague and global descriptions. If she were describing an emotionally difficult event, such as an encounter with a potential male friend, fragments of representation of what happened would be gradually pieced together. Reconstructive efforts fleshed out the context of the episode and sequence of interactions. Reconstructions could be contrasted with her initially vague and perhaps distorted image representations of what happened. Similar processes clarified the patient-analyst situation. These recurrent efforts led to changes in her ability to experience an immediate situation. In addition to clearly experiencing the interrelations of meanings expressed in enactive and image modes, she was able to verbalize what was happening.

Free association is a somewhat different experience for each person. For Miss Smith, the experience was composed largely of a flow of visual images. To communicate these thoughts she had to translate the images into words, and early in treatment this translation was often blocked. She might begin to speak of her images but would quickly trail off without completing a phrase. She would say "I don't know," become silent, sigh. But the steady and basically gentle pressure of the analyst listening and asking gradually motivated her to work toward verbal translation of these images. In many ways, fantasy images dominated her conscious experience, and even when alone she did not translate these into word meanings. The long continued expectation of the analyst for verbal communication altered this pattern.

The images of the fantasies were generally disguised wish fulfillments. Since her wishes involved object relationships, in contrast to the self-aggrandizing role fantasies of more narcissistic patients, two people might be depicted in the image representations. Remarkably, neither person might be designated as "self." If she imagined a particular man she had seen as flirting with a woman, she might leave it quite unclear as to whether she was the woman or whether she imagined watching another woman. Her conceptualization could be even more vague. The idea of someone losing control and hurting someone else could be visualized without any particular awareness of whether she were the person losing control or being injured. Once again, the pressure of the analytic situation contributed to motivation to label the images as self and others. Early in treatment the request was simply for reports. Later the analyst interpreted images in terms of what she wished or feared from others. Finally she continued to elaborate images, including translation to lexical associative meanings, until the references to self became clear. Of course, interpretations of fear of activity, and of defensive switches between activity and passivity, played an important role. The central point is that the increased translation of images and enactments into words was due not only to modification of defenses and estimations of danger but was also a process of acquired skill.

While lexical representation was not exluded from her experience of thought, there was a virtual absence of some types of verbal naming. She neither spoke nor let herself think the words for genitals or bodily functions. Penis, vagina, nipple, bladder, urine, and feces were referred to as "it." She could not imagine herself as ever being able to think specifically, much less speak, in such terms. This issue of lexical vagueness was then elaborated into transference attitudes. She expected the analyst to try to force her to say sexual words and anticipated her own resistance and the excitement of the chase.

These transference meanings were worked through, along with

recognition of the general defensive function of lexical avoidances. Use of the lexical system meant a fuller orchestration of thought and a sharper designation of her own role, since in grammatical construction, the subject and object are usually specified: "I want him to do it to me." The image system may clarify what "it" is, the enactive system may clarify the intensity of doing it, the verbal system states the cause and effect sequence. Enhanced verbal communication led her to specify what she felt and wanted. At the end of the analysis she felt especially pleased with her acquired ability to speak frankly, clearly, and to the point in various contexts. She even advanced her career by taking on public-speaking engagements.

To summarize, Miss Smith accomplished repression by a series of cognitive maneuvers. Representation was inhibited in two main ways. One was the prevention of representation of any potentially threatening ideas as images, enactions, or words. The second form of inhibition was prevention of translation between modes of representation. Inhibition at the boundaries of representational systems allowed both forms of limitation of representation to work.

Automatic inhibitions changed during analysis as the deployment of attention was altered. Interventions by the analyst directed her attention to the possibility of representation. Conscious efforts, motivated by alliance and by transference attitudes, modified the automatic nonconscious inhibitory operations. As representations occurred, the situation proved safer than expected. Recurrent safety where, originally, danger had been signaled modified her automatic appraisal of threat and arousal of anxiety. Repetition of conscious efforts at representation altered the automatic "programing" of thought until representation and translation became the automatic formats.

Intrusive representations, often as images, were commonplace before and during the early phases of analysis. A loss of volitional control was an aspect of this experience because the expressions occurred in spite of inhibitory efforts. These episodes were themselves interpreted as events, and they indicated to her that she was out of control. She feared that such experiences meant insanity, yet the idea had some appeal. The secondary gain would be the opportunity to use madness to force those who neglected her to care for her.

In the course of conscious efforts at representation of usually inhibited ideas, she gained the sense of herself as active thinker of all thoughts. She tolerated threatening ideas and the resulting emotions. Because active thought was permitted, instrusive episodes lessened. The result of the increased conscious effort at representation was a sense of increased control. These various stylistic aspects of representations and the relevant changes during analytic work are shown in table 3.

TABLE 3
PATTERNS AND CHANGE IN REPRESENTATION

Style

1. Enactive forms of affect expression readily emergent with low translation to lexical mode and subjective sense of low control over contents
2. Perceptually derived images constructed with bias to fantasy of role realtionships, of sexual excitation, threat, rescue, and accusation
3. Fantasy images not designated as to which role filled by self, low translation to lexical mode, high translation to enactive mode
4. Inhibition of lexical representation of words about the sexual parts of the body
5. General inhibition of representation of conflicted ideas and feelings with occasional intrusive representations
6. Emotional representations experienced as uncontrolled and intense

Change During Treatment

Achieved more fluid and complete translations into word meanings, learned to check representations by repeated perception, learned to represent ideas about bodies, increased representation of self as agent. Reduced intrusiveness led to a sense of control.

Associational Connections and the Appraisal of Information

One can postulate that any potentially new event sets in motion a series of appraisal problems as a kind of program for thought processes (Lazarus 1966, Klein 1967, Peterfreund and Schwartz 1971). The program would continue as a conceptual tendency until the ability to fit a new event into relevant cognitive structures of schemata was exercised (Piaget 1937, Jacobson 1954, Tomkins 1962, Miller, Galanter, and Pribram 1960). Reinterpretation of new events or revision of schemata would fit new to old and so complete the process. Until such completion, codings of the event and relevant associations would tend toward recurrent representation. These representations would be experienced as intrusive if the repetition tendency were opposed by inhibitory maneuvers (Horowitz 1970, 1976).

At the onset of analysis, Miss Smith was guided by the pleasure-unpleasure principle. The reality principle also regulated cognition, but not to the extent ideal for adaptation. For example, in establishing the relationship of a new event to enduring schematic classifications she tended to short-circuit, that is, to erroneously "recognize" the new information as if it were another instance of a longstanding interpersonal fantasy.

Ever expecting a rescuer, a chance encounter with a man was appraised as if he were the rescuer and "this was it." Associations to available memories of times when similar feelings led to major disappointment were inhibited because the need for rescue was great; the idea of not being rescued was intolerable. This type of inhibition of associational possibilities was accomplished by terminating and not translating the first glimmerings of representations that threatened to arouse negative affect. In order to move away from threatening ideas, she would declare a train of thought completed or incapable of completion. These styles were reflected in her speech. Either she declared that she didn't know or she prematurely closed a topic by announcing that she knew the meanings. "I don't know," the virtual hallmark of communication of the hysterical character, was not only a statement of fact but an injunction against further thought, an injunction now internalized but once a family style.

The repeated avoidance of possible and relevant associational routes led to a low capacity for organizing and analyzing events in terms of cause and effect sequences. She was unable to predict her own actions or plan for interpersonal situations. To the extent that she recognized this impairment she suffered narcissistic injuries and also feared being out of control herself or being overwhelmed by decisiveness in others. Such fear further motivated inhibitions of thought because thinking might involve knowing her bad thoughts, knowledge would lead to peremptory action, and loss of control and powerlessness over intrusive fantasies would follow.

Because of her fears of being bad or out of control, she automatically suppressed associational lines that would amplify the meanings and implications of her own activity. If ideas were evolving that designated her as active, and if anxiety and guilt increased with such ideas, she shifted associational lines to those that designated her as passive. Sometimes inhibition and shifting were insufficient and anxiety and guilt mounted. Another operation to reduce these felt emotions was to lose her reflective self-awareness, a part of a dissociative process. In such altered states of consciousness she could not remember what she had just been thinking or perceiving. For example, after deciding to lose her virginity and aquire sexual experience, she entered impulsively into an affair. She could not, however, do so while conceptualizing herself as awake and aware. She had to be seduced while drunk. Later, while she knew intercourse had taken place, she was unsure of what it had been like. In plaintive and poignant terms, during the analysis, she described herself as psychologically a virgin because she had never actively and freely engaged in sex in a tender union.

Altered states of consciousness has the additional advantages of changing the type of mental contents she experienced. Instead of genitally tinged wishes and fears, she fantasied a kind of oceanic nurturing. The distinction between reality and fantasy was blurred, making reality less disappointing and fantasy more enjoyable. Disparate attitudes could be dissociated with ease.

To recapitulate, there are a series of cognitive options available when the person with a hysterical personality wishes to repress and avoid meanings:

1. Inhibit representation of the ideas and feelings.
2. If option one fails, then inhibit translation of those ideas into other systems of representation (for example, do not let image meanings translate into word meanings).
3. Avoid associational connections (that is, use steps 1 and 2 to avoid ideas and feelings that would be automatically elicited by information that *has* already gained representation).
4. Conclude a train of thought by early closure or by declaration of the impossibility of any solution.
5. Change self attitude from active to passive, or vice versa, depending on the direction of greater threat.
6. If the above measures are inadequate, then alter state of consciousness so as to reduce reflective self-awareness.

Each of these cognitive maneuvers could be recognized as experience. Miss Smith was, of course, unaware that these were her cognitive habits when she began analysis. But each operation could be explicitly interpreted in the context of some specific mental content and emotional response. With direction of attention to the flow of cognitive experience, she could become aware of what she was doing and try to do otherwise. A train of thought prematurely closed off could be resumed and further associations elaborated.

A complete working through of a unit of warded-off ideas and feelings would consist of several components. Usually, interpretation of each component is not necessary. The therapist simply says a few words to move the patient along. These short phrases can point to transference meanings, developmental linkages, relations to current events, cognitive avoidances, or to warded-off ideas and feelings.

To illustrate the interpretation of cognitive maneuvers with Miss Smith, a full interpretive statement will be presented. The moment illustrated is derived from working through episodes within an erotic transference neurosis. She had developed feelings of sexual excitement during the hour but was warding off recognition of such feelings. She was aware enough to communicate bodily sensations but meanings of these self-perceptions went into and out of awareness. The interpretations were aimed at increased conscious

TABLE 4

INTERPRETIVE PHRASES AND THEIR FUNCTIONS

PHRASE	FUNCTION
You say "I don't know"	Specifies the current content and cognitive maneuver
So you won't go on thinking	Says what is accomplished by the cognitive maneuver
You are feeling excited now	Labels clearly the warded-off content
In your body	Calls attention to the mode of representation of the warded-off content
You are afraid to know that in words	Identifies the cognitive maneuver of nontranslation; this also gives a suggestion that she should translate ideas into words and provides a model for doing so
Because you think it is bad and dangerous	Calls attention to and labels clearly her motives for the warding-off maneuvers; this is also a suggestion that she check to see if she does feel anxious or guilty
You felt the same way toward your father	Links the current constellation to associated developmental memories
You felt that was bad and dangerous	Explains the original threat when warding-off maneuvers were desirable
The same thing happens with your male friends	Links the immediate transference pattern to her current life experience
Even though you do not consciously want to think of sexual excitement with them as bad and dangerous	Points out the inappropriate qualities of her old attitudes and the incongruity with current values

status and acceptance of these and related meanings. A global interpretation is presented schematically in table 4. In one column are phrases always spoken in isolation but grouped here in a series as if given as one long interpretation about a warded-off erotic transference response. In the second column is the function served by the phrase. The two cognitive interpretations were that she said, "I don't know" to prevent further representation of hazardous ideas and that enactive representations of erotic excitement were not translated into words.

When Miss Smith responded to such interpretive lines with introspective effort, she reexamined her immediate experience. Was she feeling excited or afraid? If she found such information—perhaps at the periphery of conscious representation—as images or bodily enactments, she tried to translate them into words, to allow associations, to stay with the topic. If she were alone, she would not behave this way. With the analyst she now felt safe enough and also pressured enough to counteract her automatic avoidances. The pressure came from the therapeutic alliance, since she rightly believed that she and the therapist shared a value placed on full representation and communication (Greenson 1965) and from the transference relationship. She expected the therapist to be pleased and attentive if she cooperated with his wishes.

Whatever the weight of multiple motives, her conscious efforts to represent, to know, and to speak the previously unthinkable had a gradual effect. The warded-off complexes of ideas and feelings were found to be tolerable to her adult mind although they had been appraised as intolerable by her childhood mind. Avoidance was less necessary. She worked through warded-off complexes and also learned a new way of thinking by repeated trials of representation, and by cross-translation of image, enactive, and lexical representation.

Only partial changes in cognitive style occurred at any one time. Every major theme surfaced again and again, each time with additional nuances and greater clarity. During episodes of positive transference she could accept her erotic yearnings with complete understanding, as she could her anxieties and guilt feelings, her inclinations not to know, and the relevant associational networks.

TABLE 5
PATTERNS AND CHANGE IN ASSOCIATIONAL CONNECTIONS AND APPRAISAL OF INPUT

Style

1. Short circuit to active fantasy schematas, including misinterpretations of events
2. Inhibitions of associations when she experiences negative affect (which is easily aroused)
3. Tendency to deny or repress ideas of self as instigator of thought, feelings, action
4. Inhibition of threatening memories, but with concomitant tendency to intrusive representation
5. Changes meaning of events by shifting schemata of self and object between active and passive roles or by losing reflective self-awareness in altered state of consciousness
6. Easily consciously afraid of being overwhelmed or of losing control
7. Poor organization of cause-and-effect sequences

Change During Treatment

Learned to suppress and recall selectively, learned to tolerate uncertainty and continue problem solving over time, learned to allow increased network of associations, less avoidance with less intrusion of warded-off contents, more realistic appraisals of own and other's roles with ability to model and check cause-and-effect sequences and events.

With each repetition there was less resistance, less interpretation necessary, and greater definition of herself as active.

The above statements applied to periods of working through in which Miss Smith responded to an interpretation with introspective efforts. There were many times when she experienced an interpretive activity of the analyst, even simple repetitions of her own phrases, as if the analyst were teasing or exciting her. She was being forced to attend to the weird ideas of the analyst, just as her father forced his nudity upon her. Such transference projections clouded the clarity of the immediate topic but added the immediate emotionality so essential to therapeutic change.

Clarity about transference experiences was then necessary. The modifications of self- and object-schemata through transference and transference interpretation will be discussed more thoroughly in the following section, but the point to made here is that no cognitive change could occur without work on the transference. The reduction in repressive maneuvers required a combination of interpretations, trial-and-error learning, imitative learning, working through of warded-off ideas and feelings, and alteration of patterns of self- and object-relationships.

As inhibitory operations were less automatic and peremptory, Miss Smith found she could maintain conceptual time and space on a given topic. She developed increased confidence in her ability to confront conflicting topics without "runaway" emotions or thoughts. Once she was able to control her thinking about a given topic she could let herself explore it more. As Weiss (1967) has pointed out, the conscious-control ability of deliberate suppression made the unconscious defensive use of repression less necessary. As ideational-emotional complexes were worked through, conflict was reduced, and there was far less tension between emergent ideas and inhibitory operations. Correspondingly, intrusive episodes occurred less frequently, her feeling of being in control was affirmed by experience, and her self-confidence allowed her to take increased risks in behavior. These various patterns and changes in the patterns of associational connections and appraisals of input are summarized in table 5.

Resolving Incongruities

Association and appraisal do not constitute all of cognitive processing. A newly represented set of information, whether from an external event or from emergent dreams, fantasies, or memories, may not fit with existing schemata about the self, objects, or the world. Information processing would be complete only when the discrepancy between the new concepts and the enduring attitudes were reduced. Either the new concept must be revised or the enduring attitudes changed. Miss Smith had a conspicuous tendency to appraise new information so that it would fit her enduring schemata when, realistically, her schemata were inappropriate and should have been modified. Failure to change these enduring schemata led to a shallow repertoire of human knowledge, as described by Shapiro (1965).

She behaved inappropriately and these actions sometimes led to startling confrontations. Suddenly, people no longer fit her mental model of them. And if *they* were not as she believed, then *she* was not as she believed. She felt either betrayed or depersonalized. Such depersonalization experiences were sufficient triggers for anxiety attacks or shifts to alternate self-schemata. For example, if she were behaving with a man in the role of glamorous swinger and the man laughed at some trifling lack of poise, she might suddenly and globally change into a clumsy, depressed, waif-like person. This change included her inner self-experience, her actual posture, facial expression, and movement pattern and her style of thinking and speaking. Alternately, she might be unable to control a display of emotions such as panic, weeping, or vindictive and accusatory rage. These inappropriate reactions interfered with relationships and further demolished her sense of confidence.

During analysis she learned to review the fit between her inner object expectations and her perceptual analysis of current persons. Once she could think more clearly she could repeat the ideational route that led her to form an internal mode of a dyadic relationship between herself and another. These cognitive processes made it possible to revise her opinions of who she was, who the other was, and the intent of each. From her earlier limited repertoire of possible dyadic relationships she learned to model and try new ones. From a global assessment of another as fulfilling a shallow and projected role, she was able to move toward an understanding of individuals with particular traits. These repetitive learning experiences fleshed out her internal models and increased her range of possible interactions.

Another aspect of the therapeutic process should be mentioned here, although it is not part of the central focus. As Miss Smith was able to modify her degree of defensiveness and her self- and object-schemata, she was able to obtain new gratifications. Each gratification acted as a reinforcement and also provided a new learning opportunity. For example, she could enjoy new aspects of personal mastery such as public speaking with less fear of being challenged for exhibitionism or of deflation by recognition of failure.

All anticipated gratifications were not real possibilities, of course, as when she tried a new behavior because she anticipated transference gratifications. For example, she might give up some avoidances and communicate more clearly in the hope that this would please the analyst and reenact an idyllic fantasy. To some extent this hope was dashed, but it was also partially fulfilled. While the analyst did not enter into an exhilarated and excited state with her, as she fantasied, he did share with her the intimacy of working

TABLE 6

PATTERNS AND CHANGE IN RESOLVING INCONGRUITIES
BETWEEN NEW INFORMATION AND SCHEMATA

Style

1. Short circuits to apparent solutions
2. Modifies new information to fit repertoire of schemata; schemata thus tend to remain as unrevised stereotypes without depth of meanings or reality fidelity; this leads to stereotyped action plans often maladaptive to real external situation
3. Low level of checking ideational routes for reality appropriateness
4. In state of incongruity, self-schemata becomes unstable with loss of reflective self-awareness or change to another type of self-schemata

Change During Treatment

Learned to recheck ideational route and inner models for reality appropriateness; developed capacity to perceive and understand self and others and developed expanded models of dyadic relationships; current (mature) self- and object-schemata became more dominant than primitive self-and object-schemata.

together in the unique situation of a therapeutic alliance. While she could not reenact a fantasy union with her father-as-mother or father-as-lover, she could find positive uses for an improved ability to tell and understand her own story.

The same comments apply to how she listened to the analyst's efforts to counteract her vagueness of clarification and interpretation. The consistency of intervention style built a model of the real therapist in the patient's mind. This model evoked analagous or mimicked behavior and eventual partial identification with a style of clarity. But the patient also invested transference meanings in the analyst's interventions. As do many hysterical personalities (Myerson, 1969), and specifically as did a patient described by Rubinfine (1967), Miss Smith also admired the analyst's statements of fact or probability as personal and phallic exhibitions and reacted as if they were sexual overtures. This was, again, a way of continuing fantasy object relationships and of avoiding serious confrontation with the meaning conveyed by the analyst. Yet the transference enjoyment also allowed her to hear and gradually respond to these meanings. Thus each new gain provided some impulse gratification, could be used defensively, and also was used adaptively. To recapitulate, the patterns and changes in solving incongruities between new information and schemata are summarized in table 6.

Cognitive Process and Cognitive Structure

Cognitive change allows the transference situation, past memories, and current patterns of interpersonal relationship to be examined and reappraised using the tools of conscious thought. As Weiss (1967, 1971) has pointed out, the manifestations of transference may not occur until the analytic situation and the therapist have safely passed unconsciously motivated behavioral tests. For simplicity, I will call these transference tests. For example, if when Miss Smith exposed her neediness the analyst was too kind or yielded to her demands for extra care, then the pregenitally based hostility within the maternal transference might never have been fully analyzed (Wallerstein in press).

This sequence, from warding off transference based on primitive schemata to revision of schemata in the direction of maturity, can be diagramed as in figure 1. In essence, the stages are (1) warding off,

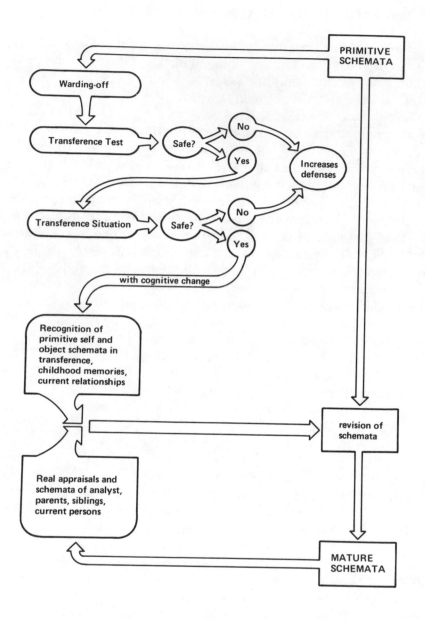

FIGURE 1

(2) transference tests (for example, asking for special times for appointments), (3) transference emergence, and then—granted changes in cognitive style—(4) recognition of what it *feels* like is happening as appriased in relation to what is *really* happening. This latter step leads to revision of primitive schemata of the self and others and relates to Loewald's (1960) view that transference interpretations that work have two elements: they take the patient to his true regressive level and they also indicate to the patient the higher integrative level to be reached.

Cognitive Structure: Self- and Object-Schemata

The original patterns of behavior and their revisions through changes of self- and object-schemata remain to be considered. Miss Smith, like all persons, operated in the world by a repertoire of self- and object characteristics. These characteristics were organized into roles, often role dyads, and imposed by her on her interpersonal relationships (Jacobson 1964, Kernberg 1966, Schafer 1968). At the onset of analysis there were a limited number of roles that could be fulfilled by her or by others. These roles can be abstracted and then discussed in terms of change during the analytic process.

Her basic models of self and object were derived from her childhood version of her family. A crude summary of the main attributes of her mental model of her family is shown in figure 2. Each central person is given a label according to the role the patient mainly attributed to him or to her. These roles were, to a large extent, agreed upon covertly within the family so that her inner model was congruent to the family communication and interaction pattern. Her father was a special exception, her mother the care-taker, her older sister the free spirit, her younger sister the defective person in a sick role, and she, the spiritually good member.

In figure 2 the main attachments are also indicated as the bonds between her older sister and her father, between her father and her mother, and between her mother and the younger sister. Her attitudes toward these bonds and toward the persons involved are also conceptualized in the arrows radiating from herself. The basic self-attribute is isolation from attachments, with envy and yearning to establish herself in a dyad. This does not mean she does not have

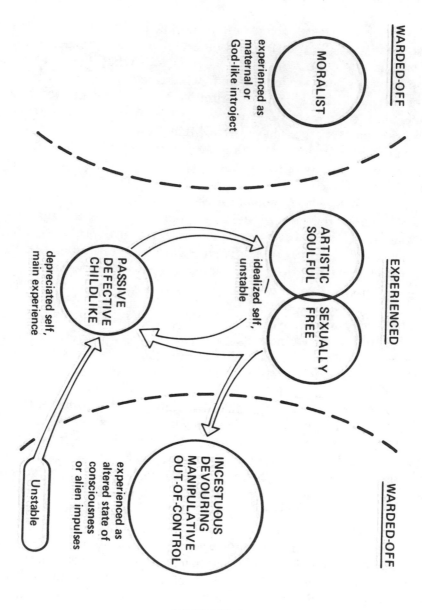

FIGURE 2

attachments with each member of the family but that these attachments, while pleasurable and exciting in part, are not entirely fulfilling. She feels rejected or conflicted in relation to every one of them, and this pattern, as suggested by Fairbairn (1954), leads her to split aspects of reaction to each family member. That is why, in figure 2, antitheses are indicated, as between contempt (withdrawal) and envy with identification (approach). Emotions such as anxiety and guilt are omitted because they are reactions to the attitudes shown, for example, anxiety over sexual interest toward her father.

Each member of the family provided a source of identification for her, both in terms of what there was in them that she could imitate and what there was in her to which they chose to react. The role structure of the family can be examined in a way that is one step more complex than the basic model of figure 2. That is, the main constructs for roles can be listed, each member of the family can be described as a personification based on these constructs, and the self roles of Miss Smith based on identification with the family member can be coordinated with these attributes (see Kelly 1955, Loevinger 1973). It is much easier to see this than to describe it in linear text, and such a chart is found in table 7.

The main constructs are goodness-badness; activity-passivity; and masculinity-femininity. The main personifications are listed as splits between good and bad versions of each family member. Her self roles are limited, then, by these personifications of others and by the matrix of family interactions that tended to view her in one or another of these roles.

Miss Smith's parents and sisters were models for her self development as well as mirrors that reflected the development of her concept of self. The defectiveness of her parents as models and mirrors interfered with her maturation, and the analytic process allowed both a resumption of construct development and an opportunity to resolve conflicts between constructs. The problem for analysis was to identify primitive roles in action and raise this to consciousness. This accentuation of awareness included recognition of precursors of more differentiated roles. By trial action within the analysis, the goal was to help her evolve her inner self and object models into forms more congruous with the real potentials for interpersonal relationships in her adult life, independent of her family (Loewald 1960).

This analytic task was complicated by her ability and tendency to take either role in a two-person dyad. As emphasized earlier, she could interchange active and passive roles in her inner experience of any given situation. She could be the moralist condemning a sexually active "swinger," or the swinger living more pleasurably than the moralist and more fully than the defective child-woman. This fluid ability to change the set for self in a given role dyad is based on childhood development. Baldwin (as reviewed by Loevinger 1973) called this the dialectic of personal growth: the child learns to perceive the traits of parents, he then can find such patterns in the self, which then permits more differentiated perception of the parents, and so on in a reciprocal process. As a result, almost everything found in the self is something found in significant others, as shown in table 7.

Cognitive processing, as described in the previous section, allowed active schemata to be reviewed. The transferences allowed here-and-now reenactments of what Knapp (1974) has called "interpersonal fantasy constellations." These could be compared with the realities of the therapeutic process and relationship. Any particular schema was labeled, known by many facets, connected with current extraanalytic relationships and with recollections of childhood.

Such reviews meant a new intergration of segregated constructs. By the end of the analysis Miss Smith could view her parents as real people with good and bad traits rather than as split-apart good and bad introjects. Clarity in perception of these patterns engendered revision of her memory of the past and of her future expectations. She gave up the hope of finding her parents transformed into ideals, developed a sympathetic understanding of their failures, and relinquished the belief that they were deliberately causing her suffering. This increased clarity about schemata derived from relationships with her family allowed her to control her development of schemata of new people. Aware of her tendencies to externalize and project, she could check supposed similarities to see if they were borne out by real behavior. With new ways to act, her relationships became increasingly fresh and real.

TABLE 7

ROLE STRUCTURE

MAIN CONSTRUCTS			PERSONIFICATIONS				SELF ROLES
GOODNESS	ACTIVITY	GENDER	MOTHER	FATHER	OLDER SISTER	YOUNGER SISTER	
good	active	female	competent childbearing caring moralistic		sensuous free child-bearing	deserving attention	sexually active swinger —vs— moralistic
good	passive	female	—vs—		—vs—	—vs—	sick and deserving child
bad	active	female	manipulator devouring		promiscuous sinful		incestuous devouring rivalrous
bad	passive	female	—vs— depressed depleted			defective	defective child-woman
good	active	male		skillful			grandiose fantasies of being skillful, effective
good	passive	male		esthetic soulful —vs— sexually intrusive out of control			esthetic, soulful artist
bad	active	male					out of control person
bad	passive	male		failure			incompetent, failure

Modifications of Self-Schemata

The various constructs of table 7 clustered into four main forms of self-experience. Two were warded off; two were commonly experienced in an oscillatory manner. The most frequent self-experience was as if she were passive, defective, and childlike. The second most frequent self-experience was of her ideal self. The components of this ideal were not fully integrated and consisted of the role of the sexual free spirit and that of the artistic and soulful person. Unfortunately, these ideal self-experiences were unstable. They changed readily into the passive, childlike, defective self or in the direction of bad activity, becoming the warded-off self with incestuous, devouring, manipulative, and out-of-control attributes. (See figure 3)

The fourth self-experience was as a moralist. In the moral schema, accusations were directed against past or anticipated acts of the self or others. This state was also warded off, and might also intrude as unbidden images or fantasies. The intrusive episodes were conscious experiences of felt presences in the form of maternal or Godlike introjects. These four types of self-experience are sufficient to pattern her self-schemata at the onset of analysis, as diagramed in figure 3. It remains to describe how they changed.

As with object schemata, changes in self-schemata relied upon concurrent change in thought. Reduced inhibitory controls allowed conscious comparisons between the current real facts and her enduring schemata. Discrepancies between schemata and real behaviors were recognized. Instead of revising the here-and-now information to fit her stereotypes, she was able in the analysis to change the schemata.

Changes in the Sexually Free Self-Schemata

Before analysis, the main manifestation of the sexually free schemata was her role of swinger. Frequent sexual liaisons revolved on a victim and aggressor dyad. She was one or the other, her partner occupied the complementary role. In the swinger role, unable to conceptualize two active persons, she invariably gave one a passive script. The aggressor takes from or seduces the victim. The victim gives up or submits. Sometimes the roles are reversed, with sadomasochistic flavorings.

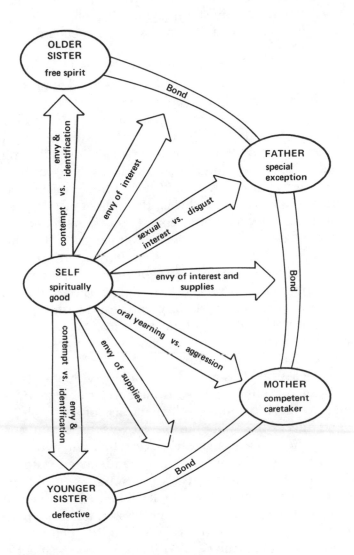

FIGURE 3

The swinger role was an adaptational attempt to defy self-images as the victim of her mother's insufficient attentiveness and her father's seductions. While she imagined herself as if she were the aggressor, luring and breaking the hearts of men and arousing the envious fury of women, she also submitted to sexual usage and was ultimately discarded. Only with older or "grayer" men, or during the vain attempts of virile men to lead her to sexual climax, could she feel as if she had actively defeated them.

The possibilities of both persons being active, as is desirable in sexual acts, or both persons being passive, as in quiet mutuality, were too anxiety provoking. If both persons were active, this meant they would excite each other too much, reviving a prototypical oedipal danger of the patient and her father arousing each other simultaneously. It was only during the course of analysis that she learned a dyad in which both persons were simultaneously active. For example, later in the analysis, she felt correctly that she and the analyst were working intensively together, attempting to understand the multiple meanings of an episode of experience. At such times she would have a "reality" experience; she would be amazed at the active cooperation, feel dizzy, and fear that she would wet the couch from a sudden loss of sphincter control. She was so sure of the risk involved, that on occasion she checked the back of her skirt for stains before leaving the office.

Before she learned this new dyad which involved activity on the part of both persons, she had to interpret the analytic situation according to more primitive schemata, as for example a dyad of victim and aggressor. Either the analyst was forcing interpretations upon her or she was the aggressor, overwhelming and draining the drab, tired analyst. The instability of the idealized state of being a sexually free person led to episodes of humiliation. When she saw another attractive female patient leave or enter the office, she fantasied that this was the exciting mistress of a famous politician or the analyst's wife, and she felt rejected and defective.

As cognitive inhibitions were reduced, every aspect of these changes in experience could be worked out. The basic schemata were recurrently confronted. As already described, she used fantasy and projective indentification to form new models. She softened the stereotype of swinger into a womanly, tender, sensuous set of traits. She daydreamed and dreamed of mutually active role relationships in an idealized projection of the analyst and his wife. After these fantasy trials proved safe, she gradually experimented in reality. The inevitable disappointments did not deter her because she could now tolerate and work them through consciously. Instead of globally imitating her ideal role models, she was able to discretely act out some idealized traits. She was no longer an actress faking a part and ready for the humiliating experience of being unmasked.

In figure 3, the ideal self also contains aesthetic and soulful qualities. These traits were not fully integrated with the concept of sexual freedom and sensuality. Because sexuality was dangerous it was isolated from other ideals. Even the aesthetic and soulful ideals, however, were unstable. She was unable to work either on artistic or career-oriented tasks, and so her self-image could not be compared with these ideals without deflation. Since she could not bolster her self-esteem with memory or anticipation of real accomplishments, she could only daydream. Even that seemed, at times, so hopeless as to lead to depression and a shift to a self-as-defective position.

In the course of the analysis, ideals were confronted. She could decide again, as an adult now, which ideal she preferred. She could equilibrate goals to realistic appraisals of possibilities, thus changing adolescent grandiose fantasies into achievable expectations. She was able to dissociate artistic enterprises from her father's behavior. For example, she reviewed memories in which her father had given her a set of oil paints, a bottle of turpentine, and some canvas boards and expected her to teach herself to paint landscapes and portraits. She tried and performed only at a mediocre and frustrating level. Since she shared her father's ideas that she ought to learn by osmosis or spontaneous talent, she had explained this failure as her own incompetence. Clear review of these ideals allowed her to reevaluate the memories. As an adult, she knew that training and practice were necessary to any skill. She then planned to take courses in technique. In executing this plan she developed an interest in color mixing and perspective, and found the step-by-step learning to be exhilarating.

These real and gratifying accomplishments provided the

necessary memories for a stable idealized self-image, and she was able to separate ideas of her own artistic interests and qualities from those ideas about her father and those ideas her father had about her. Then she was able to praise or to criticize her own work and to do so from a semirealistic basis. She could admit failure in a given effort without feeling worthless.

Changes in the Moralistic Self-Schemata

At the onset of analysis, Miss Smith was unaware that she felt guilty about her activity in general and her sexuality in particular. Her conscious thoughts dwelt on the desirability of sexual freedom. As she became aware of feeling badly about active sexual wishes, she was depressed to discover her own feelings of guilt. It seemed primitive to her, and like a submission to the weird analytic ideas she expected to have forced upon her. But the ideas became clear and tolerable.

As memories and fantasies of the past were reexamined and linked to the present, she learned to dissociate sexual and agressive aims from intrafamilial, and hence taboo, objects. Her rational thought countered the laws proclaimed in her childhood and the conditioned associations that overgeneralized them. She became the instigator of rules of behavior.

At first this process seemed artificial and also time consuming. Faced with a given decision, she had to think through many ramifications in order to deviate from her automatically imposed inhibitions and disavowals of inhibitions. But with repetition of decisions she developed new guiding principles which illuminated new ways to arrive at automatic decisions, which were then seen as self-determined feelings rather than punitive restrictions from external sources.

With these changes, there was less discrepancy between sexual self-images and the once warded off and now modified moralistic self. Attributes from both schemata could be represented consciously without guilt or anxiety. This increased the stability of the ideal self-schema and also made it unnecessary to ward off the residual aspects of the moralistic self-schema. There was thus a gradual coalescence of these two schemata and of the two others still to be discussed.

Changes in the Schemata of Self as Passive, Defective, Child

As mentioned earlier, Miss Smith typlified role relationships as a dyad between an active and a passive person. In the main version she was in the passive, waif-like role and an active person was the rescuer. In a good outcome, because of her suffering, she would be found by an idealized parental figure, given the necessary ingredients (such as gradual sexual instruction), and then become a whole person. The bad outcome was to be subjected to abuse by a malicious or sadistic person and to obtain thereby some small attention; she would accumulate pain (that by destiny would later be traded in for gratification), and relieve the guilt accumulated from various oedipal fantasies. Since this dyad was not allowed clear conscious representation, it only organized her processing of the information of her everyday life. The dyad was not revised according to realistic appraisals. She remained a passive victim or waif to be duped or rescued by active others.

Why could not two persons be thought of as being together but simultaneously passive in their relationship? She could not conceive of persons at rest with one another because her needs were experienced as too intense and peremptory. She also felt defective and unworthy of attention. She was incapable of relating and incompetent at work. To feel like that and be with another person who was not actively engaging her meant only that she had to feel alone, unworthy, empty, and neglected.

The treatment situation was ready made to fit into her rescue fantasy, as exemplified by the dream of being taken to the home-sanitorium of the analyst. As she began to reveal herself and to feel that she was understood, the fantasy of waif and rescuer took over and organized her expectations about what would happen next. The analyst would recognize her needs and fill the void in a moment of lyrical union. To repeat a central point: she expected things that did not happen, and in the vacuum of frustration her wishes emerged as conscious desires. Because of the cognitive shifts, she could appraise them as deviant from the therapeutic contract but could also understand their import as recurring patterns.

Provided that the opportunity for conceptual clarity was also present, the transference situation allowed repeated confrontation with such everyday frustrations. Every weekend and vacation there was a separation. Unexpected separations occurred with illnesses. She could, for example, see how much she wanted the analyst to take her home, how frequently she accepted intercourse with others out of a desire only to be held and cared for, how frustrated she felt when recalling childhood memories. These real experiences evoked sadness, but the sadness was related to specific instances rather than a global self-assessment. It was tolerable to feel sad when lonely on a given night, if she did not have to go from there to endless feelings of hopelessness and despair.

As she gave up the fantasy of rescue, it was necessary to fulfill the expected functions herself. Again, cognitive processing allowed both exploration of hitherto warded-off associational connections and consideration of new and possible solutions to her motivational dilemmas. Dreams often preceded the explorations of themes in the analytic hours, and may have been dreamed for the purpose of furthering the analytic process as well as for an imaginative trial of new self-images. For example, she had the intense desire to be taken to restaurants by men, and she expected this to take place after intercourse, as if, in effect, she had paid in advance. As the role schemata shifted in analysis, she began to dream of going to restaurants alone. At first the dreams ended in anxiety. After the dreams seemed satisfactory, she attempted to act them out in real life. She had always been phobic of eating out alone. Her first step was to take food home from a hamburger stand, then to eat lunch at a busy counter-service diner, finally to eat dinner in a good restaurant. She felt uncomfortable but successful after this series. Once she felt capable of being active on her own, she then felt entitled to be more assertive of her desires when dating men.

Part of this reality appraisal was also helpful in allowing her to recognize the improbability of realizing her rescue fantasy. At best, only children are rescued and cared for as children. In her relationships with older men she could be babied, but at an expense she no longer cared to pay. If being a sick child did not lead to rescue, secondary gains were no longer present. The revision of the schemata toward more adult appraisals of herself was thus encouraged by the reduction in expectation of reward.

As the swinger schema lost its utility and necessity as a disavowal of her sense of feminine inadequacy, it was possible to consciously explore her defective body image. She was surprised to realize, when she allowed herself to imagine her own genitals, that she could not visualize herself as having a vagina and other female organs. In a way, not having a speakable word like "vagina" helped preserve her childlike status. During intercourse she did not "know" her vagina. Temporarily, as she first became more distinctly aware, the experience changed. She was then afraid she would extend her body too far and become both male and female. She wanted to control and take away the penis, or even wrestle with and control all of the male body. These explorations in reality and fantasy led to an evolving sense of body image and bodily competence. She was also able to acknowledge and allow self-attributes that were masculine (as in the Jungian sense of the animus). The ideas also involved other supposedly "masculine" attributes. She became strongly contemptuous of men who did not shift the gears of cars with verve. She bought her own sports car and enjoyed her mastery of the stick shift. She imagined herself out-gunning the analyst in car races.

The projective identification with the analyst's wife also allowed her to elaborate and try out possible self-images in fantasy. She watched "Titsy" (her dream name for the fantasy wife) be sexy, maternal, and humane all at the same time and then tried to act that way herself. Again, the trials of conscious fantasy and acting according to new ideals seemed artificial at first, but with practice and confidence seemed natural.

As her experience range widened, she could become aware of attitudes related to her defective body image. She feared injury by an uncontrolled penis because of her erroneous belief in a tiny or nonexistent vagina. Her pronounced scopophilia was seen not only as a libidinal impulse and as a defensive reversal of exhibitionism but also as an intense desire to gain information about what bodies were like. Recognition of her own interest led to examination and reduction of moralistic prohibitions and exploration of her body with mirrors and her fingers. She read books on sex and experimented in erotic stimulation. Each new experience led to anxiety, but in tolerable dosages. She realized her fear of "letting go" or becoming wildly aggressive. The fear could be matched with reality. It didn't happen, and the fearful expectation was revised. As her body image evolved, she felt sexually competent. She could let her alert anxiety during intercourse wane and accumulate plateaus of erotic arousal.

The Incestuous, Devouring, Out-of-Control Self

This final set of self-attributes was warded off and experienced as intrusive, as was the moralistic self which opposed it. At the onset of analysis, Miss Smith was not aware of a self-experience as an incestuous, devouring, and dangerously out of control child. Yet the potential of such states exerted dynamic effects. Rigid controls over self-experience were fostered to avoid this state. It was, for example, better in a defensive sense to be the defective child at such times as the swinger image was not idealized but rather was associated with familial, oedipal meanings.

The rigid inhibitions gave way, and recurrent father and mother transference episodes emerged. She experienced sexual wishes toward the analyst and also devouring aims, as if the ideational and affective emergence would be tantamount to action. The rule in the analytic situation of verbalizing rather than touching and the consistent neutrality of the analyst in terms of the desires he might bring into the situation made for a safer experience of such thoughts and feelings than had been possible previously. Even her feelings of rivalry toward her sisters were given a foil in the analytic situation as she envied other patients she imagined to be more interesting or more needy than herself and as she evolved various feelings for her image of the analyst's presumed wife.

As the incestuous, devouring, rivalrous feelings emerged in dyads of self and object, it was possible for her to realize that she originated these feelings—that they were not imposed on her. As with the other roles, this out-of-control self feeling could be compared with actual experiences. She did not break the analytic rule against physical confrontations, did not injure the analyst or blow up his car, did not tear into the walls or stain the couch. She only fantasied that she or other patients might do this. The conceptual distance between fantasy and reality grew. Fantasy became self-generated and controlled. Thus the conscious experience in the present was quite different from conscious experiences in childhood.

As she learned to experience strivings for erotic and tender attentions, she was able to further contemplate plans for obtaining gratifications. Just as the reduction in anxiety and guilt responses reduced the threat, anticipation of realistic possibilities made the experience of need less painful. She came to view the analyst as a trial object. She could experiment with various ways to contemplate herself and him. Then she could have a set of ideas, plans, and responses already partially worked out when she tried to allow herself such an open range of experience with other persons, persons who would respond to her according to their own wishes.

This course of trial self-feelings reduced the incestuous quality of her erotic interests. As the connections were made through associative extensions, she was able to change the object of her erotic self-feelings. The analyst provided a safe early displacement. Then she could allow herself to experience excitement while with her male friends. She could learn to assert her sexuality without guilt or anxiety because she was able to perceive that the relationship was mutually satisfactory, that the associations to taboo or destructive components were inappropriate and could be deemphasized.

Summary of Roles

By combining the main features of her relatives in the nuclear family, a series of eight roles were seen as designators for both self- and object schemata. The basic elements in these roles were active and passive, good and bad, male and female. She had some difficulty with each role. To avoid excessive complexity, I described these roles in terms of four major and global self- experiences that were of importance at the onset of analysis. The result of changes in roles was an integrated self-experience, one which remained relatively consistent whether she was with someone active or passive or was herself active or passive in a given relationship.

Earlier, table 7 showed the main self-schemata at the onset of analysis. Change and status after the analysis can now be recorded for each of those schema. The result is table 8.

Conclusions

This chapter has described hysterical personality in terms of the interaction between a thought style centered on a lack of awareness and core schemata of self and others based upon experiencing the self as defective, childlike, and in need of rescue. These cognitive styles and structures lead to behavioral traits such as the tendency to

TABLE 8

SELF-SCHEMATA	STATUS BEFORE ANALYSIS	CHANGE	STATUS AFTER ANALYSIS
Sexually active woman	"Swinger" role used to disavow inhibition and incestuous configuration	Saw defensive function and discrepancy between reality and fantasy	Felt authentically sexual, extremes of inhibition and promiscuity reduced
Moralist	Maternal and Godlike introjects condemn her sexual and aggressive impulses; her self-attitudes are harsh but disavowed	Disavowal reduced; moralistic attitudes more clearly experienced, revised, and more realistic as patient learned to dissociate sex and aggression from familial objects	Experienced principles as self-originated and worthy of adherence
Passive, sick and deserving child	Emphasized in self-images	Lessened expectancy of rescue fantasy being realized	Less prominent
Active, incestuous, manipulative rival	Felt vaguely evil and dangerous	Unconscious sexual and aggressive motives made conscious with reduction in viewing new persons as parent figures	Felt sexual and self assertive strivings were all right
Defective child-woman	Felt as if incapable of intercourse, nurturative roles, and child-bearing; low self-esteem	Evolved body image by learning reality of bodily structures	Felt grown-up and womanly

use bodily communication of ideas and feelings rather than words or expressed images. It is these behavioral traits that have brought this typology to the attention of the helping professions throughout recorded history.

Each aspect of the hysterical personality can be amenable to change in the course of psychotherapy. The complex interaction of process styles and structural characteristics means that extended therapies are likely to be necessary. The work ahead is to review and describe the processes of change in such persons in sufficient detail so that with enough clarification of these processes it can be possible to insure a higher rate of good treatment outcome and to shorten treatment time by finding optimum intervention strategies.

Implications for a Brief Therapy

The focus here has been on change processes in the extended time available in psychoanalytic treatment. What are the implications for treatment programs that must of necessity be compressed into less time and expense? While modifications of cognitive style involve extended and repetitive episodes of learning and unlearning automatic patterns of information processing, some of the same principles apply to therapies aimed at working through a focal conflict or life problem. A therapist who is alert to the variety of avoidances and the particular interpersonal schemata that characterize the given person will be able to steer the processing of ideas and feeling toward a given goal of decision and action. For the hysterical personality, repetition and clarity will be especially helpful as will a relationship that avoids the pitfalls of excessive coldness or excessive rescue. These aspects of treatment have already been described by Allen in chapter 5, are contrasted with treatment of obsessional and narcissistic personalities elsewhere (Horowitz 1976), and are summarized for short-term treatment in table 9.

An area that needs further scientific investigation is the use of newly developed or rediscovered therapy techniques in the brief therapy of persons with hysterical personality. Would it be possible to isolate the person's form from content areas of specific emotional conflict? Could such persons benefit from training courses in awareness, clarity of thought and expression, in recognition of body

TABLE 9

SUMMARY OF TREATMENT INTERVENTIONS
FOR SHORT-TERM THERAPY AIMS IN
PERSONS WITH HYSTERICAL PERSONALITY*

Function	Style as "Defect"	Therapeutic Counteraction
Perception	Global or selective inattention	Ask for details
Representation	Impressionistic rather than accurate	"Abreaction"of details and construction of sequences Repetition
Translation of images and enactions to words	Limited	Encourage talk Provide verbal labels Designate meanings
Associations	Limited by inhibitions Misinterpretations based on stereotypes, deflected from reality to wishes and fears	Encourage production Clarification Differentiate reality from fantasy
Problem Solving	Short circuit to rapid but often erroneous conclusion Avoidance of topic when emotions are unbearable	Keep subject open Interpretations of meaning and cause-and-effect relationship Support through safety and coherence of therapeutic alliance

* From Horowitz (1976).

language? Is it possible that some of the evolutionary changes in self-image as described for sequences of dreams and fantasies in Miss Smith could be fostered more speedily by guided-imagery techniques? Could some of her progressive trial activities, such as the series of eating-out occasions, have occurred more speedily in the context of behavior therapy, role playing, or psychodrama?

Some psychoanalysts would answer these questions negatively on the grounds that every act is overdetermined, that the conflicts are too deep-seated and unconscious, that the immature development is interlocked into too many areas where one cannot change one without change in the others. Many therapists who advocate new techniques would answer positively, but they often ignore character typology in order to claim wide applicability of their methods and to promote attractively brief training for potential practitioners.

The answer will be found in empirical tests. New methods should be given a trial in the context of deep clinical understanding and objective analysis of results. This eventual psychotherapy research will, I am sure, require a careful dissection of the person's cognitive style and inner models of self and others. And our typological descriptions will have to grow more precise as will our rational prescription of potentially effective and potentially harmful interventions. For the hysterical typology, this trek has been underway throughout two thousand years of clinical practice. The slow but progressive clarifications brought by scientific objectivity indicate that the journey may usefully continue.

REFERENCES

Berne, E. (1961). *Transactional Analysis in Psychotherapy.* New York: Grove.

Easser, B. R., and Lesser, S. R. (1965). Hysterical personality: a reevaluation. *Psychoanalytic Quarterly* 34:390-405.

Fairbairn, W. R. (1954). Observations on the nature of hysterical states. *British Journal of Medical Psychology* 27:105-125.

Gardner, R., Holzman, P. S., Klein, G. S., Linton, H., and Spence, D. P. (1959). Cognitive controls: a study of individual consistencies in cognitive behavior. *Psychological Issues* 1:1-186.

Gedo, J., and Goldberg, A. (1973). *Models of the Mind.* Chicago: The University of Chicago Press.

Greenson, R. (1965). The working alliance and the transference neurosis. *Psychoanalytic Quarterly* 34:155-181.

Horowitz, M. J. (1970) *Image Formation and Cognition*. New York: Appleton-Century-Crofts.

————(1972). Modes of representation of thought. *Journal of American Psychoanalytic Association* 20:793-819.

————(1974). Microanalysis of working through in psychotherapy. *American Journal of Psychiatry* 131:1208-1212.

————(1976). *Stress Response Syndromes*. New York: Jason Aronson.

Jacobson, E. (1954). The self and the object world: vicissitudes of their infantile cathexis and their influence on ideational and affective development. *Psychoanalytic Study of the Child* 9:75-127.

————(1964). *The Self and the Object World*. New York: International Universities Press.

Kelly, G. (1955). *The Psychology of Personal Constructs*. Vol. 2. New York: Norton.

Kernberg, O. (1966). Structural derivatives of object relationships. *International Journal of Psycho-Analysis* 47:236-253.

Klein, G. S. (1967). Peremptory ideation: structure and force in motivated ideas. In *Motives and Thought: Psychoanalytic Essays in Honor of David Rapaport*, ed. R. Holt, pp. 80-128. Psychological Issues Monograph 18/19. New York: International Universities Press.

Klein, G. S., Gardner, R. W., and Schlesing, H. J. (1962). Tolerance for unrealistic experiences: a study of the generality of a cognitive control. *British Journal of Medical Psychology* 53:41-55.

Knapp, P. H. (1974). *Segmentation and Structure in Psychoanalysis*. In press.

Lazarus, R. S. (1966). *Psychological Stress and the Coping Process*. New York: McGraw-Hill.

Loevinger, J. (1973). Ego Development. *Psychoanalysis and Contemporary Science* 2:77-156.

Loewald, H. W. (1960). The therapeutic action of psychoanalysis. *International Journal of Psycho-Analysis* 41:16-26.

Marmor, J. (1953). Orality in the hysterical personality. *Journal of American Psychoanalytic Association* 1:656-675.

Miller, G. A., Galanter, E., and Pribram, K. (1960). *Plans and the Structure of Behavior*. New York: Holt, Rinehart and Winston.

Myerson, P. The hysteric's experience in psychoanalysis. *International Journal of Psycho-Analysis* 50:373-384.

Peterfreund, E., and Schwartz, J. T. (1971). *Information Systems and Psychoanalysis*: Psychological Issues, Monograph. 25/26. New York: International Universities Press.

Piaget, J. (1937) *The Construction of Reality in the Child.* New York: Basic Books, 1954.

Rapaport, D., and Gill, M. M. (1958). The points of view and assumptions of metapsychology. *International Journal of Psycho-Analysis* 40:153-162.

Rubenfine, D. (1967). Notes on a theory of reconstruction. *British Journal of Medical Psychology* 40:195-206.

Schafer, R. (1968). *Aspects of Internalization.* New York: International Universities Press.

Shapiro, D. (1965). *Neurotic Styles.* New York: Basic Books.

Tomkins, S. (1962). *Affect, Imagery, Consciousness.* New York: Springer.

Wallerstein, R. S. Case reports of the Menninger psychotherapy research project. In preparation.

Weiss, J. (1967). The integration of defenses. *International Journal of Psycho-Analysis* 48:520-524.

———(1971). The emergence of new themes: a contribution to the psychoanalytic theory of therapy. *International Journal of Psycho-Analysis* 52:459-467.

Wisdom, J. O. (1961). A methodological approach to the problem of hysteria. *International Journal of Psycho-Analysis* 42:224-237.

Zetzel, E. (1970). Therapeutic alliance in the analysis of hysteria. *Incapacity for Emotional Growth*, ed. E. Zetzel, pp. 182-196. London: Hogarth.

BIBLIOGRAPHY

Abraham, K. (1912). *Selected Papers on Psychoanalysis*. New York: Basic Books, 1960.

Abse, D.W. (1959). Hysteria. In *American Handbook of Psychiatry*, ed. S. Arieti. New York: Basic Books.

———(1966). *Hysteria and Related Mental Disorders: An Approach to Psychological Medicine*. Baltimore: Williams and Wilkins.

——— (1974). Hysteria within the context of the family. *Journal of Operational Psychiatry* 6:31-42.

——— (1974). Hysterical conversion and dissociative syndromes and the hysterical character. In *American Handbook of Psychiatry*, vol. 3, ed. S. Arieti and E. B. Brody. New York: Basic Books.

Ackerknecht, E. H. (1971). *Medicine and Ethnology: Selected Essays*, ed. H. H. Walser, and H. M. Koelbing. Baltimore: Johns Hopkins Press.

Ainsworth, M. (1973). The development of infant-mother attachment. In *Review of Child Development Research No. 3*, ed. B. Caldwell, and H. Ricciuti. Chicago: University of Chicago Press.

Allen, D. W. (1974). *The Fear of Looking: Scopophilic-Exhibitionistic Conflicts*. Charlottesville: University Press of Virginia. Virginia.

Allen, D. W., and Houston, M. (1959). The management of hysteroid acting-out patients in a training clinic. *Psychiatry* 22:41-49.

American Psychiatric Association (1952). *Diagnostic and Statistical Manual of Mental Disorders (DSM I)*. Washington, D.C.

———— (1968). *Diagnostic and Statistical Manual of Mental Disorders (DSM II)*. Washington, D. C.

Anthony, E. (1961). Learning difficulties in childhood: report of a panel. *Journal of the American Psychoanalytic Association* 9:124-134.

Arkonac, O., and Guze, S. (1963). A family study of hysteria. *New England Journal of Medicine* 268:239-242.

Aurelianus, C. (1950). *On Acute Diseases and on Chronic Diseases.* Trans. I. E. Drablin. Chicago: University of Chicago Press.

Babinski, J., and Froment, J. (1918). *Hysteria or Pithiasm and Reflex Nervous Disorders in the Neurology of War*. London: University of London Press.

Bart, P. B. (1968). Social structure and vocabularies of discomfort: what happens to female hysteria? *Journal of Health and Social Behavior* 9:188-193.

Bateson, G., Jackson, D. D., Haley, J., and Weakland, J. (1956). Toward a theory of schizophrenia. *Behavioral Science* 1:251-264.

Beall, O., and Shryock, R. (1954). *Cotton Mather: First Significant Figure in American Medicine*. Baltimore: Johns Hopkins Press.

Benedict, R. (1934). *Patterns of Culture*. Boston: Houghton Mifflin.

Berger, D. M. (1971). Hysteria: in search of the animus. *Comprehensive Psychiatry* 12:277-286.

Berne, E. (1961). *Transactional Analysis in Psychotherapy*. New York: Grove.

Bernheim, H. (1886). *Suggestive Therapeutics*. C. A. Hert. Westport, Conn.: Associated Booksellers, 1957.

Bernstein, N. R. (1969). Psychogenic seizures in adolescent girls. *Behavioral Neuropsychiatry* 1:31-34.

Beumont, P. J. V., Beardwood, C. J., and Russell, G. F. M. (1972). The occurence of the syndrome of anorexia nervosa in male subjects. *Psychological Medicine* 2:216-231.

Bibb, R. C., and Guse, S. B. (1972). hysteria (Briquet's syndrome) in a psychiatric hospital: the significance of depression. *American Journal of Psychiatry* 128:224-228.

Blinder, M. (1966). The hysterical personality. *Psychiatry* 29:227-235.

Bourguignon, E. (1968). *A Cross-Cultural Study of Dissociational States.* Columbus: Ohio State University Press.

————, ed. (1973). *Religion, Altered States of Consciousness and Social Change.* Columbus: Ohio State University Press.

Bowlby, J. (1969). *Attachment and Loss. Vol. I: Attachment.* New York: Basic Books.

Boyer, L. B. (1964). Folk psychiatry of the Apaches of the Mascalero Indian Reservation. In *Magic, Faith, Healing: Studies in Primitve Psychiatry Today,* ed. A. Kiev. New York: Free Press.

Brady, J. P. (1967). Psychotherapy, learning theory and insight. *Archives of General Psychiatry* 16:304.

Brady, J. P., and Lind, D. (1961). Experimental analysis of hysterical blindness. *Archives of General Psychiatry* 4:331-339.

Brauer, R., Harrow, M., and Tucker, G. J. (1970). Depersonalization phenomena in psychiatric patients. *British Journal of Psychiatry* 117:509-515.

Breuer, J., and Freud, S. (1893-1895). Studies on hysteria. *Standard Edition* 2.

———— (1893) On the psychical mechanisms of hysterical phenomena. *Standard Edition* 2:1-20.

Bríquet, P. (1859). *Traité clinique et thérapeutique de l'hystérie.* Paris: Ballière.

Brody, S., and Axelrad, S. (1967). *Mother-Infant Interaction No. 1: At Six Weeks.* A film.

———— (1968). *Mother-Infant Interaction No. 2: At Six Months.* film.

Bruch, H. (1965). Anorexia nervosa and its differential diagnosis. *Journal of Nervous and Mental Diseases* 141:555-556.

———— (1969). Eating disorders in adolescence. *Proceedings of the American Psychopathological Association* 59:181-196.

———— (1970). Changing approaches to anorexia nervosa. In *Anorexia and Obesity,* ed. C. V. Rowland. Boston: Little, Brown.

———— (1971). Anorexia nervosa in the male. *Psychosomatic Medicine* 33:31-47.

———— (1975). Obesity and anorexia nervosa: psychosocial aspects. *Australian and New Zealand Journal of Psychiatry* 9:159-161.

Burton-Bradley, B. G. (1974). Social change and psychosomatic response in Papua, New Guinea. *Psychotherapy and Psychosomatics* 23:229-239.

Buss, A. (1966). *Psychopathology.* New York: Wiley.

Bustamante, J. A. (1967/68). Cultural factors in hysterias with a schizophrenic clinical picture. *International Journal of Social Psychiatry* 14:113-118.

Cadoret, R. J., and King, L. J. (1974). *Psychiatry in Primary Care*. St. Louis: Mosby.

Callaway, E. (1975). Psychiatry today. *The Western Journal of Medicine* 122:349-354.

Cameron, N. (1963). *Personality Development and Psychopathology: A Dynamic Approach*. Boston: Houghton Mifflin.

Cannavale, F. J., Scarr, H. A., and Pepitone, A. (1970). Deindividuation in the small group: further evidence. *Journal of Personality and Social Psychology* 16:141-147.

Carden, N. L., and Schramel, D. J. (1966). Observations of conversion reactions seen in troops involved in the Viet Nam conflict. *American Journal of Psychiatry* 1:21-31.

Carter, R. B. (1853). *On the Pathology and Treatment of Hysteria*. London: John Churchill.

Carus, C. G. (1831). *Vorlesungen über Psychologic*. Leipzig: Gerhard Fleischer.

Cattell, J. P., and Cattell, J. S. (1974). Depersonalization: psycological and social perspectives. In *American Handbook of Psychiatry*, vol. 3, ed. S. Arieti. New York: Basic Books.

Champion, F. P., Taylor, R., Joseph, P. R., and Hedden, J. C. (1963). Mass hysteria associated with insect bites. *Journal of South Carolina Medical Association* 59:351-353.

Charcot, J. M. (1877). *Lectures on the Diseases of the Nervous System*. Trans. G. Sigerson. London: New Sydenham Society.

——— (1889). Isolation in the treatment of hysteria. In *Clinical Lectures on Diseases of the Nervous System*, vol. 3, trans. T. Savell. London: New Sydenham Society.

——— (1889). *Lecons du mardi à la Salpêtrière, Policlinique du 19 Mars*. Paris: Felix Alcair.

——— (1892). Faith healing. *New Review and Revue Hebdomadaire* December, pp.112-132.

Chodoff, P. (1954). A re-examination of some aspects of conversion hysteria. *Psychiatry* 17:75-81.

——— (1974). The diagnosis of hysteria: an overview. *American Journal of Psychiatry* 131:1073-1078.

Chodoff, P., and Lyons, H. (1958). Hysteria, the hysterical

personality, and "hysterical" conversion. *American Journal of Psychiatry* 114:734-740.

Cloninger, E. R., and Guze, S. B. (1970). Psychiatric illness and female criminality: the role of sociopathy and hysteria in the antisocial woman. *American Journal of Psychiatry* 127:303-311.

——— (1975). Hysteria and parental psychiatric illness. *Psychological Medicine* 5:27-31.

Crisp, A. H. (1965). Some aspects of the evolution, presentation and follow-up of anorexia nervosa. *Proceedings of the Royal Society of Medicine* 58:814-820.

Crisp, A. H., and Kalucy, R. S. (1974). Aspects of the perceptual disorder in anorexia nervosa. *British Journal of Psychology* 47:349-361.

Crisp, A. H., and Toms, D. A. (1972). Primary anorexia nervosa or weight phobia in the male: report on 13 cases. *British Medical Journal* 1:334-338.

Crocetti, G. M., and Lemkau, P. V. (1967). Schizophrenia II: epidemiology. In *Comprehensive Textbook of Psychiatry*, ed. Freedom and Kaplan. Baltimore: Williams and Wilkins.

Cullen, W. (1796). *First Lines of the Practice of Physic*. With practical and expository notes by John Rotheram. Edinburg, 1896.

DSM I & II. See American Psychiatric Association.

Depersonalization Syndromes (1972). *British Medical Journal* 4:378.

Dube, K. C., and Kumar, N. (1974). An epidemiological study of hysteria. *Journal of Biosocial Science* 6:401-405.

Dubreuil, G., and Wittkower, E. D. (1976). Psychiatric anthropology: a historical perspective. *Psychiatry* 39:130-141.

Duddle, M. (1973). An increase of anorexia nervosa in a university population. *British Journal of Psychiatry* 123:711-712.

Dunham, H. W. (1966). Epidemiology of psychiatric disorders as a contribution to medical ecology. *Archives of Genral Psychiatry* 14:1-19.

Early, L. F., and Lifschutz, J. E. (1974). A case of stigmata. *Archives of General Psychiatry* 30:197-200.

Easser, B. R., and Lesser, S. R. (1965). Hysterical personality: a reevaluation. *Psychoanalytic Quarterly* 34:390-405.

Ebbell, B., trans. (1947). *The Papyrus Ebers, the Greatest Egyptian Medical Document*. Copenhagen: Levin and Mucksgaard.

Ebrahim, G. J. (1968). Mass hysteria in school children: notes on 3 outbreaks in East Africa. *Clinical Pediatrics* 7:437-438.

Edelstein, E., and Edelstein, L. (1945). *Asclepios: A Collection and Interpretation of the Testimonies.* Baltimore: Johns Hopkins Press.

Edwards, J. G. (1970). The *koro* pattern of depersonalization in an American schizophrenic patient. *American Journal of Psychiatry* 126:1171-1173.

Edwards, J. G., and Angus, J. W. S. (1972). Depersonalization. *British Journal of Psychology* 120:242-244.

Erikson, E. H. (1950). *Childhood and Society.* New York: Norton (1963.)

Eysenck, H. J. (1957). *The Dynamics of Anxiety and Hysteria: An Experimental Application of Modern Learning Theory to Psychiatry.* New York: Praeger.

Faigel, H. C. (1968). "The wandering womb": mass hysteria in school girls. *Clinical Pediatrics* 7:377-383.

Fairbairn, W. R. (1954). Observations on the nature of hysterical states. *British Journal of Medical Psychology* 27:105-125.

Falret, J. (1866). *Études cliniques sur les maladies mentales et nerveuses.* Paris: Baillière, 1890.

Farley, J., Woodruff, R. A., and Guze, S. B. (1968). The prevalence of hysteria and conversion symptoms. *British Journal of Psychiatry* 114:1121-1125.

Fenichel, O. (1945). *The Psychoanalytic Theory of Neurosis.* New York: Norton.

Festinger, L., Pepitone, A., and Newcomb, T. (1952). Some consequences of deindividuation in a group. *Journal of Abnoral and Social Psychology* 47:382-389.

Feuchtérsleben, E. Von. (1845). *The Principles of Medical Psychology.* Ed. B. G. Babington. London: New Sydenham Society, 1847.

Fisher, C. (1945). Amnesic states in war neuroses: the psychogenesis of fugues. *Psychoanalytic Quarterly* 14:437-468.

Forbis, O. L., and Janes, R. H., Jr. (1965). Hysteria in childhood. *Southern Medical Journal* 58:1221-1225.

Foulks, E. (1972). *The Arctic Hysterias.* Washington, D. C.: American Anthropological Association.

Frankfort, H. (1948). *Kingship and the Gods: A Study of Ancient Near Eastern Religion as the Integration of Society and Nature.* Chicago: University of Chicago Press.

Freeman, L. (1972). *The Story of Anna O.* New York: Walker.

Freud, A. (1936). *The Ego and the Mechanisms of Defense.* London: Hogarth.

Freud, S. (1888). Hysteria. *Standard Edition* 1:39-60.

——— (1893-1899). Early psycho-analytic publications. *Standard Edition* 3.

——— (1900). The interpretation of dreams. *Standard Edition* 4/5:1-630.

——— (1901-1905). A case of hysteria: three essays on sexuality, and other works. *Standard Edition* 7.

——— (1908). Character and anal eroticism. *Standard Edition* 9:167-176.

——— (1912). Recommendations to physicians practising psycho-analysis. *Standard Edition* 12:109-120.

——— (1913). On beginning the treatment. *Standard Edition* 12:121-144.

——— (1913). On psycho-analysis. *Standard Edition* 12:205-212.

——— (1914). On the history of psycho-analytic movement. *Standard Edition* 14:3-66.

——— (1920). The psychogenesis of a case of homosexuality in a woman. *Standard Edition* 18:146-172.

——— (1925). Autobiographical study. *Standard Edition* 20:32-76.

——— (1931). Libidinal types. *Standard Edition* 12:215-222.

Friedman, T. (1967). Methodological considerations and research needs in the study of epidemic hysteria. *American Journal of Public Health* 57:2009-2011.

Galin, D. (1974). Implications for psychiatry of left and right cerebral specialization. *Archives of General Psychiatry* 31:572-583.

Gardner, R., Holzman, P. S., Klein, G. S., Linton, H., Spence, D. P. (1959). Cognitive controls: a study of individual consistencies in cognitive behavior. *Psychological Issues* 1:1-186.

Garmezy, N. (1974). Children at risk: the search for the antecedents of schizophrenia, part I. *Schizophrenia Bulletin*, no. 8, pp.14-90. National Institute of Mental Health.

Gatfield, P. D., and Guze, S. B. (1962). Prognosis and differential diagnosis of conversion reactions. *Diseases of the Nervous System* 23:623-631.

Gedo, J., and Goldberg, A. (1973). *Models of the Mind.* Chicago: University of Chicago Press.

Gedo, J., Sabshin, M., Sadow, L., and Schlessing, N. (1964). "Studies on hysteria": a methodological evaluation. *Journal of the American Psychoanalytic Association* 12:734.

Gelfman, M. (1971). Dynamics of the correlations between hysteria and depression. *American Journal of Psychotherapy* 25:83-92.

Giovacchini, P. (1975). *Psychoanalysis of Character Disorders.* New York: Jason Aronson.

Glenn, M. L. (1970). Religious conversion and the mystical experience. *Psychiatic Quarterly* 44:636-651.

Goodman, F. D. (1972). *Speaking in Tongues: A Cross-Cultural Study of Glossolalia.* Chicago: University of Chicago Press.

Greenbaum, L. (1973). Societal correlates of possession trance in Sub-Sahara Africa. In *Religion, Altered States of Consciousness and Social Change,* ed. E. Bourguignon. Columbus: Ohio State University Press.

Greenson, R. (1965). The working alliance and the transference neurosis. *Psychoanalytic Quarterly* 34:155-181.

Griesinger, W. (1845). *Mental Pathology and Therapeutics.* Trans. C. L. Roberson and J. Rutherford. London: New Sydenham Society, 1867.

Griffith, F. L., ed. (1897). *Papyri Petri, Hieratic Papyri from Kahun and Gurob; Principally of the Middle Kingdom. Vol. 1: Literary, Medical and Mathematical Papyri from Kahun.* London: Bernard Quaritch.

Group for the Advancement of Psychiatry (1966). Report of the committee on child psychiatry. In *The Psychopathological Disorders of Childhood.* New York: Scribner.

Guillain, G. (1955). *J. M. Charcot, 1825-1893: His Life—His Work.* Ed. and trans. P. Bailey. New York: Hoeber, 1959.

Guinon, G. (1925). Charcot intime. *Paris Medical* May, pp.5ll-526.

Guze, S. B. (1964). Conversion symptoms in criminals. *American Journal of Psychiatry* 121:580-583.

——— (1967). The diagnosis of hysteria: what are we trying to do? *American Journal of Psychiatry* 124:491-498.

——— (1975). The validity and significance of the clinical diagnosis of hysteria (Briquet's syndrome). *American Journal of Psychiatry* 132:138-141.

Guze, S. B., Allen, D. H., and Grollmus, J. M. (1962). The prevalence of Hyperemesis Gravidarum: a study of 162 psychiatric and 98 medical patients. *American Journal of Obstetrics and Gynecology* 84-1859-1864.

Guze, S. B., Woodruff, R. A., and Clayton, P. J. (1973). Sex, age, and the diagnosis of hysteria (Briquet's syndrome). *American Journal of Psychiatry* 129:745-748.

Halleck, S. L. (1967). Hysterical personality—psychological, social, and iatrogenic determinants. *Archives of General Psychiatry* 16:750-757

Halmi, K. A. (1974). Anorexia nervosa:demographic and clinical features in 94 cases. *Psychosomatic Medicine* 36:18-26.

Hartmann, H. (1958). *Ego Psychology and the Problem of Adaptation*. New York: International Universities Press.

Helvie, C. O. (1968). An epidemic of hysteria in a high school. *The Journal of School Health* 38:505-508.

Hinsie, L., and Campbell, P. (1970). *Psychiatric Dictionary*, 4th ed. New York: Oxford.

Hippocrates (1851). *Oeuvres complètes d'Hippocrate*. Fols. 1, 7, 8. Trans. E. Littré. Paris: Baillière.

Hirsch, S. J., and Hollender, M. H. (1969). Hysterical psychoses: clarification of the concept. *American Journal of Psychiatry* 125:909.

Hollender, M. H. (1971). Hysterical personality. *Comments on Contemporary Psychiatry* 1:17-24.

——— (1972). Conversion hysteria: a post-Freudian reinterpretation of nineteenth century psycho-social data. *Archives of General Psychiatry* 26:311-314.

Hollender, M. H., and Hirsch, S. J. (1964). Hysterical psychosis. *American Journal of Psychiatry* 120:1066-1074.

Hollingshead, A. B., and Redlich, F. C. (1958). *Social Class and Mental Illness*. New York: Wiley.

Horowitz, M. J. (1970). *Image Formation and Cognition*. New York: Appleton-Century-Crofts.

——— (1972). Modes of representation of thought. *Journal of American Psychoanalytic Association* 20:793-819.

———— (1974). Microanalysis of working through in psychotherapy. *American Journal of Psychiatry* 131:1208-1212.

———— (1976). *Stress Response Syndromes.* New York: Jason Aronson.

Horton, P., and Miller, D. (1972). The etiology of multiple personality. *Comprehensive Psychiatry* 13:151-159.

Jacobs, N. (1965). The phantom slasher of Taipei: mass hysteria in a non-Western society. *Social Problems* 12:318-322.

Jacobson, E. (1954). The self and the object world: vicissitudes of their infantile cathexis and their influence on ideational and affective development. *Psychoanalytic Study of the Child* 9:75-127.

———— (1964). *The Self and the Object World.* New York: International Universities Press.

Janet, P. (1901). *The Mental State of Hystericals: A Study on Mental Stigmata and Mental Accidents.* Trans. C. R. Carson. New York: Putnam.

———— (1901). *Psychological Healing: A Historical and Clerical Study.* Trans. E. Paul and C. Paul. New York: Macmillan, 1925.

Jones, E. (1953). *The Life and Work of Sigmund Freud.* Vol. 1. New York: Basic Books.

Kagwa, B. H. (1964). The problem of mass hysteria in East Africa. *East African Medical Journal* 41:561-566.

Kaminsky, M. J., and Slavney, P. R. (1976). Methodology and personality in Briquet's syndrome: a reappraisal. *American Journal of Psychiatry* 133: 85-88.

Kant, E. (1929). *On the Power of the Mind to Master One's Pathological Feelings Through Sheer Will Power.* Leipzig: Philipp Reklam.

Keen, W. W., Mitchell, S. W., and Morehouse, G. R. (1864). On malingering, especially in regard to simulation of diseases of the nervous system. *American Journal of the Medical Sciences* 47:367-394.

Kelly, G. (1955). *The Psychology of Personal Constructs.* Vol. 2. New York: Norton.

Kendell, R. E., Hall, D. J., Hailey, A., and Babigian, H. M. (1973). The epidemiology of anorexia nervosa. *Psychological Medicine* 3:200-203.

Kerckhoff, A. C., and Back, K. W. (1968). *The June Bug: A Study of Hysterical Contagion.* New York: Appleton-Century-Crofts.

Kernberg, O. (1966). Structural derivatives of object relationships. *International Journal of Psycho-Analysis* 47:236-253.

——— (1967). Borderline personality organization. *Journal of the American Psychoanalytic Association* 15:641-685.

——— (1970). Factors in the psychoanalytic treatment of narcissistic personalities. *Journal of the American Psychoanalytic Association* 18:51-85.

——— (1974). *Further contributions to the treatment of narcissistic personalities. International Journal of Psycho-Analysis* 55: 215-240.

Kidd, C. B., and Wood, J. F. (1966). Some observations on anorexia nervosa. *Postgraduate Medicine* 42:443-448.

Kiev, A. (1967). Psychotherapy in Haitian voodoo. *American Journal of Psychotherapy* 21: 469-476.

Kimble, R., William, J. G., and Agras, S. (1975). A comparison of two methods of diagnosing hysteria. *American Journal of Psychiatry* 132: 1197-1199.

Kirkpatrick, R. G. (1975). Collective consciousness and mass hysteria: collective behavior and anti-pornography crusades in Durkheimian perspective. *Human Relations* 28:63-84.

Kirshner, L. A. (1973). Dissociative reactions: an historical review and clinical study. *Acta Psychiatrica Scandanavica* 49:698-711.

Klein, G. S. (1967). Peremptory ideation: structure and force in motivated ideas. In *Motives and Thought: Pyschoanalytic Essays in Honor of David Rapaport*, ed. R. Holt, pp. 80-128. Pyschological Issues, Monograph 18/19. New York: International Universities Press.

Klein, G. S., Gardner, R. W., and Schlesing, H. J. (1962). Tolerance for unrealistic experiences:a study of the generality of a cognitive control. *British Journal of Psychology* 53:41-55.

Kline, D. F., and Davis, J. M. (1969). *Diagnosis and Drug Treatment of Psychiatric Disorders.* Baltimore: Waverly.

Kline, M. S. (1963). Psychiatry in Indonesia. *American Journal of Psychiatry* 119:809-815.

Knapp, P. H. (1974). *Segmentation and Structure in Psychoanalysis.* In press.

Knight, J. A., Friedman, T. I., and Sulianti, J. (1965). Epidemic hysteria: a field study. *American Journal of Public Health* 55: 858-865.

Kohut, H. (1971). *Analysis of the Self*. New York: International Universities Press.

Kolb, L. C. (1973). *Noyes' Modern Clinical Psychiatry*. 8th ed. Philadelphia: W. B. Saunders.

Kretschmer, E. (1960). *Hysteria, Reflex, and Instinct*. Trans. V. Baskin and W. Baskin. New York: Philosophical Library.

La Barre, M., and La Barre, W. (1965). The worm in the honeysuckle. *Social Casework* 46:399-413.

La Barre, W. (1962). *They Shall Take Up Serpents*. Minneapolis: Minnesota University Press.

———— (1969). *They Shall Take Up Serpents: Psychology of the Southern Snake Handling Cult*. New York: Schocken.

———— (1970). *The Ghost Dance: The Origins of Religion*. Garden City: Doubleday.

Langness, L. L. (1967). Hysterical psychosis—the cross-cultural evidence. *American Journal of Psychiatry* 124:47-56.

Laplanche, J. (1974). Panel on 'hysteria today.' *International Journal of Psycho-Analysis* 55:459-469.

Lazare, A. (1971). The hysterical character in psychoanalytic theory—evolution and confusion. *Archives of General Psychiatry* 25:131-137.

Lazare, A., Klerman, G. L. (1968). Hysteria and depression: the frequency and significance of hysterical personality features in hospitalized depressed women. *American Journal of Psuchiatry* 124:48-56.

Lazare, A., Klerman, G. L., and Armor, D. J. (1966). Oral, obsessive, and hysterical personality patterns: an investigation of psychoanalytic concepts by means of factor analysis. *Archives of General Psychiatry* 14:624-630.

Lazare, A., Klerman, G. L., and Armor, D. J. (1970). Oral, obsessive and hysterical personality patterns. *Journal of Psychiatric Research* 7:275-290.

Lazarus, R. S. (1966). *Psychological Stress and the Coping Process*. New York: McGraw-Hill.

Lee, R. B. (1968). The sociology of !Kung Bushman trance performances. In *Trance and Possession States*, ed. R. Prince. Montreal: R. M. Burke Memorial Society.

Lehmann, L. S. (1974). Depersonalization. *American Journal of Psychiatry* 131:1221-1224.

Leigh, D. (1961). *The Historical Development of British Psychiatry*. New York: Pergamon.

Leighton, A. H. (1974). Social disintegration and mental disorder. In *American Handbook of Psychiatry*, vol. 2., ed. S. Arieti. New York: Basic Books.

Leighton, A. H., and Murphy, T. M. (1965). Cross-cultural psychiatry. In *Approaches to Cross-Cultural Psychiatry*, ed. T. M. Murphy and A. H. Leighton. Ithaca: Cornell University Press.

Lerner, H. E. (1974). The hysterical personality: a "woman's disease". *Comprehensive Psychiatry* 15:157-164.

Levine, R. J., Romm, F. J., Sexton, D. J., Wood, B. T., and Kaiser, J. (1974). Outbreak of psychosomatic illness at a rural elementary school. *Lancet* 11: 1500-1503.

Lewis, A. (1975). The survival of hysteria. *Psychological Medicine* 5:9-12.

Lewis, W. C. (1974). Hysteria: the consultant's dilemma. *Archives of General Psychiatry* 30:145-151.

Lewis, W. C., and Berman, M. (1965). Studies of conversion hysteria. *Archives of General Psychiatry* 13:275-282.

Lindberg, B. J., and Lindegard, B. (1963). Studies of the hysteroid personality attitude. *Acta Psychiatrica Scandanavica* 39:170-180.

Linton, R. (1943). Nativistic movements. *American Anthropologist* 45:230-240.

——— (1956). *Culture and Mental Disorders*. Springifeld: Charles C Thomas.

Loevinger, J. (1973). Ego development. *Psychoanalysis and Contemporary Science* 2:77-156.

Loewald, H. W. (1960). The therapeutic action of psychoanalysis. *International Journal of Psycho-Analysis* 41:16-26.

Looff, D. H. (1970). Psychophysiologic and conversion reactions in children. *Journal of the American Academy of Child Psychiatry* 9:318-331.

Lower, R. B. (1972). Affect changes in depersonalization. *Psychoa-nalytical Review* 59:565-577.

Ludwig, A. M. (1972). Hysteria: a neurobiological theory. *Archives of General Psychiatry* 27:771-786.

Luisada, P. V., Peele, R., and Pittard, E. A. (1974). The hysterical personality in men. *American Journal of Psychiatry* 131:518-521.

Lyons, H. A., and Potter, P. E. (1970). Communicated hysteria—an episode in a secondary school. *Journal of the Irish Medical Association* 63:377-379.

Mc Kegney, F. P. (1967). The incidence and characteristics of patients with conversion reactions I: a general hospital consulta-tion service sample. *American Journal of Psychiatry* 124:542-545.

MacKinnon, R. A., and Michels, R. R. (1971). *Psychiatric Interview in Clinical Practice*. Philadelphia:W. B. Saunders.

Maguigad, E. L. (1964). Psychiatry in the Philippines. *American Journal of Psychiatry* 121:21-25.

Main, M. (1975). Mother-avoiding babies. Paper presented at the biennial meeting of the Society for Research in Child Develop-ment, April.

Malleus Maleficarum (1951). Trans. M. Summers. London: Pushkin.

Malmquist, C. P. (1971). Hysteria in childhood. *Postgraduate Medicine* 50:112-117.

Mandeville, B. de (1711). *A Treatise of the Hypochondriak and Hysterick*. London: Deylen Leach.

Margetts, E. L. (1976). The semantics of hysteria continued. *American Journal of Psychiatry* 133:103.

Marmor, J. (1953). Orality in the hysterical personality. *Journal of American Psychoanalytic Association* 1:656-675.

Martin, P. A. (1971). Dynamic considerations of the hysterical psychosis. *American Journal of Psychiatry* 128: 745-748.

Mead, R. (1762). *The Medical Works of Richard Mead*, Section 4. London.

Meares, R., and Horvath, T. (1972). 'Acute' and 'chronic' hysteria. *British Journal of Psychiatry* 121:653-657.

Medalia, N. Z., and Larsen, O. (1958). Diffusion and belief in a collective delusion: the Seattle windshield pitting epidemic. *American Sociological Review* 23:180-186.

Menninger, K. (1963). *The Vital Balance*. New York: Viking Press.

Meth, J. M. (1974). Exotic psychiatric syndromes. In *American Handbook of Psychiatry*, vol. 3, ed. S. Arieti and E. B. Brody. New York: Basic Books.

Meyer, J. E. (1971). Anorexia nervosa of adolescence: the central syndrome of the anorexia nervosa group. *British Journal of Psychiatry* 118:539-542.

Miller, G. A., Galanter, E., and Pribram, D. (1960). *Plans and the Structure of Behavior.* New York: Holt, Rinehart and Winston.

Millon, T. (1969). *Modern Psychopathology.* Philadelphia: W. B. Saunders.

Mitchell, S. W. (1877). *Fat and Blood: and How to Make Them.* Philadelphia: Lippincott.

―――― (1881). *Lectures on Diseases of the Nervous System, Especially in Women.* Philadelphia: Lias.

――――(1888). *Doctor and Patient.* Philadelphia: Lippincott.

Moss, P. D., and McEvedy, C. P. (1966). An epidemic of overbreathing among school girls. *British Medical Journal* 2: 1295-1300.

Muhangi, J. R. (1973). A preliminary report on "mass hysteria" in an Ankole school in Uganda. *East African Medical Journal* 50: 304-308.

Munthe, A. (1930). *The Story of San Michele.* New York: Dutton.

Murphy, H. B. M. (1973). History and the evolution of syndromes: the striking case of *latah* and *amok.* In *Psychopathology: Contributions from the Social, Behavioral, and Biological Sciences,* ed. M. Hammer, K. Salzinger, and S. Sutton. New York: Wiley.

Murphy, J. M. and Leighton, A. H. (1965). Native conceptions of psychiatric disorder. In *Approaches to Cross-Cultural Psychiatry,* ed. J. M. Murphy and A. H. Leighton. Ithaca: Cornell University Press.

Myerson, P. (1969). The hysteric's experience in psychoanalysis. *International Journal of Psycho-Analysis* 50:373-384.

Ngui, P. W. (1969). The *koro* epidemic in Singapore. *Australia and New Zealand Journal of Psychiatry* 3:263-266.

Olczak, P. V., Donnerstein, E., Hershberger, T. J., and Kahn, I. (1971). Group hysteria and the MMPI. *Psychological Reports* 28:413-414.

Opler, M. (1969). Culture and child rearing. In *Modern Perspectives in International Child Psychiatry*, ed. J. Howells. Edinburgh: Oliver and Boyd.

Orr, D. W. (1961). Lionel Blitzsten, the teacher: In *N. Lionel Blitzsten, M.D.: Psychoanalyst, Teacher, Friend 1893-1952*. New York: International Universities Press (private distribution only).

Pankow, G. W. (1974). The body image in hysterical psychosis. *International Journal of Psycho-Analysis* 55:407-414.

Perley, J. M., and Guze, S. B. (1972). Hysteria—the stability and usefulness of clinical criteria. *New England Journal of Medicine* 266:421-426.

Peterfreund, E., and Schwartz, J. J. (1971). *Information Systems and Psychoanalysis*. Psychological Issues, Monograph 25/26. New York: International Universities Press.

Pfeiffer, P. H. (1964). Mass hysteria masquerading as food poisoning. *Journal of the Maine Medical Association* 55:27.

Piaget, J. (1937). *The Construction of Reality in the Child*. New York: Basic Books, 1954.

Pinel, P. (1813). *Nosographie philosophique ou la méthode de l'analyse appliquée a la médecine*. 5th ed. Paris: Brosson.

Polk, L. D. (1974). Mass hysteria in an elementary school. *Clinical Pediatrics* 13:1013-1014.

Pollock, G. H. (1968). Bertha Pappenheim: addenda to her case history. *Journal of the American Psychoanalytic Association* 12:734.

——— (1973). The possible significane of childhood object loss in the Joseph Breuer-Bertha Pappenheim (Anna O.)-Sigmund Freud relationship: I. Josef Breuer. *Journal of the American Psychoanalytic Association* 16:711.

Prince, M. (1906). *The Dissociation of a Personality*. New York: Longmans, Green.

———(1929). *Clinical and Experimental Studies in Personality*. Cambridge, Mass: Sci-Art Publishers.

Proctor, J. T. (1958). Hysteria in childhood. *American Journal of Orthopsychiatry* 28:394-403.

Prosen, H. (1967). Sexuality in females with "hysteria." *American Journal of Psychiatry* 124:687-692.

Purtell, J. J., Robins, E., and Cohen, M. E. (1951). Observations on clinical aspects of hysteria—a quantitative study of fifty patients and one hundred fifty six control subjects. *Journal of the American Medical Association* 146:902-909.

Rabkin, R. (1964). Conversion hysteria as social maladaptation. *Psychiatry* 27:349-363.

Rangell, L. (1959). The nature of conversion. *Journal of the American Psychoanalytic Association* 17:632-662.

Rapaport, D., and Gill, M. M. (1958). The points of view and assumptions of metapsychology. *International Journal of Psycho-Analysis* 40:153-162.

Reed, J. L. (1975). The diagnosis of "hysteria." *Psychological Medicine* 5:13-17.

Reich, W. (1933). *Character Analysis*. New York: Farrar, Straus and Giroux, 1969.

Reynolds, R. (1869). Remarks on paralysis and other disorders of motion and sensation. Department on ideas. *British Medical Journal*, July.

Richman, J., and White, H. (1970). The family view of hysterical psychosis. *American Journal of Psychiatry* 127:280-285.

Riese, W. (1958). The history of the term and conception of neurosis in pre-Freudian origins of psychoanalysis. *Science and Psychoanalysis*, vol. 1, ed. J. M. Masserman. New York: Grune and Stratton.

Robertson, J., and Robertson, J. (1969). *John, 17 Months: Nine Days in a Residential Nursery*. A film. London: Tavistock Research Center.

Robins, E., Purtell, J., Cohen, M., and Mandel, E. (1952). "Hysteria" in men. *New England Journal of Medicine* 246:677-685.

Robins, L. (1966). Childhood behavior predicting later diagnosis. In *Deviant Children Grown Up*. Baltimore: Williams and Wilkins.

Rock, N. L. (1971). Conversion reactors in childhood: a clinical study on childhood neuroses. *Journal of the American Academy of Child Psychiatry* 10:65-93.

Roeder, G. (1916). *Urkunden zur Religion des alten Agyptens*. Jena.

Rosner, H. (1975). Clinical and diagnostic considerations in the analysis of a five-year-old hysteric. *Journal of the American Psychiatric Association* 23:507-534.

Rowland, C. R., Jr. (1970). Anorexia nervosa: a survey of the

literature and review of 30 cases. In *Anorexia and Obesity*, ed.
C. V. Rowland. Boston: Little, Brown.

Rubenfine, D. (1967). Notes on a theory of reconstruction. *British Journal of Psychology* 40:195-206.

Rush, B. (1809). An account of the influence. . . of the American Revolution upon the human body. In *Medical Inquiries and Observations*, 3rd ed. Philadelphia: Hopkins and Earle.

———(1812). *Medical Inquiries and Observations upon the Diseases of the Mind*. Philadelphia: Gregg.

Schafer, R. (1948). *Clinical Application of Psychological Tests*. New York: International Universities Press.

———(1968). *Aspects of Internalization*. New York: International Universities Press.

Schlessinger, N., Gedo, J. E., Miller, J., Pollock, H., Sabshin, M., and Sadow, L. (1967). The scientific style of Breuer and Freud in the origins of psychoanalysis. *Journal of the American Psychoanalytic Association* 15:404.

Schneck, J. M. (1963). Historical notes: William Osler, S. Weir Mitchell, and the origin of the "rest cure." *American Journal of Psychiatry* 119:894-895.

Shapiro, D. (1965). *Neurotic Styles*. New York: Basic Books.

Sheffield, H. (1898). Childhood as it occurs in the United States of America. *New York Medical Journal* 68:412-416, 433-436.

Shilder, P. (1939). The concept of hysteria. *American Journal of Psychoanalysis* 95:1389-1413.

Sigerist, H., ed. (1941). *Four Treatises by Paracelsus*. Baltimore: Johns Hopkins Press.

Siomopoulus, V. (1972). Derealization and déjà vu: formal mechanisms. *American Journal of Psychotherapy* 26:84-89.

Sirois, F. (1973). Les épidémies d'hystérie: revue de la litterature, reflexions sur le problème de la contagion psychopathologique. *L'Union Médicale du Canada* 102:1906-1915.

———(1974). Epidemic hysteria. *Acta Psychiatrica Scandanavica* (Suppl.) 252:11-46.

Skinner, B. F. (1953). *Science and Human Behavior*. New York: Macmillan.

Slater, E. (1965). Diagnosis of hysteria. *British Medical Journal* 1:395-399.

Slavney, P. R., and McHugh, P. R. (1974). The hysterical personality. *Archives of General Psychiatry* 30:325-332.

————(1975). The hysterical personality: an attempt at validation with the MMPI. *Archives of General Psychiatry* 32:186-190.

Slotkin, J. S. (1965). The peyote way. In *Reader in Comparative Religion: An Anthropological Approach*, ed. W. A. Lessa and E. Z. Vogt. New York: Harper.

Smelser, N. (1962). *Theory of Collective Behavior*. New York: Free Press.

Sollman, T. (1918). *A Manual of Pharmacology*. Philadelphia.

Sours, J. A. (1974). The anorexia nervosa syndrome. *International Journal of Psycho-Analysis* 55:567-576.

Sperling, M. (1973). Conversion hysteria and conversion symptoms: a revision of classification and concepts. *Journal of the American Psychoanalytic Association* 21:745-772.

Spindler, G. D. (1968). Psychocultural adaptation. In *The Study of Personality: An Interdisciplinary Appraisal*, ed. E. Norbeck. New York: Holt, Rinehart and Winston.

Spitz, R. (1965). *The First Year of Life*. New York: International Universities Press.

Stahl, S. M., and Lebedun, M. (1974). Mystery gas: an analysis of mass hysteria. *Journal of Health and Social Behavior* 15:44-50.

Stampfl, T. G., and Lewis, D. J. (1965). Essentials of implosive therapy: a learning-theory-based psychodynamic behavioral therapy. *Journal of Abnormal Psychology* 72:496-503.

Starr, P. H. (1953). Some observations on the diagnostic aspects of childhood hysteria. *The Nervous Child* 10:231.

Stephens, J. H., and Kamp, M. (1962). On some aspects of hysteria: a clinical study. *Journal of Nervous and Mental Diseases* 134:305.

Strümpell, A. (1911). *A Textbook of Medicine for Students and Practitioners*. New York.

Sydenham, T. (1848). *Works of Thomas Sydenham, M.D.* Trans. R. G. Latham. London: The Sydenham Society.

Szasz, T. (1961). *The Myth of Mental Illness: Foundations of a Theory of Personal Conduct*. New York: Hoeber-Harper.

Szurek, S. (1954). Concerning sexual disorders of parents and children. *Journal of Nervous and Mental Diseases* 120:369-378.

Szurek, S., Johnson, A., and Falstein, E. (1942). Collaborative psychiatric therapy of parent-child problems. *American Journal of Orthopsychiatry* 12:511-516.

Talmon, Y. (1965). Pursuit of the millennium: the relation between religions and social change. In *Reader in Comparative Religion: An Anthropological Approach,* ed. W. A. Lessa and E. Z. Vogt. New York: Harper.

Taylor, W. S., and Martin, M. F. (1944). Multiple personality. *Journal of Abnormal and Social Psychology* 39:281-300.

Teoh, J. I. (1972). The changing psychopathology of *amok*. *Psychiatry* 35:345-351.

Teoh, J. I., Soewondo, S., and Sidharta, M. (1975). Epidemic hysteria in Malaysian schools: an illustrative episode. *Psychiatry* 38:258-268.

Teoh, J. I., and Yeoh, K. (1973). Cultural conflict and transition: epidemic hysteria and social sanction. *Australian and New Zealand Journal of Psychiatry* 7:283-293.

Theander, S. (1970). Anorexia nervosa. *Acta Psychiatrica Scandanavica* (Suppl.) 214:1-194.

Thigpen, C. H., and Cleckley, H. (1954). A case of multiple personality. *Journal of Abnormal and Social Psychology* 49:125-151.

————(1957). *The Three Faces of Eve.* New York:McGraw-Hill.

Thomas, A., Chess, S., Birch, H., Herzig, M., and Korn, S. (1963). *Behavioral Individuality in Early Childhood.* New York, New York University Press.

Tomkins, S. (1962). *Affect, Imagery, Consciousness.* New York: Springer.

Tucker, G. H., Harrow, M., and Quinlan, D. (1973). Depersonalization, dysphoria, and thought disturbance. *American Journal of Psychiatry* 130:702-706.

Tuke, D. H. (1872). *Illustrations of the Influence of the Mind upon the Body in Health and Disease, Designed to Elucidate the Action of the Imagination.* London.

Tupin, J. P. (1974). Hysterical and cyclothymic personalities. In *Personality Disorders—Diagnosis and Management,* ed. J. R. Lion. Baltimore: Williams and Wilkins.

Vaillant, G. (1971). Theoretical hierarchy of adaptive ego mechanisms. *Archives of General Psychiatry* 24:107-118.

Veith, I. (1970). *Hysteria: The History of a Disease*. Chicago: University of Chicago Press.

Walker, J., and Szurek, S. (1973). Early childhood development of psychotic children: a study of anamnestic methods. In *Clinical Studies in Childhood Psychoses*, ed. S. Szurek and I. Berlin. New York: Brunner/Mazel.

Wallerstein, R. S. Case Reports of the Menninger Psychotherapy Research Project. In preparation.

Weingartner, H., and Faillace, L. A. (1971). Alcohol state-dependent learning in man. *The Journal of Nervous and Mental Diseases* 153:365-406.

Weinstein, E. A., Eck, R. A., and Lyerly, O. G. (1969). Conversion hysteria in Appalachia. *Psychiatry* 32:334-341.

Weiss, J. (1967). The integration of defenses. *International Journal of Psycho-Analysis* 48:334-341.

————(1971). The emergence of new themes: a contribution to the psychoanalytic theory of therapy. *International Journal of Psycho-Analysis* 52:459-467.

Wheeler, L. (1966). Toward a theory of behavioral contagion. *Psychological Review* 73:179-192.

Wholey, C. C. (1933). A case of multiple personality. *American Journal of Psychiatry* 89:653-688.

Whytt, R. (1767). *Observations on the Nature, Causes and Cure of those Disorders which have been commonly called Nervous, Hypochondriac or Hysteric: to which are prefixed some remarks on the sympathy of the nerves*. Edinburgh: Balfour.

Willis, T. (1664). *Cereleri anatome, cui accersit nervorum descripto et usus*. London.

Wisdom, J. O. (1961). A methodological approach to the problem of hysteria. *International Journal of Psycho-Analysis* 42:224-237.

Wittels, F. (1930). The hysterical character. *Medical Review of Reviews* 36:186.

Wittkower, E. D., and Dubreuil, G. (1968). Cultural factors in mental illness. In *The Study of Personality: An Interdisciplinary Appraisal*, ed. E. Norbeck. New York: Holt, Rinehart and Winston.

Woerner, P. I. and Guze, S. B. (1968). A family and marital study of hysteria. *British Journal of Psychiatry* 114:161-168.

Wolowitz, H. M. (1972). Hysterical character and feminine identity. In *Readings in the Psychology of Women*, ed. J. M. Bardwick. New York: Harper.

Wolpe, J. (1969). *The Practice of Behavior Therapy*. New York: Pergamon.

Wolpe, Z. (1953). Psychogenic visual disturbance in a four-year-old child. *The Nervous Child* 10:314-325.

Woodruff, R. A. (1967). Hysteria: an evaluation of objective diagnostic criteria by the study of women with chronic medical illness. *British Journal of Psychiatry* 114:1115-1119.

Woodruff, R. A., Clayton, P. J., and Guze, S. B. (1971). Hysteria: studies of diagnosis, outcome, and prevalence. *Journal of the American Medical Association* 215:425-428.

Woodruff, R. A., Jr., Goodwin, D. W., and Guze, S. B. (1974). *Psychiatric Diagnosis*. New York: Oxford.

Worsley, P. (1968). *The Trumpet Shall Sound*. New York: Shocken.

Wunderlick, C. (1868). *Das Verhalten der Eigenwarme in Krankheiten*. Leipzig.

Yap, P. M. (1952). The *latah* reaction: its pathodynamics and nosological position. *Journal of Mental Science* 98:515-564.

Yates, A. J. (1970). *Behavior Therapy*. New York: Wiley.

Zetzel, E. (1968). The so-called good hysteric. *International Journal of Psycho-Analysis* 49:256-260.

———(1970). Therapeutic alliance in the analysis of hysteria. In *Capacity for Emotional Growth*, ed. E. Zetzel. London: Hogarth.

Zeigler, D. K. (1967). Neurological disease and hysteria—the differential diagnosis. *International Journal of Neuropsychiatry* 3:388-396.

Zeigler, F. J., Imboden, J. B., and Meyer, E. (1960). Contemporary conversion reactions: a clinical study. *American Joural of Psychiatry* 116:901-910.

Zilboorg, G. (1941). *A History of Medical Psychology*. New York: Norton.

Zimbardo, P. G. (1969). The human choice: individuation, reason, and order vs. deindividuation, impulse, and chaos. In *Nebraska Symposium on Motivation* 17:237-307.

Zimbardo, P. G., and Maslach, C. (1971). Liberating behavior from time-sound control: expanding the present through hypnosis. *Journal of Applied Social Psychology* 1:305-323.

INDEX